WAR AGAINST THE IDOLS

WAR AGAINST THE IDOLS

THE REFORMATION OF WORSHIP
FROM ERASMUS TO CALVIN

CARLOS M. N. EIRE

University of Virginia

CAMBRIDGE
UNIVERSITY PRESS

To
the memory of my father
and to
my mother

PUBLISHED BY THE PRESS SYNDICATE OF THE UNIVERSITY OF CAMBRIDGE
The Pitt Building, Trumpington Street, Cambridge CB2 1RP, United Kingdom

CAMBRIDGE UNIVERSITY PRESS
The Edinburgh Building, Cambridge CB2 2RU, United Kingdom
40 West 20th Street, New York, NY 10011-4211, USA
10 Stamford Road, Oakleigh, Melbourne 3166, Australia

First published 1986
First paperback edition 1989
Reprinted 1990, 1997

Printed in the United States of America

Typeset in Palatino

A catalogue record for this book is available from the British Library

Library of Congress Cataloguing-in-Publication Data is available

ISBN 0-521-30685-X hardback
ISBN 0-521-37984-9 paperback

Frontispiece: Matthias Gerung, *Three Groups Engaged in
Idolatry* (1540s). From: Walter L. Strauss, *The German Single-
Leaf Woodcut, 1550-1600* (3 vols. New York, 1975),
vol. I, p. 311.

Contents

Contents

Acknowledgments

To the many who have personally aided my research and writing over the past eight years, I extend my thanks. Above all, I am indebted to Steven Ozment, who patiently directed an earlier version of the project as my dissertation advisor at Yale University, and who has since continued to support and encourage my efforts. I owe much to him. For guidance and inspiration at various times, I would like to thank Natalie Zemon Davis, William Monter, Robert Kingdon, Carl Christensen, and, in a special way, John Tedeschi. I am also indebted to the two anonymous readers for Cambridge University Press, whose perceptive comments and suggestions helped make this a better work in many ways. Peter Brown, who would be surprised to know that he unintentionally suggested the project when he came to speak about the sacred in late antiquity one April afternoon in New Haven, also deserves to be thanked. The monks of St. John's Abbey and University in Collegeville, Minnesota, where I taught for two years, were most supportive of my work, and this book, in no small way, is a tribute to their ecumenical spirit. Here at the University of Virginia, I have profited greatly from the wisdom of H. C. Erik Midelfort, as well as from the advice and encouragement of other colleagues who suggested improvements and urged me to press on, especially Martin Jaffee, James Childress, David Little, and Gerald Fogarty. Friends and associates who provided less tangible, but no less significant support, are Susan Snyder, Jure Kristo, James Latimer, Elizabeth Carroll-Horrocks, Arnold Snyder, and Thomas Safley. Gail Moore and Daniel Smith, who "keyboarded" the manuscript on a word processor, also deserve credit for making this possible. Finally, in a most special way, I want to thank Jane Ulrich, my wife, for making it all worthwhile.

The following have funded this project and helped make my research possible: The Center for Renaissance Studies at the Newberry Library in Chicago, with Fellowships from the National Endowment for the Humanities (1980) and the Exxon Educational Foundation

Acknowledgments

(1982); the University of Virginia, with a Faculty Summer Research Grant (1983); The Center for Reformation Research in St. Louis, with a Junior Fellowship; and the Council on West European Studies at Yale, with a research grant.

Portions of this book have previously appeared, in much different form, as articles. A greatly condensed version of the conclusions reached in Chapter 4 received the Carl Meyer Memorial Prize at the Sixteenth Century Studies Conference in St. Louis in 1980, and recently appeared, in a further revised form, in the *Journal of the Rocky Mountain Medieval and Renaissance Association* (1983), under the title "Iconoclasm as a Revolutionary Tactic: The Case of Switzerland 1524–1536." A section of Chapter 7 was included in "Prelude to Sedition? Calvin's Attack on Nicodemism and Religious Compromise," *Archiv für Reformationsgeschichte*, 76 (1985). Other brief portions of Chapter 7 appeared in "Calvin and Nicodemism: A Reappraisal," *Sixteenth Century Journal*, 10 (1979). I am grateful to the editors of these journals for their permission to use this material.

Abbreviations

Allen	*Erasmi Epistolae,* edited by P. S. and H. M. Allen (Oxford, 1906–1958).
ARG	*Archiv für Reformationsgeschichte.*
AS	*Erasmus von Rotterdam Ausgewählte Schriften,* edited by W. Welzig (8 vols., Darmstadt, 1968–).
CR	*Corpus Reformatorum: Joannis Calvini Opera quae supersunt omnia,* edited by W. Baum, E. Cunitz, and E. Reuss (Brunswick, 1863–80).
DS	*Martin Bucers Deutsche Schriften,* edited by R. Stupperich (Paris/Gütersloh, 1960–).
Herminjard	*Correspondance des Réformateurs dans les Pays de Langue Française,* edited by A. L. Herminjard (Paris/Geneva, 1866–97). Reissued by B. DeGraaf (Niewkoop, 1965).
Latin Works	*The Latin Works and the Correspondence of Huldreich Zwingli, together with Selections from His German Works,* edited by S. M. Jackson (3 vols., New York, 1912; Philadelphia, 1922, 1929).
Levain	Jeanne de Jussie, *Le Levain du Calvinisme ou Commencement de l'Héresie de Genève,* edited by A. C. Grivel (Geneva, 1865).
LW	*Luther's Works,* edited by J. Pelikan, H. T. Lehmann, et al. (St. Louis/Philadelphia, 1955–).
RC	*Les Registres du Conseil de Genève,* edited by E. Rivoire and V. van Berchem (13 vols., Geneva, 1900–1940).
WA	*D. Martin Luthers Werke: Kritische Gesamtausgabe* (Weimar, 1883–).
ZW	*Huldreich Zwinglis Sämtliche Werke,* edited by E. Egli, W. Köhler, F. Blanke, et al. (Berlin/Zurich, 1905–).

Unless otherwise stated, all translations are my own.

Introduction

In 1509, when John Calvin was born, Western Christendom still shared a common religion of immanence. Heaven was never too far from earth. The sacred was diffused in the profane, the spiritual in the material. Divine power, embodied in the Church and its sacraments, reached down through innumerable points of contact to make itself felt: to forgive or punish, to protect against the ravages of nature, to heal, to soothe, and to work all sorts of wonders. Priests could absolve adulterers and murderers, or bless fields and cattle. During their lives, saints could prevent lightning from striking, restore sight to the blind, or preach to birds and fish. Unencumbered by the limitations of time and space, they could do even more through their images and relics after death. A pious glance at a statue of St. Christopher in the morning ensured protection from illness and death throughout the day. Burial in the habit of St. Francis improved the prospects for the afterlife. A pilgrimage to Santiago, where the body of the apostle James had been deposited by angels, or to Canterbury, where St. Thomas à Becket had had his skull split open by knights of King Henry II, could make a lame man walk, or hasten a soul's release from purgatory. The map of Europe bristled with holy places; life pulsated with the expectation of the miraculous. In the popular mind and in much of the official teaching of the Church, almost anything was possible. One could even eat the flesh of the risen Christ in a consecrated wafer.

Fourteen years later, as Calvin began his studies at the University of Paris, it was no longer possible to take this intermingling of spiritual and material for granted. Among the many changes brought about by the Reformation, none was more visible, or tangible, where it triumphed, than the abolition of this kind of religion. Although a sharp critique of medieval piety spearheaded by the great humanist Erasmus had begun to capture hearts and minds in learned circles since the early years of the century, the impact of this critique was limited by its appeal to a rather narrow audience, and also by the fact

1

that it considered such piety only as something improper, not false or damnable. In the second decade of the sixteenth century, however, medieval Catholic piety suddenly began to be attacked in some places as "idolatry," or false religion. Wherever those who held these views acquired enough power, churches were sacked, images smashed and burned, relics destroyed, sanctuaries desecrated, altars overturned, and consecrated hosts fed to dogs and goats. The religion of immanence was replaced by the religion of transcendence; Reformers and their congregations exulted in the beauty of a newly stripped, whitewashed cathedral. The "half-hearted" critique of the humanists was left smoldering among the ashes with the images. Even Erasmus, the great critic, left Basel when the images had all been burned. As the nature of the sacred was redefined, and one holy place after another vanished from the map, first in Germany and Switzerland, later in France, the Netherlands, and England, the unity of the European religious vision was forever shattered. Within one generation, the image donors had become the image smashers.[1]

But this was not all. While some Protestants cast down the "idols" of Rome, Luther cast out the image breakers from Wittenberg. The redefinition of the sacred, then, became the watershed that separated not only Protestant from Catholic, but Lutheran from Reformed as well. By the time Calvin came to Geneva in 1536, to run his own crusade against "false religion," the streams of piety were flowing, inalterably, along three different courses. The Catholic stream continued to flow as it had for centuries, suffused with the immanence of the divine. The Lutheran stream, for all its protests, meandered close to these waters. Though they opposed much in medieval piety, Lutherans, for the most part, were not too interested in separating the material from the spiritual, or in promoting a radical change in worship. Stressing instead an opposition to "works-righteousness," they steered a middle course between transcendence and immanence, and remained open to the use of material objects in worship as long as they were regarded with indifference. The Reformed stream flowed hard and fast in a different direction, surging with transcendence. The central focus of Reformed Protestantism was its interpretation of worship – more specifically, of the relationship between the spiritual and the material. The aggressive rejection of the Catholic cult, which became the hallmark of the Reformed tradition, and reached its fullest and most enduring expression in Calvinism,

---

[1] Herman Heimpel, "Das Wesen des Deutschen Spätmittelalters," in *Der Mensch in Seiner Gegenwart* (Göttingen, 1957), p. 134.

had its foundation in Scripture, but its hermeneutic was determined by certain metaphysical assumptions. Although the Reformed were every bit as concerned with exegesis and theology as the Lutherans, and also championed the principles of *sola fides* and *sola scriptura*, they paid much more attention to the way in which the divine ought to be approached. Stressing the transcendence of God and of the spiritual realm, they adhered to a third principle: "Finitum non est capax infiniti" (the finite cannot contain the infinite). Guided by this battle-cry, the Reformed focused on piety and changed much more in the outward expression of worship than the Lutherans. Aiming to do away with any practice that compromised the "spiritual" worship commanded by God, the Reformed launched a vigorous attack on all external objects of devotion that had previously been charged with religious value. Chief among their targets were the cult of saints, with its images and relics, and the Catholic Mass, with its belief in trans-substantiation and its reverence for the consecrated host. Their posture became uncompromising and disruptive: It led to a crusade against idolatry that manifested itself in iconoclasm, civic unrest, and eventually even in armed resistance against legitimate rulers.

When Calvin took control of this stream, it was already far from the watershed; but as it fanned out through lands where it was hard to wash away the "idols," such as France, it ran the risk of losing its definition and purity. It was Calvin's task to channel the flow through Geneva, shore up embankments, dig new waterways, and build new dams. His labors would allow this stream to run clear and strong, even through bad terrain, so it could relentlessly irrigate Europe with the uncompromising waters of transcendence, and thus wash away all the "idols" from the map.

This study calls attention to the centrality of the idolatry issue for the Reformation. It traces the development of the Reformed attitude, provides a survey and synthesis of its unfolding from Erasmus through Calvin, and lays a foundation for understanding the Protestant ideology that stood in conflict with Catholicism outside of Lutheran territories. The central thesis of this work is that John Calvin, in defending the heritage of the Reformed attitude toward idolatry, forged a new, scripturally based, theological metaphysics in which the boundaries between the spiritual and the material were more clearly drawn than ever; and that his reaffirmation of the centrality of "spiritual" worship, with its consequent denial of compromise, provided a solid ideological foundation for much of the social and political unrest that accompanied the spread of Calvinism. This is an attempt to trace the development of an idea, to chronicle the way in which theology became a sociopolitical ideology, and gave rise to action, conflict, and, in some cases, change.

This work is primarily intellectual history, but not of the sort that can afford to disregard the social matrix in which ideas function. Since the ideas being studied here were of the type that called for very specific social changes, and were in and of themselves concerned with the practical aspect of religious reform, it would be impossible to consider them in isolation. This work is the history of an idea and its application: Its overarching purpose is to analyze the interrelationship between circumstances and ideas, and to probe the practical, political dimensions of one of the central concepts of the Reformed tradition. Yet, any study that aims at a broad synthesis, such as this one, needs to have clearly defined limits, and needs to have them clearly explained.

It is not my intention to chronicle the entire history of Reformation iconoclasm – or to quantify its various social components – but rather to lay bare its ideology, and to show through specific examples that a certain kind of theology, which was itself developed as a response to a particular set of circumstances, helped shape, produce, and support immediate changes in sixteenth-century society. Though concerned with explaining the process of change occasioned by the war against the idols, this study does not pursue a detailed analysis of the actual composition of the changes. The question posed here is not so much how Reformed Protestants altered the way in which late medieval society worshiped in some places, as why they came to think that certain reforms were needed. By accepting this agenda I am not arguing for the intrinsic superiority of one question over the other, but am merely defining some limits. These thematic boundaries are based on practical and theoretical considerations.

On a practical level, the current state of research on Reformation iconoclasm set the natural boundaries within which attention needed to be focused. Certain aspects of the phenomenon demand the use of very different kinds of approaches, different types of research, and different modes of presentation. For example, questions regarding such matters as the social status of the iconoclasts, or the relation between economic hardship and the rejection of Catholicism, or the symbolic content of religious violence cannot be successfully answered except on a case-by-case basis, as the result of limited, localized research. Much has already been done along these lines. Studies of this sort, which are fortunately quite numerous and generally of high caliber, have greatly increased our understanding of iconoclasm beyond the hackneyed stereotypes that were for so long maintained by confessional polemicists and shortsighted historians. In spite of the advances made by these studies, however, a certain symmetry and sense of comprehensiveness was still missing: The emphasis placed on the strictly quantitative and social-scientific approaches (intended as a corrective to the simplistic explanations of the past) had not allowed much room for a synthetic understanding of the ideological framework of iconoclasm.

This is where the practical considerations shade off into the theoretical. Convinced of the intrinsic value of intellectual history, and of the fact that a full, synthetic analysis of the ideology of the Reformed Protestant attack on Catholic worship did not need to seek its ultimate verification in an exhaustive analysis of all the material ramifications of iconoclasm, I chose a methodological approach that focused principally on what had been previously neglected, namely, the theology of idolatry. On this point I am in agreement with the historian who recently remarked that, although he did not believe that history is moved by minds alone (or any other isolated factor), he did believe that "current preoccupations with material factors and subverbal behavior have obscured the force and relevance of individual emotion, thought and discourse in the complex process of history."[2]

To study the Reformation debate over idolatry is to peer into the eye of the storm. "Idolatry" is a fighting word. It presupposes a definition of what is true and what is false in religion, for an idol cannot be universally recognized as such. Idolatry is not simply the worship of a physical object, but rather any form of devotion that is judged to be incorrect. Thus, the Reformed concern with idolatry extended not only to the use of art in worship, but also to the behavior displayed in liturgical and social settings. The concept of idolatry existed among Catholics as well as Protestants, but its meaning was very different in each camp. In the sixteenth century, one man's devotion was another man's idolatry. It is good to keep in mind that at just about the same time that the soldiers of Charles V replaced the "horrible idols" of the Aztecs with "beautiful" crosses and images of Mary and the saints in the New World, Protestant iconoclasts were wreaking havoc on these Catholic objects in lands nominally ruled by him in Europe. The grisly cult of human sacrifices led by bloodstained priests inside the Wall of Snakes in Tenochtitlán inspired the same kind of reaction among the Conquistadores as the celebration of the

---

[2] Donald Kelley has recently attempted to refine the concept of "ideology" in the study of the Reformation. *The Beginning of Ideology: Consciousness and Society in the French Reformation* (Cambridge, 1982), esp. pp. vii–viii, 1–10.

Mass in the richly decorated cathedral of Basel did among Protestants.[3] To deal with this issue, then, is to deal with the way in which the truth claims of religion are defined. The Reformed Calvinist attack on idolatry is an attack on the "corruption" of religion, a defense of a certain interpretation of Scripture against its antithesis. In studying this phenomenon, therefore, one is able to determine the axis around which the Protestant polemic was arranged.

To study the issue of idolatry in the Reformation is to realize that there is a very concrete social and political dimension to the theology of the Reformers, and that one needs to look beyond the purely theoretical aspect of their thought. In this period, the very use of the word "idolatry" inspired conflict. "Idols" are made to be cast down. One who identifies an idol, by virtue of pointing to some object of devotion as wrong or evil, is also calling for its removal. Wherever there are idolaters, there, too, lurk some iconoclasts. The theologians who pointed the finger at idols might have been iconoclasts in principle, but few of them actually knocked down an image or gouged out its eyes. There is some truth in the observation made long ago that, in the times of the Reformation, "the doctors attacked the pope and the people the images."[4] Protestant theologians attacked Catholic piety vigorously, but the success of their polemic depended largely on its acceptance by the laity. The war against Catholic worship was as much a layman's struggle as a theologian's. In fact, the war proclaimed from the presses and the pulpit by the doctors was carried out by the laity in the streets, squares, and churches. If, as has recently been said, "the original Protestant vision was of a society of religiously enlightened laymen who were no longer burdened by traditional superstition and tyranny," then the attack on idolatry may be seen as one of the most daring attempts to fulfill this vision.[5] By attacking the images, the people were also attacking the pope. When children in Geneva stormed the cathedral in 1536 – and, as one account has it, later threw pieces of the broken images at people on the street, chanting "here we have the gods of the priests, would you like some?" – they innocently laid bare the nature of the attack on idolatry: The cultic objects represented not only false religion, but also subjection to an ecclesiastical system that was resented.[6] To the icon-

[3] Bernal Diaz del Castillo, *Historia Verdadera de la Conquista de la Nueva España*, C. Saenz de Santa Maria, ed. (Madrid, 1982), p. 97; *Aktensammlung zur Geschichte der Basler Reformation*, E. Durr and P. Roth, eds.,(Basel, 1937), vol. 3, p. 66.
[4] J. H. Merle D'Aubigné. *History of the Great Reformation of the Sixteenth Century* (New York, 1846), p. 767.
[5] Steven Ozment, *The Reformation in the Cities* (New Haven, 1975), p. 165.
[6] Antoine Fromment, *Les Actes et Gestes Merveilleux de la Cité de Genève* (1544), reissued by J. G. Fick (Geneva, 1954), p. 144–5.

oclasts, the idols were not just false gods, but the gods of the Church of Rome, as represented by the priests. Protestants knew that to rid a city of "idols" was to rid it of Rome, that in destroying the images and abolishing the Mass they were also destroying the priests. Few other aspects of the Reformation lend themselves as well for studying the way in which theology inspires action, as this war on idolatry.

But how is a sophisticated, sardonic critique of medieval piety transformed into a crusade from a pulpit, or a riot in a church, or even a civil war? How does an abstract metaphysical concept about the structure of reality first articulated by learned humanists, and later applied to scriptural exegesis by theologians, ever come to have any relation with a young Swiss artisan who spit in a holy water font, or with thousands of Frenchmen who felt compelled to leave their homeland?

It is not my intention here to venture any new theses on the vexing problem of the relation between high culture and popular behavior. Instead, what I want to show is that one needs to consider the intricate correlation between ideas and situations, and that, in the writing of history, one can no more easily dismiss theology than politics, or economics. In saying this, I am far from implying some simple cause-and-effect relationship that would make all behavior depend ultimately on theological ideas, as if each and every iconoclastic act was a conscious reaction produced by the Reformed concept of idolatry. Neither am I implicitly accepting some sort of trickle-down theory proposing that the elites always and everywhere predetermine the behavior of the common people by doing their thinking for them. Yet, even when one takes into account the complexities of human behavior, and the almost infinite sets of interrelated motivations that form ideologies and produce social changes, one is struck by the fact that Reformation iconoclasm became the earmark of a movement that consciously promoted itself as a religious reform, and that the very principles of reform were at bottom theological. What concerns us here is the development and application of these principles, and it is to the unfolding of this phenomenon that we now turn.

CHAPTER 1

The state of lay devotion in the late Middle Ages

GUILLAUME Farel, leader of the Reformation in France and Switzerland, and friend and mentor to John Calvin, was deeply impressed by a pilgrimage he made as a child. As is often the case with religious converts, he could remember what life was like in the "vortex of perdition" all too clearly, and he described the event in detail years later with a certain sense of horror. The pilgrimage symbolized everything that he despised in the worship of the Roman Catholic church: He saw its objective as the misdirected veneration of material objects, and its foundation as a web of fraud, deceit, and priestly avarice.[1]

Farel reports that when he had not yet even learned to read, his family went to the Shrine of the Holy Cross at Tallard, which was not far from his native village of Gap in Dauphiné. This shrine, like countless others throughout Europe, claimed to have some fragments of the true cross of Jesus. It was not a very impressive-looking relic. The two fragments, rough and uneven, had been fashioned into a cross and were trimmed with copper. The metal trim was also an object of veneration, since it was believed to be part of the basin in which Jesus had washed the feet of the apostles. A small crucifix was also attached to the reliquary that housed these ancient, holy reminders of Jesus's life on earth, to serve as a concrete visual representation of the event of salvation in which those very same objects had played a part. But the pilgrims were not too interested in the outward appearance of the relics: They were there to seek contact with the power of God.

As soon as they reached the shrine, the pilgrims prostrated themselves in prayer before the relic. While they prayed, a priest came out and explained how the small crucifix that was attached to the reliquary also shared in their power. It was an awesome story about cosmic

---

[1] Guillaume Farel, *Du Vray Usage de la Croix* (1560), J. G. Fick, ed. (Geneva, 1865), pp. 146–9.

8

battles on a local level, which must have reinforced belief in relics as necessary weapons in the struggle against nature and the devil. Farel remembered the priest as saying:

> Whenever the devil sends hail and thunder, this crucifix moves so violently that one would think it wanted to get loose from the cross to go running after the devil . . . and all the while it keeps throwing out sparks of fire against the storm. Were it not for this, the whole country would be swept bare.[2]

When the priest had finished, a disfigured attendant also came out to make even greater claims for the power of the relic. His stories culminated in a pitch for donations to the shrine. Farel says he was terrified by all this, and it is not hard to imagine the small boy having nightmares afterward. But Farel says that his parents, too, and the other pilgrims were equally frightened, and that they believed these miracle stories. He also lamented that their understanding of religion was not much better than that of unreasoning beasts.[3]

Within the last half century a great deal has been written about lay piety in the later Middle Ages, and much continues to be written. In many ways, Farel's narrative serves as a convenient point of reference for what has been said.

In order to explain how Farel and countless others rejected the religion of their forebears in the sixteenth century, it is first necessary to make a few observations about late medieval piety. Not to do this would be as foolhardy as trying to pinpoint the cause of an earthquake without knowledge of the way in which the earth's crust moves over its molten interior. Like some impressive city perched on a quivering fault line, the edifice of late medieval religion rested on shaky ground. Beneath the deceptively calm and firm exterior, a complex series of imperceptible movements were building up pressure, mounting strain to the breaking point. Though some contemporaries may have felt minor tremors, or suspected that a major quake was long overdue, no one could predict when and where disaster would strike, or how much damage would be done.

By the same token, just as one need not become an expert geologist to recognize a photograph of the San Andreas Fault where it surges above ground, stretching like a scar across the face of the earth, so is it not necessary to delve into all the details of late medieval piety to

---

[2] Ibid., p. 147.

[3] Ibid., p. 149: "De moy i'estoye fort petit, et à peine ie savoye lire. Mon pere et ma mere croyoyent tout . . . De savoir qui sont les vrais miracles, et à quoy ils sont faits, et qui sont les faus, et à quoy ils servent, nous y entendions tous autant que des povres bestes."

become aware of the trouble that was brewing at the Shrine of the Holy Cross. A brief glance at the subsoil of the Reformation reveals enough uneven ridges and cracks, enough pressure and gradual movement of seemingly fixed structures, to convince anyone that the strain was overwhelming along those spots where the devastation was most severe. In the same way that the trail of destruction left aboveground by a quake leads a seismologist toward the epicenter, the shattered images and altars left behind by Protestant iconoclasts point a historian to disturbances beneath the ground on which they stood.

Though scholarly opinion varies concerning the quality of late medieval religion, there is little disagreement about its intensity.[4] In his essay, "Piety in Germany Around 1500," Bernd Moeller points out that the principal characteristic of the late fifteenth century was its consistent churchliness, and says it was "one of the most churchly-minded and devout periods of the Middle Ages."[5] Likewise, Lucien Febvre observes that this age was marked by an immense appetite for the divine,[6] and Johan Huizinga remarks that there was "an enor-

---

[4] Steven Ozment, *The Reformation in the Cities* (New Haven, 1975), p. 21. Ozment provides an excellent survey and analysis of the secondary literature dealing with late medieval lay piety. Ozment contrasts the work of Bernd Moeller, "Piety in Germany Around 1500," ARG 56 (1965) and Johannes Janssen, *History of the German People since the End of the Middle Ages*, vol. I (1876), who describe the late fifteenth century as one of the most spiritually sound and profound periods in German history, with that of the Roman Catholic ecumenicist Joseph Lortz, who finds true piety lacking and corruption and abuse abounding ["Probleme des kirchlichen Lebens in Deutschland vor der Reformation," in H. Jedin et al., *Probleme der Kirchenspaltung im 16 Jahrhundert* (Regensburg, 1970). Also discussed are works of Jacques Toussaert, *Le Sentiment Religieux en Flandre à la Fin du Moyen Age* (Paris, 1963) and Etienne Delaruelle, *L'Eglise au Temps du Grand Schisme et de la Crise Conciliaire (1378–1449)*, vol. 14 of the *Histoire de l'Eglise*, A. Fliche and V. Martin, eds. (Paris, 1964). Toussaert and Delaruelle find an intense and materially inclined piety that, to their opinion, was superficial. Other major works dealing with pre-Reformation piety are W. Andreas, *Deutschland vor der Reformation*, 6th ed. (Stuttgart, 1959); J. Klapper, *Deutsches Volkstum am Ausgang des Mittelalters* (Breslau, 1930); V. Hasak, *Der Christliche Glaube des Deutschen Volkes beim Schlusse des Mittelalters* (Regensburg, 1868); Francis Rapp, *L'Eglise et la Vie Religieuse en Occident à la Fin du Moyen Age* (Paris 1971); H. Schaller, *Die Weltanschaung des Mittelalters* (Munich-Berlin, 1934); G. Schnürer, *Kirche und Kultur im Mittelalter*, vol. 3 (1929); Keith Thomas, *Religion and the Decline of Magic* (New York, 1971); L. Veit, *Volksfrommes Brauchtum und Kirche im Deutschen Mittelalter* (Freiburg, 1936), and *Volkskultur und Geschichte: Festgabe für Joseph Düninger* (1970); and Raoul Manselli, *La Religion Populaire au Moyen Age* (Paris-Montreal, 1975).

[5] Translated in *The Reformation in Medieval Perspective*, S. Ozment, ed. (Chicago, 1971); and also in *Pre-Reformation Germany*, G. Strauss, ed. (New York, 1972). I have used the Ozment edition.

[6] Lucien Febvre, "Une Question Mal Posée: les Origines de la Réforme Française," in *Au Coeur Religieux du XVIe Siècle* (Paris, 1957), pp. 1–70, originally published in *Revue Historique*, 161 (1929). English translation in Peter Burke (ed.), *A New Kind of History from the Writings of Lucien Febvre* (New York, 1973), pp. 44–107.

mous unfolding of religion in daily life."[7] These scholars agree that the upsurge in piety was primarily an expression of lay fervor. As never before, says Moeller, "the folk" became not only a participant, but a determining force in the religious life of the Church.[8]

How was this appetite for the divine satisfied? A second observation may be made here about the state of piety reflected by Farel's narrative. The religious saturation of late medieval life also showed signs of tension. Late medieval religion sought to grasp the transcendent by making it immanent: It was a religion that sought to embody itself in images, reduce the infinite to the finite, blend the holy and the profane, and disintegrate all mystery.[9] By the late fifteenth century, life was so saturated with religion that the people of Western Europe ran the risk of confusing the spiritual and temporal, the sacred and the profane. It was a religion that seemed most interested in tapping supernatural power. Keith Thomas has made the blunt, perceptive observation that much of late medieval religion was magical, and that the difference between churchmen and magicians lay less in what they claimed they could do than in the authority on which their claims rested.[10] This is illustrated by the crucifix that "controlled" the weather at Tallard. Farel and his family had no trouble believing that the elemental forces of the universe could be controlled by one small object, and the priests further reinforced this belief. Late medieval piety showed an almost irrepressible urge to localize the divine power, make it tangible, and bring it under control. The relic at Tallard fulfilled these aspirations by making the divine commonplace.[11]

As one recent study of popular piety in sixteenth-century France has indicated, the word "religion" was a synonym for "devotion" in Catholic parlance. It meant the honor and respect paid to God, the Virgin, and the saints – and their images and relics – as well as to the estate of the regular clergy, who were ostensibly saintly by profes-

[7] Johan Huizinga, *The Waning of the Middle Ages* (New York, 1954), p. 151.

[8] Moeller, "Piety," p. 54.

[9] Huizinga, *Waning*, pp. 151–2: (Moeller, "Piety," p. 53). See also the essay by R. C. Trexler, "Florentine Religious Experience: The Sacred Image," *Studies in the Renaissance*, 19: 7–41 (1972). Trexler says the late Middle Ages in Florence showed a marked inclination toward a "sensuous perception of the sacred" (p. 10).

[10] *Religion and the Decline of Magic* (New York, 1971), p. 49. Thomas points out that "the magical aspects of the church's function were often inseparable from the devotional ones" (p. 50). For a fine, detailed study of the function of miracles prior to the late Middle Ages, see Benedicta Ward, *Miracles and the Medieval Mind: Theory, Record and Event 1000–1215* (Philadelphia, 1982).

[11] Huizinga, *Waning*, p. 152: "By this tendency to embodiment in visible forms all holy concepts are constantly exposed to the danger of hardening into mere externalism. For in assuming a definite figurative shape thought loses its ethereal and vague qualities, and pious feeling is apt to resolve itself in the image."

sion.[12] This devotion shown to the saints reached its peak in the fifteenth century, when the saints were brought ever closer to the individual's daily life.[13] Popular, vernacular, religious literature of the late fifteenth century was devoted largely to Mary and the saints. Most well-known preachers published at least one collection of sermons on the saints,[14] while the booklets of instruction for the parish clergy, known as *Summa Rudium* or *Summa Praeceptorium*, placed great emphasis on the cult of the saints as part of the adoration of God.[15] A "patronage system" was finally fixed whereby each saint was assigned special spheres of influence over particular social groups and particular emergencies.[16] The *cultus divorum* became, to borrow a term used by Jacques Toussaert,[17] a form of "parapolytheism" in which the realm of the saints was modeled according to the arrangement of human society and human fate.[18] The Virgin Mary, of course, continued to hold a special and leading place in this pantheon.[19]

This formal delegation of divine omnipotence gave rise to an even more curious fragmentation of supernatural power. The names of several saints became linked to the diseases they were supposed to cure. Many came to believe that if a saint could cure an illness he must have control over it and also be able to inflict it: Such was the case with skin diseases known as "St. Anthony's fire" and types of gout named "St. Maur's evil."[20] In this way, late medieval religion developed a nebulous concept of divinity: God and the saints became

[12] A. N. Galpern, *The Religions of the people in Sixteenth-Century Champagne* (Cambridge, Mass., 1976), p. 157.

[13] Moeller, "Piety," p. 55. Keith Thomas places the peak earlier for England and says it actually slackened in the fifteenth century (*Religion* p. 29).

[14] H. Siebert, *Beiträge zur vorreformatorischen Heiligen- und Reliquienverehrung* (Freiburg, 1907), p. 2.

[15] Charles Garside, Jr., *Zwingli and the Arts* (New Haven, 1966), p. 90.

[16] Peter Brown, "Society and the Supernatural: A Medieval Change," *Daedalus*, 104: 133–51 (1975). Brown argues that the sense of the supernatural began to be sharpened and delimited through this process about the twelfth century.

[17] J. Toussaert, *Le Sentiment*, p. 586.

[18] Moeller, "Piety," p. 55. A. N. Galpern argues that the multiplication of intercesors "may also in part be understood with reference to the political situation" since the fragmentation of power among feudal magnates "clouded people's understanding of divine power" (*Religions*, p. 70). This interpretation tries to make too much out of religio- and politico-social connections. A more perceptive analysis is that of Peter Brown, *The Cult of the Saints* (Chicago, 1980).

[19] W. Andreas, *Deutschland*, p. 158: Siebert, *Beiträge*, pp. 14, 29, 39. For a detailed study of the role of Mary in late medieval religion, see S. Beissel, *Geschichte der Verehrung Marias in Deutschland während des Mittelalters* (Freiburg, 1909).

[20] These diseases are listed in the poem of Robert Gauguin, "De validorum per Franciam mendicantium varia astucia." Other maladies ascribed to particular saints included: ulcers to St. Fiacrus, bladder infections to St. Damian, and paralysis to St. Pious. Huizinga, *Waning*, p. 174; Thomas, *Religion*, p. 28.

an indistinguishable source of power and wrath, not entirely unlike the *numina* of ancient Roman religion.

Bernd Moeller views this obsession with the saints as a sign of "an oppressive uncertainty about salvation together with the longing for it." He argues that by capturing the mediators between man and God, late medieval society sought to "force a guarantee of salvation."[21] Yet, the *cultus divorum* itself became a source of anxiety. The saints became the believer's friends and ever-present intercessors, but they also assumed Godlike qualities that had to be appeased in the proper way. Erasmus, for instance, would later make reference to swineherds who thought of St. Anthony as protector of their hogs and who worshiped him "for fear he should grow angry if they neglect him."[22]

The cult of the saints materialized in two forms: artistic representations and relics. Beginning in the twelfth century, the cult of images enjoyed an upsurge in Western Europe. The rise of towns, the growth of the economy and the creation of a relatively prosperous middle class greatly increased the prospects for material contributions to the devotional life of the Church. The expansion of the cult of the saints was especially aided by the rise in popularity of private and communal chantries, guilds, and religious brotherhoods, all of which donated time and money for the creation of appropriate devotional aids such as statues and paintings.[23] The chantries and guilds made possible the investment of capital in the promotion of accepted beliefs and practices, thus expanding the use of devotional paraphernalia.[24] In Zurich, for instance, the commissioning of ecclesiastical works of art increased a hundredfold between 1500 and 1518.[25]

Concern with salvation also played a role in the physical expansion of the cult. This development was intensified, of course, by the belief in the power of good works as an aid to salvation. The donation and erection of material objects of worship was in itself a way of working

---

[21] Moeller, "Piety," p. 55.
[22] *Colloquies:* "The Franciscans, or Rich Beggars."
[23] A fine, detailed analysis of this process can be found in William A. Christian, Jr., *Local Religion in Sixteenth Century Spain* (Princeton, 1981), chap. 3, "Chapels and Shrines."
[24] Delaruelle, *L'Eglise*, chap. 3, "Les Confréries," pp. 666–94. Other works dealing with chantries, guilds and brotherhoods include: Jean Deschamps, *Le Confréries au Moyen Age* (Bordeaux, 1958); Gabriel Le Bras, *Institutions Ecclésiastiques de la Chrétienté Médiévale* (2 vols., Paris, 1959–64); and "Les confréries chrétiennes: Problèmes et propositions," *Revue Historique de Droit Francaise et Etranger* 18: 310–363 (1940); Michel Molat, *La Vie et la Pratique Religieuse au XIVe Siècle et dans la Première Partie du XVe* (Paris, n.d.).
[25] Garside, *Zwingli*, p. 87.

toward one's salvation. The donor and the artist were thought to be contributing, in a very special way, to the enrichment of the spiritual life of the community. This unique expression of charity and works-righteousness was an important element of the intensification and externalization of piety on the eve of the Reformation.[26] One must not discount more basic human motives such as individual or civic pride, however. There can be little doubt that the donation of ecclesiastical art often enhanced the status of those who commissioned and installed them.[27]

As the material expansion of the cult progressed, the veneration of the saints became so tied up with images that the visual representations threatened to overshadow the spiritual element behind their worship. New images were set up nearly everywhere; they were also sumptuously decorated, given a contemporary look, and made ever larger. One scholar has observed that the Christian church had never displayed such visual splendor as it did in the late Middle Ages.[28] This visual externalization of faith became the layman's theology. Huizinga has argued that the cult of images allowed "the multitude" to have no need for intellectual proofs in matters of faith, that the mere presence of a visible image sufficed to establish the truth of holy things.[29] This development was fraught with danger. Pictures are not a good medium by which to convey qualitative distinctions in worship. The growing cult of images had no safeguard built in to prevent the people from confusing the image and what it sought to represent.[30] The reality of all spiritual things represented in wood, stone, and glass became quite vivid for the average Christian, as is witnessed by the crucifix at Tallard. Images could acquire a life of their own, work miracles, or become independent cult objects. The externalization of faith attained such earthy realism that there were even

[26] Johannes Janssen has observed that "the doctrine of good works had been one of the most powerful factors in the development of art." *History of the German People at the Close of the Middle Ages*, trans. A. M. Christie (London, 1907), vol. 2, p. 40.
[27] Carl Christensen, "Iconoclasm and the Preservation of Ecclesiastical Art in Reformation Nurenberg," *ARG*, 61: 213 (1970). Also: Andreas, *Deutschland*, p. 147.
[28] Hans Preuss, *Die Deutsche Frömmigkeit im Spiegel der Bildenden Kunst* (Berlin, 1926), p. 122. The extent to which the cult of Mary and the saints dominated Christian iconography is illustrated by C. Christensen. In an appendix to *Art and the Reformation in Germany* (Athens, Ohio, 1980), p. 207, he provides an iconographical tabulation of the themes of almost 450 German religious paintings during the years 1495–1520. Of these, 82 depict Mary as a major figure, and another 125 portray lesser saints. Combined, both categories account for nearly 50% of the sample.
[29] Huizinga, *Waning*, p. 165.
[30] Ibid., p. 166. Huizinga argues that the medieval Church overlooked the danger involved in letting people learn from images: "An abundance of pictorial fancy, after all, furnished the simple mind quite as much matter for deviating from pure doctrine as any personal interpretation of Holy Scripture."

statues of Mary that opened to reveal the Trinity concealed in her womb.[31]

Popular devotion was externalized even further in the cult of relics. All real or imagined mementos associated with the lives of Christ, Mary, and the saints were sought with fervor as special sources of divine grace.[32] As the most vivid reminders of the presence of the holy, and as physical points of contact with the divine, relics assumed wondrous powers. The cross at Tallard is only one of innumerable examples of miracle-working relics. Moreover, since relics were a source of indulgences when properly venerated, the relic-mania of the late Middle Ages was also intricately connected with indulgences.[33] This relationship, in turn, helped intensify two types of devotion: the pilgrimage and the relic collection. Farel and his family serve as witnesses to the popularity of pilgrimages, even to small local shrines; a practice which, by the late fifteenth century, had become one of the most widespread forms of devotion in Western Europe.[34] This phenomenon was accompanied by the amassment of relics by certain churches or individuals, primarily with the objective of obtaining astronomical amounts of indulgence. In Halle, for instance, Cardinal Albrecht of Brandenburg had acquired an amazingly precise 39,245,120 years of indulgence through his collection.[35] The Duke of Saxony had an equally impressive collection at Wittenberg.[36]

---

[31] Jonathan Sumption, *Pilgrimage: An Image of Medieval Religion* (London, 1975), p. 45.

[32] There is a good deal of literature dealing with saints and the cult of relics in the Middle Ages. Some of the more important works are as follow: Peter Brown, *The Cult of the Saints* (Chicago, 1980); the three books by S. Beissel, *Geschichte der Verehrung Marias in Deutschland Während des Mittelalters* (Freiburg, 1909), *Die Verehrung der Heiligen und Ihrer Reliquien in Deutschland bis zum Beginne des 13 Jahrhunderts* (Freiburg, 1892); *Die Verehrung der Heiligen und Ihrer Reliquien im Deutschland Während der Zweiten Hälfte des Mittelalters* (Freiburg, 1892); H. Fichtenau, "Zum Reliquienwesen im Früheren Mittelalter," *Mitteilung des Instituts für Osterreichische Geschichtsforschung*, 60: 60–89 (1952); and Seibert, *Beiträge.*

[33] Delaruelle, *L'Eglise*, pp. 810–20, and N. Paulus, *Geschichte des Ablasses im Mittelalter* (2 vols., Paderborn, 1922–3).

[34] J. Lortz asserts that the urge to go on pilgrimages reached almost epidemic proportions in late medieval Germany. *The Reformation in Germany* (London, 1968), vol. I, p. 114. Among the many works treating this subject: J. Sumption, *Pilgrimage* (London, 1975); R. C. Finucane, *Miracles and Pilgrims: Popular Beliefs in Medieval England* (London, 1977); S. Beissel, *Die Aachenfahrt* (Freiburg, 1902); L. Carlin, "Straf- und Sühnenwallfahrten nach Einsideln," in *Der Geschichtsfreund* (1974); B. Kötting, *Peregrinatio Religiosa* (Münster, 1950); I. Müller, *Die Churratische Wahlfahrt im Mittelalter* (1964); G. Schreiber, *Wahlfahrt und Volkstum* (Münster, 1934); and Pierre Sigal, *Les Marcheurs de Dieu: Pelerinages et Pelerins au Moyen Age* (Paris, 1974). An anthropological study by Victor and Edith Turner offers a different perspective on the subject. *Image and Pilgrimage in Christian Culture* (New York, 1978), esp. chaps. 4 and 5.

[35] Moeller, "Piety," p. 55.

[36] Paul Kalkoff, *Ablass und Reliquienverehrung an der Schlosskirche zu Wittenberg* (1907).

A consequence of the cult of relics was the widespread promotion of "pious frauds," or spurious relics, such as the ones exhibited at Tallard. No relic was more ubiquitous than the true cross. Fragments of this relic existed in almost every town and hamlet across the face of Europe. Other common pious frauds were items such as Mary's milk; Christ's foreskin, hair and nail clippings, and heads and limbs of the apostles and other favorite saints. Popular belief appears to have ignored the conflicting claims of authenticity made by duplicated relics; it was commonly believed that God multiplied these objects as He wished, for the benefit of humankind.[37] The desire to possess and venerate such objects was so overwhelming that it sometimes gave way to irreverence, crudity, and crass materialism. As Jacques Toussaert has observed, the cult of relics reached a frenzied state of "découpage millimétrique" in which the remains of holy men and women were minutely dismembered and distributed, as if the divine power inherent in their bodies could be infinitely subdivided.[38] Popular piety sought relics wherever they could be found, often without respect for the person of the saint involved. According to one account, the body of Thomas Aquinas was decapitated and boiled by the monks of Fossanova, in whose monastery he had died. The body of St. Elizabeth of Hungary was mobbed by a crowd of worshipers while it was lying in state, and was quickly relieved of its funeral shroud, hair, nails, and other parts, including the nipples.[39] The relic trade and the pilgrimage business became booming industries in the late Middle Ages. Pilgrimages created a complex network of services that would provide transportation, food, and lodging for the traveler.[40] Relics became commercial commodities and a source of profit.[41] Even the theft of relics came to be regarded as holy.[42]

The externalization of piety also focused on the Mass, and more specifically on the eucharist. It has been pointed out that the fifteenth century was not only the great age of pilgrimages and new pilgrimage shrines, but also that of bleeding hosts and the full development of the feast of Corpus Christi.[43] Popular piety seized on the theological

---

[37] C. R. Thompson, *The Colloquies of Erasmus* (Chicago, 1965), p. 295.
[38] Toussaert, *Le sentiment*, p. 291.
[39] Huizinga, *Waning*, p. 167.
[40] J. Sumption, *Pilgrimage*.
[41] H. Silvestre, "Commerce et vol de reliques au moyen age," *Revue Belge de Philologie et Histoire*, 30: 721–40 (1952).
[42] The phenomenon of pious relic stealing is treated by Patrick J. Geary, *Furta Sacra: Thefts of Relics in the Central Middle Ages* (Princeton, 1978).
[43] Herman Heimpel, "Characteristics of the Late Middle Ages in Germany," in *Pre-Reformation Germany*, G. Strauss, ed. (New York, 1972), p. 68. Appeared originally as "Das Wesen des Deutschen Spätmittelalters" in *Archiv für Kulturgeschichte*, 35: 29–51 (1953).

and liturgical idea of transsubstantiation with unrestrained fervor, but often without a proper understanding of its meaning. Instead of being a central and integrated part of Christian worship, the Mass and the eucharist became the focus of a detached adoration. Since the time of Ambrose in the fourth century, the Western liturgy had increasingly become a grand spectacle with its own visual imagery. As a standardized ritual laden with an awe-inspiring display of spiritual power through very material, and almost mechanical means, the liturgy itself had become the living image of the mystery of salvation. Regarded as the reenactment of Christ's sacrifice on Calvary (especially since the time of Gregory I, the Great), the Mass, as a ritual, could not help but become representational in a very concrete manner. Therefore, most worshipers approached the liturgy in the same way they approached images and relics, as an object of veneration and a source of power. Consequently, the Reformers would attack the ceremony of the Mass itself as an "idol."

Furthermore, as the consecrated host – believed to be the true body of Christ – became the supreme *locus divinitatis* in medieval religion, the sacrament of the eucharist became ever more remote. The laity crowded to see the host and ascribed all sorts of miracles to it, but participation in communion remained rare and infrequent. The host bled, levitated, transfigured itself into the likeness of Christ, protected itself from impious hands, and sometimes even controlled the elements.[44] Such intensity of belief was reflected in the statement made by a Dominican preacher in Geneva, who proclaimed that the priest was superior to Mary in one respect: that whereas Mary brought Jesus to earth but once, the priest could bring him forth every day.[45] Late medieval society even believed on occasion that Jews desired to steal the host so they could torture Christ anew, as if the consecrated wafer could really feel pain – in spite of the fact that Jews denied the divinity of Christ and the doctrine of transsubstantiation.[46] The belief in the objective presence of the divine in material elements could not have been intensified much further.

---

[44] For more on this subject, consult the three works by Peter Browe: *Die Verehrung der Eucharistie im Mittelalter* (Munich, 1933); *Die Eucharistiche Wunder des Mittelalters* (Breslau, 1938), and "Die Eucharistie als Zaubermittel im Mittelalter," *Archiv für Kulturgeschichte*, 20: 134–54 (1930). Also: L. Meier, "Wilsnack als Spiegel Deutscher Vorreformation," *Zeitschrift für Religions- und Geistesgeschichte*, 3: 53–69 (1951); Adolf Franz, *Die Messe im Deutschen Mittelalter* (Fribourg, 1902); and P. Geary, *Furta Sacra*, chap. 3.

[45] Henri Naef, *Les Origines de la Réforme* (2 vols., Geneva, 1967), vol. 2, p. 470.

[46] Joshua Trachtenberg, *The Devil and the Jews* (New Haven, 1944), pp. 109–23.

War against the idols

MEDIEVAL CRITIQUES OF POPULAR RELIGION

The externalization of piety in the late Middle Ages did not go un-criticized. In fact, though the material manifestations of the Christian cult were widely accepted throughout the medieval period, they had, on several occasions, caused disruption within the Church. Material expressions of devotion, such as the cult of images, had been a source of controversy long before the late Middle Ages. The Judaic heritage in Christianity passed on a legacy of animosity toward visual representations of the divine, causing tension between ideals and practices. The use of religious art as church decoration began in the third century, but rapidly developed as a devotional aid by the fourth.[47] The cult of images was principally an extension of the cult of the saints, and from its earliest days served as a physical reminder alongside the relic, which was the most effective *locus* of the holiness of the saints on earth.[48] Although some early Christian theologians, such as Vigilantius, tried to oppose the use of images in worship, others such as Augustine and Jerome accepted it with caution and rationalized it according to prevailing philosophical, hagiographical, and artistic fashions.[49]

The cult of images was dramatically expanded, especially in the Eastern Church, after the sixth century. Among the Byzantines, the icon became an increasingly powerful and almost independent cult object, but also a source of conflict. The violent and prolonged Icono-clastic Controversy of the eighth and ninth centuries showed how much resentment existed against images among some Christians, but

---

[47] Johannes Kollwitz, "Zur Frühgeschichte der Bilderverehrung," *Das Gottesbild im Abendland* (Witten-Berlin, 1959).

[48] On this point see the two excellent studies of Peter Brown: "The Rise and Function of the Holy Man in Late Antiquity," *Journal of Roman Studies*, 71: 80–101 (1971); and "A Dark-Age Crisis: Aspects of the Iconoclastic Controversy," *English Historical Review*, 346: 1–34 (1973).

[49] W. R. Jones, "Art and Christian Piety: Iconoclasm in Medieval Europe," in Joseph Gutmann (ed.), *The Image and the Word: Confrontations in Judaism, Christianity and Islam* (Missoula, Mont., 1978). For further background on the early history of images in the Christian church see the following: N. H. Baynes, "Idolatry and the Early Church," in *Byzantine Studies and Other Essays* (London, 1955); Ernst Kitzinger, "The Cult of Images in the Age before Iconoclasm," *Dumbarton Oaks Papers*, no. 8 (Cambridge, Mass., 1954); Hans von Campenhausen, "The Theological Problem of Images in the Early Church," in *Tradition and Life in the Church: Essays and Lectures in Church History*, trans. A. V. Littledale (London, 1968); Gerhard B. Ladner, "The Concept of the Image in the Greek Fathers and the Byzantine Iconoclastic Contro-versy," *Dumbarton Oaks Papers*, no. 7 (Cambridge, Mass., 1953).

the eventual triumph of the iconodules fixed the icon forever as a central part of Eastern Christian worship.[50]

The West generally tended to resist the beatification of images as cult objects, and developed no crisis of conscience like that of the Byzantines. Faint echoes of the Eastern controversy surfaced during the Carolingian age, when the discussion of images among Charlemagne's court theologians produced a negative assessment of religious imagery. The opinions of these theologians, collected in the *Libri Carolini* (ca. 790), stated that images should not be worshiped. Nonetheless, they still accepted the veneration of the cross and the commemorative and decorative use of images of the saints.[51]

The Carolingian debate had no lasting effect on the life of the Western Church. Popular acceptance and official approval from other quarters outweighed the influence of the *Libri Carolini*.[52] Already in the sixth century, Pope Gregory I had formulated a defense of images based on their educational function. Images, he said, were the *libri pauperum:* They taught the faith to those who could not read. Gregory's defense was wholeheartedly adopted by the Church and proved to be of long-lasting influence.[53]

Until the fourteenth century, Western criticism of images was sporadic and limited. The early Cistercians and Franciscans, for instance, showed contempt for lavish ornamentation and cautioned against the use of worldly symbols in the adornment of their buildings. The Waldensians and Cathars rejected the worship of images, and even the cross, but their attitude prompted no reconsideration of the cult of

---

[50] In addition to the works of Brown, Baynes, Kitzinger, and Ladner cited earlier, one might also consult: E. J. Martin, *A History of the Iconoclastic Controversy* (London, 1936); Jaroslav Pelikan, *The Spirit of Eastern Christendom (600–700)* (Chicago, 1974), pp. 51–145; and the various studies of Stephen Gero: *Byzantine Iconoclsm during the Reign of Leo III* (Louvain, 1973); *Byzantine Iconoclasm during the Reign of Constantine V* (Louvain, 1977); "Notes on Byzantine Iconoclasm in the Eighth Century, *Byzantion*, 44 (1974); "Byzantine Iconoclasm and the Failure of a Medieval Reformation" (in J. Gutmann, *Image*); also the collection of essays edited by Anthony Bryer and Judith Herrin, *Iconoclasm* (Birmingham, 1977).

[51] Stephen Gero, "The 'Libri Carolini' and the Image Controversy," *Greek Orthodox Theological Review*, 18 (1975); C. J. Hefele and H. Leclercq, *Histoire des Conciles d'après les Documents Originaux* (11 vols., Paris, 1907–52), III, pt. 2, pp. 1078–9; E. J. Martin, *History of the Iconoclastic Controversy* (London, 1936), p. 135ff.; and G. Handler, *Epochen Karolingischer Theologie* (Berlin, 1958).

[52] The *Libri Carolini* were largely forgotten by medieval theologians. It was not until the sixteenth century that they were resurrected, when the liberal French bishop Jean du Tillet published them, only to have them quickly placed on the *Index* of forbidden books. E. J. Martin, *History*, p. 230.

[53] Johannes Kollwitz, "Bild und Bildertheologie im Mittelalter," in *Das Gottesbild im Abendland* (Witten-Berlin, 1959).

images in the West.[54] Bernard of Angers in the eleventh century and Bishop William of Auvergne in the twelfth wrote against those who treated images much as the pagans had done, but did not reject the validity of religious imagery. [55] Guibert of Nogent also attacked superstitions attached to the cult of relics in the twelfth century but, again, limited his critique to abuses while still believing in the correctness of the cult.[56] These criticisms were overshadowed by the continuing expansion of the cult of saints, images, and relics throughout the Middle Ages, as well as by the ideological approval given by some of the leading theologians of the Church. Bonaventure expanded on Pope Gregory's dictum, dividing the educational value of images into three different aspects: the pedagogical, the inspirational, and the commemorative. Thomas Aquinas further exalted images as aids for communicating with the divine and distinguished the relative degrees of reverence due to the cross (*latria*), to representations of the human Jesus (*hyperdulia*), and images of the saints (*dulia*). Aquinas also adopted the theology of John of Damascus, and argued that the devotion shown the material object ascends to the spiritual reality it represents. This concept had been used since the time of St. Basil in the East to avoid charges of idolatry, and would become a standard defense of images in the West as well.[57]

These teachings led to a general acceptance of images as aids to devotion, which was so intense that by the late fifteenth century, for instance, the Augustinian Gottschalk Hollen could actually claim that people were led to piety more effectively "through a picture than through a sermon."[58] Moreover, the common worshiper found it extremely difficult to apply the theological distinctions proposed by the Church, and popular piety sunk far below the level proposed by

---

[54] W. R. Jones, "Lollards and Images: The Defense of Religious Art in Later Medieval England," *Journal of the History of Ideas*, 34: 27 (1973); Noël Valois, *Heresies of the High Middle Ages*, trans. W. Wakefield and A. Evans (New York, 1969) pp. 84, 240, 312, 313, 349; and Arno Borst, *Die Katharer* (Stuttgart, 1953), p. 219, n. 24.

[55] J. Sumption, *Pilgrimage*, p. 52; and G. C. Coulton, *Art and the Reformation* (Cambridge, 1953), p. 375.

[56] Guibert's treatise dealt with the outlandish claims made for some relics and was entitled "De pignoribus sanctorum" (ca. 1120). K. Guth, *Guibert von Nogent* [*Studien und Mitteilungen zur Geschichte des Benedikterordens*, 21 (1970)]; and A. Lenfranc, "Le traité des reliques de Guibert de Nogent," in *Etudes d'Histoire Dedieés à Gabriel Monod* (1896).

[57] Kollwitz, "Bild und Bildertheologie," pp. 125–8.

[58] Siebert, *Beiträge*, p. 22. A popular *summa praeceptorium* from the fifteenth century proposed that images were essential to religious life for four reasons: (1) They led to knowledge of things unknown, (2) They inspired imitation of the saints' lives, (3) They strengthened memory, (4) They promoted veneration (Siebert, *Beiträge*, p. 21).

the theologians.[59] The image and the prototype often became indistinguishable in the mind of the supplicant. Ulrich Zwingli later listed the acts commonly performed before images: People would kneel and bow, remove their hats, burn incense and candles, kiss them, decorate them with gold and jewels, call them merciful and gracious, touch them as if they could really heal or forgive sins.[60] Erasmus complained of people who "bowed the head before them, fell on the ground, crawled on their knees, kissed and fondled the carvings."[61] The images, in short, had come alive.

As the cult of saints, images, and relics expanded and intensified among the clergy and laity in the later Middle Ages, criticism began to develop. Pierre d'Ailly, for instance, protested against the increased attention being given to the saints and their images in his tract *De Reformatione* (1416). Jean Gerson also attacked popular superstition[62] and pointed to some of the dangers of visual imagery in his *Expostulatio adversus corruptionem juventutis per lascivias imagenes* (1402). Fredrick of Heilo wrote a special treatise *Contra peregrinantes*, and the French poet Eustace Deschamps argued that images of silver, gold, or wood should not be made, lest the people be led to idolatry.[63] These criticisms, however, were primarily academic and not aimed at the practicum of late medieval piety. Neither Gerson nor d'Ailly, for instance, argued that the cult of the saints was intrinsically wrong or that the veneration of images and relics should cease. Their critique was limited to pointing out abuses and exaggerations that they thought deviated from the true ideals of the Church. Gerson himself, for instance, was a fervent advocate of the cult of the guardian angels.

The ascendancy of the Devotio Moderna was perhaps more important for future critiques than this scholarly criticism.[64] Though they never actually rejected the medieval cult, The Brethren of the Common Life advocated an alternative sort of religion. Their emphasis

---

[59] "Dabei sinkt die Frömmigkeit der Massen natürlich vielfach weit unter das Niveau der theologischen Theorie." Hans von Campenhausen, "Die Bilderfrage in der Reformation," *Zeitschrift für Kirchengeschichte*, 68: 98 (1957).
[60] ZW 4.101, 4.102, 4.104, 4.107, 4.108–10, 4.125, 4.139, 4.146–7. Also: Trexler, "Florence," p. 18.
[61] Allen IX, no. 2433, pp. 162–3.
[62] Gerson wrote numerous treatises against popular beliefs and superstitions. For a detailed bibliography of these works see Jean Gerson, *Oeuvres Complètes* (Paris, 1973), vol. 10, pp. 73–6.
[63] Huizinga, *Waning*, pp. 153, 155, 162, 175–6.
[64] For more on the Devotio Moderna consult the two works by Albert Hyma: *The Brethren of the Common Life* (Grand Rapids, 1950), and *The Christian Renaissance: a History of the Devotio Moderna* (Hamden, Conn., 1965). Also: W. Lourdaux, *Moderne Devotie en Christelijk Humanisme* (Louvain, 1967).

was on interior piety, not the observance of the external cult. In the *Imitation of Christ*, the most famous book written in this tradition, the point is made very clear: "learn to despise outward things, and to give yourself to inward things."[65] This attitude had long been part of the Christian mystical tradition, but the Devotio Moderna popularized it in the fifteenth century. Although this inward piety did not seek to overturn external religion, it helped make it suspect and vulnerable among its adherents at the end of the Middle Ages. An heir of this tradition would be Erasmus.

The first major challenge to the *cultus divorum* in the Middle Ages took place in the late fourteenth and early fifteenth centuries in England and Bohemia with the advent of the heresies of Wyclif and Hus. Although both Wyclif and Hus were primarily concerned with theological matters such as grace and salvation, the authority of scripture, priestly power, and the structure of the Church, they also voiced specific grievances against the cult of saints, images, and relics.[66] As the ideas of Wyclif and Hus became popularized, these grievances shifted to a more central position among their followers, and the animosity expressed toward the external cult became increasingly intense and violent, leading at times to iconoclasm.

Wyclif himself did not have much to say about images, although he showed preference for a religion without many material props. He was willing to accept the veneration of the cross or modest portraits of the saints, but opposed the lavish attention proffered on images by his contemporaries.[67] It seems that Wyclif's mild skepticism regarding images was shared by many of the orthodox of his time, such as Archbishop Richard Fitzralph of Armagh, who criticized the intense rivalry among the cults of the Virgin Mary at Walsingham, Lincoln, Newark, and Leicester on the grounds that it was incorrect to address

---

[65] Thomas à Kempis, *The Imitation of Christ*, bk. II, chap. 1.
[66] Gordon Leff, *Heresy in the Later Middle Ages*, vol. 2 (Manchester, 1966); Johann Loserth, *Wiclif and Hus*, trans. M. J. Evans (London, 1884); Matthew Spinka, *John Hus and the Czech Reform* (Hamden, Conn., 1966); Howard Kaminsky, *A History of the Hussite Revolution* (Berkeley, 1965), and W. R. Jones, "Lollards and Images," *Journal of the History of Ideas*, 34: 27–50 (1973). On Wycliffite iconoclasm: J. Phillips, *The Reformation of Images: Destruction of Art in England 1535–1660* (Los Angeles, 1973), pp. 30–5. Also: Malcolm Lambert, *Medieval Heresy: Popular Movements from Bogomil to Hus* (New York, 1976).
[67] Jones, "Lollards and Images," p. 29. For Wyclif's opinion of images consult his *Tractatus de mandatis divinis*, J. Loserth and F. D. Matthew, eds. (London, 1922), p. 153ff.; *De eucharistia*, J. Loserth, ed. (London, 1892), p. 317; *Sermones*, J. Loserth, ed. (4 vols., London, 1887–90), vol. 2, p. 165. For his views on the saints see the *Trialogus*, G. Lechler, ed. (London, 1869), p. 234ff.

these images as if each were a competing divinity.[68] When Wyclifite ideology became popularized, however, it became more radical and prone to iconoclasm. Lollards published numerous vernacular pamphlets that condemned the cult of images. Occasionally, they would also destroy church decorations.[69]

Hussite opposition to images resembled that of the Lollards. Hus himself was preoccupied with doctrinal issues, not with the external expressions of the Catholic cult, and he was moderate in his criticism, calling only for an end to abuses. As Hussitism spread throughout Bohemia, however, iconoclasm became one of its distinguishing traits, especially among the Taborites, who viewed images as symbols or the "corrupt Church of the Antichrist."[70]

Though these tremors were caused by the same forces of discontent that shook Europe a century later, they presented only a limited challenge to the established piety of the late Middle Ages. The dissatisfaction expressed by the Lollards and Hussites was intense and often violent, but was restricted to certain localities in England and Bohemia. Like the Cathars and Waldensians before them, they struck out against the visible symbols of ecclesiastical authority without producing widespread or long-lasting change among the many peoples of Europe.

In spite of the fact that some similarities seem remarkable, it is very difficult to trace a direct line of development from these earlier iconoclastic movements to the Reformation.[71] Whatever resemblance exists between these first tremors and the later devastation can be attributed

---

[68] Jones, "Lollards and Images," p. 29; G. R. Owst, *Literature and Pulpit in Medieval England* (2nd ed., Oxford, 1966), p. 141.

[69] John A. F. Thomson, *The Later Lollards: 1414–1520* (Oxford, 1965), pp. 64, 100; Jones, "Lollards and Images," pp. 31–6. For an example of a Lollard tract against images and pilgrimages, see *Selections from English Wycliffite Writings*, Anne Hudson, ed. (Cambridge, 1978), pp. 83–8; on the eucharist, pp. 17–18, 110–14. The Lollard tracts and the defenses written by orthodox clergymen constitute a significant body of literature and are a rich source for the scholar studying the acceptance of religious art in the later Middle Ages. Jones's "Lollards and Images" provides an excellent review and analysis of the controversy on pp. 37–47.

[70] No equivalent of Jones's study on Lollards and iconoclasm exists for the Hussite phase of this phenomenon. Still, one can rely on the work of Kaminsky, *History of the Hussite Revolution;* also that of Horst Brederkamp, *Kunst als Medium Sozialer Konflikte: Bilderkämpfe von der Spätantike bis zur Hussitenrevolution* (Frankfurt am Main, 1975), pp. 231–330.

[71] Although he does not trace English Reformation iconoclasm directly to the Lollards, John Phillips does say that Lollardism (together with humanism) served "to establish intellectual precedents and practical acts that foreshadowed the iconoclasm of the sixteenth and seventeenth centuries" (*Reformation of Images*, p. 30).

to some common external factors rather than to any conscious transmission of ideology. First, the similarities can be attributed to the fact that, with the exception of the Cathars, these critiques, for the most part, drew upon a common source, namely, the Hebrew Scriptures. The Old Testament proscriptions against images are the weapons shared by these critiques. The hermeneutical principles behind their acceptance may have varied, but the language of invective against material representations of the holy was a common bond. Secondly, the medieval critiques also anticipated Protestantism by aiming their attack on social problems: corrupt piety, gross materialism, religious fraud, and clerical profiteering. Some of the Lollard attacks on the wealth spent on church decorations are remarkable close to those later voiced by Erasmus, Zwingli, and Calvin.[72]

It is no coincidence, then, that there are similarities, but the resemblance goes no further than these points. Lollards and Hussites developed no systematic theological opposition to the admixture of spiritual and material in worship, nor did they respond to Catholic worship as "idolatrous." The inconsistent and haphazard nature of their iconoclasm reveals that it had no systematically developed ideological foundation. Nonetheless, it was an indication of the way in which lay people could respond to a critique of the Church by turning against its external symbols. It was a strong tremor that revealed the pressures building up beneath the surface of medieval society.

By the end of the fifteenth century the piety of Western Europe had reached a crossroads. Although devotion was intense, dissatisfaction was fermenting, and it showed in the writings of men such as Guibert of Nogent, Jean Gerson, and Pierre d'Ailly, through the Devotio Moderna and through the heresies of Wyclif and Hus. Although the cult was challenged in a limited way, there were factors working to make it vulnerable to attack in the sixteenth century.

By all accounts, piety was abundant, intense, and materially oriented in the late Middle Ages. But was it satisfying? Although this question cannot be answered in quantifiable terms, it is possible to say that the religious atmosphere immediately preceding the Reformation showed some flawed characteristics. Bernd Moeller has argued that the anxious, craning gestures suggested by the externalization of piety in the fifteenth century indicate a "spiritual destitution" and "misery of existence" much greater and intense than at any other time in Christian history.[73] The fragmentation of supernatural power

---

[72] Jones, "Lollards and Images," p. 35.
[73] Moeller, "Piety," p. 56.

and the search for material points of contact with the holy reflect the
weak points of late medieval piety. It seems that the intensification of
external religious ritual and devotion failed to quiet the inner anguish
that drove the laity to seek grace and salvation through an ever-
increasing multitude of intercessors and material objects.[74]

The line between Christian priciples and heathen magic was not
clearly established in the popular mind, and the clergy who controlled the *cultus* offered little guidance on this point. Magic is an
awesome and frightful thing to the unsophisticated; it does give some
assurance of control over fate, but also makes one depend upon fickle
and unpredictable powers. Late medieval religion looked for these
powers in a panoply of lesser, but supposedly more accessible
sources: in saints, their images and relics, and in the consecrated
host.[75]

But as the divine became ever more fragmented, so did the chan-
nels for grace, mercy, and salvation. Religious anxiety must have
increased proportionally to the distancing of God through materialism and "parapolytheism." Paradoxically, in seeking divinity
through more immediate means, late medieval religion only succeeded in making it ever more distant.[76] This is why Farel's family
could cower so helplessly before the fraudulent relic at Tallard: They
participated in a worldview that had fragmented the holy into inde-
pendently powerful material manifestations. It is this development
that also led Farel and many others to respond so violently in the
sixteenth century against the ecclesiastical system that supported and

---

[74] Steven Ozment, *The Reformation in the Cities*, pp. 21–2. Ozment argues that the
objectification of late medieval piety was unsatisfying and that the intensification of
external religious ritual failed to quiet inner anguish (as shown by the work of
Toussaert and Delaruelle).

[75] R. C. Trexler has made a similar observation: "The belief in powerladen natural
objects . . . stretched from the host, through the image, to the relic, from the body of
the dead to that of the living saint" ("Florentine Religious Experience," p. 9). Also:
Keith Thomas, *Religion*, chap. 2, "The Magic of the Medieval Church." Thomas
studies the difference between prayer, which he defines as a supplication dependent on the will of God, and charms, whose efficacy is dependent on the correctness
of ritual (p. 41). For a more general study of superstitious practices and their place in
medieval religious thought see Dieter Harmening, *Superstitio: Überlieferungs und The-
oriegeschichtlich Untersuchungen zur Kirchlichtheologischen Aberglaubensliteratur des Mittelalters* (Berlin, 1979).

[76] On this point I disagree with Huizinga, who claims that the saints "acted on the
exuberant piety of the Middle Ages as a salutary sedative" (p. 168). Peter Brown has
remarked on this point: "Increased impersonality and a tendency to delimit what is
above man to a fragile extension of his own good intentions are not necessarily the
recipe for human happiness." "Society and the Supernatural," *Daedalus*, 104: 147
(1975).

promoted such beliefs. The greater a deception is, the greater the disappointment is bound to be when it is perceived.[77]

Though no single explanation can fully account for the dissatisfaction engendered by late medieval piety, it might be argued in a general way that certain types of devotion and certain expectations about the church reached a saturation point, and that as they intensified, the returns began to diminish. Iconoclasm and the rejection of the externalized cult would be the anguished response of those who had anxiously invested much in late medieval piety, but received little in return.[78] The *cultus divorum*, as well as the theological assumptions that supported it, had become charged with expectations that became increasingly difficult to fulfill. Moreover, the *cultus* had become very "churchly" as well, in a very literal sense: It was the physical expression of the promises made by the institutional church. Though never strictly limited to the church building itself, the physical dimension of medieval piety was most intensely evident in churches, chapels, or shrines, and was also ostensibly under direct priestly guid-

---

[77] Steven Ozment argues that iconoclasm was the response of a people whose piety had been sincere, but who suddenly realized they had been hoodwinked (*Reformation*, p. 44). Similarly, William Stafford writes: "Iconoclasm is not random destructive behavior; it was a slap in the face of medieval piety. People broke statues not because they hated beauty, but because the objects had been holy to them, a holiness which had been discredited, which they had come to hate." *Domesticating the Clergy: The Inception of the Reformation in Strasbourg 1522–1524* (Missoula, Mont.: Scholars Press, 1976), p. 2. Huizinga observes that the rapid abandonment of the cult of the saints in the Reformation was possibly due to the fact that nearly everything connected with the saints had become "caput mortuum," that piety had depleted itself through excessive externalization (*Waning*, p. 177).

[78] Lionel Rothkrug disputes this assertion. His position, if it is possible to summarize at all, is that the Reformation can be explained by geographic differences in worship. Northern Germany, because it was converted at "sword point," never developed the intimate relationship with the dead that found expression in saints' shrines. In contrast, Bavaria developed an intense piety firmly based on the relics of its native saints. As a result, he claims, the Reformation triumphed easily in the North, where shrines were uncommon, and Catholicism remained strong in the South, where such shrines were popular. Rothkrug's study is well documented: He analyzes over 1,000 pilgrimage sites. Though it cannot be easily dimissed, his thesis tends to oversimplify a continental phenomenon on the basis of German evidence. His overwhelming documentation needs to be double-checked and compared with similar data from other countries where the Reformation spread and iconoclasm surfaced, especially Switzerland, France, the Netherlands, and England. *Religious Practices and Collective Perceptions: Hidden Homologies in the Renaissance and Reformation* [entire volume of *Historical Reflections/ Reflexions Historiques*, VII (Spring, 1980)]. Also the shorter summary of this work: "Popular Religion and Holy Shrines: Their Influence on the Origins of the German Reformation and Their Role in German Cultural Development," in James Obelkevich (ed.) *Religion and the People, 800–1700* (Chapel Hill, 1979). H. C. Erik Midlefort has written a perceptive review of Rothkrug's "dizzying" thesis in *Historical Reflections*, VII: 255–8.

ance. As a complex system of symbols, from the consecrated host held aloft in the Pope's hands at Rome, to the crucifix over some widow's bed in a Swiss village, the *cultus* was inextricably bound in myriad ways to the salvational system of the Roman Catholic church. It is not surprising, then, that the symbols became "idols" in the eyes of those who rejected this salvational system and that, in seeking to dismantle the institution of the Roman Catholic church, they often began by dismantling the symbols that had come to fill the churches.

CHAPTER 2

Erasmus as critic of late medieval piety

W HEN the city of Basel erupted into a violent iconoclastic riot in February 1529, Erasmus remarked in one of his letters: "I am greatly surprised that the images performed no miracle to save themselves; formerly the saints worked frequent prodigies for much smaller offenses."[1] Unlike the pilgrims at Tallard, the great humanist had difficulty believing in the power of images. In fact, few men in Europe had done as much to discredit the materialism of medieval piety as had Erasmus. When Guillaume Farel rejected everything his childhood pilgrimage stood for, his decision was formed, to a large extent, by ideas that can be traced directly to Erasmus.

One of the most hackneyed aphorisms concerning the relationship between humanism and the Reformation is that which blames Erasmus for laying the egg that Luther hatched. Risking all the dangers that attend the stretching of metaphors, I think it is possible to say that Erasmus laid more than one egg; and that those hatched in succession by Karlstadt, Zwingli, Farel, and Calvin resembled their parent more closely in some respects than Luther's ever did.

Regarding the issue of worship, or piety, a clear line can be traced between Erasmus and the Reformed tradition. Though Erasmus, the sardonic pacifist, could not stomach the "virulence" of Protestant iconoclasts, he was at heart in agreement with some of their basic assumptions regarding worship. The search for the roots of the Reformed Protestant attitude toward worship must begin with Erasmus, since it is he who gave rise to a new Christian interpretation of the relationship between the spiritual and the material.

ERASMUS AND HUMANISTIC PRIMITIVISM

The principal characteristic of the life and thought of Erasmus was his desire to restore Christianity to its primitive purity, both in theology

---

[1] Allen VIII, 162.

and piety.[2] Erasmus sought to achieve this religious renaissance, or rebirth, by means of a "fresh" exposition of Christ's teachings set against the background of the Golden Age of the early Church. Erasmus was taking the primitivistic impulse to renew the *studia humanitatis* of antiquity, which was common among humanists as a model for a reform of the Church: Christianity was to be cleansed from all accretions and distortions.[3]

The instruments of Erasmus's program were the writings of the New Testament and the early Fathers. "It is at the very sources," he maintained, "that one extracts pure doctrine."[4] Theology and piety could therefore never be reformed without a knowledge of the languages of antiquity, especially those of the Bible. In reference to Greek, for instance, he said:

for we have in Latin only a few small streams and muddy puddles, while they have pure springs and rivers flowing in gold. I see that it is utter madness even to touch with the little finger that branch of theology which deals chiefly with the divine mysteries unless one is also provided with the equipment of Greek.[5]

---

[2] Secondary studies of Erasmus's life and work are quite numerous. Roland H. Bainton's *Erasmus of Christendom* (New York: Scribner's, 1969) is perhaps the best English biography. Bainton provides an excellent bibliography as well. Among the many other works on Erasmus, the following are indispensable: Alfons Auer, *Die Vollkommene Frömmigkeit des Christen, nach dem Enchiridion Militis Christiani des Erasmus von Rotterdam* (Düsseldorf, 1954); Louis Bouyer, *Autour d'Erasme* (Paris, 1955); Jacques Etienne, *Spiritualisme érasmien et Théologiens Louvanistes* (Louvain, 1956); E. W. Kohls, *Die Theologie des Erasmus* (2 vols. Basel, 1966); J. Huizinga, *Erasmus of Rotterdam* (London, 1952); John B. Payne, *Erasmus: His Theology of the Sacraments* (Richmond, 1970); Augustin Renaudet, *Erasme: Sa Pensée Religieuse et Son Action (1518–1529)* (Paris, 1939); and L. W. Spitz, *The Religious Renaissance of the German Humanists*, chap. 9, "Erasmus, Philosopher of Christ" (Cambridge, Mass., 1963). Also, Robert Stupperich, *Erasmus von Rotterdam und Seine Welt* (Berlin, 1977); James D. Tracy, *Erasmus, the Growth of a Mind* (Geneva, 1972); Marjorie O'Rourke Boyle, *Erasmus on Language and Method in Theology* (Toronto, 1977).

[3] Paul Joachimsen deals with the issue of primitivism as part of the humanistic program. He traces this attitude to Petrarch, for whom, he claims, the return to the past was more a matter of individual psychology. This is in contrast to Erasmus, for whom the attitude assumes social implications. "Humanism and the Development of the German Mind," in Gerald Strauss (ed.), *Pre-Reformation Germany* (New York, 1972), pp. 164, 190. For more on the concept of primitivism and its classical, humanistic, and religious manifestations see Franklin H. Littel, *The Origins of Sectarian Protestantism* (New York, 1964), pp. 46–51. Erasmus's involvement with classical antiquity has been analyzed by Rudolph Pfeiffer in *Humanitas Erasmiana* (Leipzig-Berlin, 1931), esp. pp. 1–24.

[4] Allen II, 384. Also: Albert Rabil, Jr., *Erasmus and the New Testament: the Mind of a Christian Humanist* (San Antonio, 1972), esp. p. 49ff.

[5] Allen I, 352.

Ancient language, ancient learning, and ancient Christian piety were undisputed models of clarity, wisdom, and truth; and nowhere was the contrast between past and present as stark as in the case of scholasticism.[6] Erasmus marked off Christian antiquity as a sphere within history and gave it a privileged place in his thought.[7] His favorite model among the "splendid host" of the ancients was St. Jerome, and he also had high regard for Origen, and, of course, the apostle Paul, but the purest crystalline source was the Gospels.[8]

This contrast between the ancient sources and the contemporary situation transcended merely philological considerations. Erasmian primitivism was above all historically conscious, and it used the past as a practical measure against the present.[9] When Erasmus viewed the medieval Church against the backdrop of the Apostolic Age, it appeared to him as corrupt. The early Christian centuries were, in effect, idealized at the expense of the contemporary situation.[10] Medieval piety, which was centered on so many external practices such as pilgrimages, eucharistic devotions, and the veneration of saints, images, and relics, appeared to Erasmus as a gross deviation from the simple Christocentric worship of the early Church. This historically conscious critique was directed just as much against the parish priest as it was against the doctors of the Sorbonne. Erasmus aimed at a reform of the everyday life of the Church,[11] and he emphasized the point that the aim of theology was practical instead of speculative.[12]

---

[6] AS I, 88.

[7] P. Joachimsen, "Humanism," p. 191.

[8] "Unde potius consilium sumamus, quam ab Evangelio?" (preface to the Paraphrase of the Gospel of Matthew). J. Coppens has collected this and several similar passages where Erasmus proclaims the supreme authority of Scripture. "Les Idées Réformistes d'Erasme dans les Préfaces aux Paraphrases du Nouveau Testament," *Scrinium Lovaniense,* E. van Cauwenbergh, ed. (Louvain, 1961), p. 353, nn. 3, 4.

[9] Henri Hauser has observed that the critical philology of the humanists was "l'arsenal où les réformateurs puisseront leurs armes les plus terribles contre la vielle Eglise." *Etudes sur la Réformation Française* (Paris, 1909), p. 15.

[10] Charles Garside, Jr., *Zwingli and the Arts* (New Haven, 1966), p. 29.

[11] *Paraclesis* (cited by Huizinga, *Erasmus,* p. 110): "Christ desires that his mysteries shall be spread as widely as possible. I should wish that all good wives read the Gospel and Paul's epistles; that they were translated into all languages; that out of these the husbandman sang while ploughing, the weaver at his loom; that with such stories the traveller should beguile his wayfaring."

[12] This attitude was also accompanied by a primitivist impulse. In the *Enchiridion,* for instance, Erasmus contrasts the warm piety of the Fathers with the dry theology of the scholastics: "Tu si mavis spiritu esse vegetior quam ad contentionem instructor, se saginam animae quaeri magis quam ingenii pruritum, veteres potissimam evolve, quorum et pietas spectatior et eruditio uberior antiquiorque et oratio neque ieiuna neque sordida et interpretatio sacris mysteriis accomodatior." AS I, 88–90.

Erasmus's transcendentalism

Aside from considering the disparities between the past and the present, Erasmus also paid a great deal of attention to certain metaphysical principles in his critique of medieval piety. His concern with *pietas*, and his desire to see a warm, living faith among all Christians also forced him to criticize any kind of worship that concentrated its attention on the outward form rather than the inner substance of religion. Erasmus insisted that the inner life of the spirit was superior to any material or formal considerations; and this principle formed the basis for his interpretation of the nature of worship. More specifically, it gave rise to a strident transcendentalism that was opposed to external ritualism or juridicism.

The *Enchiridion Militis Christiani*, written by Erasmus in 1503, is the clearest exposition of his predilection for the spiritual and inward as opposed to the external and material in religion.[13] In the *Enchiridion* Erasmus attempts to show that the actions of the individual must always reflect what is in the heart. The *Enchiridion* is a handbook that teaches the Christian how to avoid dry formalism by placing mind, spirit, and will beyond the visible world. Erasmus plays upon the title word "enchiridion" which can mean either a dagger or a handbook. This is in keeping with the martial imagery of the treatise: The *Enchiridion* is a weapon as well as a manual for the Christian soldier. But why such imagery? What is the "war" about? It is a war between *caro* and *spiritus*, between the things of this world and those of heaven. It is a battle against the world and its seduction.

This conception of piety draws partly on Erasmus's primitivism and biblicism, but its principal intellectual roots are clearly Platonic. The Platonic tradition maintains a dualism of matter and spirit. Not only is the material world regarded as a shadow of the world of ideas: The human self is seen as a duality composed of body (matter, flesh) and spirit. The spirit, being the superior component of the self, is

---

[13] Alfons Auer sees the *Enchiridion* as the key to all Erasmian thought, and maintains that the foundation of Erasmiam piety is the basic theme "per visibilia ad invisibilia" (*Frömmigkeit*, pp. 73–94). J. Etienne also maintains that Erasmus' theology is dominated by his spiritualism (*Spiritualisme Erasmien*). A different interpretation is proposed by Ernst W. Kohls, who sees the *Enchiridion* as a soteriological piece, concerned primarily with the place of Scripture in God's redemptive works. "The Principal Theological Thoughts in the *Enchiridion Militis Christiani*," in R. L. DeMolen (ed.), *Essays on the Works of Erasmus* (New Haven, 1978). Also: Jean Boisset, "Le Christianine d'Erasme dans l'*Enchiridion Militis Christiani*," in Margolis (ed.), *Colloquia*, vol. II, pp. 647–56.

believed to be imprisoned in the body. The chief end of human existence, then, is the emancipation of the spirit from the material world.
Erasmus adopted these basic Platonic motifs and incorporated them
into the *Enchiridion*, further reinforcing his own religion of in-
wardness.[14] It appears that Erasmus developed this outlook most
intensely during his first stay in England, where his close friends
John Colet and Thomas More were deeply involved in a renewal of
Neoplatonism.[15] Upon his return to the Continent, Erasmus applied
himself to the study of Greek and, after having finished the *Enchiridion*, in 1504, to a more intense study of Origen. Erasmus found the
allegorical, Neoplatonic interpretation of scripture practiced by Origen quite congenial, and had praised it in the *Enchiridion*.[16] The Neoplatonism absorbed by Erasmus in England further reinforced and
influenced the spirituality he had already inherited from the New
Testament, and the Devotio Moderna. This so-called modern devotion, which had been promoted by the Brethren of the Common Life,
and which Erasmus had first encountered at Deventer while still a
schoolboy, stressed the inner life of the spirit and was more con-

---

[14] Auer pays attention to Erasmus's platonism and his use of sources (*Frömmigkeit*, pp.
80–94). The English translation of the *Enchiridion* by Raymond Himelick (Bloom-
ington, Ind., 1963) identifies references to several of Plato's dialogues: *Timaeus,
Phaedo, Phaedrus, Symposium, Protagoras, Republic*, and *Gorgias*.

[15] English Neoplatonism owed much to the Neoplatonic revival of the academy of
Florence headed by Marsilio Ficino and Pico della Mirandola. Colet had corre-
sponded with Pico, and More had translated a life of Pico and one of Pico's letters to
his nephew. For more on the English Neoplatonic revival see Jane Sears, *John Colet
and Marsilio Ficino* (Oxford, 1963); Leland Miles, *John Colet and the Platonic Tradition*
(LaSalle, Ind., 1961); Lewis Spitz, *The Religious Renaissance of the German Humanists*
(Cambridge, Mass., 1963), p. 335, n. 13.; and P. O. Kristeller, *Renaissance Thought*
(New York, 1961), chap. 3, "Renaissance Platonism." In the first edition of the
Adagia, Erasmus speaks of Pico as "endowed with a certain felicity of temper" (Allen
I, 126). In listening to Colet's lectures, Erasmus exclaimed he could hear Plato
himself speaking (Allen I, 118). Tracy (*Erasmus*, p. 92ff) argues that Erasmus' critique
of medieval piety was not really centered on this Platonic metaphysics. "Erasmus
was never anxious about the underlining of his thought . . . the suspicion of matter
qua matter in Erasmus must not be overstressed; Colet, for example, took his Neoplatonism more seriously" (p. 93). He thinks "personal attitudes" and "moral convictions" played a stronger role in forming Erasmus's critique of ceremonies. (I
disagree with Tracy on this point, and think that Neoplatonic metaphysics were the
foundations of Erasmus's critique, as well as of later Protestant interpretations of
worship.)

[16] Erasmus applied himself to the study of Greek after his visit to England, and, after
1504, to the study of Origen. The allegorical, Neoplatonic interpretation of scripture
and reality seemed right to him: Allen I, 405 (to Colet, Dec., 1504): "Origenis operum bonam partem evolui; quo praeceptore mihi videor non nullum fecisse operae
precium. Aperit enim quasi fontes quosdam et rationes indicat artis theologicae."
Also: A. Godin, "L'origenisme d'Erasme," in Michel Péronnet (ed.), *La Controverse
Religieuse (XVI - XIX Siècles) Actes du Premier Colloque Jean Boisset* (Montpellier, 1980).

cerned with *pietas* than doctrine. Through the influence of some strains of medieval mysticism, this modern devotion had absorbed a considerable amount of Neoplatonism, particularly in regard to metaphysical assumptions. In the *Imitation of Christ*, which is the best known treatise produced by this tradition, the contrast between "flesh" and "spirit" is very strong, even to the point of advising: "wean your heart from the love of visible things, and attend rather to things invisible."[17]

The central theme of the *Enchiridion* is the interiorization and spiritualization of religion, and the development of a more intimate relationship between the individual soul and God.[18] The entire work is controlled by the scriptural dictum: "The flesh profits nothing, it is the spirit that gives life."[19] Erasmus claims that the law of the Christian is spiritual, and that spiritual things should not be made carnal. From the very start, Erasmus proposes a piety that has little need for material objects of worship. Never content with what he calls the "barren letter" in religious matters, Erasmus encourages the Christian to "pass on to the more profound mysteries."[20] Erasmus thus sets the stage for a Neoplatonic ascent of the soul: from the visible to the invisible.

The first section of the *Enchiridion* establishes the basis for Erasmus's teaching on the nature and scope of piety – a notion that dominates his critique of medieval religion. Erasmus begins with a thoroughly Neoplatonic anthropology. The framework is clearly revealed in chapter four of Book One: "Of the inner and outer Man." The body is here compared to a "brute beast," while the soul is referred to as "a kind of divine will." The soul is the divine principle: It enables humans to climb above the minds of angels and to become one with God. Tragically, this divine element is "imprisoned" in the beastly

---

17 *The Imitation of Christ*, chap. 1, pt. 5. On the influence of the New Testament on Erasmus, see Bainton, *Erasmus*, p. 61. Bainton lists some of the Pauline and Johanine texts that are most dualistic in their interpretation of the conflict between "flesh" and "spirit." For more on the Devotio Moderna consult R. R. Post, *The Modern Devotion: Confrontation with Reformation and Humanism* (Leiden, 1973).

18 AS I, 232. "Spiritus est deus, et spiritalibus victimis flectitur . . . Mens est, et quidem purissima simplicissimaque. Proinda potissimum mente pura colendus est." This after quoting a poem by Cato "Si deus, inquit, est animus, nobis ut carmina dicunt, hic tibi praecipue sit pura mente colendus."

19 AS I, 90. This dictum is taken from the Gospel of John 6:63; and from 2 Corinthians 3:6.

20 Erasmus points out, however, that he is not condeming those who, "from weakness of mind," can only worship according to the flesh. Those who are ignorantly entangled in outward observances still worship God effectively as long as they have "sincere faith and pure affection." *Enchiridion*, AS I, 90–1.

body[21]: "The soul, remembering its heavenly nature, wrestles stren-
uously against the bulk of this earthly body to push up toward the
heights."[22] Erasmus expands on this anthropology in the following
chapters. In chapter six, entitled "Of the inner and outer man and his
two parts as found in Holy Scripture," Erasmus exegetes the scriptural notion of the struggle between flesh and spirit in a Neoplatonic
fashion. This is the conclusion he reaches: "If you are flesh alone, you
will not see God; if you do not see him, then you will not be saved.
Take care, then, to become spirit."[23]

This dualism forces Erasmus to propose a highly transcendental
conception of worship. Although he does not become a spiritualist by
denying the value of external worship completely, he stresses the
superiority of the spirit over matter to such an extent that the outward
forms of worship are subjected to the demands of interior devotion.

The full impact of Erasmus's transcendentalism is made evident in
Book Two, where he deals specifically with ceremonies in Christian
worship. Here he openly attacks those who try to turn religion into a
series of outward motions, and in doing so, he spells out the central
dictum of his transcendentalism:

> You can only establish perfect piety when you turn away from visible things,
> which are for the most part either imperfect or of themselves indifferent, and
> you seek instead the invisible, which corresponds to the highest part of
> human nature.[24]

This is a concise summary of Erasmus's metaphysics. Two spheres of
existence, the material and the spiritual (visible and invisible), are
juxtaposed, and it is clearly stated that true religion can only be expe-
rienced in the invisible realm. The material, visible world can never
be the focus of true piety, since it is a distortion of reality or, at best,
incapable of bringing one to the truth.[25] Human beings are caught

---

[21] *Enchiridion*, AS I, 108. For more on Erasmus' anthropology: David Marsh, "Erasmus
on Body and Soul," *Journal of the History of Ideas*, 37 (1976), pp. 673–88. Marsh cites
relevant passages from writings spanning thirty years of Erasmus's life, but he does
not provide much analysis.

[22] *Enchiridion*, AS I, 110. Erasmus makes his debt to Plato clearly known when he adds:
"The divinely inspired Plato wrote all these things in his *Timaeus*" (AS I, 112).

[23] AS I, 138. Also: *The Praise of Folly* (1509), H. H. Hudson, ed. and trans. (Princeton,
1974), pp. 123–4.

[24] AS I, 180. This interpretation of the nature of worship is by no means limited to the
Enchiridion. In the *Praise of Folly*, for instance, Erasmus has Folly say: "in all of his life
the pious man sincerely forsakes whatever has alliance with the body and is drawn
to eternal, invisible and spiritual objects." (Hudson, *Folly*, p. 122).

[25] AS I, 182, 184. "Sic autem existina adeo non esse nullas res invisibiles, ut eae, quae
videntur, prae illis vix umbrae quaedam sint tenuem modo quaedam imaginem

between these two realms, and they participate in both, living in "a third sphere," as it were. The only way to break out of this situation, says Erasmus, is to transcend the world of the senses and rise to the realm of the spiritual and intelligible.[26] Erasmus applies this conception of reality to all aspects of religious life. In the reading of scripture, the spiritual meaning of the text is to be drawn from the merely external narrative, especially in regard to the Old Testament (which contains so many scandalous stories). Allegory becomes the key to understanding Erasmus's hermeneutic at this point. As he is discussing metaphysics, Erasmus points out that the poetry and philosophy of the pagans is very useful. In the first place, because of its method; secondly, because of its content. Regarding the first point, method, Erasmus says that all poetry – even Homer's and Virgil's – can only be properly interpreted allegorically. Then, emulating Origen, he says that this makes it similar to Holy Scripture, which should only be interpreted in the same way.[27] Erasmus does not stop here, though. This principle is also a metaphor for existence itself: In good Neoplatonic fashion, all that is visible and tangible becomes an allegory of sorts, a reflection of that highest reality, God, who is pure mind, pure spirit, and in whom all creation is contained. Following Origen and Dionysius,[28] Erasmus expresses reality in terms of reflections. God is most clearly revealed in Christ; Christ is most clearly revealed in scripture. Yet scripture itself is to be interpreted allegorically. One is always to search for *spiritus*, not for *caro*.[29] The key to religion and life is to accept all that is visible as a representation of a higher, invisible reality.

Although other Christian theologians had used this principle to defend the practical use of religious imagery, Erasmus inverts the argument. Instead of admitting any real connection between image and prototype, Erasmus downplays the representative value of physical reality. Images are not needed, it seems, because the spiritual

---

illarum oculis repraesentantes." Similar thoughts are also expressed in the *Sileni Alcibiades*, written by Erasmus in 1515: "suffice it to say that in both the domains of nature and faith, you will find the most excellent things are the deepest hidden, and the furthest removed from profane eyes." J. C. Olin, ed. and trans., *The Catholic Reformation: Savonarola to Ignatius Loyola* (New York: 1969), p. 76.

26 AS I, 182.

27 AS I, 188. On the place of allegory in Erasmus' theology: O'Rourke Boyle, *Language and Method*, esp. pp. 40ff, 118ff. "Theology is not a disciple of rigorous exploration into God, as in the scholastic *quaestio*, but a linguistic appropriation of the archetypal text: Christ, *oratio*" (p. 118).

28 AS I, 194.

29 Kohls, "Thoughts," p. 66.

reality is reachable without matter. Accepted theology, dating back to
the Byzantine iconoclastic controversy stated it differently. Accepting
a Neoplatonic system of a hierarchy of reflections alongside with
vivid incarnational principles, this theology (especially as formulated
by John of Damascus) argued that it was indeed possible for matter to
convey spiritual values. After all, ran the argument, had not God
divinized matter through his incarnation?[30]

In worship, the spiritual or inner life is to be given preference over
the external elements of devotion. Since it is the spirit alone that gives
life, then every action should tend toward the spirit. When Christ
spoke to the Samaritan woman about the worship of God being in
spirit and in truth, says Erasmus, he was speaking against the very
same problems that plagued medieval piety.

> To whom do you think he said 'the flesh profits nothing; it is the spirit that
> gives life?' Certainly not to those who hang the Gospel about their necks and
> think that perfect religion consists of a copper cross that can protect them
> against evils, but rather to those to whom he revealed the great mystery of
> enjoying his body. If something so great as receiving his body is counted as
> nothing, nay even dangerous, when it is lacking in spirit, why, then, should
> we trust in other fleshly things?[31]

Erasmus insists that religion is best when it does not depend on
visible things. He has a Neoplatonic frame of reference behind this
interpretation of worship, and it leads him to believe that the proper
end of human beings lies in the realm of the invisible. The goal of
existence is to stop crawling on the ground with the brute beasts
(even the "brute beast" of one's own body), and rise to the world
above. Only when one has made a sincere effort to escape from the
"chains" that bind human nature to earth, will one be able to enjoy
the presence of God.[32]

ERASMUS'S CRITIQUE OF LATE
MEDIEVAL PIETY

Erasmus's primitivism and transcendentalism were the framework of
an intense indictment of medieval religion. Erasmus deplored the fact

---

[30] John of Damascus, *On the Divine Images*, trans. D. Anderson (Crestwood, N.Y., 1980), p. 23.

[31] AS I, 198.

[32] AS I, 238–40: "Tu igitur, mi frater, ne tristibus laboribus non multum promoveas, sed mediocri exercitio cito grandis et vegetus evadas in Christo hunc regulam dili- genter amplexus, ne velis cum animalibus humi reptare, sed semper alis illis nitens,

that so many of his contemporaries focused on the external aspects of worship, and he generously sprinkled much of his work with an acid, burning condemnation of all practices that seemed to reverse the proper order of devotion. The excessive ceremonialism and materialism of his day was especially dangerous, he said, because it had a veneer of virtue and fooled the believer into thinking he or she might really be religious. The sad truth, he added, was that all these practices were "the ruin of all Christendom."[33]

Erasmus's indictment of medieval piety was intense and detailed, but he always insisted he was only attacking superstition. "Superstition" meant for Erasmus a misplaced faith in the external forms of religion. He was especially upset by practices in which the sacred was treated as magical, as if divine favors could be obtained by following prescribed formulae.[34] One of the principal sources of superstition was the *cultus divorum*. It engendered so many errors, said Erasmus, that it could be seen as an "ocean of superstition."[35]

Erasmus objected to numerous aspects of the medieval *cultus divorum*. His primary objection was that the worship of the saints distracted people from the true worship of God. The excessive attention paid to the saints by his contemporaries struck Erasmus as a fragmentation of the deity. Instead of placing their faith in God and His Son, Erasmus complained, most Christians sought the aid of a whole panoply of lesser deities. According to Erasmus, superstition triumphs over true piety whenever favors are sought from the saints as if Christ were dead, or whenever they are believed to be more compassionate than God.[36] The practice of assigning specific functions to each saint was proof of this triumph of superstition. Every fear or desire of man had been assigned to a corresponding deity: St. Christopher could ward off sudden death, St. Roch could cure certain diseases, St. Apollo could cure toothaches, St. Barbara could protect the soldier in

---

quas Plato putat in animis amoris calore elicitas denno pullulascare, a corpore ad spiritum, a mundo visibili ad intelligentia, a compositis ad simplicia temetipsum quasi gradibus quibusdam scalae Jacob erige." Also: AS I, 370.

[33] AS I, 206: "hunc errorem communem esse pestem totius Christianismi" ("pestis" can mean either "ruin" or "plague").

[34] Allen IX, 162–3: "I have never condemned one or the other (saints or images), but only superstition, as that a soldier going out to butcher should pray for a safe return, that St. Barbara should be invoked as if Christ were dead, that particular saints should be given specialties so that Catherine would grant what Barbara would not, that images be treated as if they were alive, and that folk should bow the head before them, fall on the ground, crawl on knees, kiss and fondle the carvings" (trans. by Bainton, *Erasmus*, p. 255).

[35] Hudson, *Folly*, p. 58.

[36] Allen IX, 163.

battle, and so on.[37] Erasmus leveled a charge against this practice that would later be picked up by the Reformers, saying that it was no more than a shallow revival of paganism:

This kind of piety, since it does not refer either our blessings or troubles to Christ, is hardly a Christian practice. As a matter of fact, it is not very different from the superstitions of the ancients . . . The names have been changed, indeed, but the purpose is the same in both cases.[38]

The cult of the saints, he insisted, had many of the same qualities as the religion of the ancient heathens. He observed that when Venus gave up protecting sailors, the Virgin Mary relieved her of her duties.[39] In short, the saints had become the successors of the pagan gods.[40]

The basis of the *cultus divorum* was the belief in the intercession of the saints, and Erasmus aimed some of his sharpest barbs against this principle. Although he never openly attacked the intercession of the saints as theologically incorrect, he continually tried to lessen their importance. The Sorbonne interpreted some of Erasmus' satires against the saints as unorthodox.[41] One example of the type of satire that disturbed the Paris theologians is the following passage from "The Shipwreck," written in 1523:

[The Character Adolph, who has just been shipwrecked, is being questioned by the character Anthony, who asks what Adolph did when he saw that the boat was about to sink . . . :]

Anthony: But you called on some saint for help?
Adolph: Not even that.
Anthony: But why?
Adolph: Because heaven is a large place. If I entrust my safety to some saint – St. Peter, for example, who perhaps will be first to hear,

---

[37] *Enchiridion,* AS I, 177. In 1514 Erasmus published a poem dealing with this problem. It was entitled "Expostulatio Jesu cum homine," and featured a dejected Christ to whom no one prayed any longer: "Dives item et facilis dar magna et multa roganti,/ Rogari amo, nemo rogat." Cornelius Reedijk (ed.), *The Poems of Desiderius Erasmus* (Leiden, 1956), pp. 294–6.

[38] *Enchiridion,* AS I, 178.

[39] C. R. Thompson, *The Colloquies of Erasmus* (Chicago, 1965), "The Shipwreck," p. 141.

[40] *Opera omnia,* Leiden ed., vol. V, pp. 1099–1133, "Modus orandi": "The cult of Proserpine became the cult of the Virgin. Apollo and Aescalapius became St. Roch and St. Anthony. Juno was invoked for a safe delivery, now St. Jocodus. The sailors used to call on Venus and the Gemini, now they cry 'Salve Regina'."

[41] In 1526 the Sorbonne condemned the *Colloquies* as well as selected passages from other works. Noel Beda attacked Erasmus and Lefèvre d'Etaples together the same year in a work entitled "Annotationum Natalis Bede . . . in Jacobum Fabrum Stapulensem libri duo, et in Desiderium Erasmum Roterodamum liber unus" (Paris and Cologne, 1526).

since he stands at the gate – I may be dead before he meets God
and pleads my case.

Anthony: What did you do, then?

Adolph: Went straight to the Father himself, reciting the Pater Noster. No
saint hears sooner than he, or more willingly grants what is
asked.[42]

It is in this manner that Erasmus lampooned the simple beliefs of his
contemporaries while providing instruction about the "proper" way
to worship. Always keeping his eye on the "higher," spiritual realm,
Erasmus insisted that God was the only proper object of worship. In
place of the intercessional *cultus divorum* of the medieval Church,
Erasmus proposed an emulatory piety. The only way to honor the
saints was to follow their example.[43]

The cult of the saints manifested itself in outward forms, and its
principal characteristic was the veneration of images and relics. The
Erasmian critique of these practices anticipates much of the criticism
later leveled by the Reformers. Erasmus, in the first place, considered
religious images as powerless. Many may seek aid from the images of
the saints as if they had a power of their own, observed Erasmus, but
there is no sound basis for such expectations. No painted or carved
image of Christ, or Mary or any other saint, could ever begin to
approach the holiness it sought to represent. Instead of venerating
images and statues as ends in themselves, he said, the Christian
ought to revere the portrait of God's mind that the skill of the Holy
Spirit has portrayed in the writing of the Gospels.[44] In fact, even the
litteris, the letters, are specifically mentioned as the best representation, the best "picture" of God. If the Father is perfectly revealed in
the Son, he argued, then the words of the Son are the closest image of
God. Since God is the only true source of spiritual power, all other
images are worthless. Biblicism and spiritualism combine in this instance to provide a strong argument against the cult of images. In the
Praise of Folly Erasmus provides another argument against images,
saying that they are not aids to piety, but rather distractions. Erasmus
has Folly say that images often prevent the worshiper from seeking
the spiritual reality they represent:

---

[42] "The Shipwreck," Thompson, *Colloquies*, p. 142.

[43] *Enchiridion*, AS I, 200. "Nullus cultus gratior Mariae, quam si purae exempla. Nulla
religio sanctis acceptior magisque propria, quam si virtutem illorum exprimere
laboris."

[44] Ibid., AS I, 202: "multo religiosius honoranda mentis illius imago, quae spiritus
sancti artificio expressa est *litteris* evangelicis."

I am not so foolish as to ask stone images, painted up in colors; they would but hinder the worship of me, since by the stupid and dull those figures are worshiped instead of the saints themselves. And it would come about with me exactly as it does with the saints – they are thrown out of doors by their substitutes.[45]

Physical representations of spiritual things hinder true piety because they attract attention to themselves: Instead of proceeding from the external to the inward, as Erasmian piety demands, images do just the opposite.

Relics are even worse, because they were venerated as direct points of contact with the divine power, which was thought to flow through the blessed objects. Erasmus objected to such a materialization of religion, saying there could be nothing more disgusting than the cult of relics.[46] Erasmus aimed against relics with the same transcendentalist scope he used against images. He insisted that physical contact is nothing in itself without faith in the higher spiritual reality surrounding the sacred object, and he supported this argument by pointing to the example of Christ's presence on earth. If His material presence was really an undeniable source of divine power and an end in itself, then why was He betrayed, tortured, and crucified? If the external things associated with Christ were really sources of holiness, he reasoned, then certainly there could never have been a nation more religious than the Jews. They lived with Christ, heard his words, touched him and saw him, but still rejected him, and had him crucified. "Who could be more fortunate than Judas," asked Erasmus, "who pressed the divine mouth with his lips?"[47]

This same principle is consistently applied to Christology by Erasmus. Christ is, above all else, the "archetype" that all should follow.[48] He is not so much God *incarnate*, changing the structure of material reality, but rather a spiritual reflection, temporarily enfleshed, whose primary purpose seems to be to point humans in the direction of the spiritual realm. Though he is far from docetic, Erasmus lends an ephemoral quality to Christ's incarnation that comes close to denying the humanity of Jesus. In fact, throughout the *Enchiridion* he refers to "Christ" most often, not to "Jesus" or "Jesus

---

[45] Hudson, *Folly*, p.66.
[46] Bainton, *Erasmus*, p. 244 (quote from Erasmus's "Modus orandi").
[47] *Enchiridion*, AS I, 204. Erasmus adds: "Christi corporea praesentia inutilis ad salutem, et in ulla praeterea re corporali audebimus perfectam pietatem statuere?" In the colloquy "Cyclops," he provides a similar argument, saying through one of his characters: "Obviously those who smote Christ touched him too" (Thompson, *Colloquies*, p. 418).
[48] AS I, 240.

Christ." The apostles, he says, are a good example of the "stupidity" that afflicts all Christians. They got bogged down in their crass material sphere "because the flesh of Christ stood in their way." After all, had not Christ described his own physical presence as "inutilis ad salutem" (useless to salvation)? According to Erasmus, this was the reason Christ had to leave the earth and send the Holy Spirit: His human body was not only distracting, but also incapable of convincing anyone of the truth. If Christ's physical presence had really made any difference, Erasmus asks, then why did his contemporaries crucify him?[49] Erasmus, then, stresses the *textual*, scriptural dimension of the incarnation. By insisting on the superiority of the spiritual realm, the Word is not so much enfleshed as written. This is why he even goes as far as to say that the *litteris*, the written symbols of Scripture, are the most faithful picture of God.[50]

We can see clearly at this point how Erasmus's transcendentalism led him to promote a shift from concrete *visual* images to strictly *verbal* ones; from the sensual to the intellectual. The barrier between the visible and the invisible, according to Erasmus, could be most effectively crossed through the symbolic, representational power of words. In this way, language replaces the plastic arts as the medium of imagination.

But as much as Erasmus separated the spiritual from the material, and as much as he interiorized religious expression, he never completely disembodied or silenced the life of faith. The spiritual is indeed invisible and interior, but it is certainly expressible. This is what keeps Erasmus from being a thoroughgoing spiritualist. Taking to heart the notion that human beings were the "image and likeness" of God principally in their invisible spiritual and intellectual capacities, Erasmus allowed for language to serve as the primary link between the human and the divine. This notion would become the heart and soul of the Reformed Protestant crusade against material objects of worship; and later, through the success of this crusade, it would give shape to a general and profound cultural change.

The example of Christ's life is again used by Erasmus when he tries to argue against the distracting nature of relics. He proposes that Christ ascended to heaven so that men might love him spiritually and lift their minds above the earth. Had the risen Christ remained on earth, says Erasmus, then no one would have been able to worship him correctly. If men are so easily distracted by the paltry relics now

---

[49] AS I, 204–6.
[50] AS I, 202.

bandied about the world, how much worse would things not have been if Christ had remained on earth?:

For if men now take such pleasure in the color and the shape of garments and boast so much of the blood of the foreskin of Christ, and the milk of the Virgin Mary, what do you think would have happened had He abode on earth clothed, eating and discoursing? What dissensions would those peculiarities of His body have not occasioned?[51]

In addition to attacking the cult of relics on theological grounds, Erasmus also condemned some of its most blatant irrationalities. Among the most pointed barbs of Erasmus stand those that mock the frauds perpetrated on the faithful in the name of religion, and the credulity with which they were accepted. There is a decidedly rationalistic strain in this part of Erasmus's critique.[52] Erasmus maintains that there is no excuse for insulting the reason of the believer when dealing with sacred objects. It was not enough to say that when dealing with the sacred the natural order may be subjected to the miraculous. In the colloquy "A Pilgrimage for the Sake of Religion," Erasmus tried to expose fraudulent claims with his biting wit. Witness the following dialogue between his two characters, Menedemus and Ogygius, who are talking about the relics of Christ and Mary:

Menedemus: O Mother most like her son! He left us so much of his blood on earth; she left so much of her milk that it's scarcely credible a woman with only one child could have so much, even if the child had drunk none of it.

Ogygius: The same thing is said about the Lord's Cross, which is exhibited publicly and privately in so many places that if the fragments were joined together they'd seem a full load for a freighter. And yet the Lord carried his whole Cross.

Menedemus: Doesn't it seem amazing to you, too?

Ogygius: It could be called unusual, perhaps, but "amazing" – no, since the Lord, who multiplies these things as he wills, is omnipotent.

Menedemus: You explain it reverently, but for my part, I'm afraid many such affairs are contrived for profit.[53]

---

[51] *Inquisitio de fide* (1524), Thompson, *Colloquies*, p. 185.

[52] It would be going too far, however, to see his rationalism as a foreshadowing of the Enlightenment. His critique is still dominated by the demands of faith and piety. With Erasmus it is not a question of faith and reason being incompatible, but rather of childish credulity being incompatible with true faith.

[53] "A Pilgrimage for the Sake of Religion" (1526), Thompson, *Colloquies*, p. 295. This colloquy is based on visits made by Erasmus to the great English shrines of Our Lady of Walsingham and St. Thomas of Canterbury, probably between 1512 and 1514.

Erasmus also mocked some of the more gruesome aspects of the cult of relics, since his refined sensibilities were offended by the coarseness that was often disguised as reverence. Broken bones, bloody flesh, and dirty rags were all displayed before the people as objects of devotion. At Canterbury, for instance, one could venerate the linen rags with which the martyr Thomas had wiped the sweat from his face, the dirt from his nose, "or whatever other kinds of filth human bodies have." Erasmus shows his disgust through the character of Menedemus, saying: "I consider it shameful to push soles, shoes and girdles at one to be kissed."[54] Instead of seeking the truth of the spirit, men pressed their faces to filthy objects. Erasmus looked upon the scene with despair; piety could sink no lower than this.

Another target of Erasmus's critique was the pilgrimage. The various practices involved in this form of piety were criticized in two colloquies, "On Rash Vows" (1522) and "A Pilgrimage for the Sake of Religion" (1526), as well as in other works. Erasmus was opposed to pilgrimages for several reasons. First, he objected to the false sense of holiness that they engendered. Like the veneration of images and relics, they made the individual feel that he was religious, when in truth he was merely carrying out a formal observance. Furthermore, the traveling involved in pilgrimages was more often than not an occasion for sin and irresponsibility: "Qui peregrinatur raro sanctificatur." Erasmus charged that the name of religion was used as a cover for superstition, faithlessness, foolishness, and recklessness among pilgrims.[55] Erasmus also objected to the way in which people made pilgrimage vows to the saints. Especially repulsive was the "bargaining" nature of most vows, which he condemned as "making deals with the saints" and as a shallow understanding of divine mercy. Such a notion was a total misunderstanding of prayer and divine assistance; it turned piety into a commercial transaction. Even more repulsive was the theology of localization that served as the basis of the pilgrimage. It is on this point that Erasmus's spiritualism enters his critique of pilgrimages. He objected to the idea that the divine power could be sought in one place as opposed to another. Was not God omnipresent? Why should He be more merciful in Santiago or Walsingham than in one's home town? Just as Erasmus objected to seeing the divine power subdivided among the saints, so did he condemn its being parceled out to different spots on the globe.[56]

---

[54] Ibid., p. 310.
[55] Thompson, *Colloquies*, p. 626 ("De utilitate colloquiorum," 1526).
[56] "The Shipwreck," and "Pilgrimage," Thompson, *Colloquies*, pp. 141, 291, respectively.

Erasmian piety always demanded that spiritual reality be sought *above* the things of this earth, not *in* them.

A final point to consider in Erasmus's critique of medieval piety is his opposition to the economics of the *cultus divorum*. Since Erasmus regarded material objects of worship as distractions from true piety, he saw no point in the amassment of religious treasure. His argument for a change in priorities is presented in "A Pilgrimage for the Sake of Religion." In this colloquy, Erasmus remarks that the shrine built to St. Thomas at Canterbury is really a blot upon the memory of the martyr. St. Thomas, he argues, was always a friend to the poor, and, even in death, would have wanted to relieve the wants of the needy with his riches. If a poor wretched woman with hungry children at home were to sneak into the cathedral and carry off a small part of its wealth, St. Thomas would gladly consent.[57] Erasmus maintained that the excessive wealth surrounding the *cultus divorum* contradicted the claims of Christian charity. It was detestable, therefore, not only because it kept men from practicing true piety, but also because it made a mockery of the spirit of Christianity itself. Erasmus raised an argument which had earlier been made by Bernard of Clairvaux, and would later be repeated by many Protestant Reformers:

> Seriously, I wonder sometimes what possible excuse there could be for those who spend so much money on building, decorating, and enriching churches that there is no limit to it. Granted that the sacred vestments and vessels of the church must have a dignity appropriate to their liturgical use; and I want the building to have grandeur. But what is the use of so many baptistries, candelabra, gold statues? What is the good of the vastly expensive organs, as they call them? . . . What is the good of that costly musical neighing when meanwhile our brothers and sisters, Christ's living temples, waste away from hunger and thirst?[58]

Erasmus, however, was typically ambivalent about his commitment to this idea. He was not proposing an immediate redistribution of Church treasure, but rather commenting on its inappropriateness. He also remarked that since the fault sprang from excessive devotion it was not all that bad, and that since the treasure was generally given

---

[57] "Pilgrimage," Thompson, pp. 306–7.

[58] Ibid., p. 307. Erasmus had made the same statement earlier in his 1522 colloquy, "The Godly Feast," where he had also said that those who poured money into churches while the poor starved seemed "almost guilty of a capital crime" (Thompson, *Colloquies*, p. 70). Zwingli would adopt this argument, even using some of the same language, in his 1525 treatise, *De vera et falsa religione* (*Latin Works*, 3.331). Calvin, in turn, also borrowed the argument, either from Zwingli or Erasmus, or maybe from both of them (*Institutes*, IV. 5. 18.)

by kings and potentates it was better to see it spent on religion than on gambling and war.[59] Nonetheless, he urged the "thickheaded" donors to spend their money secretly for the support of those who really needed it.[60] Little did Erasmus suspect in 1522 that within a few years his advice would be taken literally by iconoclastic mobs in Zurich, Bern, Basel, and other Swiss and German cities.

THE LIMITATIONS OF THE ERASMIAN CRITIQUE

The barbs flowing from Erasmus's pen were viewed with increasing impatience by Church authorities, especially after 1521, when the threat posed by Luther began to make itself felt. Those who defended the *status quo* against the Wittenberg professor soon turned their attention to the man who had been criticizing the Church for years, and it began to be rumored in some circles that Erasmus had laid the egg that Luther hatched.[61] As early as 1522, the Inquisitor of Louvain called for a public burning of the *Colloquies*, saying they were infected with Lutheran heresy.[62] The most significant opposition to the Erasmian critique of medieval religion came from the Sorbonne. In a petition to Parlement in May 1526, the theological faculty of Paris condemned the *Colloquies* and a few other Erasmian writings, denouncing sixty-nine passages as "erroneous, scandalous and impious" and describing Erasmus as a pagan who mocked the sacred rites and customs of the Christian religion. The Sorbonne requested that the *Colloquies* be forbidden to everyone, but above all to youths, whose morals might be corrupted by them "a finibus eliminaretur Christianorum."[63] That same year, Noel Beda launched an attack on Erasmus.[64] In 1528, the Sorbonne explicitly prohibited the *Colloquies* from being used in teaching by the faculty. The *Colloquies* were long included in various inquisitorial lists, and when the Roman *Index librorum prohibitorum* appeared in 1559, all of Erasmus's scripture com-

---

[59] "Pilgrimage," Thompson, *Colloquies*, p. 307. Erasmus added: "I'd rather see a church abounding in sacred furnishing than bare and dirty, as some are, and more like stables than churches."

[60] "The Godly Feast," Thompson, *Colloquies*, p. 70. Erasmus was well aware that he who gives can also take away. With foresight, he made one of his characters say: "I'd rather have this superfluous wealth spent on the poor than kept for the use of officials who will plunder it all sooner or later."

[61] Allen V, no. 1528.

[62] Ibid., p. 88.

[63] C. DuPlessis d'Argentre (ed.), *Collectio iudiciorum* (Paris, 1728–36), vol. II, pp. 47–52.

[64] AS I, 202.

mentaries, annotations, and translations were condemned, along with the *Colloquies*.[65]

Roman Catholics were not the only ones who saw similarities between Luther and Erasmus, however. Protestants who had been inspired by his critique of the medieval Church also tried to make him join their struggle. Ulrich von Hutten, for instance, saw Erasmus as a precursor of Luther, saying that since he had "first bestirred the minds of men for liberty" he had better beware of persecution.[66] Albrecht Dürer, the great German artist, was similarly aware of Erasmus's radicalism. Upon hearing the rumor that Luther had been assassinated, he wrote in his diary:

O God, if Luther is dead, who will so clearly teach us the Gospel? O Erasmus of Rotterdam, where are you staying? Ride forth, you knight of Christ. Defend the truth and win the martyr's crown.[67]

Dürer and Hutten were in for disappointment. Even though the evangelicals and the Catholics both clamored for the inclusion of Erasmus in the Protestant fold, he staunchly refused to be drawn into the camp of the religious rebels.[68] Erasmus's critique of medieval religion was not as radical as some of his readers thought it was, and he tried hard to defend himself against all charges of heresy. The same man thought by many to have denounced "the universal hypocrisy" and "the cesspool of Roman crimes," now did his best to dull the sharper edges of his critique.

Though cutting and pervasive, Erasmus's critique of medieval piety had an intentional element of ambiguity. Some attributed this to indecision, others to deviousness, but the fact is Erasmus was neither confused nor insincere. For the most part, he knew exactly what he was doing, and refused to compromise with any viewpoint that lacked the subtlety he so highly favored. Several factors dulled the edge of Erasmus's critique, and it is difficult to single out any of them as a primary guiding principle. No one has ever considered Erasmus

---

[65] H. Reusch, *Der Index der Verbotenen Bücher* (Bonn, 1883–5), vol. I, pp. 347–67; and *Die Indices Librorum Prohibitorum des 16 Jahrhunderts* (Tübingen, 1886), pp. 183, 259; also M. and P. Grendler, "The Survival of Erasmus in Italy," *Erasmus in English*, 8: 2–21 (1976).

[66] Allen, IV, no. 1161. Hutten wrote to Erasmus: "Do you think you are secure now that Luther's books have been burned? Flee, Erasmus, flee!"

[67] Hans Rupprich (ed.), *Dürer-Schriftlicher Nachlass* (Berlin, 1956), p. 171.

[68] E. Bocking (ed.), *Ulrich Hutteni Opera* (Leipzig, 1859), vol. II, pp. 180–248. Hutten wrote he was "stupefied and shaken" over Erasmus's failure of nerve. Bainton, *Erasmus*, p. 176. Also: Karl H. Oelrich, *Der Späte Erasmus und die Reformation* (Münster, 1961).

a simple man. His propensity for sarcasm, for example, led him to seek a very high, almost unreachable middle ground from which he could lash out at folly on all sides. His irenic personality also tempered his sarcasm and prevented him from becoming too intolerant. His elitism, in turn, allowed him to accept a wider range of acceptable gradations in faith and practice. His aversion to theological speculation and precise definitions, finally, also moved him naturally toward complexity and ambiguity. Taking these factors into consideration, it becomes easier to see why it is that Erasmus acted as he did when faced with the consequences of his critique.

Erasmus had an aversion to theological speculation and precise definitions, and his critique of medieval piety, though cutting and pervasive, shared in this lack of precision. In his later years Erasmus did not withdraw the criticisms he had made; on the contrary, he intensified his attack at the same time he was trying to deny his association with the Lutheran "heresy." Some of his most biting colloquies appeared between 1522 and 1526. However, when he was pressured by Church authorities, he found himself stressing the limited nature of his attacks on medieval piety, saying he did not *completely* condemn any doctrine or practice of the Church. His defense, though legitimate, was rather lame. In the *Enchiridion*, for instance, he had tempered his criticism, but the disclaimer was always a "footnote" of sorts.

Erasmus cautioned he was not denying the value of any aspect of Church life, but merely exposing a distorted sense of values:

Truly, I do not condemn those who do these things with a guileless sort of superstition, so much as I despise those who, looking out for their own profit, prey upon the ignorance of the common people and raise things that are barely tolerable to the level of the highest, perfect piety. I really cannot endure it when they turn what is indifferent into what is best; what is of smallest value into the greatest.[69]

This passage captures the essence of the Erasmian critique: It was sharp and cutting; it opened the eyes of many a reader to some deficiencies of medieval piety; it gave rise to an aggressive transcendentalism in theology; but it was not very radical. And it is this last point which makes all the difference. Erasmus saw the material piety of the medieval Church as an *indifferent* thing. Religious materialism corrupted true piety, but it was not a sinful evil. It was dangerous – in the sense that it engendered a false sense of holiness – but it was

---

[69] *Enchiridion*, AS I, 178–80.

not worth the price of schism, or heresy. In the *Enchiridion* he argued that material objects of worship sometimes serve as "signs and supports" of piety. They were necessary for those who were not ready to accept a more mature spiritual faith, for "children in Christ." His approval rested, he said, on the assumption that they are only steps that lead to a more appropriate means of salvation.[70]

Erasmus, therefore, presented a limited critique. On the one hand he refers to material objects of worship as "dangerous," while on the other hand he says they are necessary for the weak. This is a good example of Erasmus's disdain for theological precision. Erasmus attacks and retreats at the same time. His objection to materialism in religion is quite strong; he says that to place the whole of religion in external ceremonies is not only "sublime stupidity," but also against the spirit of the Gospel. Still, Erasmus refused to deny the value of material objects of worship. His criticism is clearly tempered by his respect for authority and his abhorrence of contention. He says it is "wholesome" to observe some unimportant things in religion, and asks: "What, then, should the Christian do? Should he neglect the mandates of the Church? Should he despise the honorable traditions of the ancients? Or condemn godly customs?"[71] Erasmus's transcendentalism was not very aggressive: The observance of honorable traditions and godly customs could override any metaphysical objections.

Moreover, close below the surface of Erasmus's critique one can also detect a certain elitist attitude that contributed to his retreat from intolerance. Steeped as he was in Origen, Erasmus could not help but subscribe to the elitist principles that his mentor had applied alongside his transcendentalist theology. After all, had not Origen proposed a certain hierarchy of spiritual perfection within the Christian community, a hierarchy that was related directly to the interpretation of the truths of scripture, with the pneumatic elite being the only ones capable of understanding its hidden meanings?[72] To some extent, this

---

[70] AS I, 206: "tum indicia tum adminicula pietatis."

[71] AS I.,230. Erasmus adds: "Non damnatur opera corporalia, sed praeferentur invisibilia. Non damnatur cultus visibilis, sed non placatur deus nisi pietate invisibili. Spiritus est deus, et spiritalibus victimis flectitur."

[72] Origen, *On First Principles*, trans. R. Greer (New York, 1979), Bk. IV, chaps. 2–3, esp. IV.2.4. This elitist attitude seems to be part of a larger pattern in religious history. In systems that carry their transcendental principles to the point of dualism, it has often been the case that two distinct classes of believers are created. This was true of the Manicheans, as well as many gnostic groups, and also the Cathars. A discussion of this intriguing problem is beyond the scope of this study, but the general pattern should be kept in mind. Though Erasmus never advocated the

can be openly detected in Erasmus's reference to "children in Christ" for whom material aids are still necessary as "signs and supports" of piety. Just as Origen was willing to tolerate a complex gradation of faith within the Christian community, even to the point of including thickheaded materialists who actually insisted that God had planted individual trees in the Garden of Eden, "like some farmer"; so was Erasmus willing to tolerate a complex gradation of practice, even to the point of allowing for some merit to be found in simple-hearted pilgrims who showed true devotion before a spurious relic.

The limitations of Erasmus's critique become most apparent in the defense he raised against specific charges of unorthodoxy, especially in regard to saints, images and the eucharist. Erasmus carefully disassociated himself from the Protestant attack on medieval piety, sometimes defending his orthodoxy point by point.

Not unreasonably, Erasmus was suspected of discouraging prayers to the saints. He denied this charge on several occasions, and apparently continued to believe they could be invoked.[73] Erasmus believed that St. Genevieve had once saved him from a deadly fever, and continued to venerate the Virgin Mary as a merciful mother.[74] Three years before his death, he cautiously defended prayers to the saints.[75] Erasmus, though, had a unique flair for blending his support of traditional beliefs with criticism; and for being able to distribute praise and blame at the same time. In "A Pilgrimage for the Sake of Religion," he has the Virgin Mary writing a letter to Zwingli. This provides him with an opportunity to take a swipe at both the Protestants and the Catholics. Mary thanks Zwingli for persuading people not to invoke her. She was exhausted from hearing the "shameless" petitions of mortals who demanded everything from her as if her Son were always a baby.[76] However, Mary also takes umbrage at being denied her rightful place. She says she hears Zwingli is trying to remove

creation of a class of "pneumatics," or "perfecti," it is possible that his avoidance of radicalism could have been related (as it was in these other movements) to an awareness of the rigors of a transcendental theology, and of the fact that most Christians needed an education in words, rather than pictures, before becoming truly capable of a full, spiritual, interior faith.

[73] Bainton, *Erasmus*, p. 69.
[74] Léon E. Halkin, "La Mariologie d'Erasme," *ARG*, 68 (1977), 32–55.
[75] *De Sarcienda Ecclesiae Concordia* (1533), ed. and trans. J. P. Dolan, *The Essential Erasmus* (New York, 1964), p. 380. His defense is typically elitist: "If our prayers are not heard by the saints, Christ, who loves *simple* souls, will give us what we request through the saints."
[76] "Pilgrimage," Thompson, *Colloquies*, pp. 289–90. The letter from Mary is addressed to a certain "Glaucoplutus," which is a play on Zwingli's first name, "Ulrich" ("Owl-rich").

from the churches whatever belongs to the saints, and asks him to consider what he is doing. Erasmus has Mary defend her exalted position:

But me, however defenseless, you shall not eject unless at the same time you eject my Son whom I hold in my arms. From him I will not be parted. Either you expel him along with me, or you leave us both here, unless you prefer to have a Church without Christ.[77]

As much as Erasmus detested the abuses involved in the cult of the saints, he was not willing to see it abolished.

Erasmus was also quite clear about his opposition to iconoclasm. Defending himself in *De utilitate Colloquiorum*, Erasmus remarked that in "A Pilgrimage" he had reproached those who "with much ado have thrown all images out the churches."[78] In *De sarciendia ecclesiae* (1533) he presents the clearest expression of his position regarding iconoclasm. Here he says that those who rage against images may have had good reasons for doing so, but were still too immoderate. Statuary and painting have a place in the Church as "a kind of silent poetry," since they occasionally catch the emotional state of man far better than words.[79] This is not to say, he continues, that abuses should be tolerated. Foolish and obscene depictions should be removed and the people should be taught to see the images in the right perspective. One must be careful to distinguish between what is proper and improper. And above all, remarks Erasmus, one must respect the peace of the Church.[80]

In his treatise *Against the Pseudo-Evangelicals of Strasbourg*, Erasmus complained that it was useless to destroy existing piety if no better reform plan was at hand, and if morals were not also improved. He seemed disturbed not so much because the old practices were any good, but rather because nothing better had replaced them. "Your object is not to reform as to destroy," he told the evangelicals. "Images are thrown out of the churches, but what good is that if the idols of vice remain?" He seemed to chide the reformers not so much for doing something wrong, but rather for doing something badly.[81]

Erasmus places limitations not only on his transcendentalism but on his primitivism as well. Just as he is willing to accept a reverent and detached use of material objects, he is willing to grant that it is

---

[77] Ibid., p. 291.
[78] Thompson, *Colloquies*, p. 631.
[79] *De sarcienda*, Dolan, *Essential Erasmus*, p. 380.
[80] Ibid., p. 381. Also *Opera omnia*, Leiden ed., vol. V, p. 504.
[81] trans. Bainton, *Erasmus*, p. 260.

impossible to return the Church to a pristine condition. Iconoclasts often argued that the Church had to return to its primitive state in every respect. Erasmus rejects this argument on the principle that the primitive state was not altogether ideal. "There was drunkeness at the Lord's Supper, debauchery at midnight vigils, and riots attending the election of bishops."[82] In spite of these disclaimers, though, the ambivalent Erasmus occasionally expressed a desire to see the images removed. In one of his later works he wrote: "Images are the books of the unlearned, but so readily lend themselves to externalism that it might be well if bishops, in an orderly fashion, should remove them all except the cross."[83]

Another point on which Erasmus had to defend himself was on his interpretation of the eucharist. As with the case of saints and images, Erasmus pressed for a more spiritual understanding without rejecting the teaching of the Church. Although he showed sympathy for the spiritualistic interpretation of Oecolampadius, he continued to deny any association with sacramentarian views.[84] On this point, again, the strength of the Church's teaching authority seemed to be the reason for Erasmus' defense: "Never have I said joking or serious that the Eucharist is nothing but bread and wine . . . I do not despise the Roman church, especially when supported by the consent of all the churches."[85]

Erasmus maintained that there was no ambiguity about the presence of Christ's body in the eucharist. The only point where there was room for doubt was the manner in which Christ made himself present.[86] Men were commanded to be spiritual, he argued, but the presence of Christ's flesh could never prevent anyone from being spiritual.[87] There was no need, therefore, to stamp out the Mass as if it were a pestilence. Erasmus was even willing to accept the adoration of the consecrated elements, within limits, of course. "If Christ is totally present in the sacrament, why should it not be adored?" he asked.[88] Erasmus might have interpreted the spiritual and material as

---

[82] *Opera omnia*, Leiden ed., vol. X, pp. 1577–87.
[83] Ibid., vol. V., pp. 1187–8.
[84] Allen VI, no. 1717. Erasmus remarked: "The opinion of Oecolampadius [concerning the eucharist] would not displease me if it were not contrary to the consensus of the Church."
[85] Allen VI, no. 1637.
[86] Allen IX, no. 2631.
[87] Allen VI, no. 1637.
[88] *Opera omnia*, Leiden ed., vol. V, p. 503. Still, Erasmus cautioned, it is not proper to engage in exaggerated devotion, such as "parading the host around in a cart for everyone to adore."

contrasting spheres, but he certainly did not regard them as completely antithetical.

Erasmus remains an enigmatic figure in the history of the Reformation. On the one hand, it is difficult to deny that he made a positive
contribution to Protestantism through his critique of medieval piety.
His primitivism, biblicism, and, above all, his spiritualism deeply
affected a whole generation of younger humanists, many of whom
later became ardent enemies of Roman Catholic worship.[89] Heinrich
Bullinger, for instance, praised Erasmus as "a truly great man,
worthy of eternal praise" in his treatise against images, *De origine
erroris* (1539). He commended Erasmus for having shed the clearest
light on the question of images in the *Enchiridion*, *The Praise of Folly*,
the *Colloquies*, and other writings, and for having spoken "truthfully,
piously, wisely and justly" about the superstition surrounding the
cult of images.[90] On the other hand, it is not possible to trace the
Protestant attack on Catholic worship directly to Erasmus. Although
he stressed the spiritual over against the outward and material in
worship, he never denied the absolute value of external religion. A
certain tension is apparent in Erasmus. Though he formulated a new
metaphysical foundation for the interpretation of worship, and spoke
freely against what he thought was wrong in medieval piety, he
refused to follow his own logic to any kind of practical conclusion.
When it came to questions of worship (as was the case with most
things), Erasmus refused to consider extremes. Instead, he fixed
upon an axis of criticism that ran through the opposite poles of indiscriminate worship and intolerance. Erasmus saw much of the materially oriented piety of the medieval Church as misdirected and superstitious, but not as evil. His indifference toward outward forms of

---

[89] Roland Bainton comments on this point: "The Erasmian spiritualizing of religion,
though utterly gentle, led to the drastic measures of Zwingli, Oecolampadius, and
Pellikan, and though Erasmus disowned his children, they were not altogether
wrong in regarding him as their sire" (*Erasmus*, p. 282; also p. 61).

[90] H. Bullinger, *In librum de origine erroris circa invocationem et cultum deorum ac sim-
ulachrorum* (Zurich, 1539) Bullinger says: "Erasmus Roterod., vere magnum & aeterna laude dignum virum, mirror quo vultu pro se adducere audeant adversarii. Nam
luce clariora sunt quae ille scripsit de imaginum usu in Enchiridio militis Christiani,
in Morias encomio, in Colloquiis & multis aliis locis . . . Ut imagines sint in templis
nulla praecipit vel humana constitutio. Et ut facilius est ita tutius quoque est omnes
imagenes e templis submovere, quam impetrate ut nec modus praetereatur nec
admisceatur superstitio. Iam ut animus sit ab omni superstitione purus, tamen non
caret superstitionis specie orantem ad ligneum simulachrum procumbere, in hoc
intentos habere oculos, ad hoc verba facere, huic oscula figere, nec orare, prorsus
nisi coram imagine . . . Hec Erasmus prudenter, pie, vere & sancte pronunciavit"
(pp. 153r–153v).

worship, therefore, distanced him as much from Protestants as from Catholics.

Moreover, Erasmus actually did no reforming of his own, and limited his critique to the printed page. His sophistication distanced him from the masses, and the impact of his critique was restricted to learned circles. By writing exclusively in Latin, and always poking fun at the "simple folk," Erasmus circumscribed his own plan for reform, and necessarily left the actual task of change to his readers. Though he had many admirers and disciples, he had no way of directing them along clearly defined paths. The Erasmian critique provided intellectual and spiritual guidelines for his followers, but these guidelines were themselves elitist at heart and limited in scope. So it is that when the images and the Mass were abolished in Basel, Erasmus fled, unable to accept the intolerance he had engendered in spite of himself.[91]

[91] John Phillips correctly traces some of the attitudes that led to Protestant iconoclasm to the thought of Erasmus. *The Reformation of Images: Destruction of Art in England 1535–1660* (Los Angeles, 1973).

CHAPTER 3

Early reformers and the question of idolatry

At one point during the First Zurich Disputation, Ulrich Zwingli said the following about Protestant guidelines for religious reform:

We desire to speak of the truth [to find out], whether a man is bound by divine ordinance to keep that which on account of long usage has been set up as law by men. For we of course think that custom should yield to truth.[1]

The question for Zwingli was no longer one of rejecting the misuse of "good and honorable customs," as had been the case with Erasmus, but rather of separating human customs from divine ordinances. Zwingli's statement focuses on the foundations of the Protestant attack on medieval piety. Unlike Erasmus, Protestant Reformers drew a sharp distinction between "good" and "evil," or "true" and "false" worship. This distinction often involved separating the heavenly from the earthly as well.

Protestantism claimed that the medieval Church had fallen into idolatry, and this judgment had a dual perspective. In the first place, as is indicated in Zwingli's argument, a distinction was made between rites of divine origin and humanly devised observances. The externalized cult of medieval Catholicism was attacked as a human institution that was opposed to the worship revealed by God in scripture. In other words, the Church had set itself up as an idol, substituting its own decrees for those of God.

Secondly, the Catholic cult was attacked as improperly directed. Instead of worshiping God the creator, the medieval Church worshiped the creature; not only because it set up its own prescriptions against God's, but also because it directed the worshiper's attention to the material world. The Church was idolatrous because it used idols in the most concrete sense. Like some vast Augean stable, the medieval Church was ankle-deep in the "filth" of images, relics, al-

[1] Ulrich Zwingli, *Selected Works*, ed. and trans. Samuel Macauley Jackson (Philadelphia, 1972), p. 54.

tars, holy places, and miraculous hosts. The Protestant attack on medieval piety sought to flood the ground and cleanse the Church from the accumulated debris. Consequently, iconoclasm, the destruction of sacred images and objects, became one of its most visible characteristics.

Yet, this holy war against "false religion" was far from unified. Differences of opinion on theology and reforming policy led to struggles within Protestantism itself, pointing to divisions that would plague the Reformation for years to come.

KARLSTADT AND THE IDOLS AT WITTENBERG

The Protestant attack on Roman Catholic "idolatry" begins with Andreas Bodenstein von Karlstadt, Luther's colleague at the University of Wittenberg. It was he, not Luther, who first criticized medieval piety as misdirected and evil, and who first implemented a plan to do away with the Catholic *cultus*.[2] Although Karlstadt's opposition to Catholic worship may be seen in part as an extension of the Erasmian critique of late medieval piety, it may also be regarded as an expression of a distinctly Protestant ethos, apart from humanism.

There is little doubt that Karlstadt was influenced by Erasmus.[3] As early as 1518, he was engaged in an Erasmian attack on externalized piety – an attack that would intensify and become more radical after 1520.[4] Karlstadt began to strike out against the prevailing religious externalism of his day, hoping he would be able to reassert the primacy of the Word. He became convinced of the contingency of created elements, and said that since God is a spirit, visible and external acts of worship were of little value in themselves. These attacks on externalized piety were based on the Gospel text of John 6.63 (also quoted often by Erasmus): "it is the spirit that gives life, the flesh is of no avail."[5]

Yet, Karlstadt's opposition to the externalization of worship was not entirely "Erasmian." In the first place, Karlstadt began to regard

---

[2] Of the numerous works on Karlstadt, I cite those that are most helpful in dealing with his opposition to externalized worship: Gordon Rupp, *Patterns of Reformation* (Philadelphia, 1969), pp. 47–153; James S. Preus, *Carlstadt's "Ordinaciones" and Luther's Liberty: A Study of the Wittenberg Movement 1521–22* (Cambridge, Mass., 1974); Ronald J. Sider, *Andreas Bodenstein von Karlstadt: The Development of his Thought 1517–1525* (Leiden, 1974); Margarete Stirm, *Die Bilderfrage in der Reformation* (Gütersloh, 1977), pp. 24–44; and Carl Christensen, *Art and the Reformation in Germany* (Athens, Ohio, 1980), pp. 13–65.

[3] Rupp, *Patterns*, pp. 59, 81–3, 117, 124; and Sider, *Karlstadt*, pp. 85, 149, 240.

[4] Sider, *Karlstadt*, p. 149.

[5] Ibid., pp. 149, 151.

as evil those things which Erasmus considered indifferent. Secondly, Karlstadt's thought was centered on an uncompromising biblicism – one that was significantly more legalistic in its interpretation of the letter of the Law than that of Erasmus or even Luther.[6] Even though Karlstadt admitted that the ceremonial proscriptions of the Old Testament were no longer binding on Christians, he interpreted the application of this principle much more narrowly than Erasmus or Luther, and refused to believe that the prohibition of images had been invalidated by the New Covenant.[7]

Karlstadt's attack on Catholic piety developed gradually. His earlier opposition to externalized worship was generally limited to the use of material props in worship, such as holy water, sacred salt, and images. Although he was concerned with reforming the Mass as early as 1520,[8] and carried out liturgical reforms in 1521, these measures were directed not so much against "idolatry" as against unscriptural practices. Karlstadt initially attacked the Roman Mass as worthless worship rather than as an evil corruption of the true worship of God. It is not until 1523 that he parted with Luther on the question of the real presence and began to attack eucharistic adoration and the notion of sacrifice as idolatrous.

Karlstadt's initial attack on popular religion

One of the earliest expressions of Karlstadt's opposition to the externalization of worship is his treatise "On Holy Water and Sacred Salt," first published in 1520.[9] In this treatise one finds him proposing that material elements are unable to convey spiritual benefits, and that they are merely "signs" that lead the worshiper to a higher spiritual reality, much as a hand painted on a road sign points the way to a traveler's destination.[10] Just as the hand does not push the traveler along, but merely shows the way, so do external religious objects

---

[6] Friedel Kriechbaum, *Grundzüge der Theologie Karlstadts* (Hamburg, 1967), pp. 108, 115. Also: Sider, *Karlstadt*, pp. 167, 280. Sider warns, however, that "great care will need to be exercised in the definition and use of this epithet ['legalism']," p. 4.

[7] Sider, *Karlstadt*, pp. 111, 278–9.

[8] George H. Williams, *The Radical Reformation* (Philadelphia, 1962), p. 40.

[9] "Von Gewychtem Wasser und Saltz, Doct. Andreas Carlstadt: Wider den Unvordienten Gardian Francisus Seyler" (Wittenberg, 1520). Karlstadt's pamphlet was quickly attacked by Johannes Fritzhans in 1520, in his own "Von dem Geweichten Wasser Widder Andream Bodenstein von Karlstadt Doctor zu Wittenberg." Karlstadt counterattacked with yet another tract on the same subject, "Antwort Andreas Bodenstein von Carolstadt Doctor: Geweicht Wasser Belangend: Wider Einen Bruder Johannes Fritzhans Gennant: Holtzuger Ordens" (Wittenberg, 1521).

[10] *Gewychtem Wasser* (1520), p. 2.

help the worshiper along without having any power of their own.[11] Karlstadt criticized his contemporaries for approaching holy water as unreasoning beasts, and warned that such abuses must cease.[12]

Karlstadt continued his attack with a condemnation of the cult of images in a work entitled "Instruction Concerning Vows,"[13] first published in June 1521. In the foreword to this pamphlet, Karlstadt presents a "pathology" of popular religion.[14] Karlstadt now viewed images as part of a religious atmosphere whose function and impact was to retard the intellectual and spiritual growth of the laity, and – even more heinous – to misdirect and corrupt Christian worship at its core. Karlstadt charged that the *cultus divorum* diverted faith and prayer, expecially in time of need, from their proper object, God. Karlstadt itemized a long list of patron saints who supposedly protected against specific evils, and criticized those who addressed their prayers to this new pantheon of "lesser deities." He said God wanted to drive all lesser gods from men's hearts, because it was not so much the outer, but the inner image that led people to worship falsely.[15]

During the rest of the year 1521, Karlstadt continued voice his opposition to images. In July, for instance, he condemned the makers of religious images in his exegesis of a passage from the Gospel of Matthew.[16] Around the same time, one of his students also defended a disputation calling for the destruction of all images of Christ, the Virgin, and the saints.[17]

Karlstadt's strongest indictment against religious art appeared in early 1522, when he wrote "On the Abolition of Images" to justify iconoclasm at Wittenberg.[18] This pamphlet was the first major Protes-

---

11 Ibid., p. 5: "Ausserlich wasser/ ist nur zu eynem zeychen/ wie ein hand an eynem stock den weg zuweysen/ geben und angericht ist. Die hultzere hand macht dich nit geen/ sie gibt dir auch nit den weg/ sie tregt dich auch nicht/ sie teudt und weyset allein."

12 Ibid., p. 3: "Also geen sie zu dem geweychten wasser wie ein pferdt zu der trenck/ das keyn vornunfft hat."

13 "Von Gelubden Unterrichtung" (1521).

14 Preus, *Ordinaciones*, p. 35.

15 "Von Gelubden Unterrichtung," Ci,v: "gott wirt von deynen herzen alle creaturen und fremde gotter abschneyden auff dastu yhn alleyn mit vollem herzen liebest." This distincion between "inner" and "outer" idols would become an inportant part of Zwingli's theology.

16 Preus, *Ordinaciones*, p. 14, n. 6.

17 The thesis is printed in Theodor Kolde, "Wittenberger Disputationsthesen aus den Jahren 1516–1522," *Zeitschrift für Kirchengeschichte*, XI (1889–90), p. 463, thesis 12.

18 "Von Abthung der Bylder und das Keyn Bedtler unter Christen Seyn Sollen" (Wittenberg, 1522). This tract has been reprinted in an annotated edition edited by Hans Lietzmann ("Kleine Texte für Theologische und Philologische Vorlesungen und Übungen," no. 74, Bonn, 1911). Page numbers given for the "Abthung" shall refer to the Lietzmann edition.

tant treatise on the question of religious imagery, and proved to be one of the most influential in the development of a Protestant "theology of idolatry."[19]

Karlstadt begins with the enunciation of three theses: (1) that the presence of images in churches and houses of God is wrong and contrary to the first commandment; (2) that the carved and painted idols on the altars are even more devilish and dangerous; and (3) that it is therefore good, necessary and praiseworthy to abolish them, and to give scripture its proper right and judgment. Although the work is far from systematic, the three theses divide the tract into three distinct parts. The first concentrates on the scriptural prohibition of images. Karlstadt argues that God has forbidden all religious images, and cites numerous Old Testament passages to prove this point. Included in this argument is the assertion that men are always inclined to idolatry and that images "murder the spirits of their worshipers" by drawing them away from God.[20] Because he relies so heavily on the Old Testament, Karlstadt has to answer the claim that the Mosaic Law had been abrogated by Christ. Karlstadt denies this "heretical" viewpoint and presents a series of counterarguments. Above all, Karlstadt contends that Christ did not come to destroy, but to fulfill the Law. Since the command against images is included in the Decalogue, along with other essential moral commands, then it must be as important as all the others. If one ignores the command against images, then why not also those against murder, adultery, or theft? Furthermore, Karlstadt continues, since the image prohibition appears at the beginning of the Decalogue, is it not to be considered even more important that the rest? Karlstadt proposed an uncompromising interpretation of the image prohibition: "I say to you that God has forbidden images with no less diligence than killing, stealing, adultery and the like."[21] This interpretation of the biblical proscription is the heart of Karlstadt's attack, and the foundation of subsequent Protestant arguments against the use of religious imagery.

But it is not enough to say that Karlstadt interpreted scripture in such an uncompromising fashion. To understand this kind of exegesis, one must turn to the hermeneutic of transcendence that domi-

---

[19] Carl Christensen provides an excellent analysis in *Art and the Reformation in Germany*, pp. 23–35. Other studies include: C. F. Jager, *Andreas Bodenstein von Carlstadt* (Stuttgart, 1856), pp. 263–74; Hermann Barge, *Andreas Bodenstein von Karlstadt* (Leipzig, 1905), vol. I, pp. 386–91; G. Rupp, *Patterns*, p. 103; Sider, *Karlstadt*, pp. 110–11; Preus, *Ordinaciones*, pp. 36–9.

[20] "Abthung," pp. 4–5.

[21] Ibid., p. 22.

nated Karlstadt's opposition to images. Throughout his arguments against the Catholic cult, Karlstadt repeats a constant theme: Images serve no good religious purpose. The reason for this, he says, is that images are bound to the flesh and cannot transcend it. The spiritualist hermeneutic employed by him is clearly revealed in this dictum: Only the Spirit vivifies, and the Spirit works through the Word, not through material objects. "The Word of God is spiritual, and it alone is useful to believers."[22]

This dualism between matter and spirit allows Karlstadt to reject the distinctions between the image and its prototype. How can one say that worship is not being offered to the image itself when one sees that men bow and genuflect before them, remove their hats in their presence and bring wax figures and other votive offerings to them when they wish to be healed? Are all these gestures really intended for the "prototype," or the image? Karlstadt argues that there can be no "prototype" represented in the image, since material objects cannot objectify a spiritual reality, and that worship offered to images is therefore offered only to the artistic representation, not to the person represented by it.[23]

In condemning the veneration of images, Karlstadt also condemns its theological foundation, the cult of saints. Karlstadt argues that God alone can help man, and that He will not tolerate that anyone or anything be given a place of honor in his stead. He then continues: "if the saints cannot help you, how can their fraudulent images help you?"[24]

One of the most common arguments raised in defense of images was the *libri pauperum* dictum of Pope Gregory. Karlstadt denies that images can be the books of the unlearned, saying that the use of images kept the laity ignorant and dependant on the clergy.[25] In fact, he adds, the clergy fear that if the laity begins to read the Bible its "rubbish mart" will collapse. Since Karlstadt was now beginning to emphasize the role of the laity, he saw the cult of images as one of the principal obstacles that separated the clergy from the laity, and he charged that those who argued that images were the books of the

---

[22] Ibid., p. 9: "Aber das wortt gottis ist geistlich/ und allein den glaubigen nutze."
[23] Ibid., pp. 5–8, 11, 12, 14.
[24] Ibid., p. 13.
[25] Ibid., p. 9: "Ich merke aber warumb die Bebst soliche Bücher den Leyen für gelegt haben. Sie haben vermeckt wan sie die schefflein ihn die bücher furtten ihr grempell marckt wurd nichst tzunehmen. Und man wurt wellen wissen was gotlich oder ungotlich, recht oder unrecht ist."

untutored were really saying that the laity ought not to be full disciples of Christ.[26]

Karlstadt challenges the Gregorian dictum on another point as well. He denies that images can teach anything of spiritual value, since they lead the worshiper no further than the flesh. Even a crucifix, he says, focuses a man's attention on how Christ was killed, not on why. Little is learned about salvation from a crucifix. People learn about Christ's body, beard, and wounds, but "his power they learn not one bit."[27] Again, it is a question of the material being unable to convey spiritual value. Images are "deaf and dumb"; they signify nothing but the flesh, and since the flesh is of no avail, they are worthless.

Another defense of images proposed that they served as reminders of holy things and inspired the faithful to prayer and meditation, Karlstadt refutes this argument on the same grounds as the *libri pauperum* argument. God is a spirit, he says, and all who wish to worship Him correctly must do so in spirit, not through material props. Those who are inspired to pray by images worship lies, and think of God only in "semblances and external reports."[28] Moreover, he continues, prayer is itself a divine work, and can only result from God's initiative – since only God can draw men to Himself.[29]

Karlstadt thus insisted that instead of being aids to devotion, images were a corruption of religion.[30] In reference to this point, Karlstadt maintains that man has a perverse psychological need for images. Once they are set up in churches, he warns, it is impossible to prevent people from committing idolatry. As long as the images are present before man – even if he knows that they are not the true object of worship – they will sit deep in his heart, and prevent him from attaining a true spiritual faith.[31]

Outward religious structures were not neutral for Karlstadt. He insisted that as long as externals existed in worship, they ought to

---

[26] Ibid., p. 9.

[27] Ibid., p. 10: Karlstadt is not yet arguing against crucifixes as would Zwingli, saying that it is impossible to represent Christ's divinity. Karlstadt merely objects to the superficiality of the religious feelings endendered by crucifixes: "Aber unsser bildpreisser wellen den leyhen Christum im fleisch tzuerkennen geben/ das nicht nutz ist sie wellen lieber leren wie Christus gehangen hat, and warumb er gehenckt ist. Sein leip/ bart und wunden leren sie. Die krafft Christi leren sie gar nit."

[28] Ibid., p. 16.

[29] Ibid.

[30] Preus, *Ordinaciones*, p. 38.

[31] "Abthung," p. 19: "Ich forcht kein bilde. Aber iszt weiss ich/ wie ich in dissem vall/ gegen gott und den bildern stehn/ und wie vest und tieff bilder in meinem hertzen sitzen."

conform to the new evangelical message of the Reformation, and to any ordinances that may result from the implementation of that message.[32] In the case of images, Karlstadt was well aware of the power they exerted over the common people. It was the laity who were most deeply affected by the externalization of piety. Since they depended on public worship rather than on scripture for their religious life, they could not help but regard the material elements of worship as the focal point of their religion. Images seemed to tell the laity that the saints were closer to God than they were and could therefore be more helpful than the distant God. It is this dependence on externals that Karlstadt sought to put in step with the new message of the Gospel.[33]

Karlstadt and the mass

In addition to opposing images as idolatrous, Karlstadt also attacked the Catholic eucharist as a form of idolatry. Karlstadt's opposition to the Mass was at first largely a question of liturgical reform: He wanted a vernacular Mass and communion in both kinds. In July of 1521, he argued this position in his treatise "On Both Forms of the Holy Mass."[34] Though not yet opposed to transsubstantiation, he was beginning to display a more spiritualized understanding of the sacrament. Certainly, his understanding of externals as "signs," which he expressed about the same time in "On Holy Water," is an indication of Karlstadt's growing distrust of material objects as bearers of divine grace.[35]

---

[32] Ibid., p. 20: "Drum sollen Christen sie [Bilder] abthun/ nach inhalt der schrifften. Ungeacht das eusserliche ding seind. Dan wan du got eusserlich wilt eheren/ oder in Ceremonien ansuchen/ solstu seine ceremonien und seinem gesetz nach volgen."

[33] Preus, *Ordinaciones*, p. 38.

[34] "Von beiden Gestalten der Heilige Messe," Barge, *Karlstadt*, vol.II, p. 147. Other treatises by Karlstadt on the subject of the Mass include the following: "Wider die Alte und Neuwe Papstliche Messen" (1524); "Von dem Widerchristlichen Missbrauch des Herrens Brot und Kelch" (1524); "Dialogus, oder ein Gesprechbüchlin von dem Grewlichen und Abgötishen Misbrauch des Hochwirdigsten Sacraments Jesu Christi" (1524); "Auslegung dieser Wort Christi: 'Das ist Meyn Leyb . . . Das ist Mein Blut'" (1524); and "Erklerung wie Carlstadt Sein Lere von dem Hochwirdigen Sacrament und Andere Achtet und Geacht Haben Wil" (1525).

[35] Williams, *Radical Reformation*, pp. 31, 41. The spiritualistic tendencies voiced by Karlstadt in 1521 can be traced to one possible outside influence. George H. Williams has shown how medieval Netherlandish sacramentism developed a theological opposition to the doctrine of the real presence. Williams traces this attitude to Wesel Gansfort (ca. 1420–89), whose "De Sacramento eucharistiae" he describes as "the first major link in the development, or recrudescence, of subjectivist Eucharistic theology."

Karlstadt's adoption of sacramentist principles, however, is not fully evident until his break with Luther in 1523. Beginning with his treatise, "On the Priesthood and Sacrifice of Christ," in which he denied the real presence, Karlstadt began to oppose the Roman Mass as an idolatrous service – one in which men paid reverence to mere bread and to their own inventions rather than to God.[36] This interpretation of the eucharist would become the basis for the Reformed opposition to the Mass as idolatrous. Since it is a straightforward argument, in line with opposition to the worship of any material object, Karlstadt's eucharistic theology needs no further explanation in connection with his attack on idolatry. Once Karlstadt's attitude toward external aspects of worship is understood, it is easy to see why he considered the eucharistic elements as unworthy of adoration. The debate between the Reformers on the issue of the real presence is related to the issue of the relationship between the material and spiritual in worship, but it is a problem separate from the attack on idolatry.

Karlstadt's iconoclastic policy

Karlstadt's attack on externalized piety was not limited to the sermon and the printed page. His opposition to the Catholic *cultus* was also expressed in concrete terms through a program of iconoclasm and through a radical conception of the individual's duty to destroy "false" worship.

In the development of the Protestant attack on idolatry, tension developed between those who insisted that iconoclasm could only be carried out by a legal process and those who made it a duty of the people, regardless of its legality. Karlstadt can rightly be called the father of the latter type of iconoclastic policy. From the beginning, Karlstadt's policies at Wittenberg showed impatience with the pace of legal reform measures. The iconoclasm that occurred in Wittenberg was a violent, revolutionary opposition to established authority: It was a way of bringing a theological concept to fruition in spite of legal hesitancy and opposition. Karlstadt's reforms at Wittenberg, though later overturned by Luther, set a precedent followed by many other communities throughout Europe.[37]

---

[36] "Von Priesterthumb und Opfer Christi" (1523).

[37] Aside from Preus, Sider, Rupp, and Barge, there are other significant studies dealing with Karlstadt and the Wittenberg Movement: Mark Edwards, *Luther and the False Brethren* (Stanford, 1975); Karl Müller, *Luther und Karlstadt: Stücke aus Ihrem Gegenseitigen Verhältnis* (Tübingen, 1907); Nikolaus Müller, *Die Wittenberger Bewegung 1521 und 1522*, 2nd ed. (Leipzig, 1911). Christensen also provides a good summary of iconoclasm in Wittenberg in *Art*, pp. 16–42.

Late in 1521, as Luther was hiding at the Wartburg, Karlstadt began to assume an influential position at Wittenberg. With the cooperation of Philip Melanchton, Karlstadt sought to implement many reforms that had heretofore only been espoused theoretically. On 3 December 1521, for instance, a group of students and townspeople forced their way into the parish church, destroyed the missals, and drove the priests from the altar. The next day another group stoned the Franciscan cloister and pulled down its altar.[38] The attack on the Roman *cultus* was no longer strictly verbal; it had now been vividly expressed by the people who listened to Karlstadt's sermons or read his pamphlets.

The Elector Fredrick was lenient with the rioters, but ordered that no innovations be introduced concerning the Mass. Popular support for innovation increased, however. In mid December, a crowd stormed the council meeting and demanded that the Mass be suspended and that it be replaced with a scriptural celebration of the Last Supper. On Christmas Eve the violence continued as another crowd broke into the parish church again, destroyed the lamps, intimidated the priests and sang popular songs, such as "My maid has lost her shoe." After this incident the mob marched over to the castle church, where they interrupted the priest's benediction by wishing him pestilence and hellfire.[39] The next day, without legal permission, Karlstadt celebrated the first reformed eucharistic service at Wittenberg, wearing a plain cloak and addressing his flock as fellow laymen. In addition, he simplified the Latin canon, omitted reference to sacrifice, spoke the words of institution in German, and distributed the bread and the cup in the parishioners' hands after telling them they had no need to go to confession to receive the sacrament. This evangelical service was again repeated on New Year's Day, the next Sunday, and on Epiphany.[40]

In response to these innovations, the Wittenberg magistracy enacted what was, in effect, the first municipal Reformation ordinance. The decree, issued on 24 January 1522, sanctioned Karlstadt's previously illegal service and banned all private Masses. More significantly, it also called for a governmentally directed removal of all images in the near future. A few days later, Karlstadt published his influential tract "On the Abolition of Images," in which he warned the magistrates that unless they took swift action against the images they would incur the wrath of God.[41]

---

[38] Müller, *Wittenberger Bewegung*, pp. 73, 152–3.
[39] Ibid., pp. 133–4.
[40] Ibid., pp. 132, 154, 170.
[41] "Abthung," p. 20: "Uber ess ist noch kein execution geschehen, villeicht derhalben,

In early February the council satisfied Karlstadt's demand by announcing a date on which the images were to be removed, but this only served to incite some Wittenbergers to take the law into their own hands. A band of iconoclasts, reportedly led by the preacher Gabriel Zwilling, pulled down and destroyed many images in Wittenberg.[42] The Elector's representative in Wittenberg later reported that Karlstadt and Zwilling had worked the crowd to a fury through "tumultous preaching," saying that if the magistrates refused to act, then "the common people" ("die gemeyn") had the power to remove the images.[43] An aggressive revolutionary precedent was being established in Wittenberg, which argued that the common people were empowered by God to wage war on the idols if their rulers refused to do it.

The tumult soon subsided, however, since the iconoclastic riot prompted restrictive measures from Fredrick and also hastened Luther's return from the Wartburg. Upon his arrival on 6 March, most of the old customs were restored and further iconoclasm was prohibited.

Although Karlstadt was soon forced to leave Wittenberg, he continued to develop a revolutionary iconoclastic theory. In his 1524 treatise, "Whether One Ought to Behave Peacefully and Spare the Feelings of the Simple," Karlstadt argued that any delay in the removal of images was sinful disobedience to God's commands.[44] He rejected the argument that one should postpone the abolition of images and other corrupt practices until the entire community agreed on a common policy: "I ask whether one should not stop coveting another's goods until the others follow? May one steal until the thieves stop stealing?"[45]

Calling on the individual to assume responsibility, Karlstadt further stated that every believer and every community had to act on its own against images.[46] Defending the rights of his new fellow towns-

---

das Got seinen tzorn ausstzuschüden, wo wir allso blind bleiben, und forchten unss vor dem, das uns nicht kan thun. Das weiss ich das die Obirsten derhalben gestrafft werden."

[42] The actual extent of destruction is not known. Müller, *Wittenberger Bewegung*, pp. 191, 195; R. Sider, *Karlstadt*, p. 168; Christensen, *Art*, p. 32.

[43] Müller, *Wittenberger Bewegung*, p. 186: "Sye sagenn, das dye gemeyn woll macht habe, in Nachlessigkeyt der oberkeyt." Sider insists that this remark could only have applied to Zwilling, not to Karlstadt, but he only refers to Karlstadt's previous call on the magistrates in the "Abthung" as proof of his assertion (*Karlstadt*, p. 169).

[44] "Ob Man Gemach Faren und des Ergernüssen der Schwachen Verschonen Soll" (1524) in Erich Hertzche (ed.), *Karlstadts Schriften aus den Jahren 1523–1525* (Halle, 1956), vol. I.

[45] Ibid., pp. 76–7.

[46] Ibid., p. 85: "Ja so wir sie in unser gemein finden [bilder], ein iglche gemein in irer stadt, gleicher weyss ein iglche gemein schuldig ist die ire zu enthalten."

men of Orlamunde, Karlstadt asserted that they did not have to wait until the neighbors and "guzzlers at Wittenberg" were ready to follow them. Everyone, he continued, whether great or small, "should see to it that he does what is right and proper, without waiting for anyone."[47]

This argument was summarized with a powerful metaphor. Karlstadt proposed that dangerous things should be removed from the weak, even against their wishes, to prevent them from hurting themselves. To illustrate his point he used the example of a child who wants to play with a sharp, pointed knife. Even though the child will cry if the knife is taken away, is it right to allow the child to keep the knife, when one well knows that he can injure or kill himself? Since images are just as dangerous to the soul of the individual and to the community as the knife is to the child, should they not be removed by those who know them to be harmful?[48]

Karlstadt had developed a fully revolutionary concept of iconoclastic violence. According to him, it was a Christian's duty to effect the removal of images from his community, even against opposition, because it was a divine commandment to abolish such pollution. The opinion of the magistracy or of one's fellow citizens should not be taken into acount, since legal restrictions placed on iconoclasm are like the crying of a child who does not know that a harmful object is being taken away from him. The intellectual basis for revolutionary iconoclasm had been established. We shall soon see how it was put to practice.

LUTHER'S RESPONSE TO KARLSTADT'S ICONOCLASM

In 1525 Luther charged: "Doctor Andreas Karlstadt has deserted us, and on top of that has become our worst enemy."[49] The rift between Luther and Karlstadt was caused primarily by Karlstadt's reform of

---

[47] Ibid., p. 80.
[48] Ibid., p. 88: "Wir solten den schwachen soliche schedliche dinge nemen, und auss iren handen reyssen, unnd nicht achten, ob sie drumb weinten, schryhen, oder flüchten. Es wirdt die zeit kommen, das sie uns dancken werden, die uns ietz fluchen unnd verfluchen, der auch würd den narren die rechte und beste brüderliche lief beweysen, der iren willen mit gwalt bräch . . . Demnach frag ich, wenn ich sehe das ein klein unmündig kindlein ein spitzig scharpff messer in seiner handt hett, und wölt es gern behalten, ob ich im denn brüderliche lieb beweiset, wenn ich im das schedlich messer und seinen willen liess, damitt sichs verwundet oder ertödt, oder denn, wenn ich im seinen willen breche, und das messer näm? Du must ie sagen, wenn du dem kind nibst, das im schaden brengt, so thustu ein väterlich oder brüderlich Christelich werck."
[49] "Against the Heavenly Prophets," LW 40, 79.

the cultic life of Wittenberg. Outwardly, the fundamental issues dividing the two men in 1521–2 seem to have been issues of religious policy, not so much of theology, but inwardly their disagreement stemmed from differing interpretations of the nature of worship.

Luther's return to Wittenberg was a reassertion of his role as leader of the reform he felt he had started.[50] From the first day of his return, Luther began to distinguish between the disturbances that had occurred and the principles of the refomed movement itself, setting the tone for his disagreement with Karlstadt over the issue of "externals." In his "Invocavit Sermons," preached immediately upon his return (9–16 March), Luther pointed out that although he agreed in theory with Karlstadt's views on the reception of the sacrament in both kinds, confession, and the removal of images, he opposed the manner in which these reforms had been carried out.[51]

On the surface, then, it would appear that Luther had no theological disagreement with Karlstadt. But in spite of Luther's disclaimers, the truth is that both men were viewing the problem of reform from very different theological perspectives. While Karlstadt had formulated a program of change based on his transcendentalist interpretation of scriptural commands concerning worship, Luther refused to accept these metaphysical issues as central. In fact, when he condemns Karlstadt's policies, he carefully sidesteps discussion of the points that Karlstadt had tried to raise to prominence, thus undermining his rival's enterprise in a most powerful way. Luther may have claimed to agree with Karlstadt's theology, but in fact refuted the key ideas with which Karlstadt was defending his policies. The theology developed by Luther in response to Karlstadt's attack on externals in worship was never fully systematic, but it proved to be a great parting of the ways, and came to have a profound influence on the way in which Lutherans viewed ceremonies and church art.

Luther's "theology of externals" (if one may speak of a "theology" at all) seems inconsistent at first sight. This stems from the fact that Luther was not developing a systematic theology of externals against Karlstadt, but was instead trying to undermine his policies by negating the centrality of the spiritual–material issue. In 1524, when Luther wrote to the Strassburg church to warn them about Karlstadt, he claimed that his own writings had "done more to overthrow images

---

[50] Preus, *Ordinaciones*. Preus argues that during the brief period 1521–2, questions of policy and polity played a central role in defining the nature of Luther's reform. Margarete Stirm, in contrast, devotes her attention almost exclusively to the theological differences between Luther and Karlstadt (*Bilderfrage*, pp. 38–60).

[51] Preus, *Ordinaciones*, p. 51.

than Karlstadt will ever do with his storming and fanaticism."[52] Luther also protested in a later treatise that he was not entirely opposed to iconoclasm, as long as it was carried out in a proper manner.[53] In spite of such statements, however, Luther's position in regard to the use of images differed greatly from Karlstadt's.

As is the case with other aspects of Luther's theology, his position on the question of externals undergoes a slight redefinition as it is challenged; the younger Luther speaks about externals in a different tone of voice than the Luther of 1525.[54] Luther's initial position on religious images shows a certain skepticism about their ultimate value, and a concern over the morality of spending money on material objects while the poor suffer from want. In the *Lectures on Romans* (1515–16), Luther criticized the cost of church decorations and called material objects of worship "mere shadows and tokens of reality" and "childish things."[55] One of the Ninety-five Theses condemns the use of indulgence revenues for the building of churches, a purpose referred to as "most trivial."[56] Other works from the period 1518–22 contain similar references to the impropriety of lavish church decorations.[57] Luther also showed spiritualistic tendencies in this early period. The *Church Postils* of 1522, for instance, contains a passage about the nature of true worship that seems as iconoclastic as anything written by Karlstadt:

See, that is the proper worship, for which a person needs no bells, no churches, no vessels or ornaments, no lights or candles, no organs or singing, no

---

[52] LW 40, 69.

[53] LW 40, 85: "Furthermore, I have allowed and not forbidden the outward removal of images, so long as this takes place without rioting and uproar and is done by the proper authorities."

[54] Carl Christensen shows that Luther moved from an originally critical and even somewhat negative opinion of church decorations to an ultimately positive one. Christensen deals with Luther's theology of religious art in detail in *Art*, pp. 42–65. Another scholar who has dealt with this subject is Hans von Campenhausen: "Die Bilderfrage in der Reformation," *Zeitschrift für Kirchengeschichte*, 68: 96–128 (1957). The same article (only slightly altered) also appears in *Das Gottesbild im Abendland*, W. Schöne et al. (eds.) (Witten/Berlin, 1959), under the title, "Zwingli und Luther zur Bilderfrage." Margarete Stirm examines Luther's theological position on the question of images in some detail, but gives a more unified picture than might be acceptable. She concludes that Luther was not opposed to official Catholic teaching in the earlier years, but rather to abuses in the image cult (*Bilderfrage*, pp. 36–7). Stirm's study provides a thorough overview of Luther's theology and can be useful in referring the reader to numerous passages in Luther's writings where he deals with the image question.

[55] Christensen, *Art*, p. 62. For Luther's treatment of images and the problem of idolatry in the *Lectures on Romans*: LW 25, 157–9, 164–5, 192.

[56] LW 31, 32.

[57] Christensen, *Art*, pp. 62–3.

paintings or images, no panels or altars . . . For these are all human inventions and ornaments, which God does not heed, and which obscure the correct worship, with their glitter.[58]

In addition, Luther attacked some of the abuses surrounding the cult of the saints,[59] and lashed out at the practices surrounding some of the more popular pilgrimage sites of his day.[60]

By 1522, however, it is possible to see a change in Luther, as he returns to Wittenberg and gains control of his reform. The "Invocavit Sermons" are a strong indictment of Karlstadt's liturgical and iconoclastic policies, and mark the beginning of the development of Luther's mature position on the role of externals in worship. In the sermon dealing with images, Luther charges that Karlstadt's policies are wrongheaded. Instead of removing the idols by force, he argues, it would have been more effective to preach against them.[61] More significantly, Luther argues that "outward things" are really indifferent and can do no harm to the faithful if they are not trusted in.[62] Christians are then free to have images or not. Luther says religious artworks are "neither here nor there, neither evil nor good," and adds, "we may have them or not, as we please."[63]

Luther apparently did not yet think of images as indifferent. He says elsewhere that he is "not partial" to images, calls them "unnecessary," and avers that "it would be much better if we did not have them at all" and that "because of the abuses they give rise to, I wish they were everywhere abolished."[64] Whenever images are worshiped in an idolatrous manner, he maintains, "they should be put away and destroyed."[65]

Nonetheless, Luther continued to develop his argument that images were indifferent things in his letter to the Strassburg church

---

[58] WA, 10¹ , 39. (trans. of this passage by Carl Christensen).
[59] "Sermons on the Ten Commandments" (1518), WA 1, 413–14.
[60] "Address to the German Nobility" (1520), LW 44, 185–6.
[61] "Third Lenten Sermon" (1522), LW 51, 83: "Therefore it should have been preached that images were nothing and that no service is done to God by erecting them; then they would have fallen of themselves . . . And you rush, create an uproar, break down altars, and overthrow images! Do you really believe you can abolish the altars in this way? No, you will only set them up more firmly. Even if you overthrew the images in this place, do you think you have overthrown those in Nuremberg and the rest of the world? Not at all."
[62] Ibid. "Without a doubt he [St. Paul] wanted to show that outward things could do no harm to faith, if only the heart does not cleave to them or puts its trust in them. This is what we must preach and teach."
[63] LW 51, 86.
[64] LW 51, 84.
[65] LW 51, 82.

(1524). Here he charges Karlstadt with pouncing on "outward things" with great violence as if the essence of Christianity consisted in the destruction of images and the overthrow of the Mass.[66] Luther insists that Karlstadt's concern over externals not only detracts from the true purpose of Christianity, but also impinges on the freedom of the Christian as much as the laws of the Pope.[67] This is Luther's first statement attacking Karlstadt's policies as a form of works-righteousness. By adopting this view, Luther developed a unique argument in the Reformation debate over externals. He charges that by making the destruction of religious paraphernalia a necessity, Karlstadt is stressing iconoclasm as a religious work, as an action that will ensure spiritual well-being. If the images are harmless, he asks, then why make faith depend on their removal?[68] Arguing from one of his central vantage points, Luther thus lumps Karlstadt with the Catholics as a proponent of works-righteousness. In doing this, Luther is able to sidestep metaphysical considerations about the nature of worship and its place in the Christian life. By taking up the familiar cudgel of Christian freedom, Luther found he could fight Karlstadt with the weapon he was most skilled at wielding. As he had demolished the Catholics and their power structure with the issue of justification, so would he demolish the radicals. Luther and Karlstadt were really saying very different things about the nature of reform, and Luther showed his genius for polemics by making it seem as if the debate were a matter of policy rather than theology. By saying that Karlstadt's interpretation of worship was a misguided denial of *sola fides* rather than a wrongheaded view of reality, Luther managed to take the edge off of the iconoclast's sword. But by doing this, Luther also revealed that he was not all that interested in the relationship between the spiritual and the material as a focus of reform.

This is evident in the treatise which culminates Luther's attack on Karlstadt. In "Against the Heavenly Prophets" (1524–5), Luther marshals several arguments against Karlstadt's concern with "outward things."[69] Luther begins by expanding on the charge he had

[66] LW 40, 67. Luther's letter was prompted by Bucer's and Capito's request for advice concerning Karlstadt, who had come to Strassburg in October of 1524, after his expulsion from Saxony.
[67] LW 40, 69: "I will not endure any one inciting and driving Christians to works of this kind, as if one cannot be a Christian without their performance. Nor can we tolerate anyone imprisoning Christian freedom by laws and laying a snare for consciences."
[68] Ibid.: "why should the Christian conscience be ensnared and tortured on account of something that has no reality?"
[69] The first part of this treatise, which deals with the image question, was completed in December 1524. The second part, which deals with the eucharist, in January 1525.

already made in his letter to Strassburg, saying Karlstadt had made iconoclasm a "work" necessary for salvation. By forcing the issue of externals, which is really trivial, says Luther, Karlstadt has bound consciences to the "work" of iconoclasm and has ironically made the act of destroying images an idol in itself: "Such legalism results in putting away outward images while filling the heart with idols."[70]

Luther also strikes out against Karlstadt on another theological point, charging that his former colleague has not interpreted the Old Testament command against images properly. First, Luther believes that the Mosaic proscription applies only to "an image of God which one worships," not to other images or statues that are made without idolatry.[71] Secondly, Luther says that the prohibition of images, like the Sabbath regulations and other ceremonies of Judaism, is not binding for Christians. The reference to images in the first commandment is interpreted by Luther as strictly a temporal law that has been abrogated by the New Covenant. Luther sets up a contrast between the ceremonial laws of Moses and the natural laws of mankind, that is, those commandments that pertain to the governing of society: laws against murder, theft, and adultery.[72] Consequently, he argues, it is wrong to insist upon the continued validity of the Mosaic proscription against images. If one were to follow the logic of Karlstadt's argument against images, says Luther, then it would be necessary for all Christians to be circumcised as well.[73]

Since matters of policy were foremost in the outward power struggle between Luther and Karlstadt, it is not surprising that Luther focuses on this issue in "Against the Heavenly Prophets." Against Karlstadt's call for the removal of images from the Churches, Luther argues that it is more effective to first "tear them out of the heart through God's Word," for when they are no longer in the heart, "they can do no harm when seen with the eyes."[74]

---

[70] LW *40*, 85. Luther charges that Karlstadt has made iconoclasm a "work of the law" and taught "works and the free will all over again" (p. 89).

[71] LW *40*, 85.

[72] LW *40*, 97: Luther concludes that "Therefore, Moses' legislation about images and the sabbath, and what else goes beyond the natural law, since it is not supported by the natural law, is free, null and void, and is specifically given to the Jewish people alone."

[73] LW *40*, 94.

[74] LW *40*, 84. Aside from challenging the theological assertions of Karlstadt, Luther also defends images in a more traditional way. He defends the use of imagery as reminders of holy things (p. 91), and argues for their use as aids in teaching, agreeing in part with the Gregorian dictum (p. 99). These two arguments are supported by an anthropology that allows for the use of material objects in worship. Luther proposes that image making is a natural part of man's psychology. Men, he says, are sentient beings who must form images in their minds in order to comprehend anything.

Luther defends his own policy against Karlstadt, saying that he does not protect images, but rather destroys them in a more effective way, both "outwardly and inwardly."[75] Yet Luther is not consistent. On the one hand, he says that no one is obligated to destroy images: Since everything is free for the Christian, one is only obligated to destroy confidence in them through the Word. Beyond this, he says, it is really indifferent whether images stand or fall: "It is all the same and makes no difference, just as when the poison has been removed from a snake."[76] On the other hand, Luther praises those who have destroyed images at Eichen, Grimmental, and Birnbaum, or any other place where pilgrimages were made for the adoration of images, "for such are truly idolatrous images and the devil's hospices."[77] Thus, though Luther says that the best way to destroy images is by driving them from men's hearts, he is willing to concede that there are times when images are not really indifferent and that there are occasions when is is best to remove them. Luther thought it was commendable to destroy images that had become objects of idolatry, but did not want to make iconoclasm a strict command for all Christians.

Continuing the attack on matters of policy, Luther reveals much about his fear of Karlstadt by also accusing him of sedition. Luther was aware of the revolutionary tendencies of Karlstadt's iconoclasm and argued against him that the removal of images is the prerogative of the government, not of the common people.[78] Luther contends that when people want the images removed, they should calmly petition those in authority. If the magistracy refuses to destroy the images, then the people must content themselves with preaching against the images and with trying to remove them from men's hearts. At a time when the early phases of the Peasants' War and Thomas Müntzer's campaigns were beginning to disrupt German society, Luther made every effort to disassociate his reform program from revolution. Not surprisingly, then, Luther argues that Karlstadt's policies are wrong because they will only lead to rebellion and social upheaval. Luther saw the unauthorized destruction of images as a preliminary to more serious revolution:

Where God tells the community to do something and speaks to the people, he does not want it done by the masses without the authorities, but through the authorities with the people. Moreover, he requires this so that the dog does not learn to eat leather on the leash, that is, lest accustomed to rebellion in connection with the images, the people also rebel against the authorities.[79]

[75] LW 40, 85.   [76] LW 40, 91.
[77] LW 40, 92.   [78] LW 40, 90.
[79] Ibid, pp. 89, 90.

Luther feared the revolutionary implications of Karlstadt's iconoclastic policies, and argued that once the common people learn to
disobey the authorities on one point – even if it is for religious reasons – then they begin to forget civil discipline. The iconoclastic policies of Karlstadt, charged Luther, were nothing more than "pretty
preliminaries to riot and rebellion, so that one fears neither order nor
authority."[80]

Though these fears were well-founded, the disagreement over iconoclasm was not exclusively over policy. The most important dif-
ference between Luther and Karlstadt remained their understanding
of the relationship between the spiritual and the material in worship.
Luther strongly rejected any inclination toward body–spirit dualism.
For him, the spiritual life could never be totally disembodied. In
"Against the Heavenly Prophets," Luther had argued against Karlstadt that people need to worship with the aid of material objects.[81]
This principle is explained more clearly in another treatise, where
Luther proposes that God always meets humans on their own level,
that is, through outward, material means:

Now when God sends forth his holy Gospel, He deals with us in a twofold
manner, the first outwardly, then inwardly. Outwardly he deals with us
through the oral word of the Gospel and through material signs, that is,
baptism and the sacrament of the altar. Inwardly He deals with us through
the Holy Spirit, faith, and other gifts. But whatever their measure or order the
outward factors should and must precede. The inward experience follows
and is effected by the outward. God has determined to give the inward to no
one except through the outward.[82]

This understanding of the relationship between spiritual and material
in worship gave the Lutheran church its distinctive ceremonial and
liturgical life. It is the principal theological reason why Luther and his
Church stand alone in the history of the Reformation debate over the
proper way to worship.[83]

This was brought out most clearly in 1529, at the Marburg Colloquy, when the Lutherans and the heirs of Erasmus and Karlstadt
came together to discuss the issue of the presence of Christ in the
material elements of the eucharist. When Luther said to Bucer and the
Swiss, "our spirit has nothing in common with your spirit," he was
referring precisely to this issue. Earlier in the debate Zwingli had

[80] LW 40, 101.
[81] LW 40, 84.
[82] LW 40, 146.
[83] For a detailed discusssion of the place of images in the Lutheran church, see Margarete Stirm, *Bilderfrage*, pp. 69–129, esp. 124–9.

affirmed the incompatibility of spirit and matter by citing one of Erasmus's favorite passages (John 6:63), "the flesh is of no avail," and
even told Luther that this text would "break his neck." Luther
snapped back, reminding Zwingli that he was in Hesse, where necks
did not break as easily as in Zurich, and refused to budge on the issue
of Christ's physical presence. When Oecolampadius said "don't cling
so fast to Christ's humanity and flesh; raise your thoughts to Christ's
divinity," Luther responded: "I know God only as he became
human, so shall I have him in no other way." Zwingli pleaded for
unity with tears in his eyes, but to no avail. The division between
Protestants had been sealed. For Luther and his followers, there
could be no strict separation of spiritual and material. Luther told
Zwingli: "Call upon God, that you may receive understanding."
Oecalampadius retorted: "Call upon Him yourself, for you need it
just as much as we."[84] This is the great watershed of the Reformation.
Let us now follow the course of the other stream, to see how it waged
war on idolatry in defense of its transcendentalism.

ULRICH ZWINGLI AND THE REFORMATION OF WORSHIP AT ZURICH

Whether or not Karlstadt's iconoclastic theory had any direct effect on
events in Switzerland is hard to prove. Doubtless, his works could
have been read by any literate person in German-speaking
Switzerland, and there is no evidence suggesting that their circulation
was geographically limited in any way. In studying the development
of the Reformed Protestant attitude toward externalized piety, one is
faced with the oft-asked question: What influence did Wittenberg
have on Zurich? To answer this question in connection with the attack on idolatry, one must deal with two different issues, iconoclastic
policy and iconoclastic theology. Let us deal first with policy, since it
is the less complex issue.

It is difficult to establish a direct connection between Karlstadt and
the Swiss in regard to iconoclastic policy for one major reason: His
work is overshadowed by that of the major Swiss Reformers, none of
whom advocated as radical a policy as he did. Zwingli, Bullinger,

---

[84] W. Köhler, *Das Marburger Religionsgespräch 1529: Versuch einer Rekonstruction*
(Leipzig, 1929), p. 27; also LW *38*, 3–90. Gottfried Locher has aptly summarized the
difference as follows: "Luther's Reformation was directed against the Judaistic heresy. For him, the alternative to faith is works. Zwingli's Reformation was directed
against the false doctrine of the pagans. For him, the alternative to faith is every
kind of idolatry." *Zwingli's Thought: New Perspectives* (Leiden, 1981).

Oecolampadius, and Calvin never called on the common people to ignore the authority of the magistracy. The major Continental Reformers always insisted that the removal of *idolotramenta* was the duty of the magistrate, not of the people. Although their attack on the cultic objects of Catholicism was every bit as vehement as Karlstadt's, it was not as revolutionary in nature. This is not to say, however, that their moderate approach was followed in Switzerland. On the contrary, one finds Karlstadt's policies employed more often than those of Zwingli.

One is thus faced with a puzzling situation. Although Karlstadt's theories about revolutionary iconoclasm are not acknowledged by those who dominate the intellectual heritage of the Swiss Reformation, they are followed in a very concrete manner by lesser figures and by many of the common people. Why the dichotomy in theory and practice? One reason is that it is not really a dichotomy in theory, insofar as the objective is concerned (that is, the removal of idolatry), but rather in method. The major Swiss Reformers fanned the fires of iconoclasm with their sermons and tracts against the cultic objects of Rome. The people adopted the course of action proposed by Karlstadt because a revolutionary tactic, by definition, does not need the approval of the established authorities. Zwingli, Oecolampadius, and Calvin led the people to violence indirectly. They never sanctioned illegal acts because disregard for authority would eventually erode their own position. In other words, by sanctioning illegal iconoclasm they would diminish respect for the concept of authority that supported their leadership of the Reformation. To use Luther's phrase, they did not want the dog to learn to eat leather on the leash. They would rant and rave against the idols, and work up their congregations to a fever pitch while telling them that they had to wait upon the magistracy to see the idols removed, only to turn their heads away when iconoclastic rioting occurred – never saying that the people had obeyed a principle that ought to be followed everywhere, but also never saying that the people had committed an act for which they should repent. The *fait accompli* was accepted by the major Reformers with some regret over the methods employed, but it was always viewed as a good thing. Consequently, although there is no direct evidence proving the spread of Karlstadt's policies to Switzerland, it is difficult to deny his influence.

Though Karlstadt's influence is undeniable in regard to theology (as opposed to practice), it is still risky to assert that the Swiss are *wholly* indebted to him. Evidence suggests that opposition to externalized worship existed in Switzerland before Karlstadt's rise to

prominence. One of the most convincing proofs is the pseudony-
mous tract, "On the Old and the New God," first published at Basel
in 1521.[85] The authorship of this work is still disputed, but some
scholars have attributed it to Joachim Vadian, the Reformer of St.
Gall.[86] The author of this tract provides one of the earliest theological
analyses of the issue of idolatry as a corruption of worship: many
points that would later become central to the Protestant attack on
Catholic piety are found here for the first time. "On the Old and New
God" was an immensely popular work in its time, going through
numerous editions and translations.[87] Its objective is to prove that
Protestant evangelism is not a new religion, but rather a renewal of
primitive Christianity. It is divided into two parts. The first is a relatively brief history of the Church (one of the first of its kind among
Protestants) in which the author tries to distinguish between true
religion and false worship. The second part is an exposition of the
"old religion," outlined in twenty catechetical propositions.[88]

One of the most significant contributions of this tract is its exposition of the origin and nature of idolatry. The author begins his study
from an anthropological perspective, pointing to the inborn re-
ligiousness of humankind and to the great number of deities it has
created.[89] Because man is fallen, he cannot escape error. Consequently, false belief and false worship are a natural condition of the
descendants of Adam and Eve.[90] The source of this false belief is

85 *"Vom Alten und Neuen Gott, Glauben und Lehre"* by Judas Nazarei (pseud.); ed. and
reissued by Eduard Kück ("Neudrucke Deutscher Litteraturwerke des XVI und XVII
Jahrhunderts – Flugschriften aus der Reformationszeit, vol. XII," Halle, 1896).
Hereafter cited as Kück. For a recent discussion of this treatise see H. G. Hofacher,
"'Vom Alten und Neuen Gott, Glauben und Ler," Untersuchungen zum
Geschichtsverständnis und Epochenbewustein einer Anonymen Reformatorischen
Flugschrift"; and Heinz Scheible, "Das Reformatorische Schriftverständnis in der
Flugschrift, 'Vom Alten und Neuen Gott.'" Both articles appear in *Kontinuität und
Umbruch, Theologie und Frömmigkeit in Flugschriften und Kleinliteratur an der Wende vom
15. zum 16. Jahrhundert* (Tübinger Beiträge zur Geschichtsforschung, vol. 2), 1977.
86 The modern editor of the pamphlet, Eduard Kück, argues that Vadian was indeed
the author (pp. iii–v). This has been denied by T. Schiess, "Hat Vadian Deutsche
Flugschriften verfasst?" in *Festgabe für Hermann Escher* (Zurich, 1927), pp. 66–97.
Conradin Bonorand also claims that the authorship can be disputed. *Vadians Weg
vom Humanismus zum Reformation* (St. Gall, 1962), p. 73.
87 Kück, pp. vi–xi.
88 For a discussion of a different aspect of this pamphlet see Steven Ozment, *The
Reformation in the Cities* (New Haven, 1975), pp. 62–3. Ozment concentrates on how
this tract expresses the new social ethic espoused by early Protestantism.
89 Kück, p. 4: "So finden wir warhafftig anzeigen, das sich die menschen in allen
zyten, sonderlich zuvor, in eerebietung gots vast seltzam unterscheidlichten
gehalten."
90 Ibid.: "Die art haben wir all uss den brüsten Eve gesogen, und des so starck, das alle
menschen (nach gemeinem lauff) in unglauben erborn werden."

attributed to man's desire to search for divinity in the created world: "The evil way of unbelief and disobedience has been inherited by all of Adam's children, so that we seek out, raise up and establish our own selves, nature itself, and all things as new gods for ourselves."[91]

Idolatry, therefore, is defined in "On the Old and New God" as "a raising of the creature over God through the deception of the devil."[92] This would become the standard Reformed definition of idolatry.

On a less theoretical plane, the author of "On the Old and New God" also lashes out at some of the more materialistic aspects of Catholic piety. He condemns the "temples of Rome" and all their ceremonies, calling them idolatrous, and juxtaposing them against the "true" worship that ought to be offered to God. Catholic worship has set up a new god, a god invented by men, not the God of scripture and of the early Church.[93] He proposes that Christians should not seek religion in outward things, but rather in scripture.[94] In regard to images, he says that it is impossible to erect images in churches without having the people fall prey to idolatry.[95] The second part of the tract expresses a command that would become the hallmark of the Reformed interpretation of true Christian worship. The author proposes here that God is to be honored only according to his commands, not by human inventions.[96]

Zwingli and iconoclasm at Zurich

The originality of the Swiss attack on externalized piety is also testified to by Zwingli himself, who is of central importance in the development of the Reformed Protestant attitude toward idolatry.

Although Zwingli is a direct heir of the more radical aspects of the humanist critique of late medieval piety, he also displays an indepen-

---

[91] Ibid., p. 5.
[92] Ibid., p. 3.
[93] Ibid., pp. 36–7, 38–9.
[94] Ibid., p. 8.
[95] Ibid., p. 6: "In summa was besonders by eim menschen von erstem uffkam, erfunden ward, der empfieng den namen das er ein got were; Und dann so bald bilder der selben kunstrichen menschen, oder gewaltigen künig, uff gericht wurden, so schmuchket sich der tüfel dorin, und hüb etwan ein gerümpel an, etwan spey er füer, etwan so troumbt den lüten (durch des tüfels ingeben) wann sy ire kranchen für das bild brachten, und ein opffer theten, würden sy gesund. Also sind die abgött die nüwen gott entstanden und uffkomen by den alten."
[96] Ibid., p. 54: "Die höchst zierd, glory und ere so got der almechtig von allen menschen ersücht und begerd ist, das eyn yeglich mensch dem mundt gots seinen worten uff das aller eynfaltigest glaub on allen menschlichen züsatz."

dence that shows that the origins of the Reformed opposition to Catholic worship were based on theological principles inherent in the evangelical movement itself, apart from humanism. The relationship between Zwingli and the humanist critique of late medieval piety is very clear.[97] Zwingli was himself a humanist. He had been educated at Vienna and Basel by great humanists such as Bünzli, Wölflin, and Celtis. During the decade 1506–16, when he served as parish priest at Glarus, he continued his classical studies and began to correspond with some of the leading humanists of his day, such as Glareanus, Vadian, Froben, and Beatus Rhenanus. Finally, while at Einsiedeln, Zwingli came under the influence of Erasmus and became a disciple of the great Dutch humanist. When Zwingli adopted Erasmus' primitivism, transcendentalism and Christocentrism, he began his spiritual pilgrimage away from the piety of his day. We have Zwingli's own testimony about Erasmus' influence on him to verify this point. Zwingli long remembered Erasmus' poem "The Complaint of Jesus" as the work that opened his eyes to the "error" of the veneration of the saints. In 1523, Zwingli wrote the following:

> I shall not conceal from you how I arrived at the opinion and the lasting belief that we need no mediator other than Christ, moreover that no one other than Christ alone can mediate between God and us. I read eight or nine years ago a comforting poem by the most learned Erasmus of Rotterdam, in which in many beautiful words Jesus laments that men did not seek all good in Him in order that He might be a fountain for all good for them, a Saviour, solacer, and treasure of the soul. Here I thought, if that is indeed true, why then should we seek help from any other creature. And although I discovered other hymns or songs to St. Anne, St. Michael and others by this same Erasmus, in which he addresses those to whom he is writing as intercessors, still these could not deprive me of the knowledge that for our poor souls Christ was the only treasure. I began, nevertheless, to look through Scripture and the Fathers in order to find in them evidence for the intercession of the saints. In short, I have found in the Bible none at all; among some of the Fathers I have found it; among others I have not.[98]

Thus, while Zwingli's initial break with Catholic piety was inspired by Erasmus, it is clear that he soon went beyond the humanist critique. It was the reading of scripture, not of Erasmus, which led

---

[97] Locher, *Zwingli's Thought*, pp. 233–255; Charles Garside, Jr., *Zwingli and the Arts* (New Haven, 1966); J. Rogge, *Zwingli und Erasmus: Die Friedensgedanke des Jungen Zwingli* (Stuttgart, 1962); E. W. Kohls, *Die Theologische Lebensaufgabe des Erasmus und die Oberrheinischen Reformatoren* (Stuttgart, 1969), esp. pp. 30–5; A. Rich, *Die Anfänge der Theologie Huldrych Zwinglis* (Zurich, 1949); W. Köhler, *Zwingli und Luther*, 2nd ed. (Gutersloh, 1953); and *Huldrych Zwingli* (Stuttgart, 1952).
[98] ZW 2.217. Trans. by Garside, *Zwingli and the Arts*, p. 94.

Zwingli to believe that the cult of the saints was not truly Christian. To say, as Charles Garside does, that Zwingli's attitude towards the role of images in worship "eventually derives from his humanism," is to place too much emphasis on one aspect of Zwingli's background.[99] Garside himself says that Zwingli broke with humanism in his insistence upon the exclusive authority of scripture. Humanism had guided Zwingli to the scriptures; Erasmus in particular had provided the lens with which he could interpret passages related to worship; but Zwingli himself invested the scriptural texts with a different kind of authority. The commands of scripture, especially those concerning worship, were taken as a blueprint for behavior. Any tradition that did not square with these commands was therefore to be disregarded.[100] Herein lies a principal clue to the origins of Zwinglis's "theology of idolatry": It was guided by the hermeneutic of transcendentalism he had picked up from Erasmus, but it was unrestrained by any kind of compromise with nonscriptural authority.[101]

Zwingli began to preach against the cult of the saints shortly after his arrival in Zurich in 1519. His attack was at first limited against adoration as opposed to "invocation," apparently because he still believed in the traditional distinction made between *dulia* and *latria*. By 1522, though, his critique of the *cultus divorum* had become a full-scale attack.[102] All in all, during his first four years in Zurich, Zwingli often preached on two themes: the centrality of Christ, and the worthlessness of "invented external worship."[103] Zwingli's theology

---

[99] Charles Garside emphasizes the Erasmian influence on Zwingli. He says that "Although he [Zwingli] no longer understood the doctrine of 'Christ Alone' in terms of the Erasmian philosophy of Christ from which he had originally appropriated it, the Christocentric position from which he argued either explicitly or implicitly throughout the debate was ultimately based on the concept formulated by Erasmus, as was his attack on the intercession of the saints." The question remains, however: did Erasmus really "formulate" any concrete concept about the centrality of Jesus in worship to the total exclusion of the saints? Erasmus continued to worship the saints, as Zwingli himself observed. What Erasmus expressed was an attitude, not a concept. There is a definite relationship between Erasmus and Zwingli, but Garside perhaps credits Erasmus with something that the humanist himself never fully advocated (*Zwingli and the Arts*, p. 98).

[100] ZW 1.148–53.

[101] Richard Stauffer analyzes some of the more salient differences between Zwingli and his humanist background in "L'Influence et la Critique de l'Humanisme dans *De vera et falsa religione* de Zwingli," *Interprètes de la Bible; Etudes sur les Reformateurs du Seizième Siècle* (Paris, 1980). Stauffer argues that by 1525 Zwingli had radicalized his heritage to the point where he was more inclined to criticize humanism than to admit its influence. For an excellent summary of the range of scholarly opinion on this topic see Locher, *Zwingli's Thought*, esp. pp. 42–71, 142–232.

[102] Locher, *Zwingli's Thought*, p. 95.

[103] Ibid., p. 98.

of idolatry cannot be fully understood without first taking into account the events that took place in Zurich between 1523 and 1524. Zwingli's opposition to the Catholic *cultus* developed gradually. Although he attacked the theology behind the cult of saints, denied the usefulness of external objects of worship, and rejected transsubstantiation, he did not at first formulate any policies against existing practices.[104] It was the iconoclastic activities of some of his fellow townsmen, who seemed to be following Karlstadt's advice about taking the law into their own hands, that finally brought Zwingli's attack on Catholic piety to its fulfillment.

Although preaching against images in Zurich did not begin in earnest until 1523, there are indications that opposition to images was being publicly taught before this date. There is one report dated in October of 1523, that says that Zwingli and his colleague Leo Jud had "for a long time now" preached "that idols and images should not exist."[105] As early as June of 1520, in Zwingli's native Duchy of Toggenburg, a certain farmer named Uli Kennelbach defaced a painting of the crucifixion and defended his action by saying that "images are useless and of no help." There are other similar cases indicating that iconoclastic sentiment was beginning to grow among the people prior to 1523.[106]

Opposition to images was now being taught in and around Zurich, but the churches remained full of "idols." Theology and practice were at odds. On 1 September 1523, Leo Jud preached a particularly forceful sermon against images. This event was a turning point in the attack on material objects of worship in Zurich. A week later, a Mass helper of St. Peter's church damaged a panel of the *Pietà*.

As if to increase tension and further encourage iconoclasm, there appeared at this time from the press of Christopher Froschauer a small pamphlet directed against images, written by Ludwig Haetzer, entitled "A Judgment of God Our Spouse Concerning How One Should Regard All Idols and Images."[107] The "Judgment" was a col-

---

104 Garside says that Zwingli formulated his policy "slowly and cautiously" (*Zwingli and the Arts*, p. 77), and states that Zwingli seems to have been "entirely unprepared to deal with the practical consequences of iconoclasm," which resulted from his attack on the saints (p. 137).
105 Ibid., p. 102.
106 Ibid., p. 102.
107 "Ein urteil gottes unser eegemahels wie man sich mit allen götzen und bildnussen halten soll" (Zurich, 1523). Garside claims that the exact date of publication is not known, but the copy of this treatise in Beinecke Library at Yale University has the following information: "Getruckt zum Zürich durch Christophorum Froschower/ am XXIII tag des ersten Herbstmonats. Anno MDXXIII Jar."

lection of scripture passages condemning the worship of images, accompanied by some arguments based on Karlstadt's "On the Abolition of Images" (1522). The "Judgment" of Haetzer is divided into two parts. The first consists of scripture passages collected under three theses: (a) God our Father and Spouse forbids us to make images; (b) God intends to destroy images as well as those who possess them and honor them; and – most significantly – (c) the deed of those who have done away with images and idols will be praised and glorified.[108] The scripture passages chosen as proof-texts were the most radical Old Testament condemnations of image worship. The significance of this section of the "Judgment" is obvious; it provided arguments against images and made searching for texts unnecessary. Here, in one compact pamphlet, they were available in the vernacular for all to study and use.[109] The third thesis had an especially inflammatory emphasis, since it collected scripture passages that praise those who destroy idols. Although Haetzer was not being as openly revolutionary as Karlstadt, he was hinting that iconoclasm in general was praiseworthy without specifying that it should only be carried out by magistrates. The second part of the work is a theological refutation of three Catholic arguments in defense of image worship, all of which had been previously attacked by Karlstadt.[110]

In early autumn 1523, as Haetzer's pamphlet was coming off the presses, iconoclastic violence suddenly increased in Zurich. On 13 September, a group of men entered the Fraumünster, destroyed some lamps, and disrespectfully sprinkled holy water on themselves, saying they would "exorcise one another."[111] Only two men could be

---

108 "a) Got unser vatter und Eegemahel verbüt uns die bilder zemacht. b) Got heisst die bild zerbrechen und von der straff deren die sy habend und eerend. c) Die that deren die bild und götzen abgethon hand wirt gerümpt und prisen."

109 In 1524 Clement Ziegler, the Strassburg preacher, published a similar "Register" of scripture passages condemning images: "Ain Kurz Register und ausszug der Bibel in wölchem man findet was Abgöttery sey/ und was man yedes süchen soll" (Strassburg, 1524).

110 The three arguments challenged by Haetzer are (a) that the Old Testament prohibitions against images are not binding on Christians; (b) that the images are not adored, but rather the saints whom they represent; (c) that the images serve as books for the ignorant.

111 Emil Egli, *Actensammlung zur Geschichte der Züricher Reformation in den Jahren 1519–1533* (Zurich, 1879), doc. 415. The men were seen reading "a little book" before entering the church. Could it have been Haetzer's pamphlet? Garside thinks it was, "in all likelihood" (*Zwingli and the Arts*, p. 115). The dating of the document raises problems here. If the "Judgment" was first published on 23 September, as the Yale copy seems to indicate, then the "little book" might not have been Haetzer's. It is possible, however, that it could have been made available a few days before its official publication date.

positively identified as having committed this act. Both were arrested and imprisoned for three days. Iconoclasm was still illegal in Zurich, but the verbal assault on images continued in the churches, and the people to whom the sermons were directed began to take matters into their own hands. On 23 September, three men destroyed a large crucifix in Stadelhoffen, a village near the lower gate of Zurich. According to the testimony of one of the men arrested in connection with this act, the crucifix was destroyed with the intention of selling the wood and turning the proceeds over to "the poor people who could best use it."[112]

As the month of September progressed the tension between theory and practice in Zurich remained unresolved. Zwingli condemned images from the pulpit, Jud called for their removal, and Haetzer praised iconoclasts, warning that those who allowed images to exist would be punished by God. Zwingli and Jud reluctantly supported the hesitancy of the magistrates, restraining themselves from openly approving of illegal iconoclasm, but fomenting discontent with their sermons against images. As the council deliberated over the fate of the images, events in nearby villages brought the issue to a crisis point.

Simon Stumpf, the village pastor of Höng, had often preached against images. On Sunday, 27 September, his regular service erupted into a heated debate over images, and ended with the removal of several cultic objects by their donors. Around the same time, perhaps a few days later, several men broke into the village church of Wippingen, where they destroyed many images. When these men were arrested, their fellow parishioners requested pardon for them, arguing that their actions were in accord with a resolution accepted at the church earlier in the day.[113] Thus, at Höng and Wippingen, the actions of the people began to circumvent the power of the magistracy. When the Zurich council met on 29 September to discuss this matter, it decided to settle the conflict by calling for a public disputation.[114] The illegal iconoclastic acts of a few people – meager though they were – had forced the legality of the Catholic *cultus* into being questioned, and would soon force Zwingli to formulate an iconoclastic policy.

[112] Egli, *Actensammlung*, doc. 421.
[113] Ibid., docs. 422, 423.
[114] Ibid., doc. 430. The Disputation was called "in order that they may hold conversation and help to make a decision, based on the Holy Scriptures of the Old and New Testament, with respect to images and the Mass; how this matter is to be resolved so that it may be done in the way most pleasing to God Almighty and in the way most satisfactory to all Christian, believing men; and in order that we shall live according to the will of God" (trans. by Garside, *Zwingli and the Arts*, p. 126).

The Second Zurich Disputation began on 26 October 1523 and finally closed with a condemnation of images and the Mass.[115] The council appointed a commission, in which Zwingli and Jud were included, to oversee the removal of images from the churches. However, no steps were taken at this time actually to do away with images and the Mass. Opposition mounted against the removal of the images, and the council stalled by calling for another disputation. The Third Zurich Disputation lasted only one day and closed without reaching a decision, calling instead for still another disputation to be held the following year. The Fourth Disputation, held in January 1524, again declared that images were evil and ought to be removed, but the magistracy continued to stall in enforcing this decision. The council made no effort to remove the images, saying it needed more time to discuss the matter and that it would rule on it no sooner than Pentecost.[116]

Those waiting for the council's decision must have been galled by its persistent hesitation. On 14 May an interim decree was issued, calling for restraint. On the next day, in the village of Zollikon, a small church had its images destroyed in spite of the council's proclamation.[117] Another interim decree was issued on the 21st, this time calling for a ban on the creation of new works of religious art and on the burning of candles and incense before images. Those who had donated images were also granted permission to remove them. Finally, on 15 June 1524, the council called for an orderly removal of all images.[118] A committee of twelve was appointed and a number of craftsmen were assigned to execute the removal of the images, and this order was swiftly carried out. The city architect and the three people's priests (Zwingli, Jud, and Engelhard) served as overseers to the project. This committee entered each Zurich church as a body, beginning on 20 June, and proceeded to remove all the images efficiently and without violence.[119] At the end of two weeks every

---

[115] The text of the Second Disputation, which is most important, is found in volume II of *Huldrych Zwinglis Sämtliche Werke* (Berlin/Zurich, 1905–). A concise and flowing narrative of this and successive disputations is provided by Garside, *Zwingli and the Arts*, pp. 129–59. It should be remarked that, by this time, sacramentarianism and iconoclasm had become inextricably interrelated. The first two days of the Second Disputation were devoted almost exclusively to the image question, but the last day was devoted to the issue of the Mass. For more on the ramifications of the eucharistic question, consult Williams, *The Radical Reformation*, p. 95 ff.

[116] Egli, *Actensammlung*, doc. 530.

[117] Ibid., doc. 535.

[118] Ibid., doc. 543. Garside, *Zwingli and the Arts*, pp. 156–7.

[119] Ibid., doc. 544.

church had been cleared of statues, paintings, murals, altar decorations, votive lamps and carved choir stalls. The walls of each church were also whitewashed. Without images and without the Mass, the preaching of the Word and the fulfillment of the Word were no longer at odds in Zurich. The physical presence of the old *cultus* had been removed after much prodding on the part of the people, and the Reformed church was now a reality. The final act of iconoclasm had been legal and peaceful, but it had not taken place without previous violence and disobedience leading the way.

Zwingli's theological argument against images

Although Zwingli formulated much of his attack on idolatry during the controversy over images in 1523–4, his most complete statement on the subject did not appear until 1525, in a work entitled *An Answer to Valentin Compar*.[120] In this work, Zwingli lays a solid foundation for his theological opposition to image veneration as idolatrous, and provides a concise "theology of idolatry." In writing the *Answer*, Zwingli must have had in mind the work he was simultaneously doing in the *Commentary on the True and False Religion*. His objective in both works is to discriminate between true and false Christian belief. Zwingli asks a central question: "What is the ultimate object of Christian belief?" His answer frames his interpretation of the problem of idolatry.

Zwingli insists that the true object of Christian belief is to have God as the ultimate focus of faith and worship. He develops his answer from a dual perspective, the divine and the human, dealing first with the uniqueness of God as the object of man's belief, and then with man's unconditional response to that object of belief. Zwingli observes that man cannot respond to God properly because of the cor-

---

[120] "Eine Antwort, Valentin Compar Gegeben." This treatise was written in early 1525 against Valentin Compar, land-secretary of the Canton Uri, who had written a critique of Zwingli's position on the Gospel, authority, images and purgatory. Compar's document is now lost, but his arguments are answered in detail by Zwingli. The "Answer" was addressed not only to Compar, but to the whole Swiss Confederacy as well. It was intended as a public document, and, as Garside says, "must thus be understood as a defense and an explanation to the rest of Switzerland of the whole Reformation as it had thus far affected the visual arts in Zurich" (p. 162). In her analysis of Zwingli's iconoclastic theology, Margarete Stirm makes no reference to Garside's pioneering work in this area (*Bilderfrage*, pp. 138–53).

ruption of human nature. In fact, he says than man persistently fails to acknowledge the supremacy of God in the spiritual life, substituting a multitude of "ends" in his worship, all of which are false.[121] Zwingli sets up a sharp distinction between creator and created in worship, and it is this interpretation of the proper response to God which underlays Zwingli's theology of idolatry. Anyone who fails to worship God alone, says Zwingli, worships falsely:

> They are not believers who go to anyone else for help other than to the one, true God. For thus are the believers differentiated from the unbelievers in that the believers, or those who are trusting, go to God alone; but the unbelievers go to the created.[122]

One of the more significant contributions made by Zwingli to the Reformation debate over idolatry was his analysis of the psychological roots of false worship. Zwingli asserts that the cause of error in religion is man's dependence on created things, and his penchant for placing trust in them. In outlining this tendency, Zwingli differentiates between the creation of inner and outer idols. The internal manifestation of false worship is what Zwingli calls an "abgott," or strange god. This word is use to describe anything in man's inner life that displaces God as an object of faith, be it money, glory, or another deity.[123] Zwingli delves into the psychology of idolatry a bit further. He asserts that as man becomes more conscious of his reliance on these strange gods, he inevitably tries to give them some specific form. The mental process, then, undergoes materialization as a result of man's need to comprehend reality through material means. What the mind of man grasps, he says, is always made into an image. Since man is by nature materially inclined, therefore, "there is no one who, as soon as he hears God spoken of, or any other thing which he has not already seen, does not picture a form for himself."[124] Since the externalization of the inner gods ("die abgötten") is inevitable, every strange god finds expression in a physical idol sooner or later. The idol, then, is defined by Zwingli as a portrait of a strange god that already existed in man's heart. The "götzen" are the end result of a human process of invention, for, as he says, "the strange god [der abgott] always comes before the idols [dem götzen]".[125]

The core of Zwingli's theology of idolatry is his opposition to any

---

[121] This idea had already been expressed in "Vom Alten und Neuen Gott," Kück, p. 5.
[122] ZW 4.88.
[123] ZW 4.97.
[124] ZW 4.96.
[125] ZW 4.133.

objects of faith (inner or outer) that usurp the place of God in worship. This principle is used in the *Answer*, but it is perhaps most clearly set forth in the *Commentary on True and False Religion*, which is a long and detailed exposition of this issue. In the *Commentary*, Zwingli says that true religion, or piety, "is that which clings to the one and only God."[126] This principle is the foundation of the Reformed interpretation of worship: "Nothing, therefore, of ours, is to be added to the Word of God, and nothing taken from his Word by rashness of ours."[127] This dictum is based on an antithesis between creature and creator – between the spiritual world of God and the material world of man. The things of earth, says Zwingli, are "carnal," and carnal things are "enmity against God." The distinction between true and false worship hinges on man's attitude toward his creator and the rest of creation: "It is, therefore . . . very easy to distinguish false religion from true. It is false religion or piety when trust is put in any other than God. They, then, who trust in any created thing whatsoever are not truly pious."[128] Later, in his *Short Exposition of the Christian Faith* (1531), Zwingli would refer to this principle as the "fountainhead" of religion and "the first foundation of faith."[129]

It has been stated that whereas Luther's Reformation sprang from a purely religious question, Zwingli's starting point was the social and political distress of his people.[130] Though it may be true that Zwingli's Reformation, so often described as "theocratic," aimed at a tighter interweaving of theology and sociopolitical concerns, this does not mean that it was any less "religious." Zwingli's concern over piety and worship, his desire to differentiate between true and false religion, derived principally from theological convictions. For Zwingli and his followers, no less than for Luther and his, the Reformation was above all a religious movement that included concrete social changes. The main difference is that, for the Zwinglians, the Reformation decision consisted not so much in finding a just God, but rather in turning away from idolatry to the true God.[131] Zwingli's theology of idolatry, especially as formulated in the *Answer* and the *Commentary*, became a powerful summons, calling evangelicals not just to reevaluate their attachment to a certain kind of piety, but to wage war against it.

---

[126] "Commentary on True and False Religion" (1525), *Latin Works*, 2.92.
[127] Ibid., p. 94.
[128] Ibid., p. 97.
[129] "A Short and Clear Exposition of the Christian Faith" (written in July of 1531, published posthumously in 1536), *Latin Works*, 3.241.
[130] Locher, *Zwingli's Thought*, p. 34.
[131] ZW 4.89.

Zwingli would eventually die on the battlefield, sword in hand, when the war on the idols led to a war between Protestant and Catholic. In what must rank as one of the greatest ironies of history, Zwingli's Catholic enemies burned his body and scattered his ashes in order to deprive the Zurichers of their leader's relics. In a further ironic twist, rumors began to circulate in Zurich that Zwingli's heart had been rescued and buried by his friends. Catholic polemicists accepted the rumor as proof that the Protestants were indeed venerating Zwingli's remains in an idolatrous manner.[132] As comic as it is tragic, this misunderstanding stemmed from the Protestant belief that Zwingli's heart could not be killed, that his spirit would live on. In a figurative sense, the Protestants were right. Zwingli's heart did keep beating, his spirit did live on; and his followers continued to be animated by it. Until Calvin emerged as the new leader of the war against idolatry, Zwingli remained the principal interpreter of "true religion," and his uncompromising transcendentalism continued to function as the heart of a rapidly growing body of iconoclasts. It is to the followers of Zwingli, to those who immediately assumed his place and spread his message, that we must now turn.

BULLINGER AND THE HISTORY OF IDOLATRY

Zwingli's attack on the worship of the Catholic church was continued and expanded upon by his successor at Zurich, Heinrich Bullinger, who wrote an encyclopedic condemnation of medieval piety. *On the Origin of Errors* first appeared in 1528 as a brief tract against the Mass. A second edition in 1529 added a section condemning the cult of images as well. Altogether, the book totaled no more than fifty-six octavo leaves, but it already contained a substantial historical analysis of the problem of idolatry in the Christian church.[133] Ten years later, in 1539, Bullinger published a revised and expanded edition, which had now grown to 260 quarto leaves.[134] Though somewhat tiresome

---

[132] G. W. Locher, "Die Legende vom Herzen Zwinglis," *Zwingliana*, IX/10: 563–76 (1953).

[133] I have not been able to consult the 1529 edition. However, a printed sermon from 1532 by a certain Woffgang Rüss contains a brief reference to Bullinger's work. Rüss recommends "De origine erroris" to his congregation, saying it has a fine section on the history of idolatry. W. Rüss, "Waher die Bilder oder Götzen mit Irem Gepreng/ Baid der Haiden und Genanten Christen Kummen" (s.l., 1532).

[134] "De origine erroris" was again published in 1563 (Zurich), and translated into French (1549), and later into Dutch and German. For more on Bullinger see J. Wayne Baker, *Henrich Bullinger and the Covenant: The Other Reformed Tradition* (Athens, Ohio, 1981).

and repetitious, it is a compendium of polemics against the images and the Mass, and could undoubtedly serve as a handy reference source for any preacher or layman who wanted to attack Catholic piety.

The first part of the work, which stands as an independent treatise, deals with the problem of the cult of images and the saints,[135] and contains the kernel of Bullinger's attack on idolatry. Bullinger begins by asserting that the purpose of the Reformation is to return to the pristine sources of ancient Christianity, and that its most important task is the renewal of true piety and pure worship among all Christians.[136] As far as theology is concerned, Bullinger adds little to the points raised by Zwingli. The greatest significance of this treatise is the way in which it treats the problem from a historical perspective.

Bullinger proceeds carefully and systematically from the divine to the human. In true Reformed fashion, he starts his analysis of idolatry with a lengthy five-chapter discussion of the nature of God and the proper worship due to Him, since, as he says, worship must always have the oneness and omnipotence of God as its vantage point.[137] Bullinger then analyzes the problem of idolatry from an anthropological perspective by dealing with those religious characteristics that are common to all men. He asserts that man is tied to earth and that it is this adherence to material things that prevents him from worshiping God correctly.[138] The *caussae idolorum*, he concludes, is that men seek the divine and infinite in the material and visible.[139]

After this general discussion of idolatry, Bullinger provides a historical analysis, tracing the history of image worship among the Jews and the early Christians. He asserts that Christian image worship developed when the bodies of the saints and martyrs began to be revered, and he places the blame on monastic piety, with its empha-

---

[135] "In librum de origine erroris circa invocationem et cultum deorum ac simulachrorum" (1539).

[136] Ibid., "Letter to the Reader."

[137] "De origine erroris," chap. 1.

[138] Ibid., p. 22r: "Quicquid anima colit ut deum necesse est ut melius esse quam seipsam putet. Animae autem natura nec terra, nec maria, nec sydera, nec luna, nec sol, nec quicquam omnino quod tangi aut his oculis videri potest, non denique ipsum quod videri a nobis non potest, coelum, eius esse credendum est."

[139] "De origine erroris," p. 43v: "Quicunque vero idola primum invenerunt institueruntque vel ad repraesentandum vel colendum deos, visum est his certe hoc medium fore congruentissimum, quo coniungerent numini. Hoc enim cum crederent esse coeleste, invisibile et impalpabile, ipsi vero cultores essent terreni, qui rebus capiuntur visibilibus, existimarum idola commodissima fore media, in quibus simul ipse colenent deus invisibilis, et ipsi afficenrent commonerenturque visibiliter."

sis on physical holiness.[140] The next few chapters are taken up with a discussion of the invocation of the saints in the early Church. Bullinger displays his erudition by using numerous patristic texts to defend his thesis, primarily from Jerome and Augustine. The treatise then returns briefly to a theological consideration of the problem of idolatry in which Bullinger states that idolatry is evil because it takes away the honor due to God.[141] In three lengthy chapters, Bullinger narrates the history of early Christian image worship, the Byzantine iconoclastic controversy, and the Carolingian opposition to images. There is really little that is new in Bullinger's attack, but his thoroughness is impressive.[142]

The second part of *On the Origin* deals with the eucharist,[143] and is somewhat shorter than the first part (66 vs. 179 leaves). In this section, which can also stand as an independent treatise, Bullinger criticizes numerous aspects of the Mass as idolatrous: the notion of sacrifice, excessive ceremonialism, the use of vestments, its unscriptural character, and, of course, transsubstantiation.

Bullinger's *On the Origin of Errors* contributed to the attack on idolatry in three ways. First, by collecting in one volume an astounding number of arguments and citations against images and the Mass; secondly, by using historical documentation to argue against idolatry, and emphasizing an identifiably explicit historical dimension; and finally, by arranging the material in a theologically systematic way. As often happens with good, solid syntheses, it became a textbook of sorts, a reference tool for theologians, pastors, and laymen, providing them with a distillation of ideas that could be used in sermons, pamphlets, and plays.

---

[140] Ibid., Chap. 13. In this chapter Bullinger also argues that the cult of images was spawned by the cult of relics.

[141] Ibid., p. 108v: "Ex istis vero obiter & illud colligimus divos extrema diabolicaque afficere ignominia quicunque hisce honoribus divinis ipsos delectari arbitrantur. Nam diabolus blasphema ambitione & audatia caecatus audet imo & gaudet id sibi quod dei solius est usurpare."

[142] Bullinger attacks all the usual arguments: "images are not really worshiped, only the subjects they represent are worshiped"; "images are the books of the ignorant"; etc. He also denies that crucifixes can represent Christ's divine nature; ridicules his contemporaries for treating images as living beings; and calls for the money spent on images to be diverted to the poor. He argues against the iconodulic Second Council of Nicaea (787); says that pagan and Christian idolatry are not really different; and devotes an entire chapter to the errors of pilgrimages.

[143] "De origine erroris circa coenam Domini sacram et missam papisticam."

MARTIN BUCER AND THE REFORMATION IN STRASSBURG

Another Protestant leader who played an important role in the development of the Reformed theology of idolatry was Martin Bucer. Although his theology differed little from Zwingli's or Bullinger's, it highlighted different issues. Bucer's attack on Roman Catholic worship has been largely ignored by scholars, even though it is a significant part of his early life and work. This might be due to the fact that Bucer maintained a middle position between Luther and Zwingli for several years, and thus seems a secondary figure. The truth is, however, that Bucer influenced the development of an attitude toward Catholic piety in southwest Germany and in France that was less tolerant than that of the Lutherans and eventually became as uncompromising as that of the Swiss. Bucer's policies at Strassburg are especially important for their impact on the development of French Protestantism. Bucer influenced not only the humanist Lefèvre, and his disciples, Roussel and Farel, but also Calvin, who later ministered to the French evangelicals of Strassburg for two years. Johann Sturm did not exaggerate too much when he said about Strassburg: "Almost everything good and pure in religion in France sprang from this source."[144]

Martin Bucer began his attack on Catholic worship by criticizing the cult of the saints and the miracles that accompanied their veneration. This point of departure is unique among the Reformers. Bucer's *Summary* of his preaching in Weissenburg contains information about the type of criticisms he made in his early sermons. He condemned the cult of saints for the same reasons as other evangelicals, saying that it detracted from the worship of Christ and had no Scriptural foundation.[145] But in attacking this form of piety, Bucer focused more on the practical aspects of the cult than on theological points. Since miracles were one of the major reasons for the popularity of the *cultus divorum*, as well as an argument for its validity, Bucer tried to expose the error of the cult by proving that the miracles performed by the cultic objects

---

[144] Johann Sturm, *Erinnerungschrift* (1581), cited by Hastings Eells in *Martin Bucer* (New Haven, 1931), p. 40. For a detailed, nearly encyclopedic account of the changes effected in Strassburg see the excellent study of René Bornert, *La Réforme Protestante du Culte a Strassbourg au XVIe Siècle (1523–1598)* (Leiden, 1981).

[145] "Martin Butzers an ein christlichen Rath und Gemeyn der statt Weissenburg Summary seiner Predig daselbst gethon" (1523), in DS I, 101.

were really demonic.[146] He charged that the miracles attributed to the departed saints were false because they detracted from the true mediatorship of Christ and made people believe that Mary and the saints could help in his place.[147] It was the devil who worked these miracles in order to pervert religion, not God. This perversion of faith, he continued, was most evident in the way in which people flocked to certain pilgrimage sites, such as Aachen, Regensburg, and Grymmental, seeking divine help as if it were present in one place and not in another.[148] People may believe that the wonders performed at these shrines were signs of divine grace, said Bucer, but they were really the work of the Antichrist.[149]

In his early sermons, as presented in the *Summary*, Bucer also brought out an issue that would become central to his attack on Catholic worship. This was a concern over the uncharitable aspects of the *cultus divorum*. Other Reformers, even Luther, had criticized medieval piety for diverting resources from the needy. Karlstadt apparently thought that the issues of iconoclasm and social welfare were inextricably related. His treatise *On the Abolition of Images* includes an entire section entitled "There Should Be No Beggars Among Christians."[150] Bucer, however, made this issue even more integral to his attack on medieval piety, and his concern over this matter shows how the "new social ethic" of early Protestantism played a role in defining his interpretation of the problem of idolatry.[151] When he criticized false miracles, for instance, Bucer added that one of their chief evils lay in that they caused people to invest more and more money into the external cult while the needy remained unattended.[152] The same

---

[146] DS I, 107. See the section entitled "Mit falschen wundern und zeichen hat man die Leüt uff des Antichrists leer gefürt und behalten, die dann krefftig yrrthumb brocht und erhalten haben bey allen, so die liebe der worheit nit haben uffgenommen."

[147] Ibid., p. 110: "Die zeichen, so man fürgibt, das sye in nammen der abgestorbenen Heilgen geschehen, seind falsch, so durch der irrthum erhalten wurd, sye seyen unser fürsprechen und mitler bey gott, das doch allein Christus ist."

[148] This criticism was part of the Erasmian critique. The question of Erasmus's influence on Bucer has been treated at length by Nicole Peremans in *Erasme et Bucer, d'après Leur correspondance* (Paris, 1970), p. 31.

[149] DS, I, 112: "Falsch und antichristlich seind alle zeichen, dadurch das volck verfurt wurt an einem ort mer gnad dann an dem andern zu erlangen."

[150] On this aspect of Karlstadt's thought see Carter Lindberg, "'There Should Be No Beggars among Christians': Karlstadt, Luther, and the Origins of Poor Relief," *Church History* 46: 313–34 (1977).

[151] Steven Ozment, *Reformation in the Cities*, pp. 63–6.

[152] DS I, 108: "Mit disen falschen wundern und zeichen ist nun das einfeltig volck auch gross fürsten und herren verfürt worden, ir güt, domit die armen solten versehen sein worden, an Stifft und Closter gegeben, die domit gebuwen und ryhlich begobet, das alles dann in bruch kummen ist, wie ir secht, das durch die

was true of pilgrimages. Bucer called them "unchristian" not only because they reflected a misplaced faith, but also because they fostered an uncharitable attitude among Christians.[153]

Bucer's opposition to Catholic piety was stated even more clearly in 1524, in his *Basis and Reason for the Innovations*, where he defended the reforms begun in Strassburg that year, and attacked images and the Mass as idolatrous. In the *Basis*, Bucer objects to the Catholic Mass because it is thought to be a sacrifice. He also condemns some of its materialistic aspects.[154] Bucer charges that Catholics have adopted pagan practices, proposes that Christians are free in regard to outward ceremonies, and again asserts that it is more important to be charitable to one's neighbor than to spend one's resources on material objects of worship.[155] Bucer neatly summarizes his unique approach to the problem of idolatry in one brief sentence: After describing the errors surrounding the cult of St. Aurelia at Strassburg, he points to the root of its falsehood, saying, "it is both against faith and love."[156]

The thrust of Bucer's theological argument against Catholic ceremonies is that they are "carnal and human statutes." Like Karlstadt and Zwingli, he contrasts the spiritual and the material, the divine and the human. In the case of the eucharist, he accuses the Catholic church of focusing on the material elements of the bread and wine instead of on the spiritual promise behind them. Bucer charges that this materialistic orientation leads the people to believe that the eucharist is a magical power, and he lists some common superstitions associated with the adoration of the host.[157] In regard to relics, which were sought as the source of miraculous cures and favors, Bucer quips, "bones are bones, and not gods."[158] Bucer maintains a sharp distinction between material and spiritual in worship: The material

---

genanten geistlichen, die Christum nit erkenen, die übrig armut dem gemeyene volck, auch den leyschen herrschafften . . . abzyehen und sye dofür nichts thun, das gottlich oder erschiesslich sey, sonder das mer seel und leib verderb."

[153] Ibid., p. 113: "Zudem verlossen die einfeltigen leüt ire arme freünd und nochburen, offt auch weib und kind wider das gebott gottes und lauffen an solche stett, tragen das ir do hyn, domitt dann, über das man an holtz, stein, wachs und mussigond leüt legt, vil grosser bubery erhalten würt."

[154] "Grund und ursach auss gottlicher schrifft der neüwerungen an dem nachtmal des herren, so man die Mess nennet, Tauff, Feyrtagen, bildern und gesand in der gemein Christi, wann die zusammenkompt, durch und auff das wort zu Strassburg fürgenommen" (1524); DS, I.

[155] DS I, 210, 218, 219.

[156] Ibid., p. 273: "Wolches alles wider glaub und lieb ist."

[157] Ibid., p. 229. Bucer reports that some thought the eucharist could bring good luck for an entire day if venerated in the morning, or that it could cure a fever if one offered a penny during the elevation of the host.

[158] Ibid., p. 274.

should lead the faithful to the spiritual, and never be the object of attention itself.[159]

Bucer's opinion on images in the *Basis and Reason* was not yet fully formulated, however. In a Lutheran vein, Bucer maintained that although the worship of images was forbidden in scripture, the images could do no harm as long as the people were properly instructed. Bucer thought, as did Luther, that images should be destroyed whenever there was danger that they may be worshiped idolatrously, but he did not think this danger was an inevitable outcome of the presence of images in churches.[160] Bucer argued that images were distracting and confusing. They were, as he says, "decoy birds [lockvögel]" that led the people away from true piety with their "magic and false miracles."[161] But, ultimately, his judgment against images was not yet as severe as Karlstadt's or Zwingli's. He agreed with Luther in saying that images caused no one any harm once they had been driven from the heart.[162] Yet, Bucer must have at this time also been aware of Zwingli's position on the problem, since shortly after the Second Zurich Disputation, in January 1523, Zwingli wrote the Strassburgers urging them to cast down their idols.[163] Bucer, however, continued to follow a more moderate course.

As far as iconoclastic policy was concerned, Bucer made it clear that he was opposed to any illegal acts. He warned that no one without authority over his fellow citizens was permitted to take the law into his own hands. The common people, he says, cannot remove the images physically without the approval of the magistracy. All they can do is teach others that images are not to be worshiped. Nonetheless, Bucer urged those in power to follow the example of King Josiah in removing all the idols, since it was the duty of the magistracy to protect the people form impiety.[164]

The Strassburg magistracy acceded to Bucer's request, but only in part. In October of 1524 they removed from the cathedral certain

---

[159] Ibid., p. 230: "das leyplich, so von gott nit auffkomen und darumb bissher so schedlich gerbracht worden ist, auss den augen thun, sye damit zum geistlichen füren." Also: "Bein seind bein und nit gott" (p. 274).

[160] Eells, *Martin Bucer*, pp. 37–8.

[161] DS I, 271: "die götzen zu lockfögeln werden, damit dem unnutzen beschoren hauffen dester mer gegen würt, ich schweig vil grosser aberglauben, zauberey und falsche wunderwerck."

[162] Ibid., p. 272: "Es ist wor, auss dem hertzen müssen die götzen erstlich gerissen werden und das durch das wort, alsdann schaden sye nicht, aber freylich, wem sye auss dem hertzen seind."

[163] ZW 8.171. Bucer shows awareness of Zwingli's theology of idolatry when he differentiates between "götzen" and "abgötter" (DS I, 270).

[164] DS I, 270, 271.

images that had become popular objects of devotion. This inspired some popular acts of iconoclasm as well. At the church of St. Aurelia, for instance, a group of iconoclasts destroyed all the statues, paintings, frescoes, and crucifixes. But, all in all, the removal of images progressed very slowly and was not completed until February.[165]

To celebrate and defend the final removal of the images from the Strassburg churches in 1530, Bucer wrote a treatise entitled *That Any Kind of Images May Not Be Permitted*.[166] This work shows a definite change in Bucer's attitude toward images, since he no longer considered them to be indifferent things.[167] He now proclaimed that images were forbidden by the first and second commandments because they always led to idolatry.[168] Before, Bucer had said that images were not harmful if properly understood; now he said that to set up images in the churches was to invite idolatry.[169] Bucer again insisted that God is to be worshiped spiritually, not through images, and that the true Christian should pay no attention to created things.[170] In regard to iconoclastic policy, Bucer remained opposed to illegal acts, but now proposed that it was necessary to overthrow the images in order to have pure worship. Whereas before he had said that one should avoid scandalizing the weak, now he said that a true Christian obeys God rather than man, and argued that obedience to God's law was more important than trying to please all men. Images are evil, he warned, and their worship makes God wrathful. Why, then, should one risk divine punishment by allowing the images to stand?[171]

In the second part of this treatise Bucer presents a collection of citations from the Fathers on the question of images, as well as a short history of their use in Christianity.[172] Bucer seemed more aware of the historical process of the acceptance of images in the Church than any other Reformer, except Bullinger, on whom he probably relied for many of these details. Bucer provides a fairly accurate history of the

---

[165] For a narrative and analysis of the process of iconoclasm in Strassburg see R. Bornert, *La Réforme*, pp. 40–153; C. Christensen, *Art and the Reformation*, pp. 79–92; and Stirm, *Bilderfrage*, pp. 156–60.

[166] "Das Einigerlei Bild bei den Gotgläubigen an Orten da Sie Verehrt, Nit Mögen Geduldet Werden" (1530), DS, IV.

[167] Eells, *Martin Bucer*, p. 38.

[168] DS IV, 167: "Des verpots aber der Bilder Mögen wir nit also frei sein, diewil am tag das Bilder haben an stetten, da sie vereret oder nun in gfar der verehrung ston."

[169] Ibid., p. 171: "Dis leugnet kein verstendiger, das man bilder haben mag, wo die nit verehrt werden."

[170] Ibid., p. 168.

[171] Ibid., p. 172.

[172] Ibid., pp. 174–7. Bucer relies most heavily on Jerome, Eusebius, Lactantius, and Athanasius.

Christian use of images through the centuries, and mentions some of the more notable controversies surrounding their acceptance. He writes about Bishop Severus of Marseilles, who destroyed all the images in his diocese in the late sixth century and prompted Pope Gregory to write his famous defense of images; describes the Byzantine iconoclastic controversy; and cites the "Libri Carolini." Bucer maintains that idolatry increased with the widespread acceptance of images after the settlement of the iconoclastic controversy in the East and the decline of the Carolingian theologians in the West. Bucer also seems aware of the way in which various cults, such as that of St. Anne, gradually increased in popularity.[173]

Bucer's *That Any Kind of Images May Not Be Permitted* is not a radical document. Bucer affirms again that only legal iconoclasm is acceptable. In addition, he covers much of the same ground as Bullinger, Zwingli, and Karlstadt. The significance of the document lies in the influence it had on those German and French communities that depended on Strassburg for religious guidance. The treatise is a strong indictment of the cult of images, and marks the final acceptance of Swiss principles in southwest Germany and the repudiation of Lutheran influence. It is also a link in the theological chain leading up to Calvin, for much of the "evangelism" he encountered as a youth in France had intimate connections with Strassburg.

FROM THEOLOGY TO PROPAGANDA: POPULAR ATTACKS ON CATHOLIC PIETY

Karlstadt, Zwingli, Bucer, and Bullinger were the intellectual leaders of the attack on Catholic piety, but the success of their campaign depended just as much on the popularization of their ideas as it did on their own writings. During the early years of the Reformation, the same arguments that flowed from the pens of the religious leaders were repeatedly echoed by less prominent figures in pamphlets, sermons, and plays. Hoping to gain the attention of the general populace, propagandists took the message of the Reformers and carried it to the pulpits, the public squares, and the streets of sixteenth-century towns, often in a more direct and homespun fashion than the theologians. This is not to say that the writings of the Reformers were not circulated, but rather that their influence was augmented by the propaganda they engendered. We shall now examine a few surviving

---

[173] Ibid., p. 178, 179.

examples of this type of literature to show how the attack on idolatry was spread among the people.

One of the greatest aids to the cause of the Reformation was the printed pamphlet. Many of these tracts contained brief references to the cult of saints and images. For instance, one pamphlet from 1523 has a son replying to his mother after she has sent him a little wax lamb to protect him while he is away from home. The letter written by the son ridicules material elements of worship in a blunt, joking manner:

> I am grateful to you for sending me the little wax Agnus Dei, to protect me against being shot, cut and from falling, but honestly, it won't do me any good. I cannot set my faith on it because God's Word teaches me to trust only in Jesus Christ. I am sending it back. We'll try it out on this letter and see whether it is protected from tampering. I don't thank you one bit less, but I pray God you won't believe any more in sacred salt and holy water and all this devil's tomfoolery.[174]

This passage is typical of the type of criticism voiced in pamphlets. The message is spoken by a character with whom the reader can identify, it is written in simple language, and stresses the practical implications of the rejection of medieval piety: The external cult is exposed as a worthless deception.

Another pamphlet from 1523, entitled "A Conversation Between Four People," uses similar methods to get across its point.[175] The characters are all familiar figures: a priest, a monk, an artisan, and a peasant. The evangelical message is carried by the artisan (who represents the urban laity to which the pamphlet is primarily directed), in a shrewd and knowing way. The message of the "Conversation" is that the deception and "foolishness [buberei]" of the *cultus divorum* has now been unmasked, and that it is time to restructure religious life in a more charitable and equitable way. This is not a theologically inclined treatise. It is an exposé aimed at bridging the gap between the clergy and the laity, one that calls attention to the "tricks" by which the clergy have deceived the laity and made themselves rich. This approach is a central aspect of pamphlet literature. Lay perception is not to be identified with the perception of the theologians. Although truth claims were important to the laity, they were at times over-

---

174 Otto Clemen, ed., *Flugschriften aus den Ersten Jahren der Reformation* (4 vols. Halle, 1907–11; reissued, Nieuwkoop, 1967), vol. I, pp. 10–17.
175 "Ein Gespräch Zwischen Vier Personnen, wie Sie ein Gezänk Haben von der Wallfahrt im Grimmental, was für Unrat oder Buberei Darans Entstanden Sei" (1523 or 1524), Clemen, *Flugschriften*, vol. I.

shadowed by more mundane concerns that affected daily life. The alleged exploitation of the laity by the clergy through the *cultus divorum* was one such lively issue.

In the "Conversation" the author has the character of the monk say that the worship of the saints is essential for maintaining the priestly class system of Rome and its luxurious style of worship. The artisan attacks medieval piety by pointing to the powerlessness of the cult. He explains, for instance, that the weeping image of Mary at Grimmental, which attracted hundreds of pilgrims, was a sham: Its head was hollow and had holes in its eyes to allow water to gush out.[176] The artisan also echoes a theme which struck a responsive chord among some sixteenth-century burghers. He tells the peasant it is better for him to stay home and take care of his family or "the poor sick people" than to waste his time and money on pilgrimages.[177] He also tells the peasant not to pay attention to the priests and monks, who peddle their endless ceremonies and devotions in order to gain power and wealth: "they seek a bishopric, not Christ, and they crave to bamboozle you out of your money."[178]

A similar charge is made by Sebastian Meyer in his "Retractation," addressed to the residents of Strassburg.[179] Meyer says that the pope is interested in canonizing saints only for the sake of profit, since the cult of saints creates church revenue through festivals, indulgences, and pilgrimages.[180] Meyer also attacks the cult of relics in a humorous vein, much as Erasmus had done in his Latin *Colloquies*. Meyer says than even the three largest trees in the Black Forest could not provide enough splinters to account for all the particles of the true cross being shown in Germany. He quips that most saints must have had at least two bodies, and then lists some duplicated corpses to prove his

---

[176] Ibid., 143.

[177] Ibid.: "Darumb, liebes beurlein, lass furbas dein wallen unterwegen, bleyb do heym, bey deim weyb und kindern und wardt deyner arbeyt, hab got vor augen, der ist der recht helffer."

[178] Ibid., p. 160: "Darumb so ker dich nit an aller pfaffen und München geschwetz, lass sie sagen, was sie wöllen! . . . sie süchen Bystum und nit Christum, sie gegeren dich umb das gelt tzu betriegen."

[179] "D. Sebastian Meyers, Etwan Predicantum zum Barfussern zum Strassburgk/Widerruffung, an ein Löblich Freystatt Strassburgk" (s.l. 1524). Sebastian Meyer had been a priest in Strassburg for twelve years before he became the first Protestant preacher in Bern. This work is an apology in letter form to the residents of Strassburg, telling them why he had been in "error" during his stay in that city.

[180] Ibid.: "Der Bapst mit seinen Canonizirem umb gelts willen/ den fest uffrichten/ abloss geben/ denen die dahin walfarten/ Also uns das gelt by unserm dencken/ vil neuwer heylen uffgerichtet."

point.[181] The laity may have thought that they were venerating holy relics, he adds, but all they were probably doing was kissing the bones of dogs and asses. He accuses the clergy of having no shame when it comes to deceiving the simple folk: Where in the world, he asks, could they have obtained such improbable items as Jesus' beard clippings or Mary's milk?[182]

Pamphlets may have attacked the Catholic cult from a practical angle, but this does not mean that theology was ignored. Although the practical implications of the rejection of the cult remained prominent in popular literature, pamphlets also sought to explain theological principles in a simpler and more entertaining way than was done by theologians. One example of this kind of tract is the "Dialogue Between Christ and Adam," written by Ulrich Eckstein in 1525.[183]

Eckstein's "Dialogue" is intended to serve as a Protestant primer on worship. It aims to present the Zwinglian conception of true piety in such a way as to hold the reader or listener's attention, and smoothly force him to recognize his present point of view as mistaken. Eckstein, for example, explains why it is that humans have sought divine help through images in a very personal way. The character of Adam speaks in a way that not only parrots the common Catholic teaching, but also expresses sentiments that were assumed to be quite proper:

> It seems not wrong to me
> that without pictures I seldom
> think of thee;
> Since my nature is so unruly
> I pray much more when a picture
> stands before me in the church . . .
> As long as I a crucifix can see
> thy sorrows are real to me.

---

[181] Ibid.: "Es sind auch nicht drey böum so gross in dem schwarzwald/ sy gegen nit so vil stück als vil man deren vom heyligen creütz zeigt allenthalben/ die weil es solichen nütz treit. Also hat auch mänger heylig zwey oder mer corper."

[182] Ibid.: "Haraus auch gewachsen/ das wir heüt diss tags/ vil schelmen beyn/ ia esel und hunden beyn für heyltumb küssen/ ia auch holz von galgen oder vom rad in sylber und gold fassen. Denn beschämen sy sich nit fräuntlich zu lügen/ das sy haben von unsers herrn bart der doch nie bart geschart/ unser Frowen milich/ hembd/ usw."

[183] "Dialogus: Ein Hüpsche Disputation die Christus Hat mit Adam Thon/ darinn ein Mensch Erlernen Mag nach Welchem Wercken Gott Frag von Liebe/ Glauben/ Güten Wercken und Bätten/ Bildern/ was Gott uns Erfordre" (1525). For a capsule biography of Eckstein see *Allgemeine Deutsche Biographie* (Berlin, 1968), vol. 5, p. 636.

If the reader has been lulled into thinking that this makes sense, or is even praiseworthy, as was commonly accepted, the passage that follows shatters these assumptions. Christ denies that any of this is necessary, and instead speaks to Adam in a very Zwinglian manner:

> If you really loved me the right way
> you would not offer honor to images.
> Why not? Because I am myself in you,
> and whoever loves me is also in me;
> So if I am in you spiritually,
> why do you turn away
> and seek me in another place?[184]

Similarly, the character of Christ attacks other points of the Catholic cult throughout the "Dialogue." He explains, for instance, that the Old Testament commands against images apply to Christians as much as to the Jews, and proposes that Christian idolatry has outstripped that of the pagans.[185] Sebastian Meyer does not use the dialogue form in his "Retractation," but he, too, raises fundamental theological issues in a simple manner. He points to the contrast between the spiritual and material, denies the argument that images are not really offered worship, and speaks of the necessity of doing away with images.[186]

Aside from the pamphlet, perhaps the most common way of spreading the Reformation message was through preaching. It is quite likely that the major theologians spread their message abroad more effectively through their sermons than through their writings. The congregations at Zurich, Wittenberg, and Strassburg were all incited to reject Catholic worship directly from the pulpit, and so were congregations in other communities. Although very few of these sermons against idolatry were printed, enough have survived to give us an idea of their content.

One is the sermon preached by Diepold Peringer, published under

---

184 Ibid. Eckstein also writes a passage in which he explains the Zwinglian teaching on the theological error of image worship in concrete, personal terms: "Wenn denn schon kein gschrifft wär/ so ist doch das ein uneer/ Das man zü holtz sagt: Herr Gott/ nun macht man ye uss gott ein spott/ Also gibt man dem holtz die eer/ die selb solt han gott der Herr/ Bilder sind wider all gschrifft veer."

185 Ibid.: "Denn was die Juden botten ist von bildern/ das selb sol ein Christ . . . Denn man findt nit by den alten/ das sy sich habind so styff gehalten In den götzen wie die Christen thund."

186 Meyer, "Widerrufung": "Denn so ziehen dise eüsserliche ding uns ab von der rechten waren gottes eer und dienst so allein gott zu gehört/ und mit hertzen geschicht/ denn als Christus selber sagt/ das fleysch ist kein nutz was sollen denn die beyn der todten oder die götzen nütz sein."

the title "Sermon Against Idolatry Among the Peasantry Who Can Neither Write nor Read."[187] This sermon provides a glimpse into the practical orientation of Protestant preaching against idolatry among the common people. In this case the congregation is made up of peasants, but the message differs little from that addressed to the urban laity on the printed page.

Peringer's aim in the sermon is to criticize the peasants for their naïve belief in the power of the saints. He charges that although the Gospel has been preached among them for two years, they still need to be warned about idolatry, because they ignore the supremacy of Christ and continue to show devotion to crosses, and to saints Marx, Leonard, and Wolfgang, hoping that these devotions will bring them good weather and bountiful harvests. Peringer says, "in language peasants understand," that the saints are nothing more than "decoy birds of the shorn people." Priests and monks use saints and material objects of worship to draw the simple people into their "thorn-bushes," that is, shrines, cloisters, pilgrimages, and ceremonies, where they fleece them at will under the guise of holiness and the promise of salvation.[188] Peringer's message is similar to that found in the "Conversation." It is a testament to the practical orientation of the attack on idolatry among the laity, and of the "new ethic of service to one's neighbor" that permeated the early Protestant movement.[189]

Another sermon is that preached by Wolffgang Rüss at Riethen in October of 1532.[190] Rüss makes reference to the great number of sermons already preached against idolatry, and, like Peringer, complains that the people are still attached to superstition.[191] Unlike Peringer, however, Rüss does not concentrate on the abuses of the cult, but rather on its theology, and in doing so provides us with a concrete example of the way in which the work of major theologians made its

---

[187] "Eyn Sermon von der Abgötterey/ durch den Pawern/ der weder Schreyben noch Lesen Kan/ Gepredigt zu Kitzing im Franckenland auff Unsers Herren Fromleychnams Tag" (1524). For more on Peringer and this sermon see Ozment, *Reformation in the Cities*, pp. 66–7.

[188] Peringer, "Sermon," p. A 3a. Bucer makes the same comment in the "Grund und Ursach" (1524), n. 5, pp. 140–1.

[189] Ozment, *Reformation in the Cities*, p. 61 ff., esp. p. 67.

[190] "Waher die Bilder oder Götzen mit Irem Gepreng/ Baid der Haiden und Genanten Christen Kummen. Wie lang derselbigen mysbrauch gewert/ Wer sy auffpracht/ Wie haiden und Christen die selben verantworten/ Was underschayd zwischen der Hayden und genanten Christen Bilder sey/ Unnd was die hailig schrifft/ und die gar uralten vätter und lerer davon sagen und halten/ Durch Wolffgang Rüss zum Riethen/ In weckthung der Bilder gepredigt" (1532). For a brief biography of Rüss see C. G. Jöcher, *Allgemeines Gelehrten Lexicon* (Leipzig, 1751), vol. 3, col. 2323.

[191] Rüss, "Waher die Bilder," p. A 2.

way to the laity. Most of Rüss's arguments are borrowed from Bull-inger's *On the Origin of Errors*, which he recommends to the congregation, much as a professor recommends a colleague's work in a lecture. He begins by dealing with man's innate tendency to create idols, saying that man always wants to make things better then God had made them.[192] He compares pagan idolatry with the medieval cult and tells his congregation that there is no difference between the two religions. Like Peringer and Bucer, he calls the images "decoy birds," and denies that any one can be taught religion through images.[193] The rest of the sermon is rather academic and dull. Rüss narrates Bullinger's history of idolatry and ends abruptly, without a conclusion, after finishing the story of the Byzantine iconoclastic controversy. This type of sermon is perhaps a good example of how the work of major theologians was used by local pastors: It is not as exciting as a satirical pamphlet, but it still got the message across to the people. The fact that the congregation seemed unwilling to give up "idolatry," both here and in the case of Peringer, points, perhaps, to the slower pace of the Reformation in the countryside, and to the greater effort that had to be made to transform the new theology into some kind of propaganda that the peasants could understand.

The Protestant message was also often announced on the stage through dramatic poems or plays, which often combined sharp satire with theological argumentation. One of the most aggressive critics of the Catholic cult was the Bernese painter and playwright, Nicholas Manuel. His play, *Die Totenfresser* (*Those Who Feed Upon the Dead*), does not deal directly with the issue of idolatry, but is a wholesale indictment of the clerical system of Masses and ceremonies surrounding the cult of the dead.[194] Another play by Manuel, *On the Illness and Last Testament of the Mass*, which was produced in 1528 to celebrate the abolition of the Mass in Bern, is a biting satire of the Catholic ceremony of the eucharist. The Mass, deathly ill and pale, goes seeking a cure among physicians. After trying a number of treatments – including a steambath to sweat out the illness – the Mass dies. On its deathbed, the Mass distributes its ceremonial paraphernalia to the people, and when the holy oil is handed out, it is used as shoe polish.[195] The

---

[192] Ibid., p. A 3.
[193] Ibid., pp. A 5 and A 6.
[194] *Niklaus Manuels Spiel Evangelischer Freiheit: Die Totenfresser*. "*Vom Papst und Seiner Priesterschaft*," 1523, F. Vetter, ed. (Leipzig, 1923). For a discussion of this play see Ozment, *Reformation in the Cities*, pp. 111–16.
[195] "Von Krankheyt der Messe" and "Von Testament, der Messe," both written, published, and performed in 1528. *Niklaus Manuel, Schriften*, Bächtold and Vögelin, eds., "Bibliothek Älterer Schriftwerke der deutschen Schweitz," vol. II (Frauenfeld, 1878).

play, written in simple rhyme, is a cutting exposé of the "errors" of the Catholic cult and it drives its message home with sarcasm and humor. It invites its audience to revel in the unmasking of fraud and deception.

Entirely different in tone and content is the play by Hans von Rüte that was performed in Bern four years later, in 1532.[196] Von Rüte's play is little more than a long lesson in theology, spoken by one-dimensional, unimaginative characters such as "Lady Confusion" and "the Devil." The playwright's intention is to provide a survey of pagan and Christian idolatry, and to speak of its demise in the present day. Stock theological themes are presented by various characters. "The Herald," for example, opens the play by announcing that idolatry begins when men turn from the creator to worship the created.[197] "The Devil" boasts that he has been able to draw men away from God to worship saints and images instead. The Reformed position is defended by a "Theodorus Gottlieb" ("God-lover God-love"), who argues against images and the saints, calls for the distribution of church treasure among the poor, and demands that the creator/creature distinction must be maintained in worship.[198] It is a wooden script but, in an age deeply concerned with religious matters, it might have provided some entertainment as well as edification. All in all, as a public celebration of ideology, it was an effective way to reach and indoctrinate the people.

As a whole, the popular literature of the 1520s and 1530s reflected one important aspect of the Protestant attack on medieval piety: its relationship to disaffection with contemporary religion. The pamphlets, sermons, and plays that ridiculed Catholic worship are genuine expressions of popular feeling. Most are not the work of theologians trying to distill their ideas for the people, but rather the work of the laity themselves. The attack on the cult touched a raw nerve in the early sixteenth century, drawing on widespread religious anxieties and disappointments. The feeling evoked by the popular literature is one of sudden enlightenment after years of deception.

[196] "Ein Fastnachspil den Ursprung Haltung und das End Beyder Heydnischer und Bäptslicher Abgötteryen Allenklich Verglychende/ zu Bern durch die Jungen Burger Gehalten" (Basel, 1532). Why the play should have been produced at this time is not entirely clear, since images and the Mass had been abolished in Bern in 1528. Perhaps it was intended as a reminder of the struggle that continued to be carried out in other nearby cities, such as Geneva, which was then under the aegis of Bern.

[197] Ibid.: "Uss einem grund sind beyd fäler entsprunger/ Sy sind glichlich vom Schöpfer uff die gschöpfften drungen."

[198] Ibid.: "Den Schöpffer sol man eeren mit fromckeit/ Die gschöpfften ding syent all zruch gleit/ Wie wol er unser nathur ist minder glych/ Dann der himmel syg dem erdtrych."

The popular literature of the Reformation voices a strong sense of rebellion against a religious life that is viewed as corrupt and oppressive. The Roman Catholic church becomes a realm of darkness, the kingdom of the Antichrist. In the popular mind, to turn away from the idols was also to turn away from a church mired in sin and corruption. Even among Lutherans, who had no great interest in overturning idols, and instead focused on justification, Christian freedom meant freedom from Rome and its laws, not so much from the power of the Law. This is clearly pointed out in one pamphlet:

> Jesus Christ, son of the pure virgin Mary,
> Free us from the darkness of the Antichrist in Rome,
> Who does not tend his sheep but burdens them
> With his oppressive tyranny and laws.
> Your commands and writings he despises totally
> And raises his own laws with great pomp,
> So that we are unable to love, believe or hope in you.[199]

To the individual, then, the issue became which Church to believe. And the question faced by many in Germany and Switzerland in the 1520s is the question raised by one character in a widely circulated pamphlet of 1521: "Should I then consider the Pope and his cronies to be the Christian Church?"[200] Those who made it their task to win people over to the Protestant side focused on this point as a way of converting the faithful to "true" religion. A sermon preached by Heinrich von Kettenbach in 1522 makes it obvious: "Christ has his Church, and the Antichrist also has his Church, and the Church of the Antichrist is nowdays often mistaken for Christ's Church."[201]

Such a clear-cut distinction points to the break people had to make with their past. It was not enough to understand what true worship meant; a conscious commitment had to be made to a new Church. A pressing concern voiced in many Reformation tracts is that one's salvation depends on following one church or the other. In the pamphlet "Neuw Karthans" a thought is expressed that may have echoed in the mind of many who chose to become Protestant. Karthans, the main character, laments that all his life has so far been wasted on the wrong religion:

---

[199] "Ein Clag und Bitt der Deutschen Nation an der Almechtigen Got umb Erlosung auss dem Gefenknis des Antichrist," in Oskar Schade (ed.), *Satiren und Pasquille aus der Reformationszeit*, vol. I (Hanover, 1856), p. 1.

[200] "Ain Schöner Dialogus Zwischen aim Pfarrer und aim Schulthaisz" (1521), Schade, *Satiren*, vol. II, p. 136.

[201] Heinrich von Kettenbach, "Ein Sermon von der Christlichen Kirche" (1522), in Clemen, *Flugschriften*, vol. II, p. 83.

Oh God, to you we lament, that for such a long time we were robbed of the true knowledge of your holy teachings and instead were taught fables and useless prattle. If I had been able to hear the true teaching as a youth, I would have led a different kind of life.[202]

In popular literature, the objection to the burdens laid by Rome on people's shoulders is strong, but a stronger complaint is voiced against the damning power of the burdens themselves. Guillaume Farel would point out in his 1525 *Sommaire* that Rome's "human" laws were especially dangerous because they had an appearance of sanctity and thus deceived people by making them feel they were obeying God's law:

The more a human doctrine appears to be holy, the more dangerous it is. As is the case with the doctrines of the Pharisees and above all those of the Antichrist, which seem to be from Jesus and are more effective in deceiving and fooling than any other.[203]

In the "Dialogue Between Peter and a Peasant" (1523), one of the most important tenets of the Reformation is expressed by the character of St. Peter: "Christ alone is our helper, intercessor and mediator, and without him there is no other." Not only is the Catholic church seen as false and unable to dispense grace, but also, along with the saints, as unable to mediate between God and human beings. The advice given by one propagandist was well taken by many lay people:

Thus every Christian I advise
Who is not steeped in lies,
That far from these he run apace,
And in his house depend on grace.[204]

It was Christ who interceded for all before God. The individual now faced God directly in faith, at home, as part of a new community of believers, not through a host of intercessors in a church. The falsehood of the "idols" was therefore also proof of the falsehood of the entire institution that supported them. It was not just a question of removing idolatry from the institution, but rather of removing the insititution itself. A cult that made many demands but apparently did not give commensurate satisfaction was now under attack, and those most deeply affected by the proposed changes, the laity at large, reveled in removing the blinds from their eyes.

---

202 "Neuw Karthans," Schade, *Satiren*, vol. II, p. 15.
203 Guillaume Farel, *Sommaire et Briefve Declaration* (1525), in J. G. Baum (ed.), *Le Sommaire de Guillaume Farel Reimprimé apres l'Edition de l'An 1534* (Geneva, 1867).
204 "Von dem Jubeljahr" (1525), Schade, *Satiren*, vol. I, p. 42.

DRAWING THE BATTLE LINES

By 1525, when Zwingli wrote his *Answer to Valentin Compar*, the Protestant position against the medieval cult had crystallized into a well-
established pattern. First, the difference of opinion between Lutheran
and Reformed was fully evident. Although a final division on the
question of the eucharist was not to be reached until the Marburg
Colloquy in 1529, it was clear by 1525 that Luther embraced a less
radical theological and tactical approach to the rejection of the medieval cult than did Karlstadt or the Swiss.

In addition, the theological attack against the cult was fairly well
developed by 1525. Karlstadt, Zwingli, and others had drawn a sharp
dividing line between "true" and "false" worship, clearly delineating
the "errors" of Catholicism, and drawing up numerous arguments
against "idolatrous" religion. Though much of this theology would
be expanded upon throughout the following decades it contained the
heart and soul of many future arguments. Essential distinctions and
fundamental arguments had been brought to light that would later be
employed as Protestants continued to attack Roman Catholicism.

Another significant pattern was the fact that the Protestant rejection of Catholic worship was not strictly a theologian's affair. More
than any other aspect of the Reformation, the war against the idols
called and depended upon the support of the lay community: It drew
upon dissatisfaction with contemporary religion and sought popular
acceptance in order to triumph. The attack on Catholic piety was
aimed at changing the worship of the entire *corpus christianorum*, and
such a change could not take place without the participation of the
people. The iconoclastic events at Wittenberg and Zurich bear witness to this, as does some of the popular literature of the early 1520s.

Moreover, the phenomenon of iconoclasm had begun to be closely
associated with Reformed ideology, radically transforming the outward appearance of Christianity in several communities. The worst
fury had not yet been unleashed in 1525, but events in and around
Wittenberg and Zurich already foreshadowed the impending
destruction.

CHAPTER 4

Iconoclasm, revolution, and the Reformation in Switzerland and Geneva, 1527–1536

It is one thing to preach against idolatry, and quite another actually to smash an altarpiece. As has already been pointed out, iconoclastic theology and iconoclastic policy were not always in agreement during the early days of the Reformation. We have seen how the policies of Karlstadt and Zwingli were reduced to practice in Wittenberg and Zurich. It is now time to examine the phenomenon of iconoclasm in greater detail.

Older studies of the Reformation often display a keener awareness of the significance of iconoclasm than modern interpretations.[1] J. H.

---

[1] Although several studies have been written on the subject of Protestant iconoclasm in general, none provides a systematic analysis of this phenomenon as a pattern of Reformation in Switzerland, or tries to analyze it principally in connection with theological principles. Phyllis Mack Crew has written an excellent, detailed study of Dutch iconoclasm, but makes little reference to the broader implications of the problem or its historico-theological roots in Switzerland. *Calvinist Preaching and Iconoclasm in the Netherlands 1544–1569* (Cambridge University Press, 1978). Much the same can be said about *Les Casseurs de l'Eté, 1566, le Iconoclasme dans le Nord* by Solange Deyon and Alain Lottin (Paris, 1981), which covers an even smaller geographical area. Another localized study is that of John Phillips, *The Reformation of Images: Destruction of Art in England, 1535–1660* (Los Angeles, 1973). Like Crew, Deyon, and Lottin, Phillips largely ignores the Swiss antecedents. Martin Warnke has edited a fine collection of essays on the subject of iconoclasm, but this work is also concerned with specific examples of image destruction rather than with iconoclasm as a pattern of Reformation. *Bildersturm, Die Zerstorung des Kunstwerks* (Munich, 1973), especially Warnke's essay, "Durchgebrochene Geschichte? Die Bildersturme der Wiedertaufer in Munster 1534/1535," pp. 65–98. Julius von Vegh's *Die Bildersturmer* (Gutersloh, 1977) is an ecumenically minded theological analysis that, in trying to gloss over significant differences between the Reformers, says very little about the role of iconoclasm in the Reformation. The best synthetic study available is that of Carl C. Christensen, *Art and the Reformation in Germany* (Athens, Ohio, 1980). Christensen provides different examples of iconoclasm in Germany and Switzerland, and analyzes some of its broader implications for the history of the Reformation, but he is more concerned with the cultural aspects of the problem than with the theological, social, or political.

Merle D'Aubigné's *History of the Reformation,* for instance, describes the spread of Protestantism in Switzerland largely through a narrative of iconoclastic acts[2]; and in doing so, he only follows the lead established in the sixteenth century by chroniclers such as Johannes Stumpf and Jeanne de Jussie.[3] Although these polemical histories generally lack precision, depth, and objectivity, they sometimes offer a perceptive understanding of revealing patterns.

Iconoclasm is a phenomenon that allows us to analyze the process of the Reformation as do few other aspects of that age. It is not only the most visible change brought about by the religious crisis of the sixteenth century, but also one of the most radical and "democratic."[4] Even though there were different types of iconoclasm and various reasons for its occurrence, it is still safe to say that the destruction of Catholic cultic objects was perhaps the most intense popular expression of the revolt against Rome. D'Aubigné was not too far off target when he observed that "in the times of the Reformation, the doctors attacked the Pope and the people the images."[5] The complete destruction of the Catholic cult within a community was, in a very real sense, the triumph of the Reformation – a victory accomplished most often through popular participation in various types of iconoclasm.[6]

It is my intention in this chapter to present an analysis of iconoclasm in Switzerland and to explain how it served as one of the most important tactics in the process of religious change in some communities.[7]

By 1535 iconoclasm had become commonplace in Switzerland. In fact, the spread of Protestantism throughout the northern cantons

---

[2] J. H. Merle D'Aubigné, *History of the Great Reformation of the Sixteenth Century* (New York, 1846).

[3] *Johannes Stumpfs Schweizer- und Reformationschronik,* E. Gagliardi, H. Muller and F. Busser, eds. Quellen zur Schweizer Geschichte. Neue Folge. I Abteilung, vols. 5 and 6 (Basel, 1955).

[4] Friedrich Fischer observed in 1850: "Die Bildersturm sind meist von demokratischen Bewegungen, welche die Einfuhrung der Reformation gegen widerstrebende Regierungen zum Zwecke hatten, ausgegangen, oder von Obrigkeiten aus Nachgiebigkeit und Klugheit, um solchen zuworzukommen, angeordnet worden." "Der Bildersturm in der Schweiz und in Basel Inbesondere," *Basler Taschebuch,* vol. I (1850), p. 4.

[5] D'Aubigné, *History,* p. 767.

[6] Kurt Guggisberg, *Bernische Kirchengeschichte* (Bern, 1958), p. 133.

[7] I make no attempt here to provide a complete narrative history of Swiss iconoclasm, or to catalog and identify all iconoclastic acts. My research is based on published archival records and contemporary chronicles: Its orientation is synthetic and analytical rather than statistical.

can easily be traced through iconoclasm, for it was the destruction of images and cultic objects that sealed the triumph of the Reformation in this area. The pattern was established by Zurich, which was the first city to "cleanse" its churches in 1524. From there, the phenomenon spread in waves to smaller communities under its jurisdiction, and, in turn, to other major cities and their territories: Bern and St. Gall followed suit in 1528, Basel and Schaffhausen in 1529, Neuchâtel in 1530, and Geneva and Lausanne in 1535. In some places the iconoclasm was legal and orderly, in others unlawful and disorderly; some instances were isolated acts by one individual, others were full-scale urban riots.

It is my contention that iconoclasm, though varied, very often assumed a definite place in the pattern of Reformation: the destruction of sacred objects was used by Protestants as a way of publicly testing the legality of the Roman Catholic cultus, and, eventually, of proving that images and the Mass should be abolished and replaced by a new, "purified" religion.

Why focus on Switzerland? There are three reasons. The first is that Switzerland produced the most influential iconoclastic theology – that of Ulrich Zwingli. The second is that Switzerland was the first area where iconoclasm became a consistent policy, an established pattern of the "Protestantization" of cities. The third is that the republican structures of Swiss towns permitted a more intense participation of the populace in the process of Reformation, allowing for the use of iconoclasm as a political revolutionary tactic. This is not to say that Germany has little to offer, but rather that the sources are richer in Switzerland. In the first place, Luther's moderate position on cultic objects made the territorial Lutheran churches much less disposed towards iconoclasm than the Swiss.[8] Secondly, German iconoclasm was most prevalent in the south, where it derived principally from Zwinglian theology (which filtered in either directly from Switzerland or indirectly from Strassburg).[9] For these reasons, then, I

---

[8] Nonetheless, some Lutherans still struck out at the images. In the northern cities of Stralsund and Braunschweig, for instance, iconoclasm occurred in 1525 and 1526. On Stralsund: Alfred Uckeley, "Der Werdegang der Kirchlichen Reformbewegung im Anfang des 16. Jahrhunderts in der Stadtgemeinden Pommerns," *Pommersche Jahrbucher*, XVIII: 1–108 (1917), esp. pp. 66–73; and Johannes Schildhauser, "Der Stralsunder Kirchensturm des Jahres 1525," *Wissenschaftliche Zeitschrift der Ernst Moritz Arndt-Universität Greifswald*, vol. VII (1958/1959), pp. 113–19. On Braunschweig: Carl G. H. Lentz, *Braunschweigs Kirchenreformation im Sechszehnten Jahrhunderts* (Wolfenbütel/Leipzig, 1828), pp. 91, 95, 102–5.
[9] Two good examples of South German towns influenced by Reformed ideology are Nuremberg and Ulm. On Nuremberg: Carl C. Christensen, "Iconoclasm and the

shall focus on iconoclastic developments in Switzerland, to see what patterns emerge and to provide a working theory of the role played by iconoclasm in the Protestant attack on Catholic piety during the 1520s and 1530s.

BERN

The first major Swiss city to follow the iconoclastic policy of Zurich was Bern, where the Reformation had been making advances since the early 1520s. Iconoclastic sentiment had already been expressed by the evangelical community there, but not overtly. As early as 1518, for instance, the Bernese painter, playwright and pamphleteer Nicholas Manuel had painted a mural entitled *Solomons Götzendiest* (*Solomon's Idolatry*) in which he called attention to the scriptural prohibition of images.[10] Nonetheless, the Reformation moved relatively slowly in Bern until 1527, when new elections placed a Protestant majority in the Great Council.

Despite the efforts of Berthold Haller, Franz Kolb, and Nicholas Manuel, the Bernese government had been vigorously opposed to the permanent removal of the Catholic cult from the city. No iconoclasm occurred during the early and middle twenties, but the tension between Protestants and Catholics increased within the city as Protes-

Preservation of Ecclesiastical Art in Reformation Nuremberg," *ARG* 61: 105–221 (1970). On Ulm: J. Endriss, *Das Ulmer Reformationsjahr 1531* (Ulm, 1931); and F. Fritz, *Ulmischer Kirchengeschichte 1548–1612* (Ulm, 1934). A more general study of Protestantism in South Germany is that of H. Waldenmaier, *Die Entstehung der Evangelischen Gottesdienstordnungen Suddeutschlands im Zeitalter der Reformation* (Nuremberg, 1916). Reformed influence also caused iconoclasm in the Palatinate later in the sixteenth century. For a study of this development see H. Rott, "Kirchen- und Bildersturm bei der Einführung der Reformation in der Pfalz," *Neues Archiv für die Geschichte der Stadt Heidelberg* 6: 229–54 (1903); and W. Seeling, "Die Sogennante Calvinismus in der Pfalz: Versuch einer Klärung," *Bulletin für Pfalzische Kirchengeschichte*, 37/38: 267–74 (1970/71).

10 Kurt Guggisberg, *Bernische Kirchengeschichte* (Bern, 1958), p. 55. Nicholas Manuel was one of the greatest humorists of the Reformation, and a leading gadfly in Bern. His plays and songs ridiculed all aspects of Catholic piety, theology and ecclesiology. His dramatic poem *Die Totenfresser*, which was performed in Bern during Lent in 1523, was a uniquely perceptive indictment of Catholic concern with the plight of the dead and of the corrupt system it had engendered. For an analysis of Manuel's work see S. Ozment, *Reformation in the Cities*, pp. 111–16 . The text of *Die Totenfresser* itself can be found in *Niklaus Manuel, Schriften*, J. Bächtold and S. Vögelin, eds., in *Bibliothek Älterer Schriftwerke der Deutschen Shweiz*, II (Frauenfeld, 1878). Manuel wrote another biting dramatic satire in 1525, *Die Ablasskrämer*. In 1523–24 he had also participated in the design of a cathedral pew in which Moses was depicted pointing to the second commandment. For more on the life of Manuel consult C. A. Beerli, *Le Peintre Nicolas Manuel et l'Evolution Sociale de Son Temps* (Geneva 1953); and C. von Mandach, *Niklaus Manuel Deutsch* (Basel 1941).

tantism began to gain political strength in the latter part of the decade. By late 1527, six of the city guilds had abolished Masses,
anniversaries and prebends in their district churches, and three other
guilds had voted in favor of the Reformation, but without abolishing
the Catholic cult in their churches.[11] The remaining eight guilds were
sharply divided, except for the butchers, who appear to have been
the strongest supporters of the old faith.[12]

In the meantime, Nicholas Manuel continued using his talents to
oppose religious art. About this time he completed a suggestive glass
etching entitled *König Josias zerstürmert die Götzenbilder*, in which he
depicted King Josiah directing the destruction of idols.[13] This sketch
captures the spirit of Swiss iconoclasm, since it points to a scriptural
inspiration and represents the ideal policy sought by those who opposed the images. Staff in hand, and surrounded by religious and
civil officials, King Josiah stands authoritatively as a workman swings
an axe against a pyre of burning idols. The etching is a celebration of
government-directed iconoclasm, but it also shows one of the common people doing the actual work of destruction.

Around the same time, Manuel also penned a short satire in verse
entitled "The Complaint of the Poor Persecuted Idols," in which he
sought to place the blame for idolatry on men rather than on the
images. It was man's folly, said Manuel, that had turned the images
into gods:

> For need of fire and of water,
> For every fear and every impropriety,
> For every illness above all,
> Does man kiss us without limit.
> Man comes to us with great devotion,
> Travelling over land and ocean,
> And worshiping us as deities,
> In derison of the true God.[14]

---

[11] The guilds voting for the Reformation were those of the tanners, smiths, tailors,
shoemakers, weavers, merchants, bakers, stonemasons, and carpenters. Letter of B.
Haller to Zwingli, 4 November 1527, cited by D'Aubigné, *History*, p. 754.

[12] Ibid.

[13] Beerli, *Nicolas Manuel*, plate XXVIII. The text above the sketch reads: "Josiah der
kung zuo Jerusalemm dett, das demm Herrenn wol gfiel, der ab die altär der abgötter, verbrannt sy, zerstört die höchinen, veget uss alle warsager unnd zeichendüt-
ter, billder unnd götten, mitt für, und druog den Stoub in den bach Kidron, am
andern buch der kunig am XXIII cap." The narratives of II Kings 22–3 and II Chronicles 33–4 tell of the religious reforms of Josiah, King of Judah (640–609 B.C.) who
tried to wipe out all the aspects of gentile worship that had gradually crept into
Judaism. Josiah is the principal scriptural model of the iconoclast.

[14] "Klagrede der armen verfolgten Götzen und Tempelbilder/über so ungleich urtayl

Manuel warned that the physical removal of the idols was not enough. The greater part of the satire is devoted to preaching that one must also chase other idols from one's heart, such as drunkenness, lechery, and gluttony. This highly moralistic work was illustrated by an Ernst Schön woodcut depicting the removal of images from a church.[15]

In order to put an end to dissension and prevent violence, the Bernese government followed the example of Zurich and called for a public disputation in November of 1527. The Bern Disputation began on 6 January 1528 and lasted for twenty days.[16] Among the ten points discussed were the merits of Christ, church tradition, transsubstantiation, celibacy, the Mass, prayers to the saints, and the cult of images. Before the disputation had ended, it seemed as if the Catholics had already lost the contest. On 22 January, two days after the issue of the Mass had been discussed, attendance at Mass in the city was very low. That same evening, after the cathedral organist had finished playing, a group of men pulled down the organ and destroyed it. About the same time, an altar in the Franciscan church was vandalized.[17] These incidents, though not responsible for the outcome of the Disputation, reflect the same impatience that had been earlier displayed at Wittenberg and Zurich. The people were beginning to take upon themselves what had not yet been approved by the government.

The Disputation was a triumph for the Reformers. Immediately afterwards the Bernese council ordered all images and altars to be removed within eight days. Although this flexible schedule was intended to prevent rioting, it had the reverse effect, letting loose the fury that had simmered among the Protestants for several years. On 27 and 28 January 1528, the images and altars of the cathedral were destroyed by a mob. This riot caused no injuries or deaths, but it did produce some tense confrontations. Peter Thorman, a butcher, threatened to kill anyone who tried to tear down his guild's altar. He also complained that the stripped cathedral now looked like a stable and was only fit to store cattle on the way to market. As if to prove

---

und straffe." Reproduced by Max Geisberg, *Die Reformation im Einblatt Holzschnitt* (Munich, 1929–30) vol. XXVI, p. 27. Also available in a new edition: Max Geisberg, *The German Single-Leaf Woodcut: 1500–1550* (4 vols., New York, 1974), vol. III, p. 1092. Some scholars dispute the authorship of this document. C. A. Beerli (ed.) *Nicholas Manuel, Ecrits Satiriques* (Lausanne, 1947), p. 127.

[15] Roland Bainton, *Here I Stand* (New York, 1950), p. 207.
[16] The text of the Bern Disputation is available in *Zw* II (pt. I), 63–205.
[17] Friedrich Fischer, "Der Bildersturm," *Basler Taschenbuch* vol. I (1850), p. 9.

Thorman's point, one of the council members, Johannes Zehender, rode into the cathedral on an ass, and began to heap insults on the iconoclasts, who were still busily engaged in their task. A Protestant turned to Zehender and defended himself by saying: "It is God's will that the images have been pulled down." In response, Zehender huffed, "Say rather by the devil's. When have you ever been with God so as to learn his will?"[18] This incident – which cost Zehender his post on the council and a fine of twenty gulden – captures in one brief scene the essence of the conflict between Catholics and Protestants in regard to cultic objects.

As the iconoclasts continued their destruction, some children celebrated the Protestant victory by singing in the streets: "We have been freed from a baked god," meaning, of course, that the "idol" of the consecrated host had also been overthrown.[19] Nicholas Manuel enlivened the celebration with a new satirical play in which the fatally ill Mass tries to find a cure, but finally dies, leaving its so-called *idolotramenta* to posterity.[20]

The removal of images in Bern was a legal act, but it had turned into a popular act of rebellion against the cultic objects of medieval piety. On the second day of the rioting, Zwingli declared the triumph of the Reformation in an emotional sermon at the cathedral. Walking past the rubble of generations of piety, Zwingli mounted the pulpit and exclaimed, "Victory has declared for the truth." Directing the attention of the congregation to the broken remains of the images and altars, Zwingli continued his paean over the idols:

There you have the altars and idols of the temple! . . . Now there is no more debating whether we should have these idols or not. Let us clear out this filth and rubbish! Henceforth, let us devote to other men, the living images of God, all the unimaginable wealth which was once spent on these foolish idols. There are still many weak and quarrelsome people who complain about the removal of the idols, even though it is clearly evident that there is nothing holy about them, and that they break and crack like any other piece of wood or stone. Here lies one without its head! Here another without its arms! If this abuse had done any harm to the saints who are near God, and if they had the

---

[18] *Aktensammlung zur Geschichte der Berner Reformation 1521–1532*, R. Steck and G. Tobler, eds. (Bern, 1923), vol. I, pp. 612–13.

[19] Martin Luther, WA, *Briefwechsel* 4.404, no. 1236. Letter to Gabriel Zwilling (7 March 1528). Luther reports on the closing of the Bern Disputation: "Bernae in Helvetiis finita disputatio est; nihil factum nisi quod Missa abrogata, et pueri in plateis cantant, se esse a Deo pisto liberato."

[20] *Von Krankheyt der Messe* and *Von Testament der Messe*, both written and published in 1528. Text in Bächtold and Vögelin, *Schriften*.

power which is ascribed to them, do you think you would have been able to behead and cripple them as you did? . . . Now, then, recognize the freedom which Christ has given you, stand fast in it, and, as Paul says in Galatians [5:1], 'be not entangled again with the yoke of bondage.'[21]

The powerless "idols" of Rome had been overthrown, and their very destruction was sufficient proof of their falsehood; the wealth lavished on them was now to be given to the poor; the people were finally free from the yoke of "false" religion. Zwingli's sermon, like the confrontation between Zehender and the iconoclast in the cathedral, and like Manuel's "Josiah," encapsulates the spirit of Swiss iconoclasm.

THE SPREAD OF ICONOCLASM

The triumph of the Reformation in the city of Bern had a deep effect on some of the neighboring communities. In other towns of the canton of Bern (Auberg, Zofingen, Brugg, Arau, and Buren), churches were invaded by mobs and the images destroyed with enthusiasm. Heinrich Bullinger reports that at the village of Lentzburg auf dem Stouffberg, the activity of one man in particular was so frenzied that it earned him the nickname of "Idol-shearer ["Gotz-scherer"]. The name was not entirely inappropriate because he was a shearer by profession, but it gave rise to a confusing story. Because this "Idol-shearer" had thrown many images into the fire, it was reported that at Lentzburg "idols were seen carrying idols and throwing one another in the flames."[22] Whether or not the tale was believed is irrelevant (since Protestants had stopped believing in the power of images, it is not likely that the story was taken seriously). The tale is significant because it evokes a vivid picture of the fury with which the images were destroyed.

Other cantons soon began to follow the example of Bern, and the first of these was St. Gall. Upon returning home from the Bern Disputation, Joachim von Watt (Vadianus), burgomaster of St. Gall, pressed for the removal of the images. On 23 and 24 February 1528, less than one month after the iconoclastic riot of Bern, the government of St. Gall ordered the abolition of the images. With the approval of the magistracy and under the leadership of Vadianus, the

[21] ZW 6/1.497–8.
[22] J. J. Hottinger and H. H. Vögeli (eds.), *Bullingers Reformationsgeschichte* (2 vols., Frauenfeld, 1838–40), vol. II, p. 1: "Wenn Götz scherer ein götzen in das fhüwr trüg und warf . . . ward ein gemeine sag darus, zü Lentzburg hätte ein götz dem anderen in das fhüwr getragen und verbrent."

people of St. Gall stormed the cathedral and the other churches in town to wage war on the idols. From the cathedral alone forty-six wagons full of rubble were carted to the Bruhl square to be burnt.[23] The more valuable items were melted down, and some of this wealth was distributed among the poor, while the rest was deposited in the town treasury.[24] At the cloister church of St. Mang, the previously revered bodies of Saints Wiborad and Rachild were dug up, as was the arm of St. Mang, but the "bodies" and the "arm" were never found. What had stood in their place all those years was a cache of wooden images, some rags, a skull, a large tooth, and a snail's shell.[25] The people of St. Gall then rejoiced over this unmasking of the deception of the old cult.

The legal, but somewhat disorderly iconoclasm of Bern and St. Gall was carried out by a substantial part of the citizenry. In other communities where the magistracy was less willing to cast down the images, or where there was stronger Catholic opposition, iconoclasm was accomplished by the illegal and sometimes violent actions of a few individuals. Zwingli reports that at Toggenburg, on 13 and 14 September 1528, some youths marched into the cathedral of St. John during vespers. The young Protestants interrupted the service by singing a roguish song and by overturning the tabernacle containing the consecrated hosts. On the next day, some more youths returned to the cathedral to destroy the altars and images.[26] At Wesen, a town that lay under the shared jurisdiction of the Catholic canton of Schwyz and the Protestant canton of Glarus, the Protestants chose to defy the government of Schwyz. A group of young men removed the images from the churches and piled them up outside, in the presence of some Catholic deputies from Schwyz. As the deputies looked on, the iconoclasts mocked the images, telling them they had better walk away if they wanted to escape the flames; then they set them on fire.[27]

---

[23] F. Fischer, "Bildersturm," p. 10ff.

[24] The charitable impulse of the iconoclasts was a strong driving force. In Bern, for instance, so much wealth was distributed to the poor that the town treasury received very little from the church spoils, if anything at all. When the council sought to pay the annuities of the former monks and nuns, it had to borrow the money. Haller confided in Zwingli that for eight days there was not a single crown in the Bernese treasury (ZW 10.415).

[25] Fischer, "Bildersturm," p. 13. Also: D'Aubigné, *History*, p. 766.

[26] A heated dispute erupted between Schwytz and Glarus as a result of this incident. Zwingli describes this episode and its consequences in detail (ZW 6/2.272–8), as does John Stumpf, *Schweizer- und Reformationschronik*, vol. II, pp. 8–9.

[27] Stumpf, *Reformationschronik*, vol. II, p. 25.

Protestant efforts were sometimes resisted with violence. At the village of Schwanden, for instance, a Catholic mob interrupted the Protestant service and destroyed the stoves and windows of the Protestant pastor's house. His congregation retaliated by breaking the images in the town church.[28] At Aeschi, when the Protestants tried to destroy the images, a contingent of armed women staved off the would-be iconoclasts, and even forced the Protestant preacher to flee the church.[29]

At Schaffhausen, the process of iconoclasm shows not only how the citizenry sometimes tried to force the government to remove the images, but also how external political pressure could help accomplish the task. Sebastian Hoffman, preacher at Schaffhausen, had attended the Second Zurich Disputation in 1524. After returning home, he, Erasmus Ritter, and Sebastian Hoffmeister began to press for the removal of the images. The magistracy was overwhelmingly Catholic, however, and refused to grant their requests. Sporadic illegal acts of iconoclasm began to occur, but the perpetrators were swiftly punished. In an effort to force the magistracy to accede to their wishes, many citizens and the entire guild of vinedressers refused to swear allegiance to their government on the day appointed for that purpose in 1525, saying that they would withhold their pledge until the images were removed. At first it seemed as if the Protestant ploy had worked. The council ruled in favor of the protesters and proclaimed that the images would be removed in the near future. Before any action could be taken, however, armed agents of the council overpowered the protesters and prevented them from removing the images.[30] The Schaffhausen revolt was crushed, but the Catholic victory was only temporary. Four years later, in the Autumn of 1529, the Schaffhausen magistracy finally gave in to demands from Zurich and Bern, and ordered that the images be taken out of the churches in an orderly fashion.[31] Although the popular revolt had failed, the passage of time and the political pressure of Bern and Zurich finally prevailed in favor of the Reformation.

BASEL

The next major Swiss city to wage war on the idols was the great cultural center of Basel, home of Erasmus and Oecolampadius.[32] By

---

[28] D'Aubigné, *History*, p. 766.
[29] Guggisberg, *Bernische Kirchengeschichte*, p. 134.
[30] Lewis Mayer, *History of the German Reformed Church* (Philadelphia 1851), pp. 407–14.
[31] Guggisberg, *Bernische Kirchengeschichte*, p. 141. Appropriately enough, Nicholas Manuel served as the leader of the Bernese delegation.
[32] The history of the Reformation in Basel is richly documented. Primary source mate-

1528, Protestants had been preaching for about five years, but the efforts of the Reformed party could not effect a legal decision on the abolition of the old cult for the entire city. The city council, in Oecolampadius' words, tried to "sit on two stools," allowing religious pluralism in the city, but not deciding for either the Catholics or the Protestants.[33] In an age not given to religious toleration, such an arrangement was doomed from the start. Perhaps it is fitting that Erasmus, who had himself also been accused of sitting on two stools, should have lived in Basel at this time.

Sporadic acts of iconoclasm began to plague the city in 1525, and by 1528 religious tension had reached fever pitch.[34] The Protestants, heartened by the success of the Reformation at Bern, clamored for the abolition of the Mass and the removal of images, but the Basel magistrates continued their moderate policy. As had happened before at Wittenberg, Zurich and Bern, some of the citizens decided to ignore the proscriptions of the stalling magistracy. On 10 April 1528, a group of men from the carpenters' and masons' guild entered the church of St. Martin (where Oecolampadius preached and the Mass had already been abolished), and removed all the images.[35] Three days later the same scene was repeated at the Augustinian church, but the iconoclasts were arrested and questioned. One of them defended himself by saying that what they had done was intended "for the honor of God and the edification of their neighbors."[36] The men were imprisoned for their crime, but were soon released at the insistance of their fellow guild members.[37]

---

rial can be found in the detailed *Aktensammlung zur Geschichte der Basler Reformation,* E. Durr and P. Roth, eds., esp. vol. III (Basel 1937). The iconoclastic riot is described by Erasmus: Allen VIII, 161ff.; Oecolampadius, *Briefe und Akten zum Leben Oekolampads,* E. Stahelin, ed. (Leipzig, 1934), vol. II, pp. 280–2. Other eyewitness accounts are those of Johann Stolz in *Quellenbuch zur Schweizergeschichte,* W. Oechsli, ed. (Zurich, 1918), pp. 330–1; Niklaus Rippel in *Basler Taschenbuch,* 1: 17–37 (1850); and Frydolin Ryff in *Basler Taschenbuch,* 6/7: 193–6 (1855). Secondary histories are also plentiful. Among the best are those of P. Roth, *Durchbruch und Festsetzung der Reformation in Basel* (Basel, 1942); R. Wackernagel, *Geschichte der Stadt Basel* (Basel, 1916); and Friedrich Fischer, "Der Bildersturm in der Schweiz und in Basel Insbesondere," *Basler Taschenbuch,* 1: 3–16 (1850). More recently, Hans R. Guggisberg has provided us with a good, analytical sketch in *Basel in the Sixteenth Century: Aspects of the City Republic before, during and after the Reformation* (St. Louis: Center for Reformation Research, 1982).

33 ZW 9.414: "Vereorque ne dum semper utraque sella sedere velit, utraque extrudatur aliquando."

34 For a good narrative of the history of iconoclasm in Basel see Christensen, *Art and the Reformation,* pp. 93–102.

35 Durr and Roth, *Aktensammlung,* vol. 3, p. 65; Wackernagel, *Geschichte,* p. 496.

36 Christensen, *Art and the Reformation,* p. 96

37 Durr and Roth, *Aktensammlung,* vol. 3, p. 66.

To prevent further disturbances and appease the Protestants, the council also granted permission for the removal of images from the five Reformed churches of Basel. This measure pleased the Protestants, but only as an intermediate step. The magistracy continued to be assailed with requests for the abolition of the Catholic cult throughout the entire city, and the Reformed churches – now cleared of "idols" – rang with sermons calling for the removal of the other idols that still "polluted" the city, especially those in the cathedral.[38]

As the religious settlement remained stalled at Basel, citizen involvement in the process of Reformation began to increase. On 23 December 1528, several hundred guildsmen met at the gardeners' guild hall and drew up a petition calling on the council to arrange a public debate on the question of the cult, so that the city might finally be rid from "public profanation."[39] As the council deliberated, a riot erupted on Christmas night, and although the trouble soon subsided, the city was left on the brink of civil war.

In early January, the council decreed that the Mass was to be celebrated only in three churches, and announced that a debate would be held in June.[40] This announcement was not well received by either side, however. The Catholics were angered by the concessions it made to the Protestants, and the Protestants were disappointed by its dilatory spirit. As both sides continued to pressure the council, which was itself divided on the religious issue, armed bands began to roam the streets of Basel, with those of one side nervously watching the movements of the other. Serious rioting was somehow avoided for a month, but in early February, violence finally erupted. On 8 February 1529, a large crowd approached the town hall and petitioned the council to abolish the Mass, remove the idols, reform the city's political constitution, and dismiss twelve of its most fanatically Catholic members.[41] Since the Catholic core in the inner council was composed of high officers in the four merchant guilds,[42] the revolt may be seen as directed not only against the Catholic church and the Basel magistracy, but also against the leaders of the guild structure. Images and the Mass served as the focus of a wide-ranging feeling of discon-

---

[38] Ibid., pp. 67–9 (removal of images); Bullinger, *Reformationsgeschichte*, vol. II, p. 36 (sermons).

[39] Durr and Roth, *Aktensammlung*, vol. 3, p. 197ff. This petition was supported by all the guilds except for the bread-bakers, the smiths, and the sailors and fishermen (P. Roth, *Durchbruch*, pp. 12–14). As Gordon Rupp has observed, this is "a nice problem for the Marxist historian." *Patterns of Reformation* (Philadelphia, 1969), p. 36.

[40] Durr and Roth, *Aktensammlung*, vol. 3 p. 234ff.

[41] Ibid., p. 268.

[42] G. Rupp, *Patterns*, p. 31.

tent in Basel: in clamoring for the removal of the old cult, the citizens of Basel also asked for a transformation of the oligarchical structure that had so far prevented them from having their Reformation.

The council was hastily called that morning and deliberations continued throughout the entire day, as an anxious crowd awaited its answer outside. Night approached, and no decision had yet been reached. Some in the crowd, fearing that the council might be preparing a plot to overpower the protesters, began to spread rumors about the council's apparent duplicity. Many men took up arms, guards were placed in front of all the guild halls, and chains were stretched across the streets leading to the town hall.[43] Throughout the night Basel remained in an internal state of siege.

On the next morning, 9 February, the council met again while thousands congregated outside. As one of the armed patrols roaming the city passed near the cathedral, one of the men in the group opened a door to a room in which many images had been hidden, and one image fell out, breaking into many pieces as it hit the ground. With the opening of that door, to paraphrase Erasmus, the torrent hidden underground for so long burst forth with violence "to commit frightful ravages."[44] The broken image inspired the men to storm the room and destroy everything in it. Soon afterwards, another contingent of three hundred men joined the iconoclasts, and together marched to the cathedral, where they broke down the doors and began smashing every cultic object in sight.[45]

As the destruction was being carried out, the magistrates entered the cathedral and unsuccessfully tried to stop the rioting. In a tense confrontation that summarized the spirit of Basel's iconoclastic revolt, the assembled mob told the magistrates: "All that you failed to effect in three years of deliberation we have completed within this hour."[46] The rubble from the cathedral was taken outside to the surrounding squares, where it fueled several bonfires around which the armed burghers warmed themselves.[47]

The riot in the cathedral was only the beginning of the destruction. The four remaining Catholic churches were also sacked. In the

---

[43] Stahelin (ed.), *Briefe und Akten*, vol. 2, p. 280: Letter of Oecolampadius to Wolfgang Capito, 13 February 1529.

[44] Allen VIII, 231: "Basilica torrens quidem, qui sub terra labebatur subito errumpens" (to Willibald Pirckheimer, July 1529).

[45] Christensen, *Art and the Reformation*, pp. 100–1.

[46] Stahelin, *Briefe und Akten*, vol. 2, p. 281: "Vos intra triennium deliberando nihil effecistis; nos intra horam hec omnia absolvemus."

[47] Zurich manuscript, cited by D'Aubigné, *History*, p. 771. "Lignis imaginum usi sunt vigiles, pro arcendo frigore nocturno."

staunchly Catholic quarter of Klein Basel, the Protestant mob intimidated the Catholics into doing their work for them. As the iconoclasts approached the Klein Basel church, the Catholics pleaded that their images be spared. The Protestants naturally refused, but allowed the Catholics to clear the church without doing damage.[48]

To complete the revolt, the iconoclasts marched over to the town hall and demanded that the magistrates finally consent to what was being done. The power of the city government had been vanquished by them. Faced with a fait accompli, the council had no choice but to accede to the demands of the mob. The twelve Catholic magistrates resigned, the Mass and images were legally abolished, and concessions were made to the guilds concerning their future role in the governing of Basel. Among the concessions, the most significant stated that henceforth the burghers were to participate in the election of the two councils and that any future deliberations concerning "the glory of God or the good of the state" would require the opinion of the guilds. Nowhere else had iconoclasm been used so effectively to bring about change. The power of Rome and that of the established oligarchy had been simultaneously swept away along with the images.[49]

Now that the Reformation was established, the people completed their war on the idols. On 10 February, Ash Wednesday, the destruction of cultic objects continued. As had been done in other cities, it was decided to distribute the spoil from the ravaged churches to the poor. Unburned wood was allocated to the needy and precious metals were reserved for charitable purposes. However, since the revolt in Basel had been so disorderly, the intentions of the iconoclasts could not be efficiently carried out. Those who came to claim the shattered images as firewood soon began to fight over the spoils. To prevent further trouble, the distribution was called off; the debris was piled up, and burnt in a public square. Thus, quipped Oecolampadius, were the idols reduced to ashes on Ash Wednesday.[50] The

---

[48] Erasmus reports a very thorough destruction in the city: "Statuarum nihil relictum est, nec in templis nec in vestibulis nec in porticibus nec in monasteriis. Quidquid erat capax ignis, in rogum coniectum est; quod secus, frustulatim comminutum. Nec pretium nec ars impetravit ut cuiquam omnino parceretur" (Allen VIII, 162). See also D'Aubigné, *History*, p. 771.

[49] Durr and Roth, *Aktensammlung* vol. 3, p. 286: "zu lob der eren gottes unnd nutz eins cristenlichen burgerlichen wesenns." The political gains made by the guilds were gradually reversed over the next few years, however, so that by 1533 the city had once again reverted to an oligarchic government. Guggisberg, *Basel in the Sixteenth Century*, pp. 30–1.

[50] Stahelin, *Briefe und Akten* vol. 2, p. 282: "In die cinerum, quum idola secta distribui

Catholics, griefstricken at the sight of the iconoclastic ravages, shed "tears of blood" over this "saddest of all spectacles of superstition." "Thus did they severely treat the idols, and the Mass died of grief in consequence."[51] The hesitation of the Basel magistracy had been a "hard knot" to untangle, but iconoclasm, "the wedge of the Lord," had finally split this hard knot.[52]

NEUCHÂTEL

The German-speaking cantons were not the only part of the Alpine region to be affected by the Reformation in the late 1520s. Among those who attended the Bern Disputation was a young refugee from France who had energetically pursued the cause of the Gospel for several years. He was Guillaume Farel, and it was he who would be responsible for spreading the Reformation into the French-speaking Pays Romand under the direction of the Bernese magistracy. Farel's itinerant preaching through Aigle, Morat, Lausanne, Neuveville, and Tavannes, which began in 1526, has been perceptively described by Gordon Rupp: "This explosive person reverberated like an interminable jumping cracker as he bounced among the cities in the next months, in an aura of theological sparks and smoke."[53] The sparks might have been provided by Farel, but the smoke came most often from the images in the churches. Farel left behind him a trail of controversy and iconoclasm that was to reach its first peak during his stay at Neuchâtel from December 1529 to November 1530.[54]

Farel's work at Neuchâtel followed the pattern already established in the German cantons, and he used the images and the Mass as a focus for the process of Reformation. After his arrival in Neuchâtel, Farel quickly obtained a large following. Presaging the pattern that was later to be followed in Geneva, the growing Protestant faction first took action on 8 August 1530, when several youths posted

---

inciperent pauperibus, quidam importunius illa petebant, ita ut vulnerant se mutuum. Ea-propter visum est nostris, ut idola omnia in cineres redigantur illo ipso die cinerum. Accense igitur sunt pyre novem in campo monasterii."
51 Ibid.: "Tristissimum supertitiosis spectaculum! Et ita severitum est in idola, ac missa per dolore expiravit."
52 Ibid., p. 280: "Malo nudo suus [Domini] cuneus obvenit."
53 G. Rupp, *Patterns*, p. 21. The best work available on Guillaume Farel is the cooperatively produced biography of the Comité Farel, *Guillaume Farel 1489–1565* (Neuchâtel/Paris, 1930).
54 R. Centlivres and O. Strasser, in *Guillaume Farel:* "La première conquête de la Réforme en Pays Romand," pp. 171–90; R. Gerber, C. Simon and C. Simon, Jr., "Farel dans le Sud de l'Evêché de Bâle à la Fin de 1529 et en 1530," pp. 191–205; and J. Pétremand, "L'Apparition de Farel en Terre Neuchâteloise" pp. 206–58.

placards throughout the city bearing the inscription, "All those who say Mass are robbers, murderers, deniers of the passion of Jesus Christ and seducers of the people."[55] In addition, the placards called for a public disputation. Farel was hauled before the magistrates, but he defended himself on scriptural grounds and the court was unable to pronounce sentence on him.[56]

The Reformation had scored its first triumph in Neuchâtel. Now free, Farel continued to preach against Rome. On Sunday, 23 October, the Protestants decided to bring the religious crisis to an end through an act of disobedience. Farel, who had heretofore been banned from preaching in any of the churches, was literally carried by his congregation to the Eglise Collégiale, where he preached a fiery sermon denouncing images as evil and dangerous. The sermon made a deep impression on the congregation, and some began to murmur:

> If we take away these idols from before our eyes, will it not be aiding us in taking them from our hearts? Once these idols are broken, how many souls among our fellow citizens, now disturbed and hesitating, will be decided by this striking manifestation of the truth! We must save them as it were by fire.[57]

Karlstadt's metaphor of the child who needs to have a knife taken away from him so he will not hurt himself is now brought to life by the Neuchâtel evangelicals. Convinced that by taking the law into their own hands and removing the images they would benefit their community, the assembled crowd turned upon the images and began to smash them to pieces.[58]

That same day, by coincidence, the soldiers from Neuchâtel who had been assisting the Bernese against Savoy in Geneva returned home. These soldiers were full of tales about the iconoclastic activities of the Bernese troops quartered in Geneva.[59] This could only have served to incite further violence in Neuchâtel. On the following day, 24 October, a large crowd armed with pikes, axes, and hammers

---

[55] Ibid., p. 222: "Tous ceux qui dissent la Messe d'être méchants, meurtriers, larrons, renieurs de la passion de Jésus-Christ et séducteurs du peuple."

[56] Ibid., p. 223.

[57] Choupart manuscript, cited by D'Aubigné, *History*, p. 781.

[58] *Guillaume Farel*, p. 226. Herminjard 2.202, no. 317: Georges de Rive to the Countess of Neuchâtel: "aucuns bourgeois de la ville de Neufchastel renversèrent certaines images dans vostre église, et les rompirent par pièces . . . et aus tableaus avec instrumens ont coupé les nés aus images et percé les yeux."

[59] Herminjard 2.293. D'Aubigné cites the case of soldiers who boasted about having used the images from the Dominican cloister to keep warm at night, saying "Idols of wood are of no use but to make a fire with in winter" (*History*, p. 777). The iconoclastic ravages of the Bernese troops in Geneva are related in detail in *Levain*, p. 9ff.

marched to the Collégiale to finish the work begun on the previous day[60]: The mob destroyed every cultic object in the church, ransacked the sanctuary, and consumed the consecrated hosts as if they were common bread.[61] To testify to future generations that the Reformation in Neuchâtel has been accomplished by the citizens, not the magistracy, the following was later inscribed on a pillar in the ransacked Collegialle: "L'an 1530, le 23 Octobre, fut otée et abattue l'idolatrie de ceant par les bourgeois."[62]

The immediate result of Neuchâtel's iconoclastic riot was a hastily called general vote on the status of religion in the city. At the instigation of the Bernese ambassadors who had been called to help deal with the iconoclasts, the citizens of Neuchâtel assembled in the Collégiale on 4 November to vote on whether or not to accept the Reformation. By a slim margin of eighteen votes the Reformation was legally ushered into the city.[63] Farel, elated over the success of his war against the idols, would comment three days later on the state of the "purified" Collégiale: "Through the grace of Our Lord we now have a large and handsome place in which to preach; because it is beautiful to see all that has been cleared from the church."[64] The remaining cultic objects of the city were removed and stored in the governor's castle, and the Reformation was also carried to the surrounding countryside.[65] The iconoclasts, aided by Bern, had succeeded in effecting a religious revolution in Neuchâtel. The pattern Geneva would soon follow was now well established.

---

[60] Herminjard 2.293: "aucuns armès de pioches, de haches et de marteaus."
[61] Ibid.: "aucuns . . . vinrent en votre dite église furieusement et abbatirent le crucifix de Nostre Seigneur, l'image de Nostre Dame et Saint Jehan et prirent le paténes où estoit *corpus Domini*, et les jettérent en bas le cimitière et donnèrent à manger les hosties commme simple pain les uns aus autres. Ils ont rompu les autels, sans en laisser un." The perpetrators were described as "jeunes gens de guerre, forts de leur personne, ayant le feu à la tête, remplis de la nouvelle religion et ayant part et faveur des Seigneurs de Berne" (p. 295).
[62] *Guillaume Farel*, p. 226, n. 1.
[63] Herminjard 2.294–7. George de Rive's letter describes the diplomatic maneuvers of Bern and the general vote in detail. He says the Bernese were called "pour aviser à ceste affaire" because their authority over Neuchâtel was more clearly defined than that of Fribourg, Soleure and Lucerne (p. 294). The Bernese pressed for a vote as soon as they arrived: "des dits Seigneurs de Berne n'ont jamais voulu attendre que le peuple fût bien ensemblé, pour voir de quel costé y auroit plus de voix" (p. 294). After the vote was taken, he reports, it was the Bernese who proclaimed that "chacun dût vivre selon le contenu de leur Réformation, et qu'on ne dût point dire de messe" (p. 296).
[64] Cited in *Guillaume Farel*, p. 227: "Par la grâce de Notre Seigneur, nous avons (maintenant pour prêcher) lieu beau et large; car il fait beau voir ce qui a été nettoyé de l'église."
[65] Ibid., p. 230. Also: D'Aubigné, *History*, p. 786.

ICONOCLASM AND THE REFORMATION
IN GENEVA, 1530–6

As we have seen so far, the unfolding of the Reformed Protestant theology of transcendence into the actual creation of a new church and a new society is largely a story about iconoclasm; and it is the word "story" that needs to be stressed here, because it is the *process* of change that concerns us. In telling the story of iconoclasm in Bern, Basel, and Neuchâtel, it is possible to observe how teaching and preaching against medieval piety turned into direct action: how the formulations of theologians were echoed in public debates; how their words were repeated by laymen, or even more significant, how their vision of "true" religion tested the social fabric and led to violent change in the outward expression of piety. Much as time-lapse photography reveals natural processes normally hidden from the eye by breaking a fluid sequence of movements into shorter segments, the narration of details surrounding Swiss iconoclasm helps make visible a social process that is otherwise hard to see.

At this juncture, in order to see more clearly how theologians produced very concrete social changes by promoting iconoclasm, it will be useful to employ this narrative method of analysis with an even greater eye for detail. Few cities provide as good an opportunity for studying the revolutionary dimensions of iconoclasm in this way as does Geneva.

First, one must consider the wealth of materials available. Geneva has preserved not only most of its official documents relating to the Reformation, but also an incredibly rich set of chronicles.[66] The quality, variety and number of documents is such that one can provide an accurate narrative with a reasonable degree of confidence.

The second reason for Geneva's usefulness to the historian is the identity of the individuals involved with its Reformation, most nota-

---

[66] In addition to Jeanne de Jussie's *Levain*, one can consult: Antoine Fromment, *Les Actes et Gestes Merveilleux de la Cité de Genève* (1544), reissued by J. G. Fick (Geneva, 1954); Michel Roset, *Les Chroniques de Genève* (ed. and pub. by H. Fazy, Geneva, 1894); the *Journal du Syndic Balard 1525–1531*, J. J. Chaponnière, ed. (Geneva, 1954); the *Texte Inédit de Savion*, 1529 and 1531–45, thought to be the continuation of Balard's *Journal*, P. F. Geisendorf, ed., in *Les Annalistes Genevois du Début du Dix-septième Siècle* (Geneva, 1942); and the painstakingly edited *Registres du Conseil de Genève* (RC) vols. *12, 13*. In addition, there are numerous excellent histories of Reformation Geneva written by later scholars. Among the most significant: Emile Doumergue, *Jean Calvin, Les Hommes et Choses de son Temps* (Lausanne, 1902), vol. III; J. A. Gautier, *Histoire de Genève*, vols. II, III (Geneva, 1896, 1898); E. William Monter, *Calvin's Geneva* (New York, 1967); H. Naef, *Les Origines de la Réforme à Geneve* (Geneva/Paris, 1936); A. Roget, *Histoire du Peuple de Genève* (Geneva, 1870–87); P. Guichonnet (ed.), *Histoire de Genève* (Toulouse, 1974); and C. Borgeaud, "La Conquête Religieuse de Genève," in *Guillaume Farel*, pp. 298–337.

bly Guillaume Farel and, later, John Calvin. The triumph of Protestantism in Geneva was largely due to the efforts of Farel, who represents the same school of thought in which Calvin was instructed in regard to Catholic worship. As shall be seen in the next chapter, he is an important link between Zwingli (by whom he was definitely influenced)[67] and Calvin in regard to the question of true worship. What Farel said and did in Geneva, therefore, allows the historian to peer into the sources of Calvin's opposition to Catholic piety. Moreover, as the future home of Calvin and citadel of the Reformed faith, Geneva assumes a singular importance. Since Geneva became a model city in the eyes of other communities, its history is very influential. It might be observed that the Geneva later emulated by the French, Dutch, Scottish, and English Reformed Protestants was the Geneva of Calvin and not of Farel, but this does not diminish the special significance of the city's earlier history. Calvin's Geneva owed much to that period before Calvin's arrival, since its revolutionary turmoil helped shape many of the institutions and policies on which Calvin would later build.[68]

Another factor weighing in Geneva's favor as a sample "laboratory" for the study of iconoclasm is its political situation. Reformation Geneva was the product of a concurrent process of religious and political revolution against the Prince Bishop of the House of Savoy. This was accompanied by a diplomatic tangle between Catholic Fribourg and Protestant Bern – a situation that sheds light on some of the political aspects of Swiss Reformation strategies.

Finally, the Reformation in Geneva can be seen as the culmination of previous developments, as a refinement of tactics previously employed. The lessons learned in other Swiss towns between 1523 and 1530 were all applied vigorously in Geneva. Because its Reformation took place so much later, relatively speaking, Geneva provides a clear picture of the patterns that evolved as the war against the idols marched across the land.

Geneva's political situation

The period of the Reformation in Geneva was one of political and religious revolution, and the triumph of Protestantism in the city cannot be understood without taking into account its revolt against

---

[67] As early as 1527 Farel was praising Zwingli for scattering the darkness with his learning. Herminjard 2.18.
[68] For an excellent account of the way in which Calvin reorganized the Genevan church see Haro Höpfl, *The Christian Polity of John Calvin* (Cambridge, 1982), p. 56–76.

the House of Savoy and its alliance with Bern. In fact, it is difficult to tell whether Geneva would have become Protestant in 1536, or even organized a Reformed congregation at all, without the constant mixture of threats and encouragements from Bern.[69] Consequently, it is necessary to preface this study of the Reformation in Geneva with a brief summary of the political background.

Geneva's struggle for political independence was not presaged by her medieval history, which has been referred to as a "study in civic retardation."[70] Medieval Geneva was controlled by two powers: the House of Savoy and the prince-bishop of Geneva, both of whom claimed to hold Geneva directly from the emperor. This jurisdictional conflict was resolved in 1444, when Duke Amadeus VIII became Pope Felix V and reserved the see of Geneva for himself. From the time of his death in 1451 to the installation of Geneva's last prince-bishop in 1522, the bishopric was occupied (mostly in absentia) by members of the House of Savoy.

It is not until 1519 that Geneva began to fight for freedom from feudal and episcopal rule. Its revolutionary fervor can be directly attributed to the westward expansion of Swiss influence at this time, particularly on the part of the Bernese.[71] The Genevan "patriots," led by a certain Besançon Hughes, even called themselves "Eidguenots," after the name for the Swiss Confederates, "Eidgennosen." Although the Eidguenots suffered a setback in 1519, they rose again in 1521, forming a political alliance (*combourgeoisie*) with Bern and Fribourg in 1526. The Bishop, who showed hesitancy in acting against the Eidguenots, fled in 1527, calling on the Duke of Savoy to put down the rebellion. The next eight years were occupied with sporadic military and diplomatic maneuvers between Savoy and the *combourgeoisie*.

When Geneva entered the *combourgeoisie* with Bern and Fribourg in 1526 there were no overt religious overtones to the struggle against Geneva's hereditary rulers, and the three cities were still Catholic. Bern, however, became Protestant in January of 1528. Fribourg remained adamantly Catholic, even to the point of imposing a profession of faith on all its citizens in 1527 and expelling all suspected "Lutherans" in 1530.[72] The history of the Reformation in Geneva is, to a large extent, also the history of the growth of Bernese influence at

[69] Monter, *Calvin's Geneva*, p. 50.
[70] Ibid., p. 30.
[71] Ibid., p. 33.
[72] Naef, *Origines*, pp. 352–9.

the expense of Fribourg. As shall be seen, the aggressive evangelizing efforts of Bern were instrumental in effecting the success of the Reformation in Geneva.

The process of Reformation in Geneva was thus inextricably joined ✓ to its political revolt, but the religious conflict was not entirely a political or diplomatic affair. The Reformation also triumphed because it gained the support of the citizenry. Without their efforts, particularly their illegal acts of iconoclasm, the Genevan Reformation could not have succeeded.

Early Protestant influence and
Bernese iconoclasm

Protestant influence in Geneva before 1532 appears to have been slight. A certain Levrier, who was executed by agents of the French king in 1524, admitted owning some of Luther's works in Geneva, and admired Luther as a "doctor of great authority" who spoke with force against the papacy.[73] Although there were probably other "Lutheran" sympathizers in Geneva at this time, they remained a weak and disorganized group.[74] Thomas von Hofen, a Bernese official, reported to Zwingli in 1527 that it would be difficult to preach the Gospel in Geneva because of the hundreds of monks who would be opposed to it.[75] Jean Balard, a Genevan citizen who kept a diary, does not note the existence of "Lutheranism" until December of 1529, and then it is only in reference to events outside Geneva.[76]

Nonetheless, a small circle of Protestants – or at least Protestant sympathizers – existed in Geneva prior to 1532.[77] The rich merchant Baudichon de Maisonneuve ate meat during Lent in 1526, and led a mock procession through the streets of Geneva in 1528 in which the priests and monks were ridiculed.[78] By October 1531, when

[73] Ibid., pp. 462–3.
[74] Monter, *Calvin's Geneva*, p. 49.
[75] Herminjard 2.9–11.
[76] Chaponière (ed.) *Journal du Syndic Balard* (Geneva, 1894), pp. 268–9 (volume 10 of the *Mémoires et Documents Publiés par la Société d'Histoire et d'Archeologie de Geneve*).
[77] Naef, *Origines*, pp. 309–41; Monter, *Calvin's Geneva*, p. 49. Monter bases his argument on the article by Hektor Ammann, "Oberdeutsche Kaufleute und die Anfänge der Reformation in Genf," *Zeitschrift für Württenburgische Landesgeschichte* 13: 150–93 (1954). Henri Naef has studied the influence of the humanist circle of the itinerant alchemist Cornelius Aggripa, who lived in Geneva from 1521 to 1523, but William Monter does not think it is possible to trace the origins of Genevan Protestantism to this group. Monter thinks it is more likely that Protestant contacts came through merchants, such as Baudichon de Maisonneuve, who frequently traveled to Protestant lands and were affected by the new doctrines.
[78] Gautier, *Histoire de Genève*, vol. 2, p. 267.

Guillaume Farel wrote to Ulrich Zwingli about conditions in Geneva, it is clear that a definite enclave of evangelicals lived in the city.[79]

Geneva's first encounter with militant Protestantism did not issue from within, but rather through the presence of Bernese troops in the city and its suburbs in October of 1530. That autumn, Geneva had applied to her Swiss allies for military aid against Savoy, and a large relief army of 12,000 men had been sent in response. Although Catholic Fribourg sent its share of soldiers, the majority were from Protestant Bern or its territories. The Bernese, who had eradicated Catholic worship from their city and canton in 1528, continued their iconoclastic destruction as they marched through other territories.

Jeanne de Jussie, a noblewoman who had joined the convent of St. Claire in Geneva, provides a vivid description of her first encounter with Protestantism in her chronicle, *Le levain du Calvinisme*.[80] According to Sister Jeanne, the Swiss "heretics" began to destroy and desecrate Catholic cultic objects even before they reached Geneva. In the village of Morge, for instance, they ravaged the Franciscan house. First, they quartered their horses on the "holy ground" of the cloister. Secondly, and even worse, they entered the chapel and made a fire in the center of the nave, into which they threw the consecrated hosts.[81] After this desecration, the soldiers destroyed the main altarpiece, the altar, and the stained glass window behind the altar. They also burned all the wooden images, smashed the stone decorations, ripped out the ironwork, and carried away every ornament they could find (including the friars' plate and linen), leaving the chapel completely empty.[82]

Although these acts might seem a normal part of warfare, they had a decidedly religious character. Every priest encountered by the soldiers was harassed, beaten, and unceremoniously stripped of his habit. In fact, the soldiers' enmity to Catholic cultic objects was so great, Jeanne reports, that they attacked every single religious representation they found, whether painted or carved. The destruction of images thus went beyond mere pillage or wanton destruction; it was a vengeful attack. Jeanne reports thay "poked out the eyes of the images with their pikes and swords, and spat on them, to deface and disfigure them."[83] The destruction was also extended to the friar's

---

[79] Herminjard 2.364–5.
[80] *Levain*, p. 9ff.
[81] Ibid., p. 9. Sister Jeanne's Catholic sensibilities were outraged by this act, which she compared to the villanies committed against Christ by Caiaphas and Pilate's soldiers when they tortured him.
[82] Ibid., p. 10: "tellement qu'il n'y demeura chose aucune, sinon l'edifice tout vuide."
[83] Ibid.

books, as well as to their pulpit. The iconoclasts, it seems, also wanted to destroy those things that helped to teach the "error" of Catholic worship.

When word of these events reached Geneva, the city government decided to close all the churches and to suspend Mass, except at the convent of St. Clare. The sisters even removed and hid a cross that adorned the entrance to their convent, lest it be desecrated by "the dogs" from Bern. Sister Jeanne provides a revealing glimpse at the contrast between Catholic and Protestant attitudes toward religious imagery: She thought it strange to hide the symbol of redemption.[84]

When the Bernese finally arrived in Geneva, their behavior confirmed the worst fears of the Catholics. The soldiers were quartered at the Dominican house near the Rhône. Though the chapel remained closed and suffered no harm, the soldiers smashed and burned all the images on the outside and even some inside the cloister.[85] Sometime during their eleven-day stay at the Convent du Palais, the Bernese also broke into the oratory, tore down an altar, smashed a window, and destroyed a stone cross. Afterwards, the soldiers marched to the Augustinian cloister, where they destroyed several images; and then to the Franciscan house, where they smashed and burned more images. Jeanne reports that they committed other "vituperations against God's honor" as well.[86]

As if it were not enough to desecrate churches, reports Sister Jeanne, the Bernese also imposed their services on the city. On a certain morning they stormed the cathedral and placed their preacher in the pulpit. Every day the "accursed" preacher delivered a sermon in German at the cathedral, and the soldiers "jumped around like goats and brute beasts, in great derision to the image of our Redemption and of the Virgin Mary and of all the other saints."[87]

Still, the Bernese showed some restraint. Although they took over the cathedral, they did no damage to the place, and satisfied themselves with merely mocking the images. None of the parish churches was attacked either. The destruction reported by Jeanne de Jussie took place only in the suburbs of Geneva and in the religious houses of the city. This may be attributed to the precautions taken by the city government before the arrival of the troops, but not entirely. Had they really wanted to, the soldiers could have caused more trouble. The Bernese incursion into Geneva left the Catholic community

[84] Ibid., p. 16.
[85] Ibid., p. 17.
[86] Ibid., p. 24.
[87] Ibid., p. 20. Jeanne incorrectly identifies the Bernese preacher as Guillaume Foret (Farel). Farel could not have preached in German, and was in Neuchâtel at the time.

badly shaken, since they had been exposed to the Protestant rejection of their cult without being subjected to a Protestant takeover. Jeanne de Jussie found the behavior of the "heretics" incomprehensible. She viewed their iconoclasm as the clearest proof of their error, and it is for this reason that she describes it in detail. Wherever the Bernese went, she said, they engaged in countless perversions "as false heretical dogs," pillaging and tearing down all the churches, monasteries, and convents, breaking all the tabernacles, stepping on the hosts, throwing them into filth, and spilling all the sacred water and ointments. They committed more crimes than a Jew or Mohammedan could ever be capable of imagining, even to the extent of feeding the sacred host to a goat and saying, "Now he can die if he wants, he has received the sacrament."[88] Viewed from a Catholic perspective, this is what the Reformation meant: the destruction of the sacred. The ravages of iconoclasm signified for the Catholics the triumph of the new heresy. Protestantism, therefore, was more than an ideological or theological threat; it was a physical threat as well, and iconoclasm was its trademark.

Iconoclasm continued to be an expression of Protestant fervor around Geneva after the Bernese troops departed, but it was confined to sporadic and isolated instances. The most celebrated case took place on 13 August 1531, when a group of about thirty Genevan Protestants shot down a bell from a suburban church, and destroyed an image of the Virgin Mary.[89] During the same month, a "Lutheran" knocked down a statue from the small chapel of St. Lawrence, cut off its arms, and threw it in a sewer.[90]

[88] Ibid., p. 23. While the Protestants always argued that the powerlessness of the images and the hosts was proven by their destruction, Catholics often circulated stories about miraculous events surrounding iconoclasm. Jeanne de Jussie tells of a Catholic who walked into a desecrated church and found the host lying on the ground. He went to get a piece of white linen to cover it reverently, but upon returning found that the host was gone, and affirmed "that he believed that the angels had taken it to heaven and placed it in an honorable place unknown to us" (p. 24). D'Aubigné cites the case of a statue of St. Blaise, which was reported to have escaped destruction by swimming across Lake Constance to the Catholic town of Mammern (*History*, p. 767). Some "miracles" were pranks of the iconoclasts themselves. D'Aubigné also tells of an iconoclast who hollowed out an image and filled it with gunpowder before a friend could burn it. The resulting explosion so terrified the poor man, that he repented for his act and became a Catholic again (*History*, p. 786).

[89] *Levain*, p. 30. Combining this act of religious iconoclasm with a demonstration of political fervor, someone in the group also took a piece of charcoal and drew a bear (the symbol of Bern) defecating on the coat of arms of Savoy. See also RC 12.572.

[90] *Levain*, p. 31. To indicate that such acts could not go unpunished, Sister Jeanne also reports that the iconoclast was infected with the plague and soon died – after having repented and confessed as a good Catholic.

In April 1532 Sister Jeanne reports the occurrence of a peculiar miracle in the town of Tornay, where a picture of Mary was mocked by a Protestant and began to bleed in response. The bleeding image was subsequently enshrined at the church of the Madeleine in Geneva, where it soon became a popular object of devotion.[91] This incident shows that even though the Protestants were growing bolder, there were still many Genevans who not only clung to the old faith, but were proud to make a display of its power over the attacks of the "heretics."

In June 1532, when Pope Clement VII proclaimed a general indulgence in Geneva, the Protestant community decided to display its displeasure openly for the first time. On 9 June, placards appeared all over the city mocking this indulgence, stating that anyone who repented with faith in the promises of Christ could have his sins forgiven.[92] At about the same time, the evangelicals of Payerne wrote to those of Geneva, congratulating them for their courage and exhorting them to keep the faith. In a passage that is full of revolutionary fervor, the church of Payerne wrote to that of Geneva: "You have done those things as true and faithful knights of Jesus Christ, without having regard for earthly goods and transitory honors, and not fearing to displease your parents and superiors, who are enemies of the truth."[93] Shortly after the affair of the placards, on 2 July 1532, the Protestants struck again, this time by destroying a large cross that stood in front of the Convent de St. Clare.[94]

The first phase of preaching
and rioting

After this incident, the process of Reformation in Geneva assumes a different character. Isolated instances of grievance against Catholic worship give way to an organized assault on the power of the Church

---

[91] Ibid., p. 43. Again, here is the Catholic counterargument to iconoclastic sentiment or violence: The sacred cannot help but defend itself, and it often does.

[92] Roset, *Chroniques*, p. 161. Also: RC 12.102, n. 1, which collects all the pertinent narratives.

[93] RC 2.427. Interestingly enough, both Jeanne de Jussie (*Levain*, p. 46) and the syndic Balard (*Journal*, p. 400) report that the placards were posted by youths (Jeanne: "mauvais garcons"; Balard: "aucuns enfans"). It is not surprising, therefore, that the evangelicals from Payerne should refer to "parens et supérieurs, ennemys de vérité." It seems that youths were on the vanguard of the Reformation in Geneva during this early stage of the religious conflict.

[94] RC 12.113. Jeanne erroneously gives an earlier date, April 1531. She also adds that two of the three men responsible for this atrocity died of the plague as heretics. The third repented and became a Catholic again, but still died (*Levain*, p. 32).

in Geneva, and iconoclasm is eclipsed, for the time being, by the effort to establish Protestantism in the city. During this phase, individual acts of rebellion are supplanted by preaching, rioting, and diplomatic maneuvering.

The one event that signals the beginning of this period is the arrival of Guillaume Farel, Antoine Saunier, and Pierre Olivetan, who came to the city in September 1532, after having attended the Waldensian synod of Chanforan in Savoy.[95] Word of their clandestine preaching soon reached some of the cathedral canons, who, in turn, reported it to the vicar, and had the three men arrested. On 4 October they faced a public hearing, where they were questioned about their illegal preaching. Farel, who assumed the position of spokesman, replied that he had come to preach the Gospel on God's authority, and that as an ambassador of Christ he needed no one else's permission to preach in Geneva. Farel was then accused of fomenting trouble in the city. He responded by saying that he had not come to disturb anyone, and that it was really the priests who caused Geneva infinite trouble with their "human traditions and inventions" and their "dissolute lives." At this point, it is already possible to see the appeal to a higher authority that would surface so often during the progress of the Reformation in Geneva. As could be expected, Farel was accused of blasphemy. After almost being lynched, the three preachers were expelled from Geneva and told never to return.[96]

Farel went to Lausanne, where he recruited a young man named Antoine Fromment to take up the task he had not been able to finish. Fromment arrived in Geneva on 3 November 1532, and established himself there as a French tutor, advertising his services throughout the city, and using this position as a cover for secretly preaching the Protestant Gospel.[97] Under his guidance, the Genevan evangelicals continued to grow in number. Encouraged by their success in attracting new members, Fromment's congregation soon tried to bring their cause out into the open. On New Year's Day 1533, they carried Fromment to the Molard square near the waterfront, which was one of

[95] "Farel et les Vaudois du Piémont" in *Guillaume Farel*, pp. 285–97. Farel had already been in touch with the Genevans, having written them a letter in July (Herminjard 2.435). These are the men named by Fromment as the nucleus of the Protestant community in 1532: Amy Perrin, Claude Paste, Claude Bernard, Jehan Chautemps, Dominique D'Arboz, Claude Savoye, Amy Porral, Robert and Pierre Vandel, Claude Roset, Jehan Golle, Estienne Dada, Jehan Sonet, Baudichon de Maisonneuve, and Claude de Genève, "avec certains aultres petits compagnions" (*Actes et Gestes*, p. 4). Herminjard 2.459–62 for a longer list; and RC 12.600 for additional names in 1533.
[96] Fromment, *Actes et Gestes*, pp. 3–9.
[97] Ibid., p. 13.

Geneva's busiest public places. Once there, Fromment began to preach a sermon from a fishmonger's bench, but as had happened with Farel a few months earlier, he was quickly forced to leave the city.[98]

Although Fromment was expelled, the Reformation pushed ahead, primarily because of diplomatic pressures exerted by Bern.[99] On 11 March, a certain Pierre Fedy was arrested and exiled for having said that those who attended Mass were idolaters and worshipers of a "god of bread."[100] Four days later, Pierre Viret would write upon arriving in Geneva, "the number of those who desire the Word of God is very great."[101]

At the end of March, the tension which had been building between Protestants and Catholics exploded into violence. A rumor began to circulate on 28 March that the Protestants were about to attack all the churches, convents and monasteries, and many Catholics assembled at the cathedral to discuss the impending peril.[102] Meanwhile, the Protestants had also assembled, fearing a Catholic attack.[103] A great riot erupted in which at least one man was killed and several wounded. Many families were so sharply divided about religion that relatives fought each other on the street.[104] Even women joined in by throwing stones at the Protestants, and so did their children, who carried little swords and also threw stones.[105]

When the syndics finally stopped the rioting, they called for a truce between the two parties. Protestants and Catholics exchanged hostages, and the council proclaimed that anyone who tried to incite more trouble would be banished from the city.[106] Two days later, the council issued a series of pronouncements intended to ensure peace in Geneva. Among the most important provisions were the following: that no one speak publicly against the sacraments of the Church, preach without a proper license, break established fasts, sing songs

---

[98] Ibid., p. 22ff.; pp. 43–4.
[99] Herminjard 3.29, 3.31.
[100] RC 12.231.
[101] Herminjard 3.31.
[102] *Levain*, p. 53.
[103] Fromment, *Actes et Gestes*, p. 50. Fromment reports that the Protestants assembled to defend themselves against a plot hatched the night before by the vicar and the clergy. Jeanne's report, which says that the Protestants assembled to destroy the Catholic churches, does not entirely agree with Fromment's version. At any rate, the conflicting reports show what each side feared from the other: The Catholics feared their churches would be damaged, while the Protestants feared for their lives.
[104] *Levain*, p. 57.
[105] Ibid.
[106] RC 12.245ff.; *Levain*, pp. 53–9; Fromment, *Actes et Gestes*, pp. 50–6.

touching religious matters, or raise any debate or complaint against such provisions. Referring to the participation of women and children in the riot, the council reminded all men that they were responsible for seeing that their wives and children also obey the law.[107] In spite of the precautions taken by the council, a much worse disturbance broke out on 4 May 1533, and the pattern followed was quite similar to that of the first riot. Fearing again that the Protestants were about to invade the churches, a large contingent of armed Catholics charged down to the Molard square to attack the Protestants.[108] Several hundred men were involved and many were wounded, including one of the syndics who was trying to restore order. A canon from Fribourg named Pierre Werly was wounded and then ambushed and killed by a group of Protestants.[109] That same day, 5 May, the Protestants boasted of their strength to the Bernese: "There are more than half as many of us as there were the previous time, and we keep growing every day."[110]

The second phase of preaching and rioting

Jeanne de Jussie correctly judged Werly's death as the turning point of the religious struggle in Geneva. After this incident, as she says, the Protestants never ceased to "torment and molest" the churches.[111] At this time, iconoclasm was renewed when two men knocked down and burned an image of the Virgin Mary that stood in the great square of the Bourg-de-Four, near the cathedral.[112] A more significant event was the return of Antoine Fromment, who arrived in Geneva with an assistant named Alexandre Canus. These two preached secretly in people's homes, or sometimes openly in the street. Their presence greatly advanced the Protestant cause, and, as Fromment says, conversely caused "great detriment" to the papacy.[113]

Canon Werly had inadvertently aided the Reformation through his excessive zeal. The next stage of the Reformation in Geneva was ushered in by the efforts of another Catholic zealot. In December

---

[107] RC 12.250–1.
[108] Fromment, *Actes et Gestes*, p. 57; *Levain*, p. 64.
[109] *Levain*, p. 64. Full accounts of the riot can be found in RC 12.264–5; 12.599–600; *Levain*, 64–7; Fromment, *Actes et Gestes*, 57–9.
[110] Herminjard 3.46–51.
[111] Herminjard 3.71.
[112] RC 12.324.
[113] Fromment, *Actes et Gestes*, p. 66.

1533, Guy Furbity, a Dominican trained at the Sorbonne, came to Geneva to preach during the Advent season. He had come to try to outpreach the Protestants, but his aggressiveness only worsened the situation. A major confrontation took place soon after his arrival, as he preached a sermon in the cathedral on 2 December in which he insulted the Protestants. Among other things, he said that the Protestants were like the drunkards who gambled for Christ's clothes, and he compared the Bernese to the Arians, Sabellians, and Waldensians.[114] He asked the congregation to avoid having contact with those who ate meat on Fridays, read scripture in the vernacular, or spoke against the pope. He also embarked on a long-winded and theologically questionable defense of transsubstantiation, arguing that priests were worthy of more honor than Mary, because they brought Christ into the world repeatedly through their celebration of the eucharistic sacrifice.[115] Fromment and Canus, who were present in the church, began to heckle Furbity, and were again chased out of the city.

This altercation provided the Protestants with a chance to push forward. The merchant Baudichon de Maisonneuve went to Bern and complained about Furbity's preaching and the treatment received by Fromment and Canus. Bern took this opportunity to place additional pressure on Geneva: On 20 December, Baudichon returned to Geneva with Guillaume Farel, who now came as an official representative of the Bernese government. In addition, the Bernese wrote a threatening letter to the Genevan council, reminding them of their war debt, and insisting that the Protestants be allowed freedom in the city.[116] This move did not please the other member of the *combourgeoisie*, Fribourg. On Christmas Eve, the Fribourg government wrote to Geneva, threatening to leave the alliance if Farel were allowed to preach.[117] The Genevan magistracy now faced alienating its two political allies.

Geneva was caught in a bind. On one side, Bern was putting on pressure to allow Protestant preaching and to silence Furbity, while on the other side Fribourg was making equally strong demands to abolish Protestantism in the city. Within Geneva, the two factions fomented against one another, and the councillors found themselves divided on the religious question. Although most council members

---

[114] RC 12.438.
[115] Fromment, *Actes et Gestes*, p. 70.
[116] Herminjard 3.119.
[117] Herminjard 3.123.

were still Catholic, many were becoming Protestant, if not openly, then secretly, as "Nicodemites." Meanwhile, no religious settlement was forthcoming.

Furbity was asked to engage in a debate with Farel, but he refused all requests, saying he could not stoop to place divine science before "such a vile and evil man."[118] The impasse was finally broken on 25 January, when the Bernese placed an ultimatum before the Two Hundred: If Furbity were not brought to trial, then Bern would break its pact with Geneva.[119] Two days later Furbity was finally brought before the councillors and the Bernese ambassadors, in whose presence he debated against Farel and Viret for three days.[120] On 11 February, the Furbity case was closed: He was found guilty of insulting the Bernese and of not having preached true to scripture on six out of seven counts. Furbity offered to revoke his insults and apologize to the Bernese in a sermon to be delivered at the cathedral, but when the appointed day arrived and he mounted the pulpit, he made no apologies and only gave "vague and vacillating" responses to the charges leveled against him. Unsatisfied with this performance, the council imprisoned Furbity.[121] Bern's persistence had finally paid off.

While Bern increased its diplomatic pressure on Geneva, the Protestants became increasingly bolder. Sometime during February, the Catholics planned a procession to the Augustinian chapel of Nôtre Dame de Grace, to the south of the city. The Protestants feared this was part of a plot to attack them again, so as the procession passed through the city, a group of men led by the nobles Amy Perrin and Jean Goullaz interrupted it, roughing up its participants and throwing their crosses and relics on the ground.[122]

Bern continued to increase its pressure at the next council meeting demanding payment for their military assistance and asking for a church in which to hold Protestant services. While Bern was using its financial and military strength to bully the magistrates, the Genevan Protestants obtained by force what the Bernese could not get through intimidation. A group of men led by Amy Perrin and Baudichon de Maisonneuve invaded the Franciscan house and seized one of its

[118] *Levain,* p. 81.
[119] RC 12.434ff.
[120] The record of Furbity's dispute and trial can be found in the RC 12.438ff.; and in a narrative written by Farel, "Lettres certains d'aucuns grandz troubles et tumultes," published in Neuchâtel in 1535 and Geneva in 1644.
[121] RC 12.479. Furbity was to spend two years in prison before being exchanged for a Protestant prisoner elsewhere.
[122] Fromment, *Actes et Gestes,* p. 93.

wings. Thrusting Farel into the pulpit, the invading congregation then heard the first Protestant sermon preached in a Genevan church since the departure of the Bernese soldiers in October 1530.[123] Through an act of open rebellion against the established laws of the ✓ city, the Protestants had finally gained a public place of worship.

The remainder of that spring, the Protestants continued to make quiet, solid advances. On 12 April, Farel celebrated the first Protestant wedding, a ceremony so simple that it prompted Jeanne de Jussie to comment on its "emptiness."[124] On 16 April, the Protestants received a letter of encouragement from Bern,[125] and the next day a certain Amy Levet was imprisoned for refusing to close his shop during a Catholic procession.[126] His arrest shows that although the Protestants had made significant advances, they were still far from their goal.

Iconoclasm and the conservative magistracy

With the coming of Spring in May 1534, the Reformation entered a new phase in Geneva, becoming more aggressive than ever. So far, the religious struggle had been largely limited to preaching and rioting. Preaching, of course, was a precondition of Reformation, since the people had to be indoctrinated before any church could be organized. This was now secured in Geneva. Rioting was a consequence of the Protestant efforts to preach. Often, but not always, it was the Catholics who instigated the violence. Religious rioting took place in Geneva only when the Protestants were a small and relatively powerless minority. It was primarily an effort on the part of the Catholic majority to remove an undesirable group from their midst. But now that the Catholics had lost so much ground, the rioting subsided and was eclipsed by iconoclasm.

As if to herald the beginning of a new phase of Reformation, a statue of St. Anthony was defaced inside the Franciscan house on the first of May. Jeanne de Jussie reports that after the Protestant sermon had ended, a certain Louis Chenevard entered the church, and, in

---

[123] *Levain*, p. 86; Roset, *Chroniques*, p. 183; *Texte Inédit de Savion*, p. 414. The *Journal* compiled by Savion – which is probably a continuation of Balard's – contains an additional piece of information: It says that the monastery was taken over "avec les enfans." This points again to the youthful character of many aggressive Protestant acts.

[124] *Levain*, p. 91.

[125] Herminjard 3.165.

[126] RC 12.525.

front of all the friars, took out the statue's eyes with his sword.[127] Chenevard's act was the first in a long series of iconoclastic demonstrations that would mark the final process of the Reformation in Geneva.

The Protestants became even more aggressive when Fribourg finally broke with the *combourgeoisie* on 15 May 1534.[128] After this date, when the predominance of Bern seemed to ensure the success of the Reformation, iconoclasm began to plague Geneva. One of the most celebrated cases occurred on 24 May, when several images in front of the Franciscan monastery were decapitated and their heads thrown into the yard of the Clarisses.[129] The council wanted to take action against the culprits, but was delayed by a lack of witnesses. Two days later, it ordered the images repaired at the expense of the perpetrators, whenever found.[130] Meanwhile, on the 25th, two angels from the cemetery at the Madeleine church were overturned and thrown into the well of the Convent de St. Clare.[131] On the same day, a priest from the cathedral visited the Protestant congregation at the Rive monastery and announced that he wanted to become one of them. He was welcomed into the community and married two days later, much to the shock of the Catholics.[132] On 12 June, the council discussed the images destroyed in May, and decided it would be best to hide them until they could be repaired. Catholicism was now under a state of siege.

Although the city government was opposed to iconoclasm and tried to punish all iconoclasts, the destruction of cultic objects continued unabated as summer approached. On the night of 22 June, as no one was watching, two images were destroyed in front of the Madeleine.[133] On 26 July, the feast of St. Anne, a group of men entered the small chapel in the Franciscan monastery known as the

---

[127] *Levain*, p. 93. (As before, Jeanne cannot allow this act to go unpunished. She adds that after enjoying his dinner at home, the impious iconoclast suddenly fell ill and died.)

[128] In April 1534 Geneva refused to receive a delegation from Fribourg that had come to renew the *combourgeoisie*. Negotiations stalled and broke down over the issue of "Lutheran" preaching in Geneva. On 15 May, Fribourg's seal was removed from the pact. RC 12.510–12; 12.523–4; 12.629–30; and Fromment, *Actes et Gestes*, pp. 119–20.

[129] RC 12.547ff.; *Levain*, p. 94. Jeanne de Jussie reports six images were decapitated, but the council records say that nine images had their heads, arms, and hands knocked off. Sister Jeanne thought it was "chose piteuse de voir les corps sans teste."

[130] RC 12.550.

[131] *Levain*, p. 94.

[132] Ibid.

[133] Ibid., p. 95.

Chapel of the Queen of Cyprus, and destroyed a large and costly image of the Virgin Mary, dismantled the four pillars before the great altar, and removed the rest of the images. They also stole the ciborium containing the consecrated hosts and took it away, as Jeanne de Jussie said, "for some unknown purpose."[134] The council records for that day show that a number of arrests were made in connection with this act, and that most of the men arrested were artisans and laborers.[135]

The council judged that even if it should come to pass that the images ought to be removed and destroyed, this would still have to be done by the proper authorities. These men had therefore committed an act that, even when legal, was reserved for the magistracy.[136] They were imprisoned, but on the following day, a certain Louis Mellier was also arrested for damaging an image of St. Anne near the Rhone bridge.[137] This iconoclastic turmoil was accompanied by another defection from the priesthood. On the same day that the images were destroyed at the Franciscan chapel, a Dominican discarded his habit in public and lamented his former adherence to the sacraments and ceremonies of the Catholic church, saying that such things were "vile and worthless."[138] Some of those who should have been defending the images were now slowly joining the iconoclasts.

Iconoclasm continued in September. On the 19th, a group of men destroyed several images; they were arrested and condemned to three days in jail on bread and water, "in order to serve as an example to others."[139] On 13 September, the council had ordered that the Genevan suburbs be razed in order to defend the city more easily against attacks from the Savoyard forces. On the 29th, as the suburban parish churches of St. Leger and St. Victor were being razed, some Protestants took advantage of the situation, and in addition to destroying all the altars (and reportedly taking the pieces home to make washbasins), they demolished all the images. A young noble,

---

134 Ibid., pp. 96–7. (This chapel had been donated by Queen Anne of Cyprus and was also known as Nôtre Dame de Bethléem.)
135 RC 13.18–19. Among those arrested were J. Blanch, cloth cutter; J. Marchand, shoemaker; J. Lambert, shoemaker; and an unnamed young servant of Etienne Dada.
136 RC 13.18: "Ibidem propositis premissis in concillio, fuit advisus quod quamvis talia simulacra et ymagines secundum legem divinam amovende et destruende venirent, dicti tamen dirruptores id sine licencia et mandato fecisse non debuerunt, quia est actus ad magistratum spectans."
137 RC 13.19.
138 *Levain*, p. 99.
139 RC 13.65, 13.68, 13.69.

Jean Goullaz, took a consecrated host and hung it around his horse's neck.[140]

Inside the city, tensions between Catholics and Protestants continued to be released through mutual acts of disrespect. Jeanne de Jussie narrates two incidents that illustrate the difference between Catholics and Protestants in their understanding of cultic objects and in their attitude toward each other. Jeanne reports that sometime during September a Protestant named Claude Testu washed his hands in a holy water font and afterwards spit into it, "in great ridicule, scorn and mockery."[141] Testu could not accept the holy water as a source of grace, and he showed his contempt for it openly. Catholics, however, regarded such *sacramentalia* as necessary for religious life, and instead desecrated the persons of the Protestants themselves. During a Protestant funeral, for instance, a group of children sarcastically displayed this attitude. Jeanne reports:

The small Christian children who had clearly seen how they had buried him said to one another: these people have not sprinkled holy water over their brother. Let us go and give him what he merits to refresh his soul. And, all together, they went over and urinated on his grave.[142]

In October, as the razing of the suburbs continued, the convent of St. Clare was invaded by some Protestants who began shouting to interrupt vespers. When they saw that the nuns would not stop praying, they removed a wooden cross, broke it in pieces, and threw it into the well outside the convent. The iconoclasts also took down an image of St. Ursula, smashed it, and threw it into the same well.[143] The following day, the nuns filed a complaint with the council, asking for protection from further assaults.[144]

During the rest of the year, religious violence in Geneva decreased. On 3 December, however, there was a brief recurrence of iconoclasm when a Bernese noble named Bischoff destroyed a stone cross and claimed that he had been ordered to do so by the syndics. His story was a lie, of course, and he was imprisoned for his impudence.[145] Jeanne de Jussie reports that during that week several other crosses were also destroyed throughout the city.[146]

---

[140] *Levain*, p. 107. The incident is also recorded in a secret report of the Bishop, RC 13.593.
[141] *Levain*, p. 105.
[142] Ibid., p. 106. Notice again the participation by children in acts of religious violence.
[143] Ibid., p. 108.
[144] Herminjard 3.222.
[145] RC 13.109.
[146] *Levain*, p. 110. Sister Jeanne mentions the one destroyed by Bischoff as well as another in front of Nôtre Dame de Grace. The others are not mentioned.

Although the departure of Fribourg from the *combourgeoisie* had inspired the Protestants to begin their war against the "idols" through the summer and early autumn, iconoclastic activity eventually subsided. This relative calm was probably due to the growing external threat posed by Geneva's enemy, the House of Savoy. On the night of 30 July 1534, for instance, the city had successfully turned back a surprise attack by the Savoyard forces.[147] The victory pleased the Genevans, but left them worried about the future, especially since the attack had been aided by the "Paneysans," that is, the episcopal partisans exiled from Geneva.[148]

During the rest of 1534 many minor skirmishes were fought outside the city, and political maneuvers carried out inside. The most significant event at this time was the legal ouster of the Bishop in October, when the council declared his seat vacant. Aside from these political and military concerns, the delay in the religious settlement may be ascribed to the persistent neutrality of Geneva's magistrates, most of whom were still Catholic or uncommitted. Although preaching continued within the city,[149] the council still persisted in punishing all acts of violence or irreverence to the old faith.[150]

The impasse reached at the end of 1534 lasted until March 1535, when a new controversy allowed the Protestants to press their cause with renewed vigor. On 6 March, the Protestant preacher Pierre Viret was poisoned, and it was soon discovered that the culprit was a servant girl in league with canons of St. Peter.[151] The incident not only exposed the canons to criticism and ridicule, but also gave the Protestants reason for increasing their efforts against Catholicism in Geneva. Three days after the poisoning, iconoclasm was again renewed, this time at Nôtre Dame de Grace (which had not yet been razed, even though it was in the suburbs). Several men broke into the Augustinian monastery, demolished a statue of St. John the Baptist, and smashed a lighted lamp that hung near the altar.[152] A week later, a certain J. Sourd was arrested, imprisoned, and fined the cost of the image. On 26 March, two more men, Claude Jacquard and Jean Col-

---

[147] RC 13.21; 13.586–90; *Levain*, p. 97; Fromment, *Actes et Gestes*, p. 123; Roset, *Chroniques*, p. 186.

[148] Monter, *Geneva*, p. 53.

[149] A secret report to the Bishop from his procurator, containing a lengthy list of suspected Protestants can be found in RC 13.591–4.

[150] Monter, *Geneva*, p. 53. Surprisingly, as William Monter has observed, it was these same conservative magistrates who supported the political revolt against the Bishop and continued the alliance with Bern.

[151] J. F. Bergier, "L'empoisonneuse de Pierre Viret," *Revue de Theologie et Philosophie* 10: 236–50 (1961).

[152] RC 13.166.

lognier, were imprisoned for having destroyed an image of St. Gregory at the Rive monastery.[153]

The public disputation

Although the Council still showed stiff opposition to iconoclasm, it soon began to bend to Protestant demands. On 2 April 1535, the council decided to legalize the Protestant occupation of the Franciscan monastery, granting the Convent de Rive as a residence for Farel and Viret.[154] The new council members elected in February 1535, in contrast to those who served through 1534, were now leaning toward the Protestant cause. But, as Michel Roset reports, the council "could not adopt the change which many of the citizens requested, because there were still varying opinions."[155] A new controversy soon provided this council with an opportunity to disturb the religious balance of the city in favor of the Protestants. On 10 and 11 May, the council discussed the miracles that had been reported at the Augustinian cloister, where dead unbaptized infants could supposedly be revived for a few moments so they could receive the sacrament.[156] This wonder was attributed to the image of Our Lady of Grace, in whose honor the monastery was named.[157] The real cause of the "miracles," however, turned out to be several old matrons who could make the corpses exhale air, urinate, or perspire, and would then cry "miracle!, miracle!" so that the "revived" infants could be immediately baptized. The syndics inspected this well-intentioned fraud in person, scolded the Augustinians for allowing such things to take place, and warned them that if they continued these practices they would be expelled from Geneva. The Augustinians did not try to argue their case and instead promised to abide by the commands of the council.[158]

While the council was occupied with these affairs, the Protestant community moved to put an end to the Catholic church in Geneva. On 23 April, Jacques Bernard, a former Franciscan, began to ask for a

---

[153] RC 13.181, 13.183, 13.184.
[154] RC 13.184; *Levain*, p. 116.
[155] Roset, *Chroniques*, p. 196: "Le Conseil pendoit fort du costé de l'Evangile et touteffois ne pouvoit pas venir au changement que plusieurs des citoyens demandoient, parce qu'il avoit encor divers advys, et cependant l'idolatrie régnoit tousiours et les abus pour ceux qui n'avoient encores entendu la vérité de l'Evangile."
[156] Ibid., p. 197.
[157] Fromment describes this painting as garish (*Actes et Gestes*, p. 154).
[158] RC 13.205; 13.206.

public debate. On that day he presented a list of "errors" still being committed in Geneva and asked the council to allow him to debate anyone who wished to show him wrong.[159] The council decided it could not bar Bernard from holding a debate and asked him to present his petition to the canons of St. Peter. Bernard also took his case to the people, posting placards throughout the city on the first of May citing the reasons for his conversion and calling for a debate.[160] The process of Reformation was now entering its final phase. On Easter 1535, Thomas Vandel, pastor of St. Germain, openly joined the Reform.[161] Three of Geneva's syndics had also turned Protestant by this time.[162]

On 10 May Bernard received permission to publish his propositions, and Sunday the 30th was assigned as the day on which the debate would begin. The disputation was opened to anyone who wished to debate the Protestant propositions, which were printed and distributed among the clergy in Geneva and in surrounding areas. All participants were given an assurance of safe conduct to and from the disputation.[163] The Dominicans tried to get the imprisoned Furbity to participate, but he stubbornly declined the offer.[164] Immediately before the debate, the atmosphere was extremely tense in Geneva. On 27 May, three days before the debate, the Catholics were prohibited from holding a procession through the streets. Instead, they were ordered to hold it inside the cathedral and to refrain from ringing any bells.[165] The Catholics were now totally on the defensive, and it was the question of the cult that was to finally seal their fate in Geneva.

The disputation began as scheduled at the auditorium of the Convent de Rive, and was very poorly represented on the Catholic side, which could only muster two debaters: Pierre Caroli, a Sorbonne doctor, and Brother Chapussi, a Dominican from the Convent du Palais in Geneva. The propositions debated, which were formulations of standard Protestant conclusions, were the following: (1) justification is by Jesus Christ alone; (2) the government of the church depends on the Word of God alone; (3) only the one God who is completely satisfied by the one sacrificial atonement of Christ is to be

---

[159] RC 13.196.
[160] *Texte Inédit de Savion*, p. 435.
[161] RC 13.149, n. 2. He had probably been sympathetic to the Reformation for a while.
[162] *Texte Inédit de Savion*, p. 433.
[163] Roset, *Chroniques*, p. 197.
[164] RC 13.227.
[165] RC 13.224.

adored; (4) Jesus Christ is the sole mediator between God and man, and no one has the power to justify himself through works, or establish human traditions or offer prayers to the saints and their statues; (5) the Mass does not aid salvation, nor do prayers for the dead; and (6) the saints cannot intercede for anyone.[166]

Among these points some were given more attention than others, and the principal issue was the Mass and all of its "idolatrous" practices. The Mass was described as the "one thing on earth that is most contrary to God," and every aspect was discussed in detail, from the use of holy water, to crosses, vestments, processions, and the consecration of the host. The Protestant summary of this part of the debate is a striking rejection of the sacred value of material objects in worship. Holy water and oil are ridiculed as superstitious and insolent attempts at trying to make material objects holier than they have already been made by God himself.[167] The use of crosses is rejected on the ground that the only cross to be borne by Christians is one of personal suffering. Vestments are criticized as effeminate, Judaizing, and ineffective: They cannot serve as spiritual armor. The ceremonial gestures of the Mass were dismissed as borrowings from the ancient pagans and Jews, and as worthless and dangerous. Concerning the nature of the eucharist, the Protestants argued in a Zwinglian vein, saying that there was no bodily presence or sacrifice, but "only commemoration."[168] The transcendentalist spirit of the Protestant argument against the Catholic cult, by now almost reduced to a stock formula, is summarized in this brief passage:

It is necessary that our treasure be in heaven, and that we look for the things that are above instead of those upon the earth, those things which are on high, where Jesus is seated at the right hand of the Father, without entanglement in the things that are here below.[169]

---

[166] Roset, *Chroniques*, p. 198. Unlike other major disputations such as those of Zurich, Baden, Bern, and Lausanne, the Dispute de Rive has not been preserved as a complete record, and there is no indication that one ever existed. All that survives is a brief summary of the Protestant position on each of the six points, probably compiled by Farel for presentation to the Genevan council and for circulation among other communities. This has been published in *Mémoires et Documents Publiés par la Societé d'Histoire et d'Archeologie de Genève*, second series, vol. II (Geneva, 1886), pp. 201–40; "Un Opuscule Inédit de Farel: Le Résumé des Actes de la Dispute de Rive, 1535." The editors think this document is the "collationem de disputa" presented to the council on 27 July 1535 and later mentioned to the priests on 12 August.

[167] "Dispute de Rive," p. 223.

[168] Ibid., p. 227. The Protestants also argued that in the Supper "seullement est faicte la memoire de Jesus" (p. 230).

[169] Ibid., p. 212.

The same otherworldly emphasis surfaced in the lengthy discussion that followed on images and the kind of worship that is to be offered to God. For instance, the Protestants argued that God can only be worshiped in "spirit and in truth," and that his honor is not to be given to anyone else.[170] Images were rejected as dangerous and worthy of God's wrath. Again, the argument hinges on a highly spiritual understanding of worship: "Seeing that we are a spiritual people, who ought to serve God in spirit and in truth, how can we have any images or honor them?"[171]

The Catholic *libri pauperum* argument was rejected on the ground that Christians need no book except the Bible and that the invisible and spiritual cannot be conveyed through the work of men's hands. The argument proposing that images are only representations of saints and not divine entities in themselves was rejected with a practical observation: if that is so, then why do some images receive more attention that others?[172] To close, the Protestants called for "the abolition of the great abuse of the Mass, images and all human inventions by which the holy name of God is greatly blasphemed and the poor people are led to perdition."[173]

The Dispute de Rive had thus challenged the value of Catholicism in a very practical way. The focus of attention was not the issue of justification, but rather that of the Mass and the images, and all their attending "abuses." Without its cult, Catholicism would cease to exist in Geneva, and it is precisely this point that the Protestants were trying to make.

As soon as the debating ended on 24 June, the Protestants began to ask the council that it declare against the Catholics and that it abolish all their rituals. On 28 June, Claude Bernard argued before a combined session of the small and great council that the populace accepted the Protestants as the victors and now expected the abolition of the Mass, the images, and other "inventions and idolatries."[174] The Catholics, however, also put in their bid before the magistrates. Roset reports that "many persons protested that they wished to continue living like their fathers."[175] The council stalled by replying that it could not reach a decision until the secretaries finished writing a full report for them to study.[176] Roset mentions that the council delayed

170 Ibid.. p. 236.
171 Ibid., p. 237.
172 Ibid., p. 238.
173 Ibid., p. 239.
174 RC 13.252: "dissimulationes et ydolotramenta."
175 Roset, *Chroniques*, p. 200.
176 RC 13.253.

because it "still hoped to avoid dangers and harmful consequences for humanitarian reasons."[177] Fromment is more specific about the council's fears. According to him, the council was frightened by some of the warnings issued by the Catholics against the removal of images and the Mass. Their main fear was the threat of war. The Catholics, led by Pierre Caroli, told the Genevan magistrates that if they acceded to the demands of the Protestants, they would only worsen their already precarious situation:

> If you tear down the images, the Masses and all the Papal things as preachers and those who favor them want you to do, know that for every enemy you now have there will be a hundred: and in place of your old and great enemy, the Duke of Savoy, you will have the King of France, who is his nephew, as your adversary, as well as the Emperor, who is also his brother–in–law . . . and they will all be against you as mad wolves chasing prey, to destroy and ruin you.[178]

Paralyzed by such fears, the council pursued a policy of neutrality as long as it could get away with it.[179] The Protestants, however, made it difficult for the council to stall. On 4 July, a Protestant named Jacob Pactu demolished a statue in front of the small chapel of Nôtre Dame du Pont, near the Rhone bridge. The council stood firm in its neutrality and imprisoned Pactu as a warning to others who might want to imitate him.[180] The Protestants felt they had successfully challenged the validity of the Catholic cult, and now they waited for a legal decision to ensure its final destruction.

The final revolt

As the council continued to stall, the Protestants increased their effort to settle the matter once and for all. On 22 July, Farel entered the Madeleine, mounted the pulpit, and preached a sermon, contrary to the city ordinance that restricted him to the Convent de Rive.[181] Illegal acts now became the policy of the Protestants. The following day, Farel was admonished and warned by the council to keep preaching only at the Rive monastery and at the church of St. Germain.[182] Ignoring the council's admonition, Farel again preached at

---

[177] Roset, *Chroniques*, p. 200.
[178] Fromment, *Actes et Gestes*, p. 143.
[179] The magistrates, still undecided by 14 July, wrote a letter to the Bernese in which they asked for advice and also reported that they were experiencing troubles because of the Gospel (Herminjard 3.316).
[180] RC 13.256.
[181] *Levain*, p. 134, *Texte Inédit de Savion*, p. 440.
[182] RC 13.270.

another forbidden church on the 28th, this time at St. Gervais.[183] On the 31st he was reprimanded once more, but to no avail: Five days later he preached at the Madeleine once more, and at the Dominican convent as well.[184] The Protestants were now confident that they could push for a settlement and break the council's stalling. On Sunday, 8 August, Farel completed his illegal preaching tour by mounting the pulpit of the cathedral, where he preached to a large crowd.[185] It is unfortunate that none of these sermons have been preserved, for they would no doubt tell much about Protestant feelings on the eve of victory.

When he was called before the magistrates to answer for his preaching in the cathedral, Farel was defiant. He argued that since the council had refused his plea concerning "a holy thing, according to God and the Gospel," he had taken it upon himself to preach to the crowd that had assembled to hear him. According to Farel, then, it was as much a people's movement as it was his, since the crowd entered the cathedral first. He asked for permission to preach in the cathedral again, but was told to wait one more day for a decision.[186] The council was not to have any more time to think about this matter, however.

The final act of religious revolt in Geneva began in the cathedral, on Sunday, 8 August 1535, sometime after Farel's sermon.[187] As the canons began to sing vespers, some boys interrupted them by staging a counterceremony of their own: Hooting and howling, they mocked the Latin chant of the service. Suddenly, the youths charged the sanctuary, overturned the chairs on which the canons usually sat, and cursed them for making images and having confidence in them. The priests stood frozen with fear as the boys, still shouting, waved the chairs at them. Outside the cathedral, others who heard the noise came running in, and, upon seeing what the children were doing, pounced on the images, knocking them to the ground and breaking them into pieces. The children dropped the chairs and joined in, collecting some of the debris and carrying it outside, where they chanted to passersby, "Here we have the gods of the priests; would you like some?" ("Nous avons les dieux des Prebstres, en voulles vous?"). Some canons ran to notify the authorities and soon returned with two syndics, but they could do nothing to stop the destruction.

---

[183] *Texte Inédit de Savion,* p. 441.
[184] Ibid.
[185] RC 13.279; *Levain,* p. 150; Fromment, *Actes et Gestes,* p. 144.
[186] RC 13.278–9.
[187] The liveliest narrative of the iconoclastic riot at St. Peter's is that of Fromment, *Actes et Gestes,* pp. 144–5.

One of the syndics expressed his exasperation by saying: "If the images really are gods, then they can defend themselves if they want; we do not know what else to do."

When the mob turned its attention to the main altar and the tabernacle, they took about fifty consecrated hosts and fed them to Mesgret's dog. Mesgret, echoing the syndic's remark, said: "If they really are gods, then they won't let themselves be eaten by a dog." The defenseless wafers – "dieux blancs," as Fromment calls them – were quickly consumed by the dog, while the mob continued wrecking the cultic objects in the cathedral.[188]

Later that same evening, the iconoclasts gathered at an inn to plan their strategy against the other churches. The following morning an alarm was sounded, and many gathered thinking it was a warning for an impending invasion. The crowd was then incited to wage battle against "all the other idols of the churches of the city."[189] Led by the nobles Amy Perrin and Pierre Vandel and the merchant Baudichon, the mob crashed through the church of St. Gervais and the Dominican house, "where they did more damage than at St. Peter's," demolishing an altar piece worth 700 ducats. The donor of the altarpiece, a Florentine named Pierre Foysseau, offered to pay the iconoclasts 100 ducats if they would spare it. They responded with a sermonizing answer:

It is written in the Law: you shall cast down the idols in the land you shall inhabit, without making exceptions . . . and cursed be him who makes them and places his trust in them . . . God's commandment says one should not make images or adore them.[190]

Foysseau could only stand helpless while the iconoclasts destroyed his altarpiece and all the other cultic objects in the church.

After finishing at the Dominican house, the crowd marched toward Nôtre Dame de Grace. The syndics, wielding their staffs, came to try to stop them from destroying the chapel donated by the Dukes of Savoy, but their efforts were fruitless. The mob destroyed every "idol" in sight, except for the famous image of Our Lady of Grace, which syndics rescued from the church and hid, apparently to avoid the wrath of the House of Savoy.[191]

To prevent further destruction, the council ordered that guards be placed at the cathedral and that no more treasure be removed from

---

[188] Ibid., pp. 144–5.
[189] Ibid., p. 148.
[190] Ibid.
[191] Ibid.; RC 13.279.

the church. The leaders of the riot were asked to appear before the syndics and the council later that evening. When questioned about their behavior, Perrin, Vandel, and Baudichon defended themselves by appealing to divine authority: "concerning the destruction of the images they answered that it was true they had done it, but that they did not think they had erred, because such things were against the Word of God."[192] Through iconoclasm the Protestants had circumvented and usurped the power of the magistracy. The council, which had stalled for so long about the destruction of the Catholic cult, was now faced with an accomplished fact. The Reformation had physically triumphed in Geneva through a rebellious act.

The iconoclasts may have accomplished what they wanted, but the laws of the city had yet to be changed. On 10 August, the council met again to discuss the turmoil of the two previous days. Three of the Protestant preachers, Farel, Bernard, and Cordelier, appeared before them and argued that the iconoclasm be judged according to the result of the Dispute de Rive.[193] The council faced the same dilemma: It still had to pass judgment on the theological debate. Again, the council stalled and, instead of declaring its position, asked for the priests to appear before it to defend the Mass and the images once more. The guardians of the cult now had to prove that the iconoclasts had broken the law and had to be punished.[194] In a momentous decision, the council also voted to suspend the Mass until the matter had been discussed with the priests. Further acts of iconoclasm were also forbidden for the time being.[195] In addition, the Genevan magistrates wrote to the Bernese, asking for their opinion on the crisis.[196] Since it had chosen to steer a middle course, the council feared unrest from both sides, and to prevent violence and guard the remaining church treasures, it ordered an inventory of all church goods and assigned some men to guard each of the churches.[197]

Two days later, on 12 August, the council began its final deliberations on the Disputation.[198] The Catholic clergy of Geneva were invited to appear before the council to hear a summary of the Disputation read to them. Those present were asked to defend images, the inter-

---

[192] RC *13*.280.
[193] RC *13*.281.
[194] Ibid.
[195] RC *13*.282.
[196] Herminjard 3.332.
[197] RC *13*.282. Turretini-Grivel, *Les Archives de Genève* (Geneva, 1878), "Inventaries des joyeaux, meubles et effets trouvés dans les eglises de Genève et leurs dependances lors de la Reformation," pp. 97–130.
[198] RC *13*.284ff.

cession of the saints, the Mass, and other ceremonies. The Reformation was to be decided, therefore, on the question of the Catholic cult. The priests, however, refused to comment on these issues, claiming that they did not have sufficient theological training to argue about them. They protested they were simple men, and asked the council to allow them to live as their fathers had done before them. The vicar and the canons of St. Peter added that they had no wish to hear about the Disputation, listen to a sermon by Farel, or much less, discuss such issues.[199] By tearing down the images, the iconoclasts had forced the priests to a confrontation, and the priests, perhaps painfully aware of the hopelessness of their situation, now refused to defend themselves. They, too, had been overthrown. Roset reports that after this meeting many of the clergy left the city, "some out of fear of their enemies, others because of their devotion."[200]

Now that the Reformation was nearly complete, the city began to take advantage of the situation created by the iconoclasts. Geneva was in desperate financial straits because of its huge war debt to Bern. On 16 August, the city began to use the spoils from the ravaged churches to fill its treasury, melting down crosses, reliquaries, and church plate to help pay the Bernese.[201] What had previously been objects of devotion now served as the source of civic revenue; iconoclasm also had its practical side. On 19 August, the remaining treasure at St. Peter's was placed under special guard, to ensure that no unauthorized use be made of it.[202]

These measures were largely ineffective, however. On 23 August, some images were destroyed at the Convent de Rive, as were the remaining altars.[203] On the following day, the Convent de St. Clare was invaded by a large contingent of men, and all of its cultic objects were ravaged.[204] Six days after this incident, the sisters left Geneva under a heavy guard provided by the syndics, but were taunted by some children as they marched out of the city.[205]

The Catholics remaining in Geneva made a final effort for their faith on 2 September, when they presented the council with a petition for the reinstatement of the Mass.[206] The council hedged, as it had done so many times before, and said it could not rule on the request until it had heard from Bern. Three days later the magistrates received a

[199] RC 13.285.
[200] Roset, *Chroniques*, p. 201.
[201] RC 13.288.
[202] RC 13.291.
[203] *Texte Inédit de Savion*, p. 446.
[204] *Levain*, p. 152ff.
[205] Ibid., p. 185ff.
[206] RC 13.301.

letter from Bern, congratulating them on their course of action and approving the abolition of the Mass.[207] The Reformation was now one step closer to legal approval. Meanwhile, iconoclasm continued to take place with impunity. On 13 September, a group of iconoclasts destroyed all the images at the small chapel of Nôtre Dame du Pont.[208] On the following day a triumphal procession of sorts was organized by the Protestants, in which the leaders of the Reformation in Geneva proudly paraded through the streets with their companions.

During that week, people continued to attack the churches – in spite of the guards placed there by the council – clearing out what had been missed before: altars, ironwork, and even the lead from stained glass windows.[209] Faced with such disobedience, the council called Baudichon, Perrin, and other leaders before them and enjoined them from commiting any more "excesses." Instead of apologizing, Claude Bernard angrily protested that the syndics had interfered with "the work of God" when they rescued the painting of Our Lady of Grace from the Augustinian monastery.[210] It seemed now that the iconoclasts were placing the magistrates on trial. On the following day, the council acted to prevent the illegal removal of treasure by the Catholics, strictly forbidding the Dominicans and Augustinians from taking any of their possessions out of Geneva, and placing another set of special guards outside their houses to ensure nothing would be taken out. Nonetheless, the turmoil continued. On 27 September, the Protestants destroyed the chapel at the Convent de Rive.[211] On the same day, iconoclasm began to spread to Geneva's surrounding territory when a party from the city tore down the images at the village church of Villete.[212]

Although the city government had yet to ratify the Reformation, all governmental actions now favored the Protestants. On 9 October, when it was reported that the Augustinians were carrying off their treasure, the council ordered Baudichon to guard the monastery and to turn over to the city everything of value he could find. On the 15th, the Augustinians were officially reprimanded for their actions.[213] On 12 October, a significant step was taken by the council. When the

---

[207] Herminjard 3.339.
[208] *Texte Inédit de Savion*, p. 446. (These images had been donated by Florentine merchants during the time of the Genevan fairs in the fifteenth century and were reported to be very costly.)
[209] Ibid.
[210] RC 13.310.
[211] *Texte Inédit de Savion*, p. 448.
[212] Ibid.
[213] RC 13.322; 13.326.

newly established public hospital requested funds, the council ordered that it receive revenue from goods taken out of St. Peter and the other parishes.[214] The hospital was also given the recently vacated Convent de St. Clare as its permanent home. On 15 October – the same day on which the Augustinians were admonished – the council prohibited the remaining priests from administering the sacraments or wearing vestments.[215] On 31 October, the council sealed its own de facto acceptance of the Reformation. The image of Our Lady of Grace, which the syndics had guarded so carefully, was taken out and publicly burned by them at the end of the meeting.[216] On 18 November, the council ensured the success of the Reformation by declaring that no "papalist" could hold public office, and on 26 November the last political prerogative of episcopal power was annulled when the city established its own mint, appropriately enough, with the spoil from the churches as revenue.[217]

The final confrontation with the remaining priests took place on 29 November.[218] The Council of Two Hundred again asked them to defend the Catholic cult, but they responded as they had done before, saying they were not learned enough to comment on theological issues. Since they failed to defend their faith, the priests were forbidden to celebrate Mass, administer the sacraments or try to "seduce" anyone. Six days later, the council gave them an ultimatum: If they did not want to accept the Reformation they had to renounce their citizenship and leave Geneva.[219] The religious revolution had triumphed, even though no specific official pronouncement had yet confirmed it.

The expulsion of the clergy gave rise to a new wave of iconoclasm in Geneva. The few remaining cultic objects of the old faith were sought out and destroyed during the following week.[220] The most dramatic event was the discovery of several "frauds" throughout the city, some of which were dramatically exaggerated. The "arm of St. Anthony" at the cathedral, for instance, was exposed as the parched "membre viril" of a stag.[221] This story is an obvious overreaction to

---

[214] RC 13.324.
[215] RC 13.326; Roset, *Chroniques*, p. 207.
[216] RC 13.340.
[217] RC 13.363.
[218] RC 13.372–3. By now only the Franciscan, Dominican, and cathedral clergy remained in Geneva.
[219] Monter (*Calvin's Geneva*, p. 54) says only six of the twenty remaining Franciscans chose exile.
[220] Roset, *Chroniques*, p. 214: Roset reports: "En ce moys de Décembre 1535, auquel la ville estoit tousiours assiégé, les cytoyens recerchoient les ydolles et reliques dans les temples pour n'y rien laisser."
[221] Fromment, *Actes et Gestes*, p. 146: Roset, *Chroniques*, pp. 214–15.

the "trickery" of Rome, but it was apparently believed by the Protestants. The spurious relic was afterwards paraded through the city streets with cries of "here is the arm of St. Anthony which we were made to adore."[222] The "brain of St. Peter," also at the cathedral, was now unmasked as a pumice stone. At St. Gervais, where the bodies of three saints buried beneath the main altar had previously worked numerous wonders, a more elaborate fraud was uncovered. The saints' voices, which had been heard by many people in the church, were revealed as nothing more than the sound of the wind passing through some pots and pipes in a subterranean chamber.[223] With the discovery of these frauds, the "error and deception" of the Catholic cult was dealt the final blow in Geneva.

On 10 March, Farel asked that the council guarantee the preaching of the Word in Genevan territories.[224] Beginning that month, and through April, steps were taken to carry out this request. This meant the removal of images from many countryside churches.[225] On 23 March, the council aided this plan by decreeing that no one was to attend Mass outside the city, or celebrate it within.[226] Almost as an anticlimax, on 25 May 1536, a General Council of the Genevan people voted unanimously to "live henceforth according to the Law of the Gospel and the Word of God, and to abolish all Papal abuses, images and idols."[227] The Reformation had made its final triumph in Geneva by declaring its war against the idols a central part of its new order of affairs. The institutional and legal triumph of the Reformation had been effected through a combination of forces, but above all, through popular revolutionary iconoclasm.

ICONOCLASM AS A REVOLUTIONARY TACTIC

Iconoclasm is a revolutionary act.[228] It is a direct act of violence  against the accepted social myth.[229] Had not the cult that supported

---

222 Fromment, *Actes et Gestes*, p. 146.
223 Ibid., p. 149–150.
224 RC 13.486.
225 Roset, *Chroniques*, pp. 227–88.
226 RC 13.503.
227 RC 13.576: "voulons vivre en ceste saincte loix evangelicque et parolle de Dieu, ainsy qu'elle nous est annuncee, veuillans delaisser toutes messes et aultres ceremonies et abusions papales, ymaiges et ydoles."
228 For a discussion of the historiographical problems involved in using this term see Perez Zagorin, "Prolegomena to the Comparative History of Revolution in Early Modern Europe," *Comparative Studies in Sociology and History*, 18: 151–74 (1976); also his *Rebels and Rulers, 1500–1660* (2 vols., Cambridge University Press, 1982), esp. vol. l, pp. 3–60. On the revolutionary aspect of Protestantism consult the brilliant new study by Donald R. Kelley, *The Beginning of Ideology* (Cambridge, 1982).
229 Robert M. Kingdon, "Was the Protestant Reformation a Revolution? The Case of

the priests been rejected, there might have been no revolution at all. In other words, the power of the priests would have been assumed, largely unchanged, by the new Protestant clergy. One must remember that Protestant ministers continued to fill the cultic role of the priests, but as guardians of a new piety. This is largely due to the successful attack waged on the piety that sustained the "social myth." The expulsion of the "idols," then, often secured the expulsion of the priests. Protestant iconoclasts, after all, did not want to destroy the churches, but to "purify" them, giving birth to a new piety and a new religious aesthetic. A beautiful church to a Swiss Protestant was one without images, relics, altars, or holy water fonts.[230]

When one looks at the phenomenon of Swiss iconoclasm in closer detail, it becomes apparent that there are several types of iconoclasm, each of which is revolutionary in a different way. In the first place, one must distinguish between two basic categories: legal and illegal. Each of these categories, in turn, may be subdivided into different types of iconoclastic activity. Let us begin with illegal acts.

Illegal acts of iconoclasm are those committed against the established laws of a community. The first type is the individual and isolated iconoclastic act. This involves a single person who strikes out against a cultic object as a private act of rebellion. Such was the case of Louis Chenevard, who entered the Franciscan chapel in Geneva in May 1534 and gouged out the eyes of a statue of St. Anthony in the presence of all the friars.[231] Chenevard's isolated act was the first in a long series of iconoclastic demonstrations that would mark the final process of the Reformation in Geneva.[232] Such acts may occur at any

Geneva," in *Transition and Revolution*, R. M. Kingdon, ed. (Minneapolis, 1974), p. 57.

[230] As evidenced in Farel's description of the newly-cleansed church in Neuchâtel. *Guillaume Farel*, p. 227.

[231] *Levain*, p. 93. In addition to Chenevard, four other individuals were engaged in isolated acts in Geneva between March 1534 and July 1535. RC *13.19*, *13.109*, *13.256*; and *Levain*, p. 105.

[232] Reported cases of iconoclasm in Geneva, 1534–5:

Date	Item(s) destroyed or desecrated	Source
* 1 May 1534	1 statue	*Levain*, p. 93
†24 May	several statues	RC *12.547*
†25 May	2 statues	*Levain*, p. 94
†22 June	2 statues	*Levain*, p. 95
†26 July	many statues, one alt. - consecrated hosts	*Levain*, p. 96–7 RC *13.18–19*

stage of the process of Reformation. By themselves they accomplish little beyond the destruction of specific objects or the disruption of certain services; but if they begin to occur regularly within a community, as happened in Geneva in the spring of 1534, then they become part of a larger protest. As a rule, isolated acts such as these do not occur with any great frequency.

A second and more common type of illegal iconoclasm is the collective protest. This takes place when two or more individuals join together in destroying cultic objects. As with the first type, such acts may occur during any stage of the Reformation. They are a bolder and more forceful type of protest than individual acts, not only because more damage can be done, but also because they serve as a display of communal solidarity among the iconoclasts. This type of iconoclasm may have either (or both) of the following aims: to destroy specific objects, or to make a public statement concerning the "error" of the Catholic cult. Such was the case at Wesen, where the young iconoclasts mocked the images before setting them on fire.[233]

Depending on the stage of the Reformation within a given community, and on how often such acts of defiance occur, the collective attack will produce varying results. For instance, if such an act is one of the first in a town, all it is likely to effect is the arrest and punishment of the perpetrators.[234] However, if many such acts are taking place within a community, then it is likely that the question of images will be brought up for public debate and that a religious settlement

(*cont.*)

Date	Item(s) destroyed or desecrated	Source
*27 July	1 statue	RC 13.19
†19 Sept.	several statues	RC 13.65; 13.68–9
†29 Sept.	several statues	RC 13.593
	altars, hosts	*Levain*, p. 107
*Sept.	holy water	*Levain*, p. 105
†Oct.	1 cross, several statues	*Levain*, p. 106
* 3 Dec.	1 cross	RC 13.109
† 4 Dec.	several crosses	*Levain*, p. 110
† 9 March 1535	1 statue, 1 lamp	RC 13.166
†26 March	1 statue	RC 13.181; 13.183–4
* 4 July	1 statue	RC 13.256

(* = individual act);
(† = group act).

[233] Stumpf, *Reformationschronik*, vol. 2, p. 25.
[234] For an example: J. Strickler, *Actensammlung zur Schweizerischen Reformationsgeschichte in den Jahren 1521–1532* (Zurich, 1884), vol. 5, p. 10, n. 20.

Group acts predominate over indiv. acts.

will be reached. In Geneva, for instance, there were ten reported cases of illegal group iconoclasm in the one year before the Dispute de Rive was held.

The third type of illegal iconoclasm is the riot. This takes place, as it did at Basel, Neuchâtel, and Geneva, when many members of the community embark upon the wholesale destruction of cultic objects without permission from the magistracy. This type of illegal iconoclasm is the most revolutionary, since it defies the power of the government and seals the triumph of the Reformation against the established laws. A good case in point is Basel, where some of the magistrates tried to stop the destruction, but failed. As one Catholic eyewitness put it, the efforts of the "fromme katholische Rat" were all in vain: The fury of the Protestants was so great, it seemed they "were all possessed by Satan," and no one even dared to try to stop them.[235] Instead of assenting to authority, the iconoclasts told the magistrates that their approval (or disapproval) no longer mattered.[236]

So far we have only looked at cases which were outside the law and aimed at changing the law through disobedience. Let us now look at another kind of iconoclasm, that which destroyed the Catholic *cultus* under the protection of the law. Legal iconoclasm is that which is effected with government approval (though not necessarily under its direction). The typology for legal acts is very similar to that for illegal acts, except that only two types are most common. The first and second types mentioned above (the isolated individual and collective acts), may still take place in a legal setting, but not too frequently. When a government pronounces judgment against Catholic worship, the ensuing destruction is usually too wild and feverish to allow for isolated acts, and when they do occur, they become part of a larger protest.[237]

The legal removal of cultic objects may be effected, first of all, in an orderly and peaceful manner, without the participation of the general populace. Zurich, where teams of craftsmen dismantled images and altars behind locked church doors, is the best example of this type of legal iconoclasm.

---

[235] "Sie taten nicht anders, als waren sie alle von dem leidigen Satan leibhaft besessen, wie es denn gar leichtig aus ihren Taten abzunehmen . . . niemand konnte oder durfte sie davon abwendig machen." Oechsli, *Quellenbuch*, p. 331.

[236] Stahelin, *Briefe und Akten*, vol. 2, p. 281.

[237] This is nicely illustrated by the story of the iconoclast who earned the name "Idol-shearer." J. J. Hottinger and H. H. Vogeli, eds., *Bullingers Reformationsgeschichte* (Frauenfeld, 1838), vol. II, p. 1.

The second and more common type of legal iconoclasm is the riot, and Bern is a good example of this type. Immediately after the Bern Disputation of January 1528, the Bernese council ordered all images and altars to be removed within eight days. Although this flexible schedule was intended to prevent rioting, it had the opposite effect.[238] The removal of images in Bern was a legal act, but it had turned into a popular act of rebellion against the cultic objects of Roman Catholicism. The legal riot is similar to the illegal, insofar as it is disorganized and violent, and is participated in by the general populace. One important difference, however, is that such rioting does not seek to disobey the law, but rather to fulfill it. Legal iconoclasm, by definition, signals the triumph of the Reformation within a given community.

The motives behind iconoclasm

There is little doubt that the principal cause of popular iconoclasm in the Reformation was religion. The images, altars, and relics of the Catholic faith were attacked not only as the symbols of a false religion, but as the physical manifestations of that very falsehood. Yet, no analysis of iconoclasm would be complete without taking into account the social and political dimensions of this religious phenomenon.

Iconoclasm may be an overtly religious act, but it has significant political implications, as is attested to by the events at Basel, where the city oligarchy was removed along with the images. Often, but not in all cases, iconoclasm was used to force unwilling governments to accept the Reformation. Basel, Neuchâtel, and Geneva are the best examples of such cases. Even when carried out by the civil authorities, iconoclasm still allows for a high degree of popular participation in the political process. In towns such as St. Gall and Schaffhausen, for instance, where the images were removed by the order of the magistrates, the final action was preceded by popular pressure and illegal acts, and was carried out with enthusiasm by many of the citizens.[239] Iconoclasm, then, is marked by its revolutionary political character, even when it is the result of government fiat.

Still, it is the case of the illegal iconoclast that best shows the revolutionary implications of this phenomenon in Switzerland. The iconoclast who destroys an image or desecrates a host against the dictates

---

[238] *Berner Reformation*, Steck and Tobler (eds.), vol. I, pp. 612–13.
[239] F. Fischer, "Bildersturm," p. 10ff.

of his (or her) own government is usurping the power of the clergy and the magistracy. It has been observed that public acts of violence by crowds in the sixteenth century were caused by a desire on the part of private individuals to assume the role of the clergy and the magistracy, "to defend doctrine or purify the religious community."[240] The illegal iconoclast acts as a religious agent by striking out against what he regards as a corrupt practice, and assumes the role of cleric, as guardian of the social myth, by taking it upon himself no longer to allow something to be venerated by the public. He assumes the role of the magistrate when he seeks to establish a situation not yet allowed by the existing political arrangement. If the government will not clear the idols, then he takes it upon himself to make de facto what is not yet de jure.

Iconoclasm, therefore, can be an act of political revolt. Illegal iconoclasts defy the magistracy through their actions: They not only break the law, as any common vandal does when he destroys public or private property, but also assert that the law supporting the "idols" is wrong and ought not to be obeyed. Those who wage war against images illegally circumvent and challenge the power of the government. The government of Geneva, for example, found it necessary to remind a group of illegal iconoclasts in 1534 that they had committed an act that, even when legal, was reserved for the magistracy.[241] A combined and sustained effort within a community to destroy the cultic objects of Catholicism thus usurps the power of the magistracy, and may even force an unwilling government to accept what it has previously forbidden. Oecolampadius was aware of this when he summarized the outcome of the religious struggle at Basel. The hesitancy of the magistracy, he said, had been a "hard knot" to untangle; but iconoclasm, "the wedge of the Lord," had finally split it.[242]

As is reflected in Oecolampadius's remark, iconoclasm is politically significant in still another way, because those who carry it out often distance themselves from it, deny personal causation, and attribute it to God instead. Oecolampadius was not alone when he interpreted iconoclasm as an act of God; to say "it is the will of God" was common practice among Swiss iconoclasts.[243] At first sight this might seem politically innocuous, but it is fraught with danger: The same

---

[240] Natalie Z. Davis, "The Rites of Violence: Religious Riot in Sixteenth Century France," *Past and Present*, 59: 90 (May 1973).

[241] RC 13.18: (note 136).

[242] Stahelin, *Briefe und Akten*, p. 280: "Malo nudo suus [Domini] cuneus obvenit."

[243] Steck and Tobler, *Berner Reformation*, vol. I, p. 613. Also: Fromment, *Actes et Gestes*, p. 145. Davis provides similar examples for France ("Rites of Violence," p. 67).

argument can easily be extended to the removal of idolatrous governments themselves. Although none of the major continental Reformers ever advocated tyrannicide or revolution as a way of effecting
religious change, their followers could not always be restrained from
applying the same rule to governments that they applied to the
"idols." As a form of aggressive disobedience to established authority, iconoclasm is closely related to the more radical forms of political
revolution.[244] This is apparent not only in Switzerland, but also later
in France and the Netherlands, where iconoclasm would be intricately connected to the process of open political revolt.[245]

Iconoclasm has three other possible motivations. First, it appears
that iconoclasts were at times also affected by class hostility[246] – at
least, that is what some Catholic contemporaries believed[247] – but as
shall be seen presently, Swiss iconoclasm was a phenomenon that
often cut across class lines. Secondly, one cannot also dismiss economic reasons, or more specifically, the desire for booty as a motive
in some iconoclastic acts. In Basel people quarreled over the spoils
from the vandalized churches; in Geneva guards had to be stationed
at each church to prevent looting.[248] Finally, one must also consider
the likely possibility of irrational motives, that is, of iconoclasm as an
act of vandalism or as an expression of the effects of mob psychology.[249] One cannot assume that every person who joined the riots in
Bern, Basel, Neuchâtel, or Geneva had previously harbored an irre-
sistible urge to smash altars, desecrate hosts, or burn images: Many,
surely, were gripped by the excitement of the moment, and vented
their fury spontaneously.

But just against whom, or what, did iconoclasts really vent their
fury when they destroyed the images and altars? Was it in fact the
"idols" themselves that were being destroyed, or was it the church
and the social system that supported it? Those who look for simple
answers, whether they be intellectual historians or sociologists, often
overlook the fact that no individual factors, when considered in isola-

244 Martin Luther was aware of the political dangers inherent in popular illegal iconoclasm, and had written about them in *Against the Heavenly Prophets*. LW 40, 89–
90.
245 Phyllis Mack Crew, *Calvinist Preaching*; and Deyon/ Lottin, *Les Casseurs de l'Eté*.
246 Christensen, *Art and the Reformation*, p. 106.
247 Johann Stolz interpreted the iconoclastic riot in Basel largely in terms of a class
conflict. Oechsli, *Quellenbuch*, pp. 330–1. Also Martin Warnke's essay, "Durchgebrochene Geschichte," *Bildersturm*, esp. p. 84ff.; and C. Verlinden, "Mouve-
ments des Prix et Salaires en Belgique au XVIe Siècle," *Annales*, 10 (1955).
248 Stahelin, *Briefe und Akten*, vol. II, p. 82; RC 13.280.
249 Christensen, *Art and the Reformation*, p. 106.

tion, can fully explain iconoclasm.[250] In trying to explain this phenomenon one has to take account of the interrelationship between abstract thought and political, social, and economic circumstances. This is clear in the case of Geneva, where the destruction of the images served multiple aims simultaneously.

On an ideological plane, the images were attacked as "idols," as false, misleading representations of divine power that needed to be removed in order to ensure the purity of religious belief and practice. But these ideas were never fully disembodied, and, in fact, became a practically oriented program for social change. In this way, iconoclasm itself became a political tactic. Farel fulfilled both of these functions at once when he climbed into the pulpit illegally to preach against the images. This was as much a political as a theological or ideological statement.

On another level, the images served as a focus for many kinds of social and economic discontent, and their removal satisfied other purposes. In Geneva, the treasure taken from the churches was used in a carefully calculated way to serve the new objectives of the rebellious Protestant city. The treasure taken from the churches was used against Savoy as much as against Rome and all it stood for. The new mint, for instance, the symbol of financial and political independence, would have been impossible without the revenue confiscated from the ravaged churches. The hospital, located in the convent vacated by the sisters of St. Clare, funded by revenue taken from the cathedral and the parishes, was a concrete expression of a new social and economic ethic, and also served as a powerful symbol of the religious transvaluation occasioned by iconoclasm.

In an age when the "religious" and the "secular" were not as easily divorced as in our own, it is misleading to speak of any motives as strictly "religious" to the exclusion of other factors. In the sixteenth century religion encompassed a rather wide and complex network of social, political, and economic relationships. To consider any one factor in total isolation, and to play it off *against* the others, as if they were truly separable, or – even worse – mutually exclusive, is to misjudge the complexity of the Reformation. It is in this comprehensive sense of meaning that I would like to argue that religion was the central issue in the ideology of iconoclasm.

It has been suggested that iconoclasm was the response of an an-

[250] M. Hagopian, in *The Phenomenon of Revolution* (New York, 1974), has observed: "those seeking simplicity should study something other than the causes of revolution."

guished lay piety.[251] Events in Switzerland support this assertion. Swiss iconoclasm was theologically motivated: It aimed to destroy the cultic objects of an ecclesiastical system that was seen as dangerous and untrue, and that was perceived as having "fooled" and "exploited" the laity. Iconoclasts not only destroyed images, they "proved" they had no power; they not only ransacked reliquaries, but delighted in unmasking frauds.[252] Iconoclasm may have in some cases produced economic and social effects that were beyond its immediate scope, but these changes are not to be seen as primary, or necessarily exclusive motivating forces. What makes it possible for us to speak of Reformation "iconoclasm" instead of "vandalism" is precisely the theological or ideological aspect of the phenomenon. Vandalism is wanton destruction; iconoclasm is the destruction of religious objects for ideological reasons.

This is not to say, of course, that every iconoclast (or even most iconoclasts) fully understood the ideological complexities behind the religiosocial change they were effecting. Perhaps it would be useful to speculate about what would have happened if Zwingli or Farel had been able to probe the minds of some iconoclasts, much as modern-day pollsters, to discover their true motives. Is it possible that they might have been surprised to discover discrepancies between their ideology and the actual reasons that compelled people to smash images and altars? No matter what the case might have been, one does have to admit that, without the underlying theological motivations around which the various streams of discontent were arranged (even in the most extreme cases of opportunism), iconoclasm could not have become such an integral part of the process of the Reformation in Switzerland. Swiss iconoclasm is principally a religious phenomenon that had significant practical implications. It is the one aspect of the Reformation in which popular participation was highest, and it is also the focus of the very process by which the religious transvaluation of the sixteenth century was effected.[253]

---

[251] Ozment, *Reformation in the Cities*, pp. 42–6.
[252] Fromment, *Actes et Gestes*, pp. 146, 149–50.
[253] In trying to arrive at a typology of early modern revolutions, Perez Zagorin distinguishes five different sets of factors: (1) the socioeconomic position of the participants; (2) the geographic extent, or focus of rebel action; (3) the aims and goals of rebellion and the targets of rebel violence; (4) the forms and degree of rebel organization; (5) the rebel mentality, justifying beliefs, or ideology. Concerning the third factor, which is what interests us at this point, he says: "The targets of violence, whether persons or property and things, generally bear some relation or correspondence to the aims of a movement." *Rebels and Rulers*, vol. 1, p. 40.

Iconoclasm and the pattern of Reformation

Because the image question is one where the impact of Protestant teachings can be measured with some confidence, the phenomenon of iconoclasm allows one to analyze the pattern of the Reformation in Swiss cities as well as popular participation in this process.

Iconoclasm is one point where Protestant preaching inspired action, and the first pattern revealed by iconoclasm is the role played by preaching in the process of Reformation. One of the first steps taken by Protestants in Swiss cities was to secure permission from the magistracy for the preaching of the scriptures.[254] The process of "Protestantization," or Reformation, in Swiss cities is a two-pronged assault, a combination of preaching and teaching, accompanied by iconoclasm. In Geneva, to mention but one example, there were distinct phases where the Protestants concentrated on either preaching or iconoclasm, though not exclusively. When John Calvin assessed the state of affairs in Geneva at the time of his arrival, he made it seem as if the Reformation had not yet triumphed, but what he said pointed, in fact, to the interdependence of preaching and iconoclasm in the "Protestantization" of the city: "When I first arrived in this church there was almost nothing. They were preaching and that is all. They were good at seeking out idols and burning them, but there was no Reformation. Everything was in turmoil."[255]

Calvin's statement sheds light on the process of Reformation in an indirect way. What he emphasizes is the fact that the Genevan church was still occupied with the destruction of the old religion rather than with the creation of an organized religious community; but by observing that preaching and iconoclasm were the main activities of this young church, Calvin testifies to the importance of these two elements of the Reformation.[256]

The pattern of Reformation in Swiss cities is laid bare by iconoclasm in still another way. The war against the "idols" often helped to bring the process of confrontation with Catholicism to a crisis point, since the political insubordination of the iconoclasts necessarily required a legal discussion of the validity of images and the Mass. Iconoclasts had to be dragged to court for their crimes, and such trials could help

---

[254] Rupp, *Patterns*, p. 30.
[255] CR 9.891.
[256] Natalie Davis maintains that the relationship between preaching and iconoclasm is even more involved. She asserts that popular acts of religious violence suggest a goal akin to preaching, insofar as they attempt to defend true doctrine and deny false beliefs "through dramatic challenges and tests" ("Rites of Violence," p. 55).

bring the religious conflict to a resolution, whether by public debate, popular vote, or magisterial decision. One of the central strategies of the Swiss Reformers was their request for a public disputation with the Catholic clergy so they could "prove" that it was necessary to remove images and abolish the Mass.[257] The Catholics, too, tried to win at this game by arranging a disputation at Baden in May 1526, but Zwingli's refusal to participate greatly hampered general acceptance of the victory claimed by the Catholics.[258]

Iconoclasm also naturally reveals much about religious violence in the Swiss Reformation, especially because it so often gave rise to disruptions beyond the destruction of cultic objects. The goal of the iconoclast was to rid the community of spiritual pollution but, as Natalie Zemon Davis has observed, this concept served as a double-edged sword.[259] The word "pollution" was used by both sides of the religious conflict, but whereas Protestants focused their enmity on the "idols," Catholics focused theirs on the "heretics." It can be said, with reservations, that while Protestants sought to overthrow Catholicism by attacking its cultic objects, the Catholics sought to defeat the Protestants by inflicting bodily harm on them.[260] Protestants would feed consecrated hosts to a goat and say "now he can die if he wants, he has received the sacrament,"[261] or spit into the holy water fonts[262]; Catholics, however, regarded such acts as attacks on the sacred, and consequently vented their anger on the persons of the Protestants themselves.

Using Geneva as an example, it becomes clear that iconoclastic violence, or merely the fear of it, often motivated the Catholics to attack the Protestants. Two of the riots that occurred in Geneva in 1533 can be attributed to Catholic fear of iconoclasm.[263] The Genevan Catholics seemed to be aware that the main target of Protestant violence was the Catholic cultus. The Protestants, who were attacked regularly, even by Catholic women and their children,[264] could not

---

[257] *Handbuch der Schweizer Geschichte* (Zurich, 1972), vol. I, p. 449.
[258] Leonhard von Muralt, *Die Badener Disputation 1526* (Leipzig, 1926).
[259] Davis, "Rites of Violence," p. 57; also her article, "The Sacred and the Body Social in Sixteenth Century Lyons," *Past and Present* 90: 40–70 (February 1981).
[260] A description of the Genevan riots of 28 March and 4 May 1533 can be found in Jeanne de Jussie's *Levain*, pp. 53, 64. On similar events in France: Philip Benedict, *Rouen during the Wars of Religion* (New York, 1981); and also his article, "The Catholic Response to Protestantism: Church Activity and Popular Piety in Rouen, 1560–1600," in J. Obelkevich (ed.), *Religion and the People, 800–1700* (Chapel Hill, 1979).
[261] *Levain*, p. 23.
[262] Ibid., p. 105.
[263] Ibid., pp. 53, 64; Fromment, *Actes et Gestes*, p. 57.
[264] *Levain*, p. 57. Apparently, the participation of women and children in Catholic

help but be aware that they themselves were the targets of Catholic violence. The difference between the two groups stems from their divergent opinion as to what constituted "pollution" within the community, or, more importantly, from their contradictory interpretations of the sacred.[265]

In addition to shedding light on theological and political aspects of the Swiss Reformation, iconoclasm sheds light on social aspects, primarily because its "democratic" nature reveals the roles played by various social groups. Although circumstances vary from place to place, the existing evidence suggests that iconoclasm was not restricted to any one social class in Switzerland. It was a truly popular movement that could involve all sorts of people.

One pattern revealed by iconoclasm is the participation of tradesmen in the Swiss Reformation. The role played by the guilds in some cities bears this out: In Basel, for instance, it was the guilds that finally brought the issue of religion to a crisis point, especially the guild of the carpenters and masons[266]; in Schaffhausen, the religious revolt was led for a time by the guild of vinedressers.[267] The eyewitness report of Fridolyn Ryff, a Catholic member of the Basel Rat, reveals this pattern in a disdainful, and not altogether impartial way. Trying to show that no worthy patrician could destroy images, Ryff claimed that the tumult at Basel was to be attributed to "common and shiftless people" and that "no prosperous or honorable citizen could be found among them."[268] Johann Stolz, a Dominican, also echoed Ryff's remarks about the iconoclasts, adding they were nothing but "scum" ("Lumpengesindel").[269]

The preponderance of working-class (or even lower-class) iconoclasts in one city does not preclude the participation of the upper class in another, however. In Geneva, class distinctions seem to have made little difference among those who wanted to wage war on the idols. Although many of the iconoclasts punished by the authorities were tradesmen such as food merchants, purse makers, cloth cutters, or

violence was so intense, it drew a public statement from the Genevan government, which reminded all men that they were responsible for seeing that their wives and children stayed out of trouble. RC 12.250–1.

[265] *Levain*, p. 106. Witness the report of Catholic children who urinated on a dead Protestant.

[266] Christensen, *Art and the Reformation*, p. 95.

[267] Jakob Wipf, *Reformationsgeschichte der Stadt und Landschaft Schaffhausen* (Zurich, 1929). Also: Mayer, *German Reformed Church*, p. 407–14.

[268] *Basler Taschebuch*, vols. V and VI (1855), p. 194.

[269] Oechsli, *Quellenbuch*, p. 330.

shoemakers,[270] the leaders of the final riot were patricians. Among these were Baudichon de Maissonneuve, a rich merchant, and the nobles Amy Perrin, Jean Goullaz, Pierrre Vandel, and Mesgret le Magnifique.[271]

Another constant and surprising pattern is the age of many iconoclasts. In numerous reports, Protestant and Catholic alike tell us that youths not only participated in, but even initiated much of the rioting. In Geneva, as we have seen, "petis enfans" played a major role.[272] In Basel we read about "Knaben" and "Buben"[273]; in Thorgau and Toggenburg they are called "jungen Knaben,"[274] in Wesen "Jüngling,"[275] in Neuchâtel "jeunes gens."[276] Martin Luther mentions boys ("pueri") who chanted in the streets of Bern as the consecrated hosts were being destroyed along with the images.[277]

Although this situation might lead some to suspect that much of Swiss iconoclasm was no more than childish vandalism (Johann Stolz certainly thought so, calling the entire tumult at Basel "bübisch"),[278] one must be cautious in jumping to conclusions. It might seem tempting to speculate whether in the age of the Reformation (to change Heimpel's dictum) "the image donors *begat* the image smashers," or even to assume that the Reformation was the revolt of one generation against another; but there are other factors to consider. Though children, or youths, played an active part in riots and disturbances, the wholesale destruction of images in cities and towns was still a very adult affair. The town councils that approved of iconoclasm were certainly not directed by children, or even young men. The theologians and preachers were certainly past adolescence. Even more significantly, there is no evidence suggesting that *all* the iconoclasts were youths. That the Reformation was aggressively promoted by the young simply means that it appealed to some of them, and that they expressed their support for it with the idealistic fervor so common to

---

270 RC 12.113, 12.324–5, n. 1, *13*.18–19.
271 Incidents involving nobles are recorded in Fromment, *Actes et Gestes*, pp. 93, 144–5, 148; *Levain*, pp. 107–8; RC 12.550, 13.279–80.
272 Fromment, *Actes et Gestes*, p. 145.
273 J. Stolz in Oechsli, *Quellenbuch*, p. 331.
274 H. Küssenberg, "Heinrich Küssenbergs Chronik," *Archiv für die Schweizerische Reformationsgeschichte*, 3: 423 (1875).
275 ZW 6/2.272. Also: Stumpf's *Reformationschronik*, vol. II, p. 8.
276 Cited in *Guillaume Farel*, p. 228.
277 WA, *Briefwechsel* 4.404, no. 1236.
278 Oechsli, *Quellenbuch*, p. 331.

them.[279] The participation of youths in Swiss iconoclasm was important, since they often acted as catalysts in public acts of violence, forcing conflicts to erupt, but it needs to be considered within a larger picture, as one component of a set of interrelated patterns.

Swiss iconoclasm is also connected to the issue of public welfare. From its inception, the iconoclastic movement was inseparably linked with the desire to redistribute the wealth of the Catholic church. The history of iconoclasm is highlighted by a concern for the needy.[280] An integral part of the iconoclastic crusade was the effort to turn the destruction of the cultic objects into a charitable and practical operation. It may be said, perhaps, that the bourgeois mind appreciated church treasure more as a source of revenue than of holiness. Wooden images were used as firewood to help keep people warm; church plate was melted down to help fill city coffers, establish charitable institutions, and pay municipal debts; vestments were given to the needy; and church buildings were turned over to secular purposes.[281] The "idols" of Rome might have been enemies of the faith, but their material value was always appreciated and put to practical use once they were cast down.

Karlstadt had argued against Luther in 1524 that to delay in removing images was to sin against God and neighbor.[282] This revolutionary argument was taken to heart in Switzerland in the 1520s and 1530s, and the destruction of images and other cultic objects became one of the most effective tactics in the "Protestantization" of many cities and towns. In removing the "idols" of Roman Catholicism by force, much as a parent removes a sharp object from a child's hand against its will, Swiss iconoclasts effected many changes that might have otherwise taken much longer to bring about, or might have never taken place at all.

By 1536, then, iconoclasm had become a significant pattern of Reformed Protestanism. Many important theological and political ques-

---

[279] This same youthful fervor expressed itself among Geneva's Catholics. *Levain*, pp. 57, 106; RC 12.250–1.

[280] This concern is expressed in Karlstadt's first iconoclastic pamphlet, "Von Abthung der Bilder und das keyn Bedtler unther den Christen seyn sollen" (1522). It was also expressed by some of the first iconoclasts in the Zurich area in 1523, who argued that they had destroyed a crucifix so they could give the wood to "the poor people who could best use it." Emil Egli, *Actensammlung zur Geschichte der Züricher Reformation in den Jahren 1519–1533* (Zurich, 1879), doc. 421.

[281] The charitable impulse of the iconoclasts was a strong driving force. ZW 10.415. For similar developments in Geneva see RC 13.288, 13.322, 13.324, 13.326.

[282] Andreas Bodenstein von Karlstadt, "Ob man gemach faren und des ergernusen der schwachen verschonen soll," *Karlstadts Schriften aus den Jahren 1523–1525*, E. Hertzsch, ed. (Halle, 1956), vol. I, p. 88.

tions connected with this phenomenon had been addressed in Switzerland in the 1520s and 1530s. As the Reformation moved more aggressively into France and other countries where the war against the idols faced much stiffer opposition, new problems arose that called for a different synthesis of the Reformed position against Catholic piety. The man who would provide the needed guidance was John Calvin.

CHAPTER 5

Humanism and reform
in France:
the seeds of Calvinism

BARELY two months after the Reformation had been legally ushered
into Geneva, in July 1536, as images were still literally smoldering,
John Calvin came to the city.[1] His visit was unplanned, a detour on
the road from Paris to Strasburg. Much to Calvin's surprise, Farel
burst into the inn where he was staying, as impetuous as ever. The
meeting that followed not only changed the course of Calvin's life,
but the history of Geneva and the Reformation as well.

Farel, who was busy organizing the Genevan church into a disciplined community, came to enlist Calvin in this hard task. The young
Frenchman (twenty years Farel's junior), was already known for his
brilliant defense and summary of the Reformed faith, the *Christianae
religionis institutio*, published at Basel in March of that same year.
Though he had fled from his native France for the sake of religion,
Calvin had no intention of getting involved in the pastoral task of
church reform in exile. His goal was to study and write in scholarly
seclusion. He told Farel he was only passing through town, on his
way to more pressing business, but Farel would not listen. Instead,
he warned him: "If you refuse to devote youself with us to this work
. . . God will condemn you."[2] Calvin was terrified by this adjuration,
and later wrote that he had felt as if God had come into his room and
laid a hand upon him. After a short trip to Basel, to collect some of his
belongings, Calvin returned to Geneva, ready to stay and assist in the
creation of a new church.

Calvin arrived in Geneva as one phase of the Reformation was
giving way to another, and to some extent his person and work are
the pivotal point of this development. The patterns followed in
Switzerland up to that time were now to change: The emphasis
would shift from expansion to consolidation. Although the Protestant
cities and cantons continued to rub shoulders uncomfortably with

[1] CR 9.891.
[2] CR 31.26.

166

Catholics, the war on idolatry within Switzerland slowed down considerably. After conquering Lausanne in December 1536 (much in the same way as Geneva had been won over), Swiss Protestants gained little more in the way of territory.[3] Protestants began to concentrate on the building of strong, unified communities in which the social order would clearly reflect the Reformed understanding of the commands of scripture. This, precisely, is the agenda Farel had in mind for Calvin in Geneva. As events would later prove, few men were better suited for such a task than Calvin.

Calvin was also well prepared to fulfill another role. While this consolidation was taking place in Geneva, a tremendous expansion was beginning in France. Though Calvin set himself to the work of organizing a disciplined church in Geneva, he also devoted attention to his native land and the rest of Europe; and as he gradually increased his control over the city, he simultaneously transformed it into a missionary base for Protestant action elsewhere, especially in France.[4]

Calvin took aim against "false religion" with no less zeal than Karlstadt or Zwingli, but the situation he faced was much different. Protestantism could not advance in France as it had in Germany or Switzerland. France was a powerful, centralized state where the monarchy took a tough stand against religious change. The dictum of "one law, one faith, one king" made it virtually impossible for Protestant communities to wage the same kind of war against idolatry that their brethren had so successfully completed in Switzerland and some parts of Germany. The social and political structure of the French state, which was controlled by a king committed to Catholicism, called for a different pattern of Reformation. The urban, revolutionary tactics previously employed could not work for a relatively small, widely scattered, and persecuted community.

Calvin knew this from first hand experience. Having converted to Protestantism in Paris, he had fled France in fear for his life. He was committed to wiping out idolatry, but knew that iconoclasm would be a suicidal policy. So, as he turned his attention to the work of Reform on a continental scale, the burden of carrying out a new kind of war fell upon his shoulders. He hoped to undermine and eventually eradicate idolatry without first causing a bloodbath. In order to do this, he

---

[3] H. Vuillemier, *Histoire de L'Eglise Réformée du Pays de Vaud sous le Régime Bernois* (Lausanne, 1927–33).
[4] Robert M. Kingdon, *Geneva and the Coming of the Wars of Religion in France, 1555–1563* (Geneva, 1956).

had to define further the metaphysics of transcendence that gave shape to the Reformed interpretation of worship, and then to apply this theology to concrete situations throughout Europe. Garnering and winnowing the thought of his predecessors, Calvin developed a new, finely nuanced attack on Catholic worship that allowed no compromise with idolatry, and inspired a crusading attitude without directly calling for iconoclasm as an explicit guiding policy.

But what are the lines of thought leading up to Calvin? What were the specific circumstances that led him to develop his theology of worship? Calvin's spiritual and intellectual development owed much to the humanistic circle led by Jacques Lefèvre d'Etaples, in which Farel had also once moved in France, and with which he still corresponded. Calvin also owed much to the more radical traditions of the Protestant Reformers who had influenced Farel. The line of development that we began to trace with Erasmus, Karlstadt, and Zwingli, finally reaches its fullest expression in Calvin. It was he who synthesized the thought of previous Reformers concerning idolatry, and laid the foundation for an enduring critique of Catholic piety among the Reformed churches of Europe. But the lines of influence leading to Calvin, and Farel before him, for that matter, were distinctly French. Their common mentor, directly and indirectly, was the humanist Lefèvre. Before going any further, it will be useful to look at this man and the beginnings of Protestantism in France.

LEFÈVRE AND LATE MEDIEVAL PIETY

The ideological and spiritual rift between humanism and the Reformation is brought to life when one reads of a meeting that took place between Erasmus and Guillaume Farel. Farel had called Erasmus a "Balaam" for refusing to carry his critique to its logical conclusion.[5] When the two met in Basel in 1524 to discuss Farel's insult, the discussion centered around the cult of the saints. Farel argued on scriptural grounds that the invocation of the saints should be totally abolished. Erasmus tried to temper Farel's radical biblicism. Since scripture makes no mention of praying to the Holy Spirit, he asked, would Farel also refuse to invoke the Spirit? The two men parted as bitter enemies. Erasmus said there was no point in arguing with a man as "ferocious" as Farel, whom he dubbed "Phallicus": "He says I am no more of a theologian than Froben's wife. I'd be a great the-

---

[5] The story of Balaam, who had revelations from God, but refused to act upon the truth he knew, is in Numbers 22:5ff.

ologian if I called the Pope Antichrist, human constitutions heretical and ceremonies abominations."[6]

Though Erasmus may have dismissed Farel as he did all the Reformers, he was, in fact, rejecting a disciple. Farel had been exposed to Erasmus's critique of late medieval piety by Jacques Lefèvre d'Etaples (also known by his Latin name, Faber Stapulensis).[7] Lefèvre's critique of medieval piety and his humanistic reform program form a vital connection among humanism, Erasmianism, and the Reformation in France and Switzerland. Ultimately, the thought and actions of Lefèvre and some of his disciples lead – directly and indirectly – to the Calvinist attack on Roman Catholic worship, as is attested by Farel's meeting with Erasmus.[8]

Unlike Erasmus, who from his earliest writings presented a straightforward critique of contemporary religion, Lefèvre was a man whose convictions and aims changed as the years progressed.[9] John Woolman Brush has traced three distinct phases in the life and work of Lefèvre.[10] In the first phase, Lefèvre showed a marked interest in the works of Aristotle.[11] During the second phase, he became immer-

---

[6] Allen V, no. 1496. Also: *Guillaume Farel, 1489–1565* (Neuchâtel/Paris, 1930), pp. 124–30; and R. Bainton, *Erasmus of Christendom* (New York, 1969), p. 217.

[7] Studies of Lefèvre are not as numerous as those for Erasmus, but the number of works is still impressive. Some of the more important research is found in articles rather than monographs, and these will be cited as the occasion warrants. The most significant monographs are as follow: J. Barnaud, *Jacques Lefèvre d'Etaples, Son Influence sur les Origines de la Réformation Française* (Paris, 1900); Guy Bedouelle, *Lefèvre d'Etaples et l'intelligence des Ecritures* (Geneva, 1976); C. H. Graf, *Essai sur la Vie et les Ecrits de Jacques Lefèvre d'Etaples* (Strassburg, 1842; Geneva: Slatkine Reprints, 1970); Henry Heller, *Reform and Reformers of Meaux* (Ph.D. dissertation, Cornell University, 1969); P. Imbart de la Tour, *Les origines de la Réforme* (2nd ed., Melun, 1944), vol. 2, pp. 488–523, vol. 3, pp. 109–53, 288–303; J. D. Jordan, *The Church Reform Principles in the Biblical Works of Jacques Lefèvre d'Etaples* (Ph.D. dissertation, Duke University, 1966); Margaret Mann, *Erasme et les Débuts de la Réforme Française* (Paris, 1933), esp. pp. 23–112; Karl Spiess, *Der Gottesbegriff des J. Faber Stapulensis* (Marburg, 1930).

[8] It will not be my purpose here to deal with the issue of Lefèvre's orthodoxy, but instead to trace the impact of his critique. The debates surrounding this issue (especially between Imbart de la Tour and Emile Doumergue) are summarized by Richard Stauffer in his article, "Lefèvre d'Etaples: Artisan ou Spectateur de la Réforme?," *Bulletin de la Societé de l'Histoire du Protestantisme Français*, CXIII: 405–23 (1967). I should state at this point that I take issue with the general thrust of Imbart de la Tour's thesis in the monumental *Les origines de la Réforme*. De la Tour tries to distance Lefèvre from some of his more radical disciples and attempts to attribute radicalism to Lutheran influences rather than to Lefèvre.

[9] A comparison of Erasmus and Lefèvre can be found in Mann, *Erasme et les Débuts*, chap. 3.

[10] John Woolman Brush, "Lefèvre d'Etaples: Three Phases of His Life and Work," in *Reformation Studies, Essays in Honor of Roland Bainton*, F. H. Littel, ed. (Richmond, 1962).

[11] Lefèvre acquired an interest in Aristotle during his visit to Italy in 1491–2, when he

sed in the writings of the mystics.[12] The third phase begins with the publication of the *Quincuplex psalter* in 1509. From this time forward the study of scripture became the dominant interest in Lefèvre's life: It occupied the center of his attention and gave shape to his reform program.[13] The three phases of Lefèvre's life are not chronologically rigid, however: Aristotle and the mystics continued to influence him for the rest of his life.[14]

Lefèvre's scriptural period can itself be divided into two stages. During the first he was primarily devoted to scholarship; during the second to ecclesiastical reform. The turning point is 1521, the year when Lefèvre followed his close friend and patron, Guillaume Briçonnet, to his bishopric of Meaux.[15] The Meaux period is marked by the promotion of an ecclesiastical reform under Briçonnet's sponsorship, and by the creation of a learned and pious circle of humanists, of whom Lefèvre was the undisputed leader. During this period Lefèvre not only intensified his biblical work, but also adopted and taught a more radical critique of contemporary piety.[16] The development of

came into close contact with the work of Ermolao Barbaro. He also became interested in Plato through Marsilio Ficino (Brush, "Three Phases," p. 118). An excellent, detailed study of the intellectual and spiritual climate of late fifteenth and early sixteenth century France is that of Augustin Renaudet, *Préréforme et Humanisme à Paris Pendant les Premières Guerres d'Italie (1494–1517)* (Paris, 1913).

[12] Brush, "Three Phases," p. 121. Some of the most significant mystical writings edited and published by Lefèvre are those of Dionysius the Areopagite (1499), Ramon Lull (1499 and 1505), St. John of Damascus (1507), and Nicholas of Cusa (1514).

[13] Margaret Mann and J. W. Brush maintain that this phase of Lefèvre's life was deeply influenced by Erasmianism at first and later by Lutheranism (Brush, "Three Phases," pp. 122–3). The most important of Lefèvre's biblical editions are the *Fivefold Psalter* (1509), the *Pauline Epistles* (1512), *Commentaries on the Four Gospels* (1522), and the French translation of the New Testament (1523).

[14] Brush, "Three Phases," p. 119.

[15] Lefèvre had joined Briçonnet in 1508 at the monastery of Saint-Germain-des Pres in Paris. Although Briçonnet was appointed Bishop of Meaux in 1516, Lefèvre did not follow him there until 1521 (Graf, *Lefèvre*, p. 92).

[16] Henry Heller has done much to dispel the notion that Lefèvre was a moderate critic of the medieval Church [*Reform and Reformers of Meaux*; and also "The Evangelicism of Lefèvre d'Etaples, 1525," *Studies in the Renaissance*, 19: 42–77 (1972)]. Heller maintains that previous scholarship on Lefèvre has been too dependent on his earlier works (the 1509 Psalter, the 1512 Pauline commentary and the 1522 Gospel commentary). By concentrating on these works, Heller argues, Fabrician scholars have overlooked one of the most crucial periods of Lefèvre's life, since between 1521 and 1525 the full effect of German and Swiss evangelical ideas began to be felt in France. Heller shows that this influence transformed the reform ideas of Lefèvre into the basis for "a serious critique of the existing ecclesiastical order" ("Evangelicism," p. 44), including the rejection of the cult of the saints and of the Mass as sacrifice. Heller's work is substantiated in part by Richard M. Cameron in his article, "The Charges of Lutheranism Brought against Jacques Lefèvre d'Etaples," *Harvard Theological Review*, 63: 119–49 (1970).

this critique, in turn, heralds the beginning of a new intellectual and spiritual climate among French humanists.

The primitivism of the Fabrician critique

Lefèvre's critique of contemporary religion shared one essential concept with humanism and Erasmianism: the desire to return to the "pristine" sources of the early Church.[17] Lefèvre's primitivism and biblicism combined to create a powerful reform ideology. Like Erasmus, Lefèvre used the past as a guideline by which to judge the present. The comparison, needless to say, was not favorable. Lefèvre expressed his primitivistic philosophy very clearly in the preface to the 1499 edition of the works of Dionysius the Areopagite:

The more nearly a light approximates the intensity of the sun, the more brightly it shines . . . , and the closer a thing is to its origin, the more purely it retains its own nature . . . It follows that of all the writings the Holy Gospels are recognized as having the greatest dignity, splendor, and authority, as writings which have emanated directly from God and have been infused into ready minds.[18]

In true Neoplatonic fashion, Lefèvre saw a hierarchy of authority in the sources of the Christian religion. It was the duty of the believer to search out the truth in those writings that were most directly related to God's presence on earth. Chief among them were the Gospels, which testified to God's Word made flesh. After the Gospels came all the other parts of the Old and New Testament, followed by the church fathers, who were chronologically arranged in order of decreasing significance.[19]

Lefèvre's primitivism challenged medieval piety on several levels.

[17] It was precisely on this point that Noel Beda based much of his attack on both Erasmus and Lefèvre. Through their biblicism and lack of appreciation for medieval theologians, charged Beda, Erasmus and Lefèvre had fallen into error. (He accused them of renewing the heresies of the Manicheans, Arians, Sabellians, Donatists, Waldensians, and Lollards.) Their principal errors concerned the veneration of the saints and the regulations and ritual of the Church. R. M. Cameron, "The Charges of Lutheranism," p. 137.

[18] *The Prefatory Epistles of Jacques Lefèvre d'Etaples,* Eugene F. Rice, ed. (New York, 1972), "Preface to the *Corpus Dionysiacum,*" p. 60. Translated by Rice in "The Humanist Idea of Christian Antiquity: Lefèvre d'Etaples and His Circle," *Studies in the Renaissance,* IX: 135 (1962).

[19] Rice, *Prefatory Epistles,* p. 62: In 1499 Lefèvre regarded the Dionysian writings as the purest of all "apostolic" writings: "Et plane litteraria monumenta ex apostolicis temporibus ad nostra derivata aeque mihi a ceteris differere videntur ac viventia a mortuis, caelestia a terrenis, et a mortalibus immortalia, aliquid vivificum atque mirificae lucis ultra cetera in se servantia."

First, by placing a great stress on the early Fathers as theological authorities, Lefèvre cast doubt on the validity of medieval religion. Moreover, like Erasmus, Lefèvre showed an aversion to formal theology: What he culled from the ancient sources was not so much *theologia* as *pietas*.[20] By proposing that the Fathers were the most eminent proponents of piety and moral insight, Lefèvre seriously undermined the authority of the scholastic theologians. The primitive Church, which according to Lefèvre had gradually declined and disappeared after the age of Constantine, was to serve as a model for his contemporaries. If the primitive Church were to be restored, he argued, then the worship of God would be pure once more.[21] This implied, of course, that contemporary worship was corrupt.

Lefèvre maintained that the correctness of the Golden Age of Christianity depended on its adherence to the New Testament. This is the second point of Lefèvre's challenge to medieval religion. Since scripture was central for all theology and piety, it became a measure for all current doctrines and observances.[22] As the Word had served for the primitive Church, he insisted, so must it serve for his contemporaries. By definition, then, anything not found in scripture was superfluous. On this point, Lefèvre maintained a sharp distinction in worship between things of divine origin and those created by human beings:

The Word of God suffices [*Verbum Dei sufficit*]. This alone is enough to effect life everlasting. This rule is the guide to eternal life. All else, on which the Word of God does not shine, is as unnecessary as it is undoubtedly superfluous. Nor should such be reckoned with the Gospel as far as the purity of pious worship and the integrity of faith are concerned, for it is not the creation of God.[23]

In this fashion, Lefèvre established one of his fundamental principles: The pure worship of God must follow His commands in scripture.

---

20 Rice, "The Humanist Idea," pp. 129, 133.
21 Preface to the *Commentaries on the Four Gospels* (1522): "And would that the model of faith be sought in that early Church which consecrated so many martyrs to Christ, which knew no rule save the Gospel, which had in short no goal save Christ, and which gave worship to no one save the Triune God . . . They depended entirely on Christ; let us also depend entirely on Him. All their faith, all their trust, all their love were gathered in Him; let ours be gathered in Him . . . And why may we not desire that our age be restored to the likeness of that primitive Church? Then Christ was worshiped more purely, and his name shone forth more widely." Rice, *Prefatory Epistles*, p. 437; trans. J. C. Olin, *The Catholic Reformation* (New York, 1969), p. 113.
22 A detailed treatment of Lefèvre's scriptural theology can be found in Bedouelle, *Lefèvre* , pp. 141–236.
23 "Preface to the *Commentaries on the Four Gospels*," Rice, *Prefatory Epistles*, p. 436; trans. J. C. Olin, *The Catholic Reformation*, p. 112.

This concept, if closely followed, would leave little room for many of the practices of the medieval Church. This Fabrician concept of the antithesis of divine commands and human inventions in worship was to become a central part of Calvin's thought.[24]

The contrast between earthly and heavenly was made even sharper by a third point of reference. In addition to pimitivism and biblicism, Lefèvre also proposed an intense Christocentricism. Jesus Christ, the word of God made flesh, was to be the central point of reference in the life of the Church. The interdependence among Christ, scripture, and the true Church in Lefèvre's thought is not difficult to explain: He interpreted Christ's role as the Word of God in a very literal sense. This perspective colored all of Lefèvre's criticisms and helped sharpen the distincton he made between true, God-given worship and humanly devised worship. The person of Jesus Christ was to be the sole point of reference for the life of every Christian:

Know that men and their doctrines are worth nothing, unless they be confirmed and supported by the Word of God. And Jesus Christ is everything; He is wholly human and wholly divine; and no man is worth anything without Him; and no word of man has any value, except in His Word.[25]

This principle was the basis for Lefèvre's opposition to the veneration of the saints.

A final point of Lefèvre's theology that runs against the grain of medieval piety is his transcendentalism. Lefèvre did not write a manifesto like Erasmus's *Enchiridion*, or ever make the distinction between spiritual and material an explicitly central part of his work, but his transcendentalism still shows through in his writings. Generally, it consists of brief assertions of the superiority of the spiritual life for the Christian, such as those in the preface to the French translation of the Gospels, where he asks his readers to leave the flesh behind and cling to the spirit instead.[26] Lefèvre's transcendentalism is more of a con-

---

24 For instance: *Institutes*, II.8.17 and IV.10.8. Lefèvre himself also asserted that without scriptural guidance man would always turn religion into a materially oriented faith: "and from the moment that these pious studies are no longer pursued, monasteries decay, devotion dies out, the flame of religion is extinguished, spiritual things are traded for earthly goods, heaven is given up and earth is accepted – the most disastrous transaction conceivable." Introduction to the *Commentary on the Psalms* (1509); translated by P. L. Nyhus in *Forerunners of the Reformation*, H. Oberman, ed. (New York, 1966), p. 267.

25 "Preface to the French Translation of the Gospels" (1523), Rice, *Prefatory Epistles*, p. 452.

26 Rice, *Prefatory Epistles*, p. 464: "en laissant la robbe charnelle qui est toute souille et maculée et prenant la spirituelle, clere et resplendissante comme le soleil, pure et nette comme la pruenelle de l'oeil, sans quelconque souilleure ou macule." Also pp. 454, 460, 462.

stant perspective than a central organizing principle. Nonetheless, it adds an important element to his critique of medieval piety, and there is little doubt that his attitude had a marked influence on some of his disciples.[27]

Lefèvre's critique might be similar to that of Erasmus, but it is not identical. Like Erasmus, Lefèvre concentrated his attention on the *cultus divorum*. Unlike Erasmus, however, Lefèvre developed a strident opposition to its validity. Whereas Erasmus continued to profess devotion to the saints – albeit in a spiritualized sense – Lefèvre seems to have completely rejected their veneration. Lefèvre's realization that the saints were not to be addressed as intercessors appears to be the logical terminus of his Christocentric biblicism. The realization was gradual, but it marks an important change in his life, as well as in the lives of those around him: The biblical humanist Lefèvre changes into the critic Lefèvre, and his reform plan takes a more radical turn.

Guillaume Farel has left a detailed account of his mentor's spiritual pilgrimage.[28] When Farel first met Lefèvre, sometime between 1509 and 1512, the great humanist was still fervently attached to the *cultus divorum*. (Farel describes Lefèvre as one of the most dedicated "idolaters" he ever encountered.[29]) The same man who so piously bowed down before the images of the saints, however, also longed for a renewal of the primitive Church and the Gospel. He even told Farel that he would soon see the face of Christendom altered for the better.[30] The turning point in Lefèvre's life apparently occurred some-

---

[27] Anémond de Coct, one of the first French nobles to become Protestant, wrote to Guillaume Farel in 1524: "Numquam in externis spiritus meus, et in sensibilibus nulla unquam mihi diuturna tranquilitas." Herminjard 1.311.

[28] There are three main narratives of Farel's dealings with Lefèvre. The most detailed is found in his "Epitre à tous seigneurs, et peuples et pasteurs" (1530), published by Abraham Ruchat in his *Histoire de la Réformation de la Suisse* (Lausanne, 1835), vol. II, p. 528 ff.; and J. G. Fick in his collection of some of Farel's works, *Du Vray Usage de la Croix de Jesus Christ* (Geneva, 1865), p. 162ff. The other narratives are in the treatise "Du vray usage de la croix" (1560) (Fick, *Du Vray Usage*, pp. 129–30); and a letter to Conrad Pellikan (1556), Herminjard 1.481 (under "Additions et Corrections").

[29] "Epitre à tous seigneurs" (Ruchat, *Histoire*, pp. 534–5; "je trouve un ['idolâtre'] qui passoit tous les autres, car jamais je n'avois veu chanteur de messe qui en plus grande reverence la chantast . . . Cestuy, afin, que je le nomme, s'appelloit maistre Jacques Faber, qui faisoit les plus grandes reverences aux images qu'autre personnage que j'age cogneu, et demeurant longuement à genoux il prioit, et disoit ses heures devant icelles." In the letter to Pellikan, he says: "Sed nihil erat nisi ipsa superstitio in qua seni (Faber) adnitebar accedere aliquantum . . . Sane stupesco, quando cogito insanam tanti viri superstitionem, qui vel floribus jubebat Marianum idolum, dum una soli murmuraremus preces Marianas ad idolum, ornari. In Missa omnes vinceret" (Herminjard 1.481). Farel says Lefèvre was "du tout plongé en idolatrie," (Fick, *Du Vray Usage*, p. 130).

[30] Herminjard 1.481: "Pius senex, Jacobus Faber, . . . ante annos plus minus quad-

time around 1518, when he began to work on a new edition of the *Lives of the Saints*. Farel reports that while Lefèvre was doing research for this project, he became convinced of the error involved in the worship of the saints and, instead of completing his hagiography, henceforward devoted himself solely to the study of scripture:

But having understood the great idolatry involved in prayers to the saints, and that their legends act as sulphur to stir up the fire, he left it all behind and forthwith devoted himself to Sacred Scripture.[31]

It appears that Lefèvre's new conviction eventually led him to reject ✓ the use of material objects of worship altogether, including the cross. In another instance, Farel reports how Lefèvre was once so disturbed by the devotion shown to an ancient statue of Isis that he replaced it with a cross. Later, according to Farel, Lefèvre came to the realization that he had only substituted one "idol" for another, and repented his action.[32]

The change wrought in Lefèvre soon began to be reflected in his works. In his preface to the French translation of Psalms, for instance, Lefèvre proclaims that the early Church never taught its members to pray to anyone but God, and he adds that the model for all Christian prayer is scripture, especially the "saintly and devout" Psalms.[33] Lefèvre made his opposition to the cult of the saints quite clear, stating that anyone who did not pray directly to God worshiped falsely:

Let your trust be upon God without solicitude, address him in every prayer and supplication; in returning thanks let your petitions be addressed to God; and the peace of God, which surpasses all understanding, will protect your hearts and minds in Jesus Christ. Anything different from this is a superstitious and human thing, not from the commandment of God.[34]

The attack on the cult of the saints became even more aggressive in the *Epistres et Evangiles* of 1525. Although it seems that Lefèvre was not the author of the entire work, it was written under his direct

raginta me namu apprehensum ita alloquebatur: 'Guileme, opportet orbem immutari, et tu viderebis.'" The same is reported in the "Epitre à tous seigneurs" (Ruchat, *Histoire*, p. 535).

[31] "Epitre à tous seigneurs" (Ruchat, *Histoire*, p. 536).

[32] Fick, *Du Vray Usage*, p. 130: "Et quant à ce qu'il fit mettre une croix au lieu de celle image d'Isis, ce fut pourtant qu'il pensoit beaucoup mieux faire à cause qui'il n'entendoit pas encore pur lors ce qu'il a bien entendu puis apres, touchant l'idolatrie qui a esté comise autour de la croix."

[33] Rice, *Prefatory Epistles*, p. 469.

[34] Ibid., p. 470.

supervision and obtained his approval.[35] Its opposition to Catholic theology and piety was so pervasive that the Sorbonne quickly condemned it, selecting forty-eight passages for explicit censure.[36] Some of the more controversial passages dealt with the cult of the saints. The sixth sermon, for example, openly stated that when St. Stephen was stoned he did not invoke the angels or Moses or Abraham, Issac, and Jacob, but only Jesus Christ. The lesson to be learned from this, continued the *Epistres*, was that "it is God and our Lord Jesus Christ who ought to be invoked, and not any angel or creature."[37] Other passages were equally explicit.[38]

Lefèvre does not devote as much attention to the cult of images as Erasmus, in spite of his apparently stronger opposition to it. Still, it is not difficult to find places where Lefèvre speaks plainly, as in this passage from his *Commentary on the Catholic Epistles* (1524):

> The superstitious have images of gold and silver, works of the hands of men which have a mouth but will not speak, eyes and will not see. All images appear to be prohibited by the apostle of the spirit, those worshiped by the gentiles at home, in the fora, harbors, temples, groves, or elsewhere as well as those which in the future might be worshiped through the custom of the pagans as a result of declining faith. By this prohibitory exhortation [I John 5:11], John forbids anything to be worshiped that is not God, for whom no image can be set up.[39]

Two of Lefèvre's central principles can be seen at work in this passage. First, there is a strong contrast between the "things of God" and the "works of the hands of men." The contrast itself is scriptural (Psalms 115 and 135), but it draws on the distinction made by Lefèvre between the worship commanded by God and that devised by men.

---

[35] *Epistres et Evangiles*, G. Bedouelle and F. Giacone, eds. (Leiden, 1976). The editors argue that although Lefèvre was ultimately responsible for the content of the *Epistres*, the real author of most of the work could have been Lefèvre's close friend and disciple, Gerard Roussel (pp. xxxix-xli). Also: Henri Meylan, "Lefèvre d'Etaples: les Themes Théologiques de les Epistres et Evangiles," in *Colloque de Tours: l'Humanisme Français au Début de la Renaissance"* (Paris, 1973), pp. 185–92.

[36] The Sorbonne condemnation was published by M. A. Screech in the facsimile edition of the *Epistres et Evangiles* (Geneva, 1964), pp. 41–51. In its summary conclusion against the entire work, the Sorbonne theologians warned: "Sanctorum insuper cultum & eorum sacros dies, cum Catholicis Scripturae sacrae expositionibus, schismatice respuens sub eiusdem Divinae Scripturae praetextu quam passim ad haereticalem pertrahit sensum: fidelem populum non parum scandalizat; schismata quae vix extirpari valeant, inducit; itaque manichaeorum haereses, Waldensium, Wiclefistarum ac Lutheranorum revocare satagit" (p. 51).

[37] Bedouelle and Giacone, *Epistres*, p. 32.

[38] Sorbonne condemnation, Screech, *Epistres*, censures 6 (p. 42), 34 (p. 48), and 44 (p. 50).

[39] *Commentary on the Catholic Epistles*, trans. by Henry Heller, "Evangelicism," p. 72.

Secondly, there is a primitivistic reference to the "decline of faith" that has allowed a resurgence of paganism among Christians. Added to this is a strong proclamation of God's transcendence. These elements work together to provide a sharp attack on the use of images in worship – the same attack leveled by the Reformers.[40]

Another aspect of medieval religion criticized by Lefèvre was eucharistic theology and piety. While his own thought on the eucharist is not fully developed, it bears traces of a transcendentalist understanding. His critique of the Catholic eucharist is of doubtful influence, however. It appears he himself was affected by the opinions of Swiss and German sacramentarians, not vice versa.[41]

The Cenacle of Meaux and Lefèvre's reform program

Another significant difference between Erasmus and Lefèvre is that whereas Erasmus restricted his criticism to the printed page, Lefèvre organized and directed a practical application of his principles, and also formed a group of disciples. Lefèvre's critique was most influential in its personal contacts – in teaching and preaching – and the setting for most of this activity was the diocese of Meaux, where Lefèvre served as the intellectual and spiritual leader of a group of humanists devoted to the reform of the Church. This reform, which has been the subject of numerous studies,[42] put to work the primitivist, biblicist, and spiritualist principles of Lefèvre.

---

[40] Lefèvre's criticism is contemporaneous with the attack being launched against images at Zurich in 1523–4. Though it is possible that Swiss theology might have influenced the French humanist at this point, he does not seem to draw from the iconoclastic writings of Ludwig Haetzer and Ulrich Zwingli. Charles Garside, Jr., *Zwingli and the Arts* (New Haven, 1966), pp. 104–78. The Fabrician critique flows primarily from principles already expressed as early as 1509 in the *Commentary on the Psalms* and as late as 1523 in the preface to the French translation of the Gospels. Lefèvre's criticisms are very similar to Calvin's in the *Institutes*, I.11.4. Although it is not possible to trace Lefèvre's influence on Calvin directly, it is worth noting that Lefèvre had already developed some of the arguments later used by him.

[41] Lefèvre's eucharistic thought is discussed by Heller, "Evangelicism," pp. 66–70. Heller points to direct influence on Lefèvre from Zwingli's *De canone Missae* (1523) and *De vera et falsa religione* (1525), as well as from personal communications with Oecolampadius, Pellikan, and Farel (p. 67). Heller exaggerates Lefèvre's radicalism at one point when he says that the Fabrician view "had *nothing* in common with that of the so-called papists." Lefèvre's eucharistic thought was highly spiritualized, but not antithetical to the Catholic understanding. Heller himself admits that Lefèvre never thought of the eucharist as a mere memorial (p. 68).

[42] Besides the major works on Lefèvre that deal with his Meaux period and have already been cited (Heller, Imbart de la Tour, and Rice), there are two important monographs on the Meaux reform: R. J. Lovy, *Les Origines de la Réforme Française*

Meaux has long had a reputation among French Protestants as the cradle of the French Reformation. The town of Meaux, which is in the region of Brie, not far from Paris, was then largely populated by "artisans and people involved in the wool trade."[43] Soon after his appointment as Bishop of Meaux in 1516, Guillaume Briçonnet began to invite various men to his diocese to help him achieve a reform of the Church according to evangelical principles.[44] Jean Crespin, the early Protestant historian, reports that Briçonnet intended to bring "the comfort of the word of God" to the common people of his diocese, the wool-trade laborers who earned a living with their hands.[45] The centerpiece of reform at Meaux was preaching and propagation of scripture. In his romantic description of the success of this project, Jean Crespin highlights those very same principles that were at the heart of the reform – primitivism, biblicism, and transcendentalism:

The working people busied themselves, especially on Sundays and feast days, with reading the scriptures and seeking out the good will of God. Many of the [surrounding] villages did the same thing, and it came to pass that one could see shining in that diocese an image of the renewed Church. Because the Word of God was not only preached, but also practiced; so that all works of love and charity were performed there, morals were reformed from day to day, and superstitions were diminished.[46]

The effectiveness of Briçonnet's program, as directed by Lefèvre, is also attested by Catholic documents. While Protestants regarded Meaux with sentimental praise, Catholics condemned its reforms as dangerous. The *Journal d'un Bourgeois de Paris* reports that Meaux became "infected" with the heresies of Luther and Lefèvre, and that the people were taught to take the images out of the churches, disregard holy water, and stop praying to the saints.[47]

(Paris, 1959) and M. Mousseaux, *Aux Sources Françaises de la Réforme: La Brie Protestante* (Paris, 1965), esp. pp. 1–129. For a brief summary of the Meaux reform: James Jordan, "Jacques Lefèvre d'Etaples: Principles and Practice of Reform at Meaux," in *Contemporary Reflections on the Medieval Christian Tradition. Essays in Honor of Ray C. Petry*, G. H. Shriver, ed. (Durham, N.C., 1974), pp. 94–115.
[43] Jean Crespin, *Histoire des Martyrs* (1564; reprinted Toulouse, 1885), vol. I, p. 493.
[44] Lefèvre was first placed in charge of the "leprosarium" of Meaux, but soon assumed greater responsibility as the leader of Briçonnet's reform program. Some of the other humanist reformers were Gerard Roussel, who was given a curacy and later became a cathedral canon; Guillaume Farel, who served as a preacher; and François Vatable, Pierre Caroli, and Martial Mazurier, who were all given curacies. Henry Heller, "Famine, Revolt and Heresy at Meaux: 1521–1525," *ARG* 68: 133–57 (1977), p. 135.
[45] Crespin, *Histoire*, p. 493.
[46] Ibid., pp. 493–4.
[47] V. L. Blourilly (ed.), *Le Journal d'un Bourgeois de Paris sous le Regne de François I (1515–1536)* (Paris, 1910), p. 233.

Lefèvre's work at Meaux became increasingly radical after 1523. At first the reform program concentrated on the revival of the parish clergy, the establishment of preaching stations, and the publication of the Gospel. (The early part of the reform also included a power struggle between the reforming humanists and the Franciscans of Meaux, who heretofore had greatly influenced the religious life of the people.) After 1523, it is a different story: Subversive doctrine from the pulpit, Lutheran pamphlets in the squares, popular heresy, and increasing repression.[48] Lefèvre grew ever closer to the German and Swiss Reformers. Some of his letters from this period show that he and his associates were much more sympathetic to Protestantism than their public avowal reveals. In April 1524, for instance, Lefèvre wrote to Farel, thanking him for some Protestant works he had sent to Meaux. Lefèvre told Farel he had passed these books on to bishop Briçonnet, and expressed pleasure over their content, saying: "All that I have received from you and from Germany pleases me greatly." Lefèvre also expressed his admiration and friendship for Oecolampadius and Zwingli.[49] Three months later, Lefèvre again told Farel of his high regard for Zwingli, Oecolampadius, and Pellikan, speaking of the great consolation he received from their works and even saying that he wished a similar enlightenment could occur in France.[50]

An earmark of the increasingly radical reform program at Meaux was its concern with piety almost to the exclusion of theology. Instead of debates over dogma, one finds an agressive attack on the outward expressions of the *cultus divorum*. The propositions of two Meaux preachers, Pierre Caroli and Martial Mazurier,[51] collected and

---

[48] Heller, "Famine," p. 137.

[49] Herminjard 1.207–8. Among the books sent by Farel to Lefèvre, Herminjard identifies the following: J. Loniecer, "Catechesis de bona Dei voluntate erga quemvis Christianum. Deque sanctorum cultu et invocatione" (Esslingen, 1523); Zwingli's "De canone Missae" (1523), "Apologia qua in publicis Helvetiorum comitiis Bernae congregatis" (1523), and "Quo pacto ingenui adolescentes formandi sint" (1523); Otto Brunfels's "Problemata Othonis Brunfelsi"; and Melanchton's commentaries on Romans and I and II Corinthians. Farel also apparently sent a copy of the *Breslau Theses*, a collection of Hussite doctrines condemned by the Catholic church.

[50] Herminjard 1.220: "O bone Deus, quanto exulto gaudio, cum percipio hanc pure agnoscendi Christum gratiam, jam bonam partem pervasisse Europae! Et spero Christum tandem nostras Gallias hac benedictione invisurum." Richard Stauffer has argued that Zwingli was one of the mentors of the Meaux movement: *Interprètes de la Bible* (Paris, 1980), p. 91.

[51] The future careers of these men are rather colorful. Mazurier was arrested in 1524 as a suspected iconoclast, but he presented a confession of orthodoxy and later went on to become a canon of Nôtre Dame cathedral as well as "Penitencier" of Paris. Caroli renounced his evangelism, returned to Paris, and became a prior at the Sorbonne. In 1535 he defended the Catholic position in a public disputation at Geneva, but quickly conceded to his opponents and became a Protestant. A year later he accused Calvin, Farel, and Pierre Viret of being Arians and Sabellians. When

condemned by the Sorbonne in 1523, bear witness to this fact. The central concern of the *Determinatio facultatis theologiae Parisiensis* (1523) is not the doctrines of sin and grace or salvation by faith, but rather the worship of the saints. The propositions condemning the *cultus divorum* are neither profound nor complicated. Their chief aim is to detract from the worship of the saints and draw worshipers to a more theocentric piety.[52] In this respect, then, the Meaux reform reflects one of the principal concerns of Lefèvre, that is, his stress on the transcendence and omnipotence of God.[53] Among the devotions singled out for condemnation at Meaux were the lighting of candles and the making of offerings to the saints, the veneration of relics, and the whole system of masses and offerings for the dead.[54]

The attack on the *cultus divorum* bore fruit at Meaux, especially among the cloth workers, and the impact of the Fabrist preachers could soon be measured in concrete terms. It appears that the leadership of the reform movement gradually slipped from the hands of Briçonnet and Lefèvre and passed on to more radical younger men, such as Guillaume Farel, Jacques Pauvant, Jean Prevost, Nicole Mangin, Matthieu Saulnier, and Jean Leclerc.[55] Two incidents in particular point to the growing radicalism of Meaux. The first took place in December 1524, when the already hesitant Briçonnet posted a papal indulgence throughout his diocese. These posters were pulled down in broad daylight and replaced with others calling the Pope "Antichrist." The second incident occurred a month later, in January 1525,

his charge was refuted, he left his pastorate and his bride and returned to France, where he once more joined the Catholic church. Caroli spent his remaining years writing against Calvin and Farel. On Caroli: E. and E. Haag, *La France Protestante* (Geneva: Slatkine Reprints, 1970), vol. 3, pp. 220–2. On Mazurier: Jean Crespin, *Histoire*, vol. 1, p. 263.

52 The *Determinatio* is a partially reproduced in: Charles Duplessis d'Argentré, *Collectio judiciorum de novis erroribus* (3 vols., Paris, 1728–36), vol. II, pp. ii–iv. Also: Heller, "Famine," pp. 137–8.

53 Spiess, *Faber Stapulensis*, pp. 82, 101–2. Spiess argues that the key to Lefèvre's theology is his concept of the transcendence of God. Also: James Jordan, "Principles and Practice," p. 96. Jordan perceives Lefèvre's insistence on the transcendence of God as one of the principal characteristics of his theology of worship.

54 Heller, "Famine," p. 138.

55 Ibid., p. 148. The future careers of some of these men, like those of Caroli and Mazurier, serve as a testimony to the impact of the Fabrician critique, but in the opposite sense. Instead of remaining Catholic, most of them became open opponents of Rome. Farel became a leader of the French and Swiss Reformations; Pauvant was arrested (along with Mazurier) as a suspected iconoclast in 1524, condemned as a heretic, and burned in public. Saulnier wrote a defense of Pauvant that was condemned by the Sorbonne in 1525; and Leclerc became the first French Protestant martyr as a result of his iconoclastic activities (Crespin, *Histoire*, vol. I, p. 263).

when prayers to the Virgin and the saints affixed to tableaux on the walls of the cathedral were defaced. This act resulted in the arrest of Pauvant and Saulnier and eventually caused the dispersion of the Meaux group. Warrants were issued during the following months calling for the arrest of Lefèvre, Roussel, Caroli, Mazurier, and other suspected clergy.[56] One of the men arrested for the first incident, a woolcomber Jean Leclerc, would soon show how radical the Fabrician critique had become. After moving to Metz, Leclerc continued to show his opposition to Catholic piety. One night he entered a shrine outside the town and destroyed all the images. He was promptly arrested and executed by the Metz authorities, becoming the first martyr of the French Reformation.[57] Leclerc, who was later described by Theodore Beza as having received "the true Christian doctrine" from the instructions of Briçonnet and the reading of the Bible,[58] had carried the Fabrician critique to a radical conclusion.

Although the Fabrician reform could produce an iconoclast like Leclerc, it also showed a marked tendency for moderation and compromise. In fact, it is the latter trait that has been used most often to describe the Meaux circle. Once again, it becomes necessary to point out the limitations of the Fabrician critique. It appears that a good number of those at Meaux were not sufficiently convinced of error in the Catholic *cultus*. Although they attacked external forms of worship, some of them did not regard these things as evil or dangerous to salvation. To them, this "corruption" did not warrant schism, or, much less, martyrdom.

---

[56] Heller, "Famine," p. 148. I disagree with the main thesis of Heller's article. Heller maintains that the radicalism expressed at Meaux resulted largely from economic considerations, and that the Meaux reformers attacked a "monetized relationship" more that they did a corrupt theology and piety. In other words, by condemning the practices that drained the artisans and merchants of income that could have been more practically spent in a time of special hardship, the Meaux reformers sought to address an "immediate and urgent question" (p. 145). Heller maintains that it was the economic crisis of 1521–2 that forced the Meaux reformers to attempt to define their beliefs for the first time. It was the hardship of the people, he says, that drove the Reformers to attack the costly *cultus divorum* (p. 147). Although Heller focuses on an important consideration, he does so at the expense of other factors. There is no denying that venality was a source of discontent, but it is extremely difficult to prove that this was the *chief* cause of iconoclasm. Discontent with theology and piety should also be considered. To state that the development of heresy and the outbreak of religious riot at Meaux was "intimately related to rises in the price of grain" (p. 156) is to oversimplify a very complex problem.

[57] Crespin, *Histoire*, vol. I, p. 244.

[58] Theodore Beza, *Icones* (Geneva, 1580), fol. Z,iii: "hic igitur animosae fidei plenus, quam partim ex Episcopi Briconeti concionibus, partim ex gallice ut cunque tum versis Bibliis, & aliis pauculis libellis diligenter lectis didicerat."

THE TWO BRANCHES OF THE FABRICIAN REFORM

The major tendencies in the thought of Lefèvre are reflected in the types of followers engendered by his critique; one group hesitant and temporizing, the other ardently opposed to medieval piety. The former remain heirs to the limitations of the Fabrician critique; the latter carry it much futher than Lefèvre.

Briçonnet, Roussel, and the limitations of the Fabrician critique

Two men in particular epitomize the hesitant nature of the Fabrician critique. One was his patron, Guillaume Briçonnet, the other his disciple, Gerard Roussel.[59] Both men worked for a reform of the Church according to evangelical principles, but were reluctant to accept the "corrupt" worship of the contemporary Church as reason for schism.[60]

One of the most dramatic setbacks of the Meaux reform was the publication of two synodal decrees in 1523 by Bishop Briçonnet in which he threatened to excommunicate anyone possessing Lutheran literature, and instructed his priests to defend the veneration of the saints, belief in purgatory, and prayers for the dead. Although Briçonnet was himself responsible for the reform program that created hostility toward the *cultus divorum*, he suddenly turned against what he initiated. One can only guess whether or not this disavowal really reflected a change of heart for Briçonnet.[61] It is known, however, that Lefèvre shared Protestant literature with his patron-bishop in 1524, and it seems that his interest in them went beyond academic or ecclesiastical curiosity. Lefèvre speaks of Briçonnet as if they shared a common understanding.[62] Yet, in his pastoral letter of October 1523, Briçonnet condemns Luther and tries to separate his own evangelicism from the radical reforms in piety being advocated by the

---

[59] On Briçonnet: Lucien Febvre, "Idée d'une Recherche d'Histoire Comparée: le Cas Briçonnet," *Au Coeur Religieux du XVIe Siècle* (Paris, 1957), pp. 145–61. On Roussel: C. Schmidt, *Gerard Roussel* (Strasbourg, 1845).

[60] Other hesitant evangelists were Pierre Caroli, Martial Mazurier, and Michel d'Arande. (Caroli and Mazurier have already been discussed in n. 51.) Michel d'Arande sought the protection of Marguerite de Navarre after the dispersion of the Meaux group, became immersed in mysticism, and eventually obtained the bishopric of St. Paul-Trois-Chateaux (Crespin, *Histoire*, p. 263, n. 3). For more on the fate of the Meaux reformers consult Lovy, *Origines de la Réforme*, chap. 8.

[61] Cameron, "Charges of Lutheranism," p. 123, discusses this point.

[62] Herminjard 1.207.

"Lutherans" in his diocese.[63] A similar indictment against "the Lutheran plague" was repeated in subsequent letters to his clergy in December 1523 and January 1525.[64]

Though Briçonnet's *volte face* is puzzling, there is no doubt he wanted to put an end to the controversy produced by his reforms so that he and his diocese as a whole could remain within the Catholic fold. The condemnation of Caroli and Mazurier in the *Determinatio Facultatis* of 1523 made it necessary for the Bishop to defend his orthodoxy. Briçonnet's reputation as a "Lutheran" was spreading quickly throughout France, especially after the affair of the indulgence placards in 1524. Shortly after this incident, a certain Pierre de Debville reported that Briçonnet and Lefèvre had burned all the images at Meaux, save the crucifix.[65] This popular rumor – which was totally unfounded – shows how radical the Meaux reforms appeared to outsiders, and how central to the program the attack on the *cultus divorum* seemed to be. Yet, though the controversy centered around the Catholic cult, Briçonnet shied away from accepting this as the focus of his reform. Briçonnet's hesitation came to be viewed by French Protestants as an act of cowardice.[66] His actions, however, stem not so much from any weakness of character as they do from the nature of the Fabrician critique itself, which, in spite of its reputation for animosity toward the *cultus divorum*, was also quite open to compromise on points of piety.

Gerard Roussel is another Fabrician who was willing to compromise on piety even though he despised the worship of the contemporary Church. Some of Roussel's letters serve as testimonies to the ambivalence of the Fabrician circle. Through them it is possible to see how far some Fabricians could come in rejecting Catholic worship while still being reluctant to act upon their convictions.[67]

---

[63] Herminjard *1*.157–8.

[64] Herminjard *1*.172, 1.321–2.

[65] Herminjard *1*.315: "Je te notifie que l'évesque de Meaux en Brie, près Paris, cum Jacobo Fabro Stapulensi, depuis trois moys en visitant l'évesché, ont bruslé tous les images, réservé le crucifix." Briçonnet's growing notoriety is also attested in a report usually attributed to Antoine Fromment ("Fragment à la Suite de la Vie de Farel," cited by Herminjard *1*.158): "il avoit le bruict d'estre l'un des plus grands Luthériens du royaume de France."

[66] Herminjard *1*.158 ("Fragment"): "Cest Evesque Brissonet, craignant perdre son Evesché et sa vie, changea sa robe et devint persécuteur de ceux qu'il aboit auparavant enseignéz, et les solicitoit a se desdire et à suivre la doctrine qu'avoyent suivie leurs prédecesseurs."

[67] Herminjard *1*, nos. 104 (to Farel, July 1524); 117 (to Farel, August 1524); 118 (to Oecolampadius, August 1524); 162 (to Farel, September 1525); 167 (to Briçonnet, December 1525); 168 (to Nicholas Le Seur, December 1525); 184 (to Farel, December 1526).

As a true Fabrician, Roussel was committed to primitivism, biblicism, and transcendentalism. His opposition to contemporary piety was very strong, and at times close to Protestant polemic. In a 1524 letter to Farel, for instance, he said he wished that the "true cult of Christ," which was "now hidden by the traditions of Rome," could be restored to its simplicity. In the same letter he said he wished France could have a man like Zwingli, and also expressed his admiration for Oecolampadius by saying: "how my soul would be fortified by personal relations with this intrepid pastor."[68] Roussel's Protestant sympathies are made even clearer in a later epistle, where he comes to the defense of Jean Leclerc, who had just been executed at Metz as an iconoclast. Roussel praises Leclerc and says that the humble woolcomber was the victim of doctors who thought themselves Christian but, in truth, were far from Christ.[69] In addition, Roussel said he agreed with Farel on the question of the eucharist, admitting that he believed the Church had abandoned the true, spiritual understanding of the Supper.[70]

During his stay in Strassburg in 1525, Roussel had a chance to see the abolition of the Catholic *cultus* firsthand, and greatly enjoyed what he observed. He wrote two glowing reports of the evangelical worship now practiced in Bucer's church, one of which was addressed to his fellow temporizer, Guillaume Briçonnet.[71] In these letters, Roussel exhibits a marked preference for spiritualized, Christocentric worship.[72] He takes immense pleasure in seeing God worshiped "in spirit" and "according to the Gospel," as opposed to human traditions.[73]

---

[68] Herminjard 1.233.

[69] Ibid., p. 390.

[70] Ibid., p. 392: "Sane nihil ad adorationem, quae in spiritu et veritate fierei debet."

[71] Ibid., nos. 167 and 168, to Briçonnet and Nicholas Le Seur, respectively.

[72] Ibid., p. 411. Roussel says in the letter to Le Seur: "Hic solus Christus colitur per suum verbum, solusque pro capite suscipitur et fundamento. Externis non defertur, . . . Ablegata sunt pene omia quae pietati incommodare videbantur: cujus generis erant imagines templis affixae, quae cultum Sanctorum ememtiebantur, missae et alia pro defunctis suffragia . . . etc . . . Et, ut semel dicam, abrasa sunt pene omnia quae per homines invecta in cultum Dei dudum fuerant, ado ut solus cultus Dei nudo synceroque Dei verbo nixus inibi visatur."

[73] The primitivist, biblicist, and spiritualist attitudes of Lefèvre are clearly reflected in his report: "Quaedam porro sunt quae plerosque offendere possent non eousque provectos in doctrina Spiritus, ut cuncta externa contemnere queant, sola interim nixi fide, quae sic in invisibilia tota rapitur, ut proximum, non negligat, sed per charitatem ad mensuram illius se summittat atque temperet. Nam imagines a templis ablegatae sunt; unicum altar omnibus patens relictum est, in quo fit communio proxime ad Christi tempora. Et ut semel omnia concludam, nullum caput a Christo inibi suscipitur: solus ibi colitur Christus, adeoque juxta suum verbum . . . . Faxit

Roussel, however, also displayed a trait all too common among Fabricians: something that prevented him from turning his inner convictions into actions. Roussel made reference to his own struggle with this problem, saying that on the one hand the flesh counseled him to dissemble, while on the other he found courage in the power of prayer.[74] His predicament, it seems, was shared by many others, and he often referred to the vacillating spirit of his companions. He complained to Farel that although the Gospel was preached in many places around Meaux, many of the people lacked the constancy that would stand up to death.[75] He also said that the letters of Zwingli and Oecolampadius were a great comfort to him, but that, unfortunately, they had less effect on him than the temptations of the flesh and the indecision of his friends, most of whom kept saying "it is not yet time for a true reform of the Church."[76] Roussel admitted to Oecolampadius that this problem was widespread in France. The Gospel had many enemies in his country, said Roussel, but few defenders: Not many were willing to take up the cross of Christ for their religion.[77]

Gerard Roussel represents those in the Fabrician circle who viewed "corrupt" worship as something *indifferent*. Many Fabricians saw the materialistically inclined religion of their contemporaries as an aberration of true piety, but not as a sinful evil, and were willing to tolerate it. Roussel eventually accepted the bishopric of Oleron, and by doing so earned the undying enmity of Calvin, who wrote him a lengthy letter warning him to stay away from the pollution of Catholic worship.[78] The estrangement between Roussel and Calvin points to the limitations of the Fabrician reform and also marks the emergence of an aggressive and uncompromising stance against Catholic piety in France, the consequences of which would be drastic.

Guillaume Farel and Fabrician-inspired radicalism

Although the Fabrician reform was limited by its indifference to external aspects of worship, it provided the spiritual and intellectual basis

Deus, ut corda populorum ita visitentur illustratione Spiritus, ut procul absint densae caecitatis tenebrae in quas hactenus prolapsi sumus, dum sivimus nos a verbo Dei ablegari ad traditiones hominum!" (Herminjard 1.411).

[74] Herminjard 1.271.
[75] Herminjard 1.236.
[76] Herminjard 1.271.
[77] Herminjard 1.276.
[78] The letter was published in 1536 as one of the two treatises in the *Epistolae duae de rebus hoc saeculo cognitu necessariis*.

for a more radical interpretation of the "errors" of medieval piety, and some who listened to Lefèvre's teachings at Paris and Meaux eventually carried his critique to its logical conclusion. Although there were several such disciples – Pauvant and Leclerc, for instance, who suffered martyrdom, and Jean le Comte de la Croix, who went on to become a Protestant pastor in Grandson, Switzerland[79] – one man in particular stands above them all in regard to the intensity of his convictions and his future influence. This is Guillaume Farel.[80] Any discussion of the development of the Protestant Reformed attack on Catholic worship has to include him, because he clearly connects the Erasmian–Fabrician tradition, Zwinglian theology, and Calvinism. Farel was deeply influenced by both Lefèvre and Zwingli, and he, in turn, drew Calvin into the work of the Reform at Geneva and remained his lifelong friend and associate. The Reformation that would later be known as Calvinist had its roots in the work of Farel and, through him, in the Fabrician critique of late medieval piety.

The differences between Farel and Lefèvre are great, but it is still possible to trace the Fabrician influence on Farel without much difficulty. Farel himself acknowledges an immense spiritual and intellectual debt to Lefèvre; he was very fond of the great humanist and long remembered him as his spiritual father.[81] Farel, in fact, traces his own "conversion" away from Catholicism to the teachings he received from Lefèvre.

Farel's conversion was a gradual and painful change in attitude toward Roman Catholic worship.[82] He recalls his youth as a time when he was addicted to "superstition" and simultaneously longed for the truth. He speaks of a "thirst of devotion" that consumed him and that he tried to quench by immersing himself in the religious life

---

[79] Pauvant and Leclerc have already been discussed. For more on de la Croix: E. Baehler, *Jean Le Comte de la Croix, Réformateur à Grandson*, trans. by E. Butticaz (Lausanne, 1912). Also: Lovy, *Origines de la Réforme*, pp. 111ff.

[80] *Guillaume Farel*, p. 12: "Mais pour que le Réforme française durât et s'étendit, il fallait qu'elle s'unifiât, s'organisat, se donnât une doctrine, une forme de culte vraiment à elle. Farel, l'une des premiers, l'a compris et s'est efforcé de grouper les évangéliques français, de les constituer en parti religieux ayant des principes et des buts communs . . . C'est Farel aussi qui, avec d'autres sans doute, dote la premiere Réforme française de libelles, d'exposés de doctrine, d'une liturgie, qui ne sont plus de simples traductions de traités allemands. Il fait bien plus encore: son esprit intransigeant a saisi que, dans la Guerre a la foi ancienne, il faut aller aux extrêmes . . . Farel fera triompher, permi les évangeliques de France, les idées de Zurich sur celles de Wittemberg."

[81] Herminjard 1.481.

[82] Henri Meylan, "Les Etapes de la Conversion de Farel," *Colloque de Tours, l'Humanisme Français au Début de la Renaissance* (Paris, 1973), pp. 253–9.

offered by the late medieval Church. He read the *Lives of the Saints*, studied Aristotle and the scholastics, and practiced all the devotions considered proper at the time.[83] It was not until he began to read and study scripture (as any good Fabrician was supposed to do) that he began to suspect something was wrong with his piety. Lefèvre's biblicism and primitivism made him think that his life as a faithful Roman Catholic had little in common with the Christian life as described in the Bible.[84] Farel claims that by reading the scriptures he acquired a more spiritual understanding of worship. Actually, what he had absorbed was a thoroughly Fabrician interpretation of the corruption of piety. Farel thought that the true worship of God, which should be based in the spiritual commands of his Word, had been supplanted by human inventions.[85] This realization, however, was not sudden. Farel says he could not immediately abandon his "superstitious" beliefs and had to struggle against them. Only little by little, he reports, were the "papal abominations" driven from his heart.[86]

In the *Epistre à Tous Seigneurs*, Farel says that through the words of Lefèvre he was "drawn away from the false opinion of merit" and brought to believe that all salvation "comes from grace and solely through the mercy of God, without anyone having earned it."[87] This insight made it much easier for Farel to rid himself of what he saw as most disturbing, that is, his devotion to the saints. As Farel tells it, Lefèvre is responsible for his final step away from this belief: As soon as Lefèvre gave up his belief in the *cultus divorum* he also was finally able to reject his own "corruption." But Farel went beyond his mentor once he had reached this conclusion:

God finally made me know that He alone ought to be invoked, that the invocation for the dead and all who have left this world, by which the absent are addressed as present, and all such worship is really idolatry. Then was

---

[83] Herminjard 2.41.

[84] "Epistre à tous seigneurs" (Ruchat, *Histoire*, p. 532): "avoir leu la bible, me trouvant fort esbai, et voyant tout au contraire sur la terre, en vie et doctrine et que tout estoit autrement que ne porte la Saincte Escripture, qui estoit un grand moyen pour venir a quelque cognoissance, et pour sortir d'une si damnable abusion.

[85] Herminjard 2.41: "J'ai voulu connaitre la cause de cette disparition de la pieté. L'étude de la Bible m'a appris, qu'au lieu d'observer scrupuleusement la loi divine, seule parfaite comme son Auteur, les nommes y ont ajouté leurs inventions, suivant ainsi l'exemple du fils de perdition, qui veut substituer sa loi à celle de Dieu."

[86] "Epistre à tous seigneurs" (Ruchat, *Histoire*, p. 539): "le jugement et affection humaines ne m'en ont point retiré, et n'ay point prins plaisir d'en laisser tant soit peu, ne desir avec de rien changer . . . et aussi (je) n'ay laisse les dites abominations papales tout à un coup, mais il a fallu que petit à petit la papauté soit tombée de mon coeur."

[87] Ibid., p. 536.

the papacy completely driven from my heart, and I began to detest it as diabolical . . . and the Holy Word of God began to have first place in my heart. And, in general, I then knew and began to discern and believe that it [papal worship] was all sinful, evil and accursed, and that the human laws and traditions that weigh down upon the conscience were all abominable.[88]

The narrative of Farel's conversion offers a unique opportunity to analyze several aspects of the Fabrician critique and its relation to Reformed Protestantism. Although Farel's spiritual journey was greatly aided by Lefèvre, its destination lay beyond the intentions of his mentor. Farel views his conversion as a turning away from sin and evil, not merely as an awareness of corruption. Farel's narrative in the *Epistre* is the tale of a pilgrimage from utter death and corruption to light and truth. In fact, Farel often thanks God for having delivered him from sure death.[89] The focus of his conversion is the problem of idolatry: For him, Catholic worship is evil, sinful and dangerous. It is not merely corrupt piety, it is false religion, and as such can bring damnation. Farel's conversion, unlike Luther's, is not centered on the problem of faith and justification.[90] His focus is false worship and the satanic influence behind it. Farel speaks of his Catholic days as a period when he was under the power of the devil; views his devotion to the cross, pilgrimages, and images as "diabolical things" and says he was immersed in them without limit "as in the depths of iniquity, idolatry and perdition."[91] He looked back on his love for the Mass as particularly heinous, especially because of his devotion to the consecrated host, which he now called, with spiritualistic disdain, "that magic morsel" and "that god of batter."[92]

---

[88] Ibid., pp. 536–7. Also: Herminjard 2.44. Farel describes here how he gave up external piety for "true worship": "Coepit ficta displicere religio exterior, polluto corde: dierum observatio, ciborum delectus, castus ablegatus lectus, incesta et membrorum Christi pollutrice subintroducta fornicatione. Video vere nulla esse vestigis pietatis . . . Video cogitatus hominum, studia et ad inventiones permixta religioni, quae cum cultu Dei stare nullo pacto possunt. Emigravit igitur pietas, Evangelium, divina lex, quae charistas est, solum relictum est humanum, quod hypocris est."

[89] For instance: Fick, *Du Vray Usage*, p. 4; "Epistre à tous seigneurs" (Ruchat, *Histoire*, p. 531).

[90] Although Farel states that he began to convert when Lefèvre drove him away "from the false opinion of merit," he viewed this only as a preliminary step. Only when he stopped believing in the meritorious intercession of the saints did Farel see himself as fully "converted." Faith and justification enter into Farel's conversion only as concepts that allowed him to see the omnipotence and transcendence of God, and that helped him away from "false worship."

[91] "Epistre à tous seigneurs" (Ruchat, *Histoire*, p. 530; also p. 534): "j'avoye bien gagné la couronne de malédiction, de tourment, de mort et de damnation, car du tout je m'employoye jour et nuict pou servir au diable selon l'homme de péché, le pape." This statement is made in special reference to his devotion for the saints.

[92] Ibid., p. 531, 537–8 ("morceau enchanté"; "dieu de paste").

Farel's conversion narrative reveals the contribution made by the Fabrician critique of the intellectual and spiritual milieu of early French Protestantism. The typical Fabrician (and Erasmian) themes can all be found here, but carried to an extreme. Primitivism, biblicism, and transcendentalism lead not only to a rejection of the Catholic *cultus*, but to the development of an aggressively spiritualistic faith as well. What Lefèvre viewed as corrupt, but perhaps indifferent and acceptable, now became for Farel something thoroughly false and evil. There could be no more compromise with Roman piety: It was the work of the devil and needed to be destroyed. By rejecting Catholic worship as evil, Farel had expanded the Fabrician critique to new dimensions. He had also taken Lefèvre's attitude toward worship and placed it in a new, aggressive context. The transcendent and jealous God of Reformed Protestantism loomed large in this conception of worship.[93]

THE AFFAIR OF THE PLACARDS

The confusion and lack of cohesion that marked the beginnings of Protestantism in France were not easily overcome by the efforts of men such as Farel, but it is possible to pinpoint the time and place where the more radical heirs of Lefèvre's legacy eclipsed their more moderate companions, making Meaux seem a rather tame affair, and irrevocably changing the direction of the Protestant cause in France. Sometime during the night between Saturday, 17 October, and Sunday, 18 October 1534, a highly organized, clandestine network of provocateurs plastered broadsheets condemning the "idolatry" of the Roman Catholic Mass in several cities throughout north-central France. According to several accounts, the distribution of these "placards" was rather thorough in Paris, as well as in Rouen, Orléans, Blois, Tours, and Amboise – so thorough, in fact, that as legend came to have it, even King Francis I awoke to find a placard posted outside his bedchamber at the chateau of Amboise (or, as another account tells it, at Blois).[94]

---

[93] Herminjard 2.45; "Vere tu solus Deus, solus sapiens, solusque bonus. Experti didiscere priores, sentimus et posteriores, quam pure tua sit lex obervanda, quam nihil subducemdum aut superaddendum, cum enim solus sis Dominus, solus et praecipere vis et debes." Also: "Epistre à tous seigneurs" (Ruchat, *Histoire*, p. 541).

[94] Among contemporary accounts of this event, the fullest and most often cited are Crespin's *Histoire des Martyrs*, pp. 128–31; and the *Chronique du Roy Françoys Ier*, Georges Guiffrey, ed. (Paris, 1860), p. 110ff. The best modern interpretations are the following: Gabrielle Berthoud, *Antoine Marcourt* (Geneva, 1973), esp. pp. 157–222; and Stephan Skalweit, "Die 'Affaire des Placards' und ihr Reformations-

This brief, but comprehensive attack on the Mass was entitled "Articles Veritables sur les Horribles, Grands et Importables Abus de la Messe Papale." Its author, it is now generally agreed, was Antoine Marcourt, a French Protestant refugee who had replaced Farel as minister at Neuchâtel in 1531. The placards had been printed at Neuchâtel, at the presses of Pierre Vingle, and apparently smuggled into France in great numbers.[95] True to sacramentarian form, this verbal attack on the material manifestations of Catholic worship denied four basic points of doctrine: The "Articles" argued that in the Mass there was no sacrifice, no real presence, no transsubstantiation, and no miracle. It was a rather bombastic, stock statement of the usual objections raised by the Reformed against the Mass, but it created a stir among certain members of French society who were not accustomed to reading such material, much less to finding it displayed in public places.

The aim of the placards, ostensibly, was to make France aware of the dangers of idolatry. Marcourt began the "Articles" by proclaiming:

I call upon heaven and earth as witnesses of the truth against this pompous and proud Papal Mass, through which (if God does not remedy the situation soon) the world will be completely destroyed, ruined, lost, and spoiled; in which Our Lord is thus outrageously blasphemed, and the people fooled and seduced. This is something which should no longer be suffered or endured.[96]

Although the placards may have intended to warn against the dangers of "idolatry," they were actually perceived as a sign of the dangers of Protestantism, and government reaction against this daring venture was as swift as it was brutal. In the eyes of many, above all King Francis, the preparation, distribution, and simultaneous posting in one night of the placards pointed to a well-organized network of dissidents who posed a threat to the nation.[97]

---

geschichtlicher Hintergund," in *Reformata Reformanda. Festgabe für Hubert Jedin* (Munster, 1965), vol. I. Shorter summaries can be found in Jean Jacquart, *François Ier* (Paris, 1981), pp. 268–73, 365–7; and R. J. Knecht, *Francis I* (Cambridge University Press, 1982), pp. 248–52, 390–407. Knecht has also analyzed the details of the story of the placards supposedly found on the king's door in "Francis I, 'Defender of the Faith'?" *Wealth and Power in Tudor England*, E. W. Ives, R. J. Knecht, and J. J. Scarisbrick, eds. (London, 1978), p. 122.

[95] Berthoud credits Guillaume Feret, a servant to the king's apothecary, with directing the smuggling operation (*Antoine Marcourt*, p. 171–6).

[96] *Chronique du Roy Francoys Ier*, p. 464. An appendix in Guiffrey's edition provides the full text of the "Articles." For an analysis of the text of the placards: Berthoud, *Antoine Marcourt*, p. 160ff.; and R. Hari, "Les Placards de 1534," *Aspects de la Propagande Religieuse*, G. Berthoud, et al., eds. (Geneva, 1957).

[97] According to Crespin, King Francis "belched forth" his anger "through his eyes and

The effect of the placards on Paris was tremendous. Rumors immediately circulated telling how the heretics were about to storm the Louvre palace, burn all the churches and massacre the faithful at Mass.[98] The Parlement of Paris ordered a roundup of suspects, and before long several Protestants had been publicly burned. King Francis set up a special commission to judge heresy cases, and by early January he was back in Paris. Soon after his arrival, however, a second verbal attack on the Mass was launched when Protestants littered Paris with copies of a longer work by Marcourt entitled "Petit Traité de la Sainte Eucharistie".[99] Since this second attempt came at a time when the authorities were beginning to think that their persecution of heresy had succesfully stifled such dissent, the response to this challenge was even more dramatic. King Francis ordered a temporary ban on the publication of new books in his realm, and also called for a general expiatory procession in Paris.

On Thursday, 21 January 1535, Paris witnessed one of the most grandiose public displays ever staged in the city up to that time, and perhaps also one of the most dramatic and revealing responses ever launched against Protestantism anywhere in Europe. Out into the streets of Paris poured forth an amazing multitude, the likes of which none could remember.[100] The royal court, the church hierarchy, the university administration, the municipal government, the religious houses, the trade guilds, and each and every parish in the city came out to witness to the Catholic faith. Appropriately enough, the most important relics were also brought out from the churches and chapels. By royal decree, the streets were cleaned and decorated with banners and tapestries. A popular motif noticed by one chronicler was a banner depicting the fabled "Jew and the Host," which was doubtlessly considered a fitting symbol for the perfidy of Marcourt's work.[101] Among the relics that were brought out to help expiate the city and the nation from the sin of the heretics, Parisians especially delighted in seeing the head of the Apostle Philip, the bodies of St. Geneviève and St. Victor, a fragment of the true cross, droplets from the blood of Jesus and the milk of Mary, and the treasured crown of

---

his mouth." *Histoire des Martyrs* (1560), fol. 65. Cited by Berthoud, *Antoine Marcourt*, p. 181.

[98] Knecht, *Francis I*, p. 249.

[99] Berthoud, *Antoine Marcourt*, pp. 223–82 for an extensive analysis of the "Petit Traité."

[100] *Chronique du Roy Françoys Ier*, p. 114ff. has a full, detailed description of this procession. P. Benedict, *Rouen during the Wars of Religion* (Cambridge University Press, 1981), pp. 62–4 has an account of a similar procession held in Rouen.

[101] *Chronique du Roy Françoys Ier*, p. 114.

thorns from the Sainte Chapelle, which made people's hair "stand on end."[102]

This lavish, richly symbolic spectacle had a triumphant as well as expiatory character. The central feature was, of course, the Blessed Sacrament attacked in the placards and the "Petit Traité." As church bells rang above, and the sound of trumpets, drums, and choral singing filled the streets and squares below, a monstrance containing the consecrated host slowly wound its way through the city to the cathedral of Nôtre Dame. The Blessed Sacrament was carried by none other than the bishop of Paris himself, "in great reverence," under a velvet canopy borne by the Dauphin, his two brothers, and the Duc de Vendome. Following immediately behind on foot, bareheaded and carrying a torch, King Francis himself paid reverence to the Sacrament and thus publicly displayed his desire to protect and defend the Catholic faith.[103]

After High Mass at Nôtre Dame, the bishop entertained the royal court at his palace. King Francis then made a speech in which he asked his subjects to denounce all heretics, even relatives and friends. The spectacle concluded with the public burning of six Protestants. From this day forward, persecution intensified. A list naming seventy-three "Lutherans" who had fled the realm was circulated, calling for their capture. An edict promulgated a few days later made those who gave refuge to heretics liable to the same harsh penalties as the heretics themselves, and also offered informers a quarter share of any property confiscated from those they denounced.[104]

The affair of the placards is a watershed in the history of the French Reformation and the Protestant crusade against "idolatry" in that country. First, as a wholesale verbal condemnation of the Mass, the affair was the most spectacular attack on Catholic piety made in France up to that time. (And the more spectacular procession staged in response showed that Catholics accurately judged the nature of the challenge.) Also, the placards were the first unambiguous expression of the turn from "Lutheranism" or Fabrician evangelism to an aggressive Reformed sacramentarianism. By signaling a clear break with the temporizing reforms of the moderate humanists, the placards made the "heretics" identifiable in a way that had not been possible before. French Protestantism had issued an open challenge to the

---

[102] Knecht, *Francis I*, p. 250.
[103] *Chronique du Roy Françoys Ier*, p. 119: "Incontinant apres ledict Sacrament, marchoit le Roy, nostre soverain seigneur, seul, tenant une torche de sire vierge en sa main, teste nue, en grande reverance qu'il faisoit merveilleusement bon voir."
[104] Knecht, *Francis I*, p. 251.

crown and the Church. In the eyes of the king, the placards were the product of a religion for rebels, one that needed to be stamped out.[105] As a result, persecution increased in France, creating an intense climate of fear among Protestants and those who were even slightly attracted to Protestant ideas. This intensification of persecution produced not only martyrs, but also refugees. Among those driven out of France by this first wave of persecution in 1534–5 none would be more important than John Calvin, who fled from Poitiers to Strassburg, and felt compelled to address in his *Institutes* of 1536 the charges of "anarchy" leveled against the Protestants by King Francis. Alongside those who suffered and fled, however, there would also continue to exist many sympathizers who refused to make a clean break with Catholicism. These so-called Nicodemites, whose behavior was largely determined by fear of persecution, would be later subjected to an intense attack on the part of Calvin, and his opposition to the compromises they favored would help give shape to the next stage of the war against idolatry. Finally, the placards implicated Switzerland in the cause of French Protestantism beyond any doubt. From this time forward, first through Neuchâtel and later through Geneva, the direction taken by French Protestants would be decided largely by refugees based in Switzerland. Consequently, it is no surprise that the more radical policies of men such as Farel would become dominant, and that the reforms of Meaux, or even those of Wittenberg, would be forgotten in favor of those dictated from Geneva.

LEFÈVRE'S CONTRIBUTION TO PROTESTANTISM

Lefèvre has held a place of honor among French Protestants since the Reformation. Theodore Beza, for instance, said that Lefèvre had "boldly begun the revival of pure religion."[106] This observation is not entirely incorrect, especially in regard to Lefèvre's attempt to "purify" worship. The practical hostility toward the Catholic *cultus* displayed by the incipient Reformed movement in France drew much inspiration from Lefèvre. Still, like Erasmus, Lefèvre himself only offered a tempered critique of medieval piety. In his capsule biography of Lefèvre, Beza also states that the lecture rooms of Lefèvre produced some of the "best men" of the age, meaning, of course, that

---

[105] Berthoud, *Antoine Marcourt*, p. 219.
[106] Beza, *Icones*, fol. xiii.

he taught many who became Protestants.[107] This observation is only partially true. Although Lefèvre's teachings produced iconoclasts such as Leclerc and Farel, it also created temporizers such as Briçonnet and Roussel. Despite its positive contributions, therefore, the Fabrician reform remains as a halfway station on the way to more radical developments. Lefèvre pointed to the "corruption" of worship, but he himself, and others around him, refused to accept this issue as a cause for schism. It would be up to others who followed Lefèvre to begin the schism, and it would be Calvin's task to seal it once and for all.

---

[107] Heller, "Famine," p. 139.

CHAPTER 6

John Calvin's attack on idolatry

THE streams of influence which we have been tracing between the
humanist critique of medieval piety and the Reformed attack on Catholic worship come together once again in April 1534, when the young
John Calvin paid a visit to the aged Lefèvre at Princess Marguerite's
court in Nerac – perhaps as a way of paying homage to the leader of
the circle with which he had been associated. He had already become
an admirer of Gerard Roussel, with whom he corresponded often.
Whether Calvin had rejected Lefèvre's circle by this time is not clear,
but there is little doubt that, within a year, Calvin had already
adopted a position that was much less conciliatory than Lefèvre's or
Roussel's. Nicholas du Chemin, Calvin's former roommate at Orleans
and a fellow admirer of Roussel, received a letter from Calvin in 1535
asking him to abandon Roman Catholic worship. Gerard Roussel also
received a similar letter.[1] The young Calvin had apparently reached
the conclusion earlier reached by Farel, and the focal point of this
change of mind appears to have been the issue of worship.

Calvin does not reveal much about the people who influenced his
conversion to Protestantism. He may have come in contact with what
was then called "Lutheranism" through personal contacts and reading during his student years at Paris, Orléans, and Bourges.[2] Theodore Beza reports that Calvin was converted before 1526 by his
cousin, Pierre Olivétan, but modern scholars doubt this story.[3] It is

[1] The letter to Chemin was really not a personal letter as such, but a treatise on the
subject of idolatry, and was entitled "De fugiendis impiorum illicitis sacris." The
same was true of the letter to Roussel, entitled "De Christiani hominis officio in
sacerdotiis papalis ecclesiae vel administrandis vel abiiciendis." Both treatises were
published together in 1537, under the title, *Epistolae duae de rebus hoc saeculo cognitu
necessariis.*
[2] For a detailed treatment of Calvin's youth: E. Doumergue, *Jean Calvin, les Hommes et
les Choses de Son Temps*, vol. I, "La Jeunesse de Calvin" and vol. II, "Les Premiers
Essais" (Lausanne, 1902); Josef Bohatec, *Budé und Calvin* (Graz, 1950); and A.
Ganoczy, *Le Jeune Calvin, Genèse et Evolution de sa Vocation Réformatrice* (Wiesbaden,
1966).
[3] Ganoczy, *Le Jeune Calvin*, pp. 43–6; and J. T. McNeill, *The History and Character of
Calvinism* (New York, 1954), p. 108.

195

more likely that Calvin gradually absorbed Protestant ideas from men such as Guillaume Cop and Guillaume Budé, whom he came to know well when he was a student at Paris. Cop was a medical scholar who served as the King's physician; Budé was the most eminent French Hellenist and a vigorous opponent of Nicholas Beda, the conservative leader of the Sorbonne faculty. Both men were radical members of the Fabrician circle.

Calvin is not as explicit about his conversion as Farel, but he does indicate that the issue of idolatry was a central concern of his spiritual transformation. Here is Calvin's only description of the event, from his Preface to the *Commentary on the Psalms* (1557):

> And first, since I was too obstinately devoted to the superstitions of Popery to be easily pulled out from so profound an abyss of mire, God by a sudden conversion subdued and tamed my heart into docility, which was more hardened in such matters than might have been expected from one at my early period of life.[4]

Although he later viewed his conversion as a "softening" to the will of God, Calvin made it clear that this change involved turning away from an "abyss of mire." As he saw it, what really stood between his will and God's was his adherence to the "superstitions of Popery." Like Farel before him, Calvin underwent a conversion experience that focused on the rejection of Roman Catholic worship as a lifesaving moment. From that moment forward, Calvin would become one of the most ardent opponents of Catholic "idolatry." He not only directed the establishment in Geneva of a church free of "pollution," vigorously punishing all offenders, but also inspired a less conciliatory attitude toward Catholicism among his fellow Frenchmen.

Calvin's conversion, then, provides us with an insight into the nature of his attack on Catholic worship. As the corruption of man's proper relationship with God, the problem of idolatry assumes a key position in the thought of Calvin. In fact, Calvin's attack on idolatry is an attack on the corruption of all religion, it is an involved defense of the truth of the Gospel against its antithesis. The significance of this defense cannot be underestimated, since it lays bare many of the central points of Calvin's theology. In studying Calvin's attack on idolatry, one is able to look at what Calvin believed to be most important in religion by seeing how vigorously he attacked its perversion.[5]

---

[4] *Commentary on Psalms*, CR 31.22.
[5] I disagree with Margarete Stirm's analysis of Calvin's position on the image question (and consequently, on idolatry). Stirm insists that "Calvin steht mit seinen positiven Aussagen des Bilderverbotes nicht im Gegensatz zu Luther" and that although the

Before analyzing the nature of Calvin's attack, however, it is necessary to lay bare its theological framework.

CALVIN'S THEOLOGY OF WORSHIP

Knowledge of God and worship of God

According to Calvin, the purpose of creation is for man to know God and to glorify him by worship and obedience.[6] Here may be seen the foundation of Calvin's theology of worship and of his attack on idolatry. Knowledge of God and worship of God are inseparable: One cannot come to know God without yielding some worship to Him.[7]

Various attempts have been made to provide a neat descriptive phrase for Calvin's principal concern in worship, but the two most commonly used are *soli Deo gloria* (to God alone be the glory) and *finitum non est capax infiniti* (the finite cannot contain the infinite). The two are interdependent. Calvin's primary concern in his struggle against Catholic piety was to defend the glory of the God who is "entirely other," who transcends all materiality, who is "as different from flesh as fire is from water,"[8] and whose reality is inaccessible.[9] Calvin's attack on idolatry was an effort to restore God's primary dignity among human beings.[10] Calvin forcefully asserted God's transcendence through the principle *finitum non est capax infiniti* and His omnipotence through *soli Deo gloria*. To make others aware of this dual realization, Calvin systematically juxtaposed the divine and the human, contrasted the spiritual and the material, and placed the transcendent and omnipotent *solus* of God above the contingent multiple of man and the created world.[11] Calvin's attack on Roman Catholic "idolatry" is a condemnation of the improper mixing of spiritual

two men held "apparently" opposing views, they did not disagree. Stirm glosses over significant theological differences to reach this ecumenically minded conclusion. While Luther thought the image question was a secondary issue, Calvin linked it to the issue of worship and made it a central part of his theology and ecclesiastical policy. Margarete Stirm, *Die Bilderfrage in der Reformation* (Gütersloh, 1977), pp. 224–8.

6 *Genevan Catechism* (1545), questions 1, 2, and 6: CR 6.9–10.
7 *Institutes of the Christian Religion* (1559), I.5.9. Subsequent references to the *Institutes* will be to the 1559 edition, unless specified otherwise. All English quotations are from the translation by Ford Lewis Battles, J. T. McNeill, ed. (Philadelphia, 1960).
8 *Commentary on John's Gospel*, CR 47.90, "cui nihilo minus est cum carne dissidium quam igni cum aqua."
9 Kilian McDonnell, *John Calvin, The Church and the Eucharist* (Princeton, 1967), p. 163.
10 Ganoczy, *Le Jeune Calvin*, p. 202.
11 Ganoczy proposes a tripartite centrality in Calvin's theology: (a) "soli Deo gloria"; (b) "solus Christus"; (c) "verbum Dei." Each of these principles defends the com-

and material in worship – an affirmation of the principle *finitum non est capax infiniti*. It is also an indictment of man's attempt to domesticate God and to rob him of his glory – an affirmation of the principle *soli Deo gloria*.[12]

Calvin speaks about the nature of worship and about the seriousness of the sin of idolatry in his 1543 treatise, *On the Necessity of Reforming the Church*, where he concentrates on the significance of worship for the Christian religion. Calvin's argument, as indicated by the title of the treatise, is that the Church had reached such a corrupt state that its reform could wait no longer. The most significant aspect of corruption singled out by Calvin is the perversion of worship, and it is in explaining this issue that he set forth the basis for his attack on idolatry.

Calvin begins by studying the place that worship holds in the Christian faith, and he concludes that it is one of the two elements that define Christianity:

> If it be asked, then, by what things chiefly the Christian religion has a standing existence amongst us, and maintains its truth, it will be found that the following two not only occupy the principal place, but comprehend under them all the other parts, and consequently *the whole substance of Christianity*, viz., a knowledge first, of the right way to worship God; and secondly of the source from which salvation is to be sought. When these are kept out of view, though we may glory in the name of Christians, our profession is empty and vain.[13]

> plete otherness and singularity of God for Calvin, according to Ganoczy. He does add, however, that "on peut affirmer sans hésiter que le principe du 'soli Deo gloria' est pour Calvin le premier et le plus fondamental" (*Le Jeune Calvin*, p. 202). François Wendel makes a similar observation: "From the beginning of his work, Calvin places all his theology under the sign of what was one of the essential principles of the Reform: the absolute transcendence of God and his total 'otherness' in relation to men . . . That is the idea that dominates the whole of Calvin's theological exposition and underlies the majority of his controversies." *Calvin: The Origins and Development of His Religious Thought*, trans. P. Mairet (New York, 1963), p. 151. McDonnell approaches the subject with more caution, stating that Calvin's transcendental premises were at the root of the majority of his theological controversies, though not necessarily at the root of all his work (McDonnell, *Calvin*, p. 165).

12 Ernst Saxer, *Aberglaube, Heuchelei und Frommigkeit. Eine Untersuchung zu Calvins Reformatorischer Eigenart* (Zurich, 1970), p. 69. Saxer thinks that Calvin based his opposition to Rome on the two Lutheran concepts of "sola fides" and "sola scriptura," and that he thus formulated his concept of "true religion" on an opposition to unscriptural beliefs and works-righteousness. I believe Saxer overlooks an important part of Calvin's theology by ignoring the principles of "soli Deo Gloria" and "finitum non ext capax infiniti." Similarly, Margarete Stirm overlooks the significance of worship in Calvin's theological opposition to image worship. Though she provides a good summary of Calvin's own arguments against images, she sees his adherence to the letter of the biblical Law as the source of these arguments (*Bilderfrage*, pp. 161–222).

13 *De necessitate reformandae Ecclesiae* (1543), CR 6.459.

Calvin, thus, asserts that one cannot be a Christian without a proper knowledge of worship, and even places worship before salvation in order of cognitive importance. Correct worship not only precedes righteousness, it precedes the true knowledge of salvation.[14] In any discussion of the relationship between religious knowledge and worship, Calvin gives prior consideration to what has been called "the existential aspect" of the knowledge of God.[15] In fact, Calvin even proposed in an earlier treatise that "genuine piety begets genuine confession."[16]

It is because he believes worship to be the foundation of theology that Calvin can answer one of the more frequent charges made against Protestantism by the Roman Catholic church. The Catholics accused the Protestants of raising disputes that were of little significance, needlessly causing a schism. Calvin responds by saying, on the contrary, that disputes over points of worship should be given precedence over all other aspects of religion.[17] Commenting further on the dispute over worship that divided Christendom, Calvin asserts that it is not an insignificant struggle at all, but rather a life-and-death combat over what is most essential to the Christian life: "For it is not true that we dispute about a worthless shadow. *The whole substance of the Christian religion* is brought into question."[18] Calvin uses equally strong language when he exhorts all Christians to assume their primary duty, that is, to struggle for the maintenance of pure worship:

> There is nothing to which all men should pay more attention, nothing in which God wishes us to exhibit a more intense eagerness than in endeavoring that the glory of his name may remain undiminished, his kingdom be advanced, and the pure doctrine, which alone can guide us to true worship, flourish in full strength.[19]

Calvin ridicules Catholics for saying that Protestants are only concerned with trifles. When the pagan idolaters spoke of fighting for their altars and sacred hearths, says Calvin, they supported what they believed to be the noblest of all causes. Catholics, though also

---

[14] *Institutes*, II.8.11.
[15] Edward Dowey, *The Knowledge of God in Calvin's Theology* (New York, 1952), p. 28. Also: E. Doumergue, "Deux Grandes Doctrines de Calvin: la Paternité et l'Honneur de Dieu," in *Foi et Vie* (1909), pp. 638–42.
[16] *De fugiendis*, CR 5.244.
[17] *De necessitate*, CR 6.502.
[18] Ibid. (italics mine) Calvin also said to Cardinal Sadoleto: "I have also no difficulty in conceding to you that there is nothing more dangerous to our salvation than a twisted and perverse worship of God." *Reply to Sadoleto* (1539), CR 5.392.
[19] *De necessitate*, CR 6.530.

idolaters, are so confused about the nature of their worship that they regard as almost superfluous a contest that is undertaken "for the glory of God and the salvation of men."[20] Calvin thus points to the contradiction in Catholic polemics: The Catholics cling tenaciously to their forms of worship, yet also try to minimize the effect of the Protestant attack by arguing that only trivial matters have been brought into question. The seriousness of their corruption, Calvin adds, is evident in their failure to see that worship is the soul of the Christian life.[21] Idolatry, then, is the very antithesis of religion.[22]

The imperative for spiritual worship

Calvin maintains that the only correct form of worship that can be offered to God is "spiritual worship," which for him means two things: worship devoid of trust in material props or humanly devised ceremonies; and worship that has been commanded by God.[23] Concerning the nature of spiritual worship, Calvin says that it must begin with an attitude of complete dependence on God as the source and endpoint of all human acts and aspirations.[24] The true foundation of proper worship, according to Calvin, is

to acknowledge God to be, as He is, the only source of all virtue, justice, holiness, wisdom, truth, power, goodness, mercy, life and salvation; in accordance with this, and to ascribe and render to Him the glory of all that is good, to seek all things in Him alone, and to look to Him alone in every need.[25]

[20] Ibid., CR 6.502.
[21] *Institutes*, II.8.11.
[22] CR 7.673. Calvin speaks of idols in *Vera Christianae pacificationis et Ecclesiae reformandae ratio* as follows: "Idolum enim erigitur, non quod externam sacrarii speciem deformet, sed quod totam ecclesiae sanctitatem inquinet ac pervertat: quod labefactet totum Dei cultum, nihil in religione nostra impollutum relinquat."
[23] CR 7.607. "Primum enim statuendum est spiritualem esse Dei cultum, se in externis vel caeremoniis, vel aliis quibuslibet operibus reponatur: deinde non esse legitimum, nisi ad eius cui praestatur voluntatem sit compositus, tanquam ad suam regulam. Utramque solus quam necessarium est."
[24] This conception of reality is only one of many Platonic influences evident in the thought of Calvin. For a detailed study of Calvin's Platonism consult: Gerd Babelotzky, *Platonische Bilder und Gedankengänge in Calvins Lehre vom Menschen* (Wiesbaden, 1977); J. Boisset, *Sagesse et Sainteté dans la pensée de Calvin* (Paris, 1959), especially "Les Thèmes Platoniciens dans la Pensée de Calvin" and "Le Platonisme de Jean Calvin," pp. 225–314.
[25] *De necessitate*, CR 6.460. In the *Institutes* Calvin expands on this point, indicating that what man owes to God may be divided into four classifications: (1) adoration; (2) trust; (3) invocation; and (4) thanksgiving (II.8.16).

The principal lesson to be learned from this knowledge is that, since God is spiritual, one should never try to form an earthly or carnal conception of Him. Man can only meet God on God's terms and at God's level, and it is the role of worship to raise men's hearts above the world. Although man searches for God in the material world, this search is always futile.[26] The sum of the matter, says Calvin, is that the worship of God must be spiritual, in order that it may correspond with His nature.[27] It is necessary to remember what God is, he cautions, "lest we should form any crass or earthly ideas respecting Him."[28]

The superiority of the spiritual dimension over the material is at the center of Calvin's teaching. Calvin insists that God is always improperly worshiped in the visible symbol, and that

whatever holds down and confines the senses to the earth is contrary to the covenant of God; in which, inviting us to Himself, He permits us to think of nothing but what is spiritual.[29]

Idolatry is interpreted by Calvin as a diminution of God's honor. Calvin repeatedly maintains that some loss of glory comes about through the improper mingling of spiritual and material in worship, since God's honor is corrupted "by an impious falsehood" whenever any form is attached to Him.[30]

Calvin's second dictum concerning spiritual worship states that God is to be honored only according to His commands in scripture. It is at this point that Calvin uses his hermeneutic of transcendence to attack Catholic worship. Calvin assails the established piety as something that had no sanction from the Word of God and was thoroughly corrupt.[31] Not once does Calvin waver in regard to his interpretation of what scripture means by "spiritual worship." The Word of God is

---

[26] *Commentary on Isaiah* (1551), CR 37.20. "Volunt enim homines praesentem habere Deum: atque hoc initium et fons idolatriae est: quia Deus per simulachrum nobis non adest, sed per verbum suum et spiritus virtutem. Quamvis autem et gratine suae et bonorum spiritualium imaginem nobis obiiciat in sacramentis, non alio tamen spectat, quam ut sursum ad se nos invitet."

[27] *Commentary on the Last Four Books of Moses* (1563), CR 24.403. "Certum enim est, Deus nunquam voluisse coli nisi pro sua natura. Unde sequitur, verum eius cultum semper fuisse spiritualem, ideoque minime situm in externis pompis."

[28] *Commentary on the Last Four Books of Moses*, CR 24.376. Also *Institutes*, II.8.17: "God wholly calls us back and withdraws us from petty carnal observances, which our stupid minds, crassly conceiving God, are wont to devise. And he makes us conform to his lawful worship, that is, a spiritual worship established by himself."

[29] *Commentary on the Last Four Books of Moses*, CR 24.387.

[30] *Institutes*, I.11.2.

[31] *De necessitate*, CR 6.463–4. Also: Peter Auski "Simplicity and Silence: the Influence

clear, he says, and as the rule that distinguishes between false and true worship, it has a universal and univocal application.[32] God's commands stand inscribed in the pages of the Bible as an unchanging rule that man must never alter in any way:

> Here indeed is pure and real religion: faith so joined with an earnest fear of God that this fear also embraces willing reverence, and carries with it such legitimate worship as is prescribed in the law.[33]

What Calvin says in the first few chapters of the *Institutes* is tightly woven around this series of facts: Scripture settles all questions and describes the truth the detail. What is this truth? That nature can lead to God, but only scripture reveals Him; that this revelation gives knowledge of God, and that worship is the result of knowledge. As Calvin says, scripture first invites to fear, then to God, and finally, "by this, we can learn to worship Him."[34] There is no escaping this hermeneutical circle in Calvin. In fact, he asserts that even the Bible itself is incapable of limiting discussion of God to a purely analytic level. All considerations of God, even the simplest mention of His name, require a response, and even more important, the *right kind* of response: "As often as Scripture asserts that there is one God, it is not contending over the bare name, but also prescribing that nothing belonging to his divinity be transferred to another."[35]

---

of Scripture on the Aesthetic Thought of the Major Reformers," *Journal of Religious History* 10: 343–64 (1979).

[32] Calvin's doctrine of scripture is best summarized in the *Institutes*, I.6–10. For further reference: J. K. S. Reid, *The Authority of Scripture* (London, 1957), pp. 29–55. Reid provides a good summary of Calvin's doctrine of scripture and supplies thorough notes in reference to the most significant scholarly debates about this subject. J. T. McNeill also provides a brief and helpful study in "The Significance of the Word of God for Calvin," *Church History*, 28: 140–5 (1959). Other studies include the following: T. H. L. Parker, *The Doctrine of the Knowledge of God* (Edinburgh, 1952), pp. 41–7; E. Dowey, *Knowledge*, pp. 86–146; W. Niesel, *The Theology of Calvin* (Philadelphia, 1956), pp. 22–38; F. Wendel, *Calvin*, pp. 156–60; and more recently, H. J. Forstman, *Word and Spirit: Calvin's Doctrine of Biblical Authority* (Stanford, 1962); and H. Kraus, "Calvins Exegetische Prinzipien," *Zeitschrift für Kirchengeschichte*, 79: 329–41 (1968). Also: W. H. Neuser, "Theologie des Worts – Schrift, Verheissung und Evangelium bei Calvin," in *Calvinus Theologus: Die Referate des Europäischen Kongress für Calvinforschung 16–19 Sept. 1974*, W. H. Neuser, ed. (Neukirchen/Vluyn, 1976), pp. 17–38; and in the same volume, A. Ganoczy, "Calvin als paulinischen Theologe. Ein Forschungsansatz zur Hermeneutik Calvins," pp. 39–70.

[33] *Institutes*, I.2.2.

[34] *Institutes*, I.10.2.

[35] *Institutes*, I.12.1.

Calvin's interpretation of the history of idolatry

The ultimate object of Calvin's theology may be knowledge of the supreme reality of God, but Calvin points out that one can only be concerned with this as it pertains to man.[36] For Calvin, God is never an abstraction that has to be related to an abstractly conceived humanity[37]; He is always the God of man, the God who reveals himself. Correspondingly, man is always described in terms of his relation to this revealing God.[38]

Calvin traces the origin of idolatry to man's fallen condition. In addition to being ontologically removed from the reality of God, man, as a result of the Fall, cannot come to know God properly. Calvin argues that fallen man is separated from God by a cognitive gulf that can only be bridged by grace and revelation, since his faculties have been impaired in two ways: His natural gifts have been corrupted and his spiritual gifts have been completely taken away.[39] Man's imperfection is greater in the spiritual part of his nature as a result of sin, since all things that pertain to the life of the soul are extinguished in him.[40]

Man, says Calvin, has been placed in a hopeless situation as a result of the Fall.[41] There is still implanted in human nature a desire

---

[36] *Institutes*, I.1.1: "nearly all the wisdom we possess, that is to say, true and sound wisdom, consists of two parts: the knowledge of God and of ourselves." This statement stands at the beginning of every edition of the *Institutes*, each time in a slightly different form. J. T. McNeill indicates that Calvin may have been following a precept used earlier by Clement of Alexandria, Augustine, and Thomas Aquinas (*Institutes*, McNeill edition, vol. I, p. 36, n. 3). Roy Battenhouse discusses the Neoplatonic overtones of Calvin's "duplex cognitio" in "The Doctrine of Man in Calvin and in Renaissance Platonism," *Journal of the History of Ideas*, 9: 447–71 (1948). Charles Trinkaus, attempting to prove that Calvin was a "modern" thinker, argues that one may see in Calvin's epistemological concerns a "healthy skepticism" derived from nominalism – the same sort of skepticism, he adds, that produced modern science. "Renaissance Problems in Calvin's Theology," *Studies in the Renaissance*, 1: 59–80 (1954).

[37] Dowey, *Knowledge*, p. 20.

[38] Dowey refers to this principle as "correlation," and insists that it is not merely a formal principle, but a reality that must be faced in treating any religious or moral category of Calvin's thought: "every theological statement has an anthropological correlate, and every anthropological statement, a theological correlate" (*Knowledge*, p. 20).

[39] *Institutes*, II.2.12, II.2.17.

[40] *Institutes*, II.2.12.

[41] Hans Engelland does not think the labyrinth is all that hopeless for Calvin. He sees the Reformer as torn between the rationalism of the humanists and the revelation theology of Christianity. This theory, however, exaggerates Calvin's indecision,

to search for the truth, but this desire can never be fulfilled. Man's mind, dulled in its intellectual capacities, and man's soul, stripped of its original capabilities, can only grope in the dark for the truth.[42] In this state of confusion man can only move in the direction of falsehood and evil. He is perpetually headed in a downward direction, towards death, ignorance, and spiritual destruction:

With respect to the kingdom of God, and all that relates to the spiritual life, the light of human reason differs little from darkness; for, before it has pointed out the road, it is extinguished; and its power of perception is little else than blindness, for before it has reached its fruition, it is gone.[43]

Just as man retains an insatiable desire for the truth he once knew before the Fall, so does he retain a longing for the relationship he once enjoyed with God. This innate desire is called the *sensus divinitatis* (awareness of divinity) or the *semen religionis* (seed of religion).[44] Calvin feels that there is ample proof for this in the fact that there is not one nation on earth that does not have some form of religion.[45] Idolatry and superstition are themselves an additional proof of this natural inclination in man. Calvin argues that the impious themselves prove through their distortion of religion that there is some conception of God present in the mind of every human being.[46]

Ironically, this seed of religion does not bring man closer to God, but further alienates him. Stressing the spiritual ineptitude of man to the point where he seems inconsistent, Calvin asserts that this seed seldom takes root, and that when it does, it only brings forth deformed and poisonous fruit. Scarcely one man in a hundred, he says, follows the inclination given by this principle; and the one who does,

since it is clear that Calvin accepts a dominant pessimism in regard to man's spiritual capabilities. *Gott und Mensch bei Calvin* (Munich, 1943), pp. 7–32, 46–59. Also: W. Kolfhaus, *Vom Christilichen Leben nach Johannes Calvin* (Neukirchen, 1949), pp. 23–68; and G. Bockwoldt, "Das Menschebild Calvins," *Neue Zeitschrift für Systematische Theologie und Religionsphilosophie*, 10: 171–3 (1968); and Richard Stauffer, *Dieu, la Création et la Providence dans la Prédication de Calvin* (Bern, 1978).

[42] *Institutes*, II.2.12.
[43] *Commentary on Ephesians*, 4.17: CR 51.204.
[44] *Institutes*, I.3.1: "There is within the human mind, and indeed by natural instinct, an awareness of divinity [sensus divinitatis]." Also: I.4.1, "God has sown a seed of religion [semen religionis] in all men." Edward Dowey maintains that outside the *Institutes*, Calvin uses the term *semen religionis* most often. Dowey, *Knowledge*, p. 52, n. 13. See also: H. C. Hoeksema, "Calvin's Theology of the Semen Religionis," *Protestant Reformed Theological Journal*, 8: 25–37 (1975).
[45] *Institutes*, I.3.1. (Calvin cites Cicero on this point, *De Natura Deorum*, I.16.43.)
[46] *Institutes*, I.3.1.

fulfills this desire in a perverted manner.[47] Because of his sinful condition, then, man can only respond to his instinct erroneously, either by suppressing its effect or by distorting its intended purpose. The "seed of religion" causes man to disparage the honor of God and to further separate him from the grace he sorely needs. The *sensus divinitatis*, in fact, is the fountainhead of superstition and idolatry among humans:

All have naturally something of religion born with them, but such is the blindness and stupidity, as well as the weakness, of our minds, that our apprehension of God is immediately depraved. Religion is thus the beginning of all superstitions, not in its own nature, but through the darkness which has settled down upon the minds of men, and which prevents them from distinguishing between idols and the true God.[48]

Calvin's interpretation of human corruption plays an important role in his assessment of the problem of idolatry. Man, in his state of corruption, strays off as a wanderer and a vagrant.[49] Although he can know God correctly in the Bible, he chooses to create his own fantasies about the divine.[50] These false conceptions lead to the development of idolatrous practices, and this process separates man from God even further. Calvin proposes a twofold corruption of worship, saying that there are two tendencies in fallen man that displease God immensely. The first is that man, though he can come to know the truth, chooses to follow his own base instincts and create his own religion. (Man's choice, however, is limited by the perversion of his nature, which will only allow him to fall into deception.) The only worship that can please God, says Calvin, is that which He has decreed as acceptable in scripture. Thus, the first step of man's audacity is to ignore the prescriptions of God.[51]

God is further displeased, adds Calvin, by the manner in which His commands are corrupted. This is the second step in man's audacity: God demands to be worshiped spiritually, but man can only devise

---

[47] *Institutes,* I.4.1.
[48] *Commentary on Psalms,* 97.7: CR 32.44. J. Ries, *Die Natürliche Gotteserkentnis in der Theologie der Krisis im Zusammenhang mit dem Imagobegriff bei Calvin* (Bonn, 1939), pp. 34–5.
[49] *Institutes,* I.5.15.
[50] At times Calvin attributes man's perversion to the direct temptation of the devil, not to man's corruption. Calvin believes that Satan's work among men is to disrupt God's plan and to estrange man from God. *Petit Traicté,* CR 5.457; *Commentary on Samuel,* CR 29.473.
[51] *Institutes,* I.11.4; *Commentary on Ezekiel,* 6.4: CR 40.140.

material forms of worship. The rebellion of man in regard to worship displeases God tremendously, not only because of the act of disobedience, but because of the form of worship it creates. It is insult added to injury.

Calvin asserts that man, in the state of sin, is continually drawn to the earthly and material. He has become a creature "of the flesh" – a selfish and self-centered creature who delights in physical gratification to such an extent that all his thoughts are dominated by material conceptions. Fallen man has become engulfed in material existence; he has completely forsaken the spiritual dimension, and has therefore removed himself from the realm of God. Calvin comments on this situation by stating that in order to approach God correctly, man must transcend his own materiality and egocentricity.

For as long as our views are bounded by the earth, perfectly content with our own righteousness, wisdom and strength, we fondly flatter ourselves and fancy we are little less than demigods. But if we once elevate our thoughts to God, and consider his nature, and the consummate perfection of His righteousness, wisdom, and strength, to which we ought to be conformed – what before charmed us in ourselves under the false pretext of righteousness, will soon be loathed as the greatest iniquity; what strangely deceived us under the title of wisdom, will be despised as extreme folly; and what wore the appearance of strength, will be proved to be most wretched impotence. So very remote from the divine purity is what seems in us the highest perfection.[52]

In this passage, Calvin makes it clear that the root of idolatry lies not in the material world *per se*, but in man himself, who is impudent enough to seek divinity on his own terms instead of the Creator's. Man reverses the order of divine reality, expecting to find the Creator in the created. As long as man remains embroiled in the material level of his own existence, and is satisfied with his own corrupt being, he is immersed in the darkest error. Man is flesh, says Calvin, and delights in those things that correspond to his own disposition; hence, he deludes himself by contriving many things in the worship of God that "are full of pomp and have no solidity."[53]

At this point Calvin further refines the theology of idolatry that had already been developed by Zwingli. Though Calvin's predecessors had also placed the blame for idolatry in human beings rather than in the material world, they had focused on this problem in isolation from the doctrine of the Fall. Calvin weaves this teaching into the *Institutes* precisely at the point where it can be turned into a categorical

---

[52] *Institutes*, I.11.1.
[53] *Commentary on John's Gospel*, CR 47.90.

judgment on the human condition: Idolatry is inescapable in the fallen state, "for each man's mind is like a labyrinth."[54]

Calvin is no dualist. The created, material world is viewed as good in itself. The material world is neutral, it seems, or indifferent. When compared to God and the spiritual realm, it is impossible to deny that ontological superiority belongs to the Creator. But what matters for Calvin is the fact that idolatry does not result from any insufficiency in matter itself, due to its contingency and ontological inferiority, but rather from a defect in human beings. It is the human mind, or "flesh," that tries to reverse the natural order. Since they are incapable of properly perceiving the superior, spiritual oneness of God, human beings continually atomize the divine by trying to create a pantheon of fictitious material deities:

Surely, just as waters boil up from a vast, full spring, so does an immense crowd of gods flow forth from the human mind, while each one, in wandering about with too much license, wrongly invents this or that about God Himself.[55]

The end result of this process is that the objective reality of God is denied by humans. Instead of understanding the true metaphysics, the human race creates an infinite number of false, subjective opinions, so that religion is atomized and men are severed from reality itself, as well as from each other. Because the "fault of dullness is within us,"[56] says Calvin, each person is to blame for creating falsehoods:

after we rashly grasp a conception of some sort of divinity, straightaway we fall back into the ravings or evil imaginings of our flesh, and corrupt by our vanity the pure truth of God. In one respect we are indeed unalike, because each one of us privately forges his own particular error; yet we are very much alike in that, one and all, we forsake the one true God for prodigious trifles.[57]

When one considers that Calvin regarded knowledge of God and of oneself to be the proper end of all human beings, it is easy to see why the idolatrous impulse seemed so heinous: It produced a complete reversal of the true, natural order, and perverted the *cognitio* that alone could make life good.

Calvin emphasizes the relative worthlessness of man's material existence (in comparison with God) and argues that the true goal of man

---

54 *Institutes*, I.5.12.
55 Ibid.
56 *Institutes*, I.5.15.
57 *Institutes*, I.5.11.

is to transcend the created world. If he is ever to attain truth and eternal life, man must then regard the world as worthless.[58] Calvin speaks of the flesh as an obstacle that must be overcome,[59] but not in a spiritualistic or dualistic sense. What Calvin opposes is the *ego-centricity* of man, that is, his attempt to worship God according to his own whims. The fault lies not in the material world, but in man, who obstinately refuses to accept the spiritual truth of God.[60] Commenting on man's corruption of worship, Calvin says that mortals are carried away by too much folly and rashness, who while "precariously drawing a fleeting breath from moment to moment" dare to devise their own form of worship.[61] The sin of corrupt worship is augmented by the fact that man tries to bring God down to the level of creation. The "crass imaginations" and materialistic conceptions of man always incline him "to try to circumscribe God's infinite essence, or to draw Him down from heaven, and to place Him beneath the elements of the earth."[62] Man tries to reverse the proper order of creation. Instead of adapting himself to the spiritual reality of the creator, man tries to make God adapt to the created world. Calvin warns that this is a dangerous error:

This single consideration, when the inquiry relates to the worship of God, ought to be sufficient for restraining the insolence of our mind, that God is so far from being like us, that those things which please us most are for him loathsome and nauseating.[63]

Since man's fallen condition has made him a slave to error, says Calvin, "every one of us is, even from his mother's womb, a master craftsman of idols."[64] When the *semen religionis* is awakened in man,

---

[58] *Institutes,* II.9.1–2.

[59] *De fugiendis,* CR 5.243. "Iam istud quoque nostri aeque ac saeculorum omnium vitium est, tam vafras esse, amabiles, captiosas, speciosisque praetextas nominibus, ad illudendum unumquemque, carnis suae illecebras, ut illam arcere a concilis nostris, abiqereque, primus sit sapiendi gradus."

[60] *De necessitate,* CR 6.461. "Scio quam difficulter hoc persuadeatur mundo, improbari Deo cultus omnes praeter verbum suum institutos. Quim potius haeret haec persuasio, et quasi in ossibus omnium defixa est, ac nedullis, quidquid agant, in eo se satis iustam approbationem habere, si modo qualemunque honoris Dei zelum obtendat . . . mendacium esse, quidquid verbo suo additur, praesertim in haec parte: ethelothreseia meram esse vanitatem."

[61] *Institutes,* I.11.4.

[62] *Commentary on the Last Four Books of Moses,* CR 24.392.

[63] *Commentary on John's Gospel,* CR 47.90.

[64] *Commentary on the Acts of the Apostles,* CR 48.562. Jean Delumeau stresses the point that Calvin, and the Reformers as a whole, were among the first armchair ethnologists of the western world. "Les Réformateurs et la Superstition," *Actes du colloque sur l'Admiral de Coligny* (Paris, 1974), p. 471.

it necessarily leads to error, because his fallen mind can only conceive of God in material terms.[65] It is no surprise, therefore, that Calvin refers to the *semen religionis* as "the beginning and source of idolatry."[66] Man persists in his search for a material divinity, and refuses to accept God on His own terms.[67] Calvin finds the origin of idolatry in man's effort to domesticate God and tailor religion to this own desires:

For this is the origin of idolatry, that when the genuine simplicity of God's worship is known, people begin to be dissatisfied with it, and curiously to inquire whether there is anything worthy of belief in the figments of men; for men's minds are soon attracted by the snares of novelty, so as to pollute, with various kinds of leaven, what has been delivered in God's word.[68]

In order to illustrate this analysis of the origin of idolatry, Calvin spends a considerable amount of time covering its history. By placing the problem in a historical perspective, Calvin shows how man has always been inclined to follow idolatry.

Calvin begins by outlining the process whereby man transfers the honor due to God to material objects.[69] He believes this tendency developed in stages, starting with the honoring of heavenly bodies and earthly idols, and progressing "by ambition" to the heaping of divine honors on mortals, culminating in the invention of a pantheon of divinities.[70] Calvin believes that the history of idolatry shows not only that man is inclined to seek God in the material world, but that he also tends to scatter the honor due to Him among various recipients.[71]

---

[65] *Commentary on the Last Four Books of Moses*, CR 24.423.

[66] *Commentary on Isaiah*, CR 37.20. "Volunt enim homines praesentem habere Deum: Atque hoc initium et fons idolatriae est: quia Deus per simulacrum nobis non adest, sed per verbum suum et spiritus virtutem."

[67] *Commentary on Acts*, CR 48.153. "quod mens humana, ut nihil nisi crassum et terrenum de Deo concipit, ita ad eandem crassiteam transfert omnia divinae preasentiae symbola . . . .nos autem, qui terrae sumus affixi illum similiter volumus in terra habere." Calvin also says elsewhere: "le source d'idolatrie est que nous sommes charnelz et apprehendons Dieu selon nostre fantasie" (CR 10a, p. 202).

[68] *Commentary on the Last Four Books of Moses*, CR 24.282.

[69] John H. Leith has remarked that "the history of religions becomes for Calvin the history of idolatry" in "John Calvin's Polemic against Idolatry," in *Soli Deo Gloria: New Testament Studies in Honor of William Childs Robinson*, J. M. Richards, ed. (Richmond, Va., 1968), p. 114.

[70] *Institutes*, I.12.3.

[71] *Institutes*, I.11.6 (Augustine, *City of God*, IV. 9; IV. 31; Varro, no longer extant). In a brief analysis three times removed from its original author, Calvin cites Augustine's use of Varro in explaining the gradual corruption of worship among men. Calvin, in agreement with Augustine, accepts Varro's interpretation of the corruption of worship.

Calvin sees all of history as a long lesson in man's propensity for idolatry. The inclination to commit false worship inherent in every individual is aggravated by society through mutual support, social conditioning, and group rebellion against God. The individual born into an idolatrous society, then, will doubtlessly also be drawn into idolatry.[72]

Moving from the history of mankind in general to that of Israel, Calvin proposes that the Jews serve as proof of his theory of the origin of idolatry. The example of the Israelites, he says, shows that men never believe God is with them unless He shows Himself physically present.[73] The history of Israel is a series of cycles wherein the chosen people keep falling into error again and again. Calvin points to the fact that God had to hide the body of Moses from the Israelites as proof of the constant caution with which the Jews had to be treated by God. Had the Israelites found the body of Moses, argues Calvin, they would have turned it into an object of worship. Calvin also cites the continuous struggle of the Old Testament prophets as a further example of the perpetual idolatry of Israel.[74]

The Christian church has not been spared the trials of the ancient Jews. In tracing the history of idolatry, Calvin wants to prove that the early Church had no images, relics, or any other type of improper material worship. As long as doctrine was pure and strong, he says, the Church rejected all such things.[75] It was only when the purity of the ministry had degenerated that images were first introduced into Christian temples, and then only for decorative purposes.[76] Calvin insists that the early fathers had kept images out of the Church in fear of the evil they could engender: It was a deliberate effort, not an oversight. The adoption of material paraphernalia resulted from and intensified the weakness of the early medieval Church.[77]

In addition to being polluted by the acceptance of the cult of im-

---

[72] *Commentary on Isaiah*, CR 37.38–9.
[73] *Institutes*, I.11.8. (Calvin is commenting here on the incident of the Golden Calf in Exodus 32:1: "We know not what has become of this Moses; make us gods who go before us").
[74] *Inventory of Relics*, CR 6.450.
[75] *Institutes*, IV.4.1, where Calvin gives a brief description of the condition of the early Church; and IV.10.19, where he treats the accumulation of "useless" rites in the post-Apostolic Church.
[76] *Institutes*, I.11.13. Calvin was a strong proponent of the "consensus of the first five centuries." For more on this point, consult: J. T. McNeill, *Unitive Protestantism* (New York, 1930), p. 271ff; Pontien Polman, *L'Element Historique dans la Controverse Religieuse du XVIe Siècle* (Gembloux, 1932), p. 74; H. Berger, *Calvins Geschichtsauffassung* (Zurich, 1955), pp. 168–70.
[77] *Institutes*, I.11.6.

ages, the Church was also irreparably damaged by the introduction of the cult of relics. Like the cult of images, the consecration and worship of relics was both the product and cause of corruption and weakness within the Church. Calvin argues that the early Church decently buried its saints and martyrs in hope of the Resurrection, and that there was no desire among the early Christians to regard the remains of holy men and women as a source of divine grace.[78]

The corruption of the early Church, Calvin argues, was completed with the adoption of pagan practices.[79] Instead of abandoning the old idolatry, as the early Christians had been taught to do, new converts and old believers alike began to retain elements of pagan religion under the guise of Christian themes. Consequently, the old idolatry continued to be observed within the Church, but under an aura of respectability. Calvin observes some of the developments that took place in Europe as it became "Christianized" in late antiquity:

So the priests of Gaul gave rise to the sacrifice of Great Cybele's celibacy. Nuns came in place of vestal virgins. The Church of All Saints to succeed the Pantheon [or the church of all gods]; against ceremonies were set cermonies not much unlike.[80]

In the *Inventory of Relics* Calvin explains in closer detail why it is that the Church abandoned itself to idolatrous practices. Referring to his theory of the origin of idolatry, Calvin remarks that man's blind search for spiritual values in the material world caused this betrayal of values. Like Erasmus before him, Calvin thinks this is proven by the case of Christ's scanty physical remains:

But the first vice, and as it were, beginning of the evil, was, that when Christ ought to have been sought in his Word, sacraments, and spiritual graces, the world, after its custom, delighted in his garments, vests, and swaddling-clothes; and thus overlooking the principal matter, followed only its accessory.[81]

The same phenomenon, he adds, occurred with the remains of the apostles and martyrs. Spiritual value began to be attached gradually

---

[78] *Inventory of Relics*, CR 6.451. "Iamais ceste mal heureuse pompe de canonizer n'a esté introduicte en l'Eglise, iusques à ce que tout a esté perverty et comme profané; partie par la bestise des Prelatz et Pasteurs, partie par leur avarice, partie qu'ilz ne pouvayent resister à la coustume."

[79] Heinrich Berger treats Calvin's polemic against images almost exclusively as a historical argument against the rebirth of paganism, overlooking other significant theological points. *Calvins Geschichtsauffassung*, pp. 47–50.)

[80] *Commentary on Acts*, CR 48.325. Also: Heribert Schützeichel, "Calvins Einspruch gegen die Heiligenverehrung," *Catholica* 35: 93–116 (1981).

[81] *Inventory of Relics*, CR 6.409.

to the material remains of those Christians most intimately connected with the success of the Church. Calvin does not pinpoint a date for this development, but he does insist that this was the first stage in the intrusion of idolatry into the Christian life.[82]

Calvin tries to drive home the point that, regardless of the intentions behind it, the preservation of relics is dangerous for the Church. The purity of worship is threatened by their presence, he says, because human nature cannot help but make relics into objects of worship. As soon as relics are admitted into the Church, the faithful begin to attach a spiritual value to them, and the process of idolatry begins to ferment:

Men cannot look upon them, or handle them without veneration; and there being no limit to this, the honor due to Christ is forthwith paid to them. In short, a longing for relics is never free from superstition, nay, what is worse, it is the parent of idolatry, with which it is very generally conjoined.[83]

CALVIN'S ANALYSIS OF REVERENTIAL ACTS

It is important to keep in mind that Calvin's theology of idolatry was not formulated as a disembodied intellectual exercise. All his writings against false worship are directed against specific practices still being observed by the Catholic church in the sixteenth century. Therefore, it is only natural that, in writing against idolatry, he would devote considerable attention to specific arguments aimed at discrediting Catholic worship and theology.

Calvin's polemic against Catholic piety is based on one fundamental principle, already widely recognized among Swiss Reformers by the time he began to write. This is the dictum that states that "nothing belonging to God's divinity is to be transferred to another."[84] But Calvin does not stop at this point. He expands on the work of his predecessors and moves beyond such categorical statements to an analysis of the reasons behind the command. Calvin is able to formulate a comprehensive theology of idolatry by carefully defining the nature of the reverential act in its metaphysical context. By examining

---

[82] *Inventory of Relics*, CR 6.410. Heinrich Bullinger had made this assertion in his 1539 edition of *De origine erroris*, chap. 13. Curiously enough, modern scholarship has revived this theory. Peter Brown argues eloquently for the function of the holy man as a cause of the acceptance of material worship in the early Church. "A Dark Age Crisis: Aspects of the Iconoclastic Controversy," *English Historical Review*, 346: 14 (1973); "The Rise and Function of the Holy Man in Late Antiquity," *Journal of Roman Studies*, 71: 80–101 (1971).

[83] *Inventory of Relics*, CR 6.410.

[84] *Institutes*, I.12.1.

what happens in the act of worship itself, Calvin is able to juxtapose human desires and capabilities with the objective reality of God. In doing so, he turns an abstract theological problem into a very practical consideration. What happens when a person kneels in church?

Calvin analyzes the act of worship by separating it into two spheres: the objective and the subjective. This is where Calvin sharpens the Reformed metaphysics of transcendence into a practical description of reality. He is going beyond a simple condemnation of "false worship" to an analysis of the relationship between the divine and the human. This is what he says: The two spheres of existence are connected by worship, which is a human act. The objective aspect is the ontological reality of the act itself. It refers to what happens in the spiritual sphere, which is God's sphere, the one real, superior state of existence. Any human motion in the material sphere that is intended as worship, or carries with it any reverence toward divinity, is an attempt to cross over from one sphere to the other, to communicate. By necessity, then, any kind of worship is really spiritual. It is the one human action that connects one sphere with the other, and since the divine can only be approached in a spiritual way, all such motions have to be charged with this value. This is the objective reality of any religious act, even of one performed for a false deity. Since every act of worship is charged with this real, spiritual sense, which relates to God, it is wasted if it does not have the true God as its object. For Calvin, this transaction is as objective as the motion of one's hand, or as anything that can be perceived by the senses in the material sphere. In fact, it is the place where the reality of the spiritual manifests itself among human beings most intensely.

What is the subjective aspect of worship? For Calvin, it is the intentions of the worshiper, what the human being has in mind while going through any religious motion. Calvin's conclusion is that the act of worship itself cannot be considered from this perspective. This is because the reality of God is unchangeable, and approachable only as He commands:

But they do not realize that true religion ought to be conformed to God's will as to a universal rule; that God ever remains like Himself, and is not a specter or phantasm to be transformed according to anyone's whim.

Religion, then, is worthless if it does not connect with the metaphysical reality of God: "no religion is genuine unless it be joined with truth."[85]

---

[85] *Institutes*, I.4.3.

The intentions of the worshiper are meaningless in defining the nature of the reverential act. Since there is only one divine reality, Calvin argues, all religious acts have reference to the one God, regardless of what is going on in the mind of the worshiper. No religious act can be separated from the supreme reality of God, he says, because every reverential act that has been joined with religion "cannot but savor of something divine."[86] The problem is that human beings continually try to supplant the divine reality with their own impulses. In this respect, Calvin inverts ordinary definitions of reality: The "real" is what goes unseen, what happens in the spiritual realm when one offers worship, the "fictitious" is what exists in the mind of the individual.

In seeking God, miserable men do not rise above themselves as they should, but measure him by the yardstick of their own carnal stupidity . . . they do not, therefore, apprehend God as he offers himself, but imagine him as they have fashioned him in their own presumption. When this gulf opens, in whatever direction they move their feet, they cannot but plunge headlong into ruin. Indeed, whatever they afterward attempt by way of service to God, they cannot bring as tribute to him, for they are not worshiping God but a figment and dream of their own heart.[87]

The strength of this argument rests, in turn, upon the assertion that there is some very real connection between actions in the material sphere and the divine reality, upon the assertion that each reverential act necessarily conveys an objective transaction of honor – a transaction that can only detract from God's glory if it is not properly carried out. Calvin states this principle clearly in the *Institutes*:

as soon as religion has been joined with an act of reverence it carries the profanation of divine honor along with it . . . whenever any observances of piety are transferred to some one other than the sole God, sacrilege occurs.[88]

Calvin emphasizes God's loss of honor so much that at times he even seems to refer to a gross transference of glory, almost as if he were speaking of an accounting ledger where the debts due to God are instead paid to the fictitious divinities dreamed up by man. This, of course, is a theological impossibility, and may be accepted only as a metaphor used to emphasize the univocal nature of reverential acts.

Calvin continues his analysis of the reverential act by focusing on the bodily gestures that constitute the act, and by explaining why

---

[86] *Institutes*, I.12.3.
[87] *Institutes*, I.4.1.
[88] Ibid.

they should be reserved for God alone. He insists that the species of adoration condemned in Exodus 20:4–6 is that in which images of wood and stone are worshiped by bodily gestures.[89] In short, he says, God forbids any physical act of reverence to images, such as prostrating, bowing, or giving any other indication of honor, such as uncovering the head or bending the knee. In defense of this position Calvin quotes Isaiah 45:23 ("Every knee shall bow to me, and every tongue shall swear by my name"). His conclusion regarding this passage is that it obviously implies that an image receives the worship due to God when any honor is paid to it through bodily gestures.[90] The same argument concerning bodily gestures is leveled against the cult of relics. In a passage that summarizes his doctrine of misdirected worship, Calvin condemns Catholic piety:

For they have prostrated themselves, and bent the knee before relics as before God, lighting torches and tapers as a sign of homage, putting confidence in them, and running to them as if they possessed a divine power and grace. *If idolatry is just to transfer the honor of God to others*, can we deny that this is idolatry?[91]

Just as God demands that all worship be in accordance with His nature, says Calvin, so does He command that it follow His clear instructions as expressed in scripture. Calvin never tires of saying that the only "lawful" form of worship is the spiritual worship that God has established "by Himself."[92] This additional point of reference completes Calvin's analysis of the reverential act: He indicates that to create one's own rules of worship is to diminish God's glory in an additional way. The very act of conceiving a rite not prescribed by God is sheer impudence and disregard for God's supreme majesty and wisdom. The foundation of this argument, says Calvin, is this: God is the sole lawgiver, and men have no right to usurp this honor from Him.[93]

Calvin broadens his analysis of this problem by urging his readers to consider God's feelings about His own honor. Calvin tries to take the reader away from a dry analysis of the problem and plant him, as it were, in the presence of God, where he may regard how the ruler of the universe feels when His honor is diminished:

---

[89] *De fugiendis*, CR 5.246.
[90] Ibid. Also: *Excuse à Messieurs les Nicodemites*, CR 6.594.
[91] *Inventory of Relics*, CR 6.411 (italics mine).
[92] *Institutes*, II.8.17.
[93] *Institutes*, IV.10.8. Also: CR 8.384.

The reason why God holds images so much in abhorrence is shown clearly by this, that He cannot endure that the worship due to Himself should be stolen from Him and given to them.[94]

Calvin speaks of God as being "disgraced" when men attempt to clothe Him in a corporeal image[95]; or as being "jealous" when men try to usurp His power.[96] But why should God be injured so deeply by man's religious practices? Calvin does not really answer this question, affirming instead that it is not a matter for human speculation. God has commanded that He be worshiped properly, and has also revealed through the prophets that He is hurt by false worship. No more need be considered. Nonetheless, Calvin hints at one reason: God's exalted position in relation to creation is disregarded by the idolater. Those who worship falsely reverse the proper order of the universe, placing the material over the spiritual, the finite over the infinite. In other words, he says, those who have tried to transform the glory of God into any "corruptible form" have served the creature and not the Creator.[97] Calvin sees misdirected worship as a reversal of the metaphysical order of the universe. Idolatry is thus the most sinister parody of man's relationship with God and the boldest affront on the divine majesty.

Calvin's interpretation of the psychology of idolatry

The objective reasons for Calvin's opposition to idolatry are found in God's commands; the subjective reasons within the realm of human behavior. One finds again that Calvin, in trying to explain his opposition to material worship, approaches the issue from an anthropological perspective.[98] We have seen how Calvin interprets the origin of idolatry as a perverted response to the inclinations of the *semen religionis*. An additional element of this perversion is that when men set up any kind of material representation of the divinity, they begin to believe that divine power resides in the idol.

---

[94] *Commentary on Psalms*, CR 32.187.
[95] *Commentary on the Last Four Books of Moses*, CR 24.382.
[96] *Institutes*, II.8.16: "God is provoked to jealousy as often as we substitute our own inventions in place of him. This is like a shameless woman who brings in an adulterer before her husband's very eyes only to vex his mind the more." (Also II.8.18.)
[97] *Petit Traicté*, CR 6.549.
[98] Leon Wencelius had divided Calvin's perspective concerning God's prohibition of idolatry into "objective" and "subjective" components: *L'Esthetique de Calvin* (Paris, 1937), p. 174. Marta Grau has also correctly identified this dual foundation of Calvin's opposition to images, but does not refer to them as "objective" and "subjective." *Calvins Stellung zur Kunst* (Würzburg, 1917), p. 18.

Calvin provides a full explanation of the psychology of idolatry in the 1559 *Institutes*. Borrowing heavily from Augustine, Calvin analyzes in detail how and why men feel that the guiding power of the universe can be sought in an insignificant lump of created matter. Men have never been so foolish, he says, as to believe that the images they create are divinities. The root of their error is not believing that they can create a deity, but rather thinking that they can harness divine power through visual representations.[99] It is this belief in the presence of a *power* in the created object that perpetuates the worship of images and relics in the Catholic church. Calvin denies the value of such belief, and declares that it is because of man's propensity toward superstition that God forbids the use of anything in worship than can invite adoration – even inscriptions in stones. Calvin insists that worship should be as free from materiality as possible, lest the human psyche begin to associate the intended representation with the divine power itself:

For just as soon as a visible form has been fashioned for God, his power is also bound to it. Men are so stupid that they fasten God wherever they fashion him; and hence they cannot but adore. And there is no difference whether they simply worship an idol, or God in the idol. It is always idolatry when divine honors are bestowed upon an idol, under whatever pretext this is done. And because it does not please God to be worshiped superstitiously, whatever is conferred upon the idol is snatched from him.[100]

By establishing that the *motive* as well as the *act* are objectively wrong in image worship, Calvin leaves no room for distinctions concerning different types of worship, such as the Catholics proposed with the concepts of *dulia* and *latria*. Calvin cannot accept image veneration as valid under any circumstances. Nor can he accept any form of material worship where men believe they can control God's power. Although Calvin concentrates on the veneration of images when dealing with the psychology of idolatry, it is clear from what he says elsewhere that the same observations apply to other objects of worship as well.[101]

---

[99] *Institutes*, I.11.9. Ulrich Zwingli had alluded to this search for power in the worship of images, and had concluded that it was the creation of lesser gods that made the image cult so despicable. *De vera et falsa religione, Latin Works*, 3.335.

[100] *Institutes*, I.11.9.

[101] Marta Grau points out that Calvin's opposition to relics is inseparably linked to his iconoclasm (*Calvins Stellung*, p. 11). This does not mean that Calvin was totally hostile toward art, however, as Karl A. Plank has observed. When not joined to worship, art had a rightful place in human affairs: "Of Unity and Distinction: An Exploration of the Theology of John Calvin with Respect to the Christian Stance

It does not matter to Calvin that images are not regarded as gods by Catholics, since no one has ever claimed the images to be the ultimate end of their religion. Calvin states that although the heathens changed images at pleasure, they always kept the same gods in mind.[102] Idolaters never have as many gods as they do images. Catholics, then, cannot excuse themselves by saying that their images are not gods.[103] All image worshipers claim that they are not worshiping the object, but rather a presence dwelling there invisibly. They claim that through the physical image they gaze upon the sign of the thing they ought to worship. The same theory is present in Catholic piety.[104] Such a distinction, though perhaps satisfying to human reason, can never be valid in the eyes of God, according to Calvin:

What then? All idolaters, whether Jews or pagans, were motivated just as has been said. Not content with spiritual understanding, they thought that through the images a surer and closer understanding would be impressed upon them, they never stopped until, deluded by new tricks, they presently supposed that God manifested his power in images.[105]

Calvin concludes with a rather negative assessment of the state of humanity, saying that the "crass errors of the multitude" are "well nigh infinite," and that "they occupy the hearts of almost all men." Humanity, he observes, has always and will always want to worship God in a material way, through wood, stone, and bone; making distinctions that are false and misleading, but that pacify the human conscience and serve to satisfy the base longings of the human heart.[106] Calvin insists that the distinction made by Catholics between *dulia* and *latria* is specious, that these terms cannot in any way

toward Art," *Calvin Theological Journal*, 13: 16–37 (1978). Charles Garside has also analyzed Calvin's attitude toward music: *The Origins of Calvin's Theology of Music: 1536–1543* (Philadelphia, 1979).

[102] *Institutes*, I.11.9. Calvin seems to depend heavily on Zwingli for this part of his analysis. The similarity between Calvin's passages and Zwingli's is too great to be merely coincidental. Calvin, for instance, mentions that "we must not think the heathen so stupid that they did not understand God to be something other than stocks and stones." Zwingli had written in *De vera et falsa religione*: "But contentiousness again objects that not the images are worshiped, but those whose images they are. I answer that neither were any of the heathen so stupid as to worship the images of stone, bronze and wood for what they were in themselves . . . everybody knew they did not in the least worship these things" (*Latin Works*, 3.332).

[103] *Institutes*, I.11.10.

[104] *Commentary on the Last Four Books of Moses*, CR 24.378.

[105] *Institutes*, I.11.9.

[106] *Institutes*, I.11.10.

refer to the existence of separate realities in the act of worship.[107] The individual, he asserts, cannot really distinguish which type of worship he is offering, because, in fact, there is only one kind of reverential act. The distinction might ease some consciences, but it will never really allow anyone to feel and know what kind of worship is being given. Just as an adulterer or a murderer cannot escape guilt by changing the name of his crime, so, too, is it the case with idolaters.[108]

The distinction between *dulia* and *latria* is neither objectively nor subjectively valid for Calvin. Viewed subjectively, from the perspective of the worshiper, it is a specious distinction: The individual can only offer up one kind of reverential act, and cannot distinguish one from another. He may be able to apply the intellectual concept to this prayer, but this will not allow him to identify one kind of worship as different from another. Viewed objectively, from a metaphysical perspective, it is also impossible to make distinctions. Calvin will only admit a univocal interpretation of reverential acts: All worship is the same, regardless of the intentions of the worshiper.

Calvin maintains that the human heart is also led into the error of idolatry through its love of ceremony and ritual.[109] Calvin atacks the excessive and improper use of ceremonies by the Catholic church as a denial of spiritual worship. First, because it is an abrogation of God's commands; secondly, because it often entails the improper use of material paraphernalia; and finally because it is often taken to be some sort of automatic communication between God and man. Humanly devised ceremonies are a bold affront to God's power, honor, and freedom. Through them men attempt to worship God as they please and to bind His power to specific situations. Consequently, Calvin deals with ceremonies as dangerous distractions that only serve to confuse man and rob God of His majesty.[110]

Calvin also carries his analysis of the psychology of idolatry to the social level. "We see," he says, "how by mutual persuasion, men urge one another to defend superstition and the worship of idols." Calvin asserts that the more the truth of God is manifested, the more obstinately man persists in following his own way against God, as if

---

[107] *Institutes*, I.11.11.
[108] Ibid.
[109] A good study of Calvin's view of ceremonies is T. W. Street's *John Calvin on Adiaphora* (Ph.D. dissertation, Union Theological Seminary, New York, 1954), pp. 208–16.
[110] Grau, *Calvins Stellung*, p. 12; Wencelius, *L'Esthetique*, pp. 221–2.

he intends to wage war against Him. Calvin is convinced that the perversion of man is such that, since the beginning of the Reformation, there has been an increase in idolatry, not a decrease.[111] Calvin attributes this rebellion against God to a form of mass hysteria in which idolaters take comfort from each other's encouragements and from the security that comes from belonging to a large group.[112] Calvin also argues that people remain steeped in idolatry out of habit and a false sense of awe resulting from the antiquity of their beliefs. It is very difficult, he indicates, to believe that anything ancient can be wrong. The older the idolatry, therefore, the harder it is to displace from men's hearts.[113]

Sounding a bit like the Luther of the *Table Talk*, though somewhat more restrained, Calvin expands upon this theme by comparing idolaters to latrine cleaners:

> Just as a "maistre Fifi" mocks those who hold their noses [in his presence], because he has handled filth for so long that he can no longer smell his own foulness; so likewise do idolaters make light of those who are offended by a stench they cannot themselves recognize. Hardened by habit, they sit in their own excrement, and yet believe they are surrounded by roses.[114]

Calvin's psychological analysis of idolatry allows him to defend Reformed worship from yet another angle. Whereas Catholics accuse the Reformers of watering down religion and of offering an easier path for men to follow, Calvin argues that the opposite is true. Reformed worship is more difficult to observe, he says, because it is based on God's commands and opposes the materialistic tendencies inherent in man. Spiritual worship does not mean for Calvin a loosening of the reins of discipline. Instead of making life easier for men, it "compels" them to follow a course opposed to their own inclinations. This thought provides Calvin with another argument against Rome. He argues against the Catholics that it is absurd to believe that the Deuteronomic prohibition of images applied only to the ancient Jews, since human nature has remained the same and men can still fall into idolatry just as easily as the Israelites did.[115]

---

[111] *Commentary on Isaiah*, CR 37.37.
[112] Ibid., CR 37.254.
[113] *Sermons on Deuteronomy*, CR 28.711. Zwingli had also made a similar reference to this phenomenon in *De vera et falsa religione* (*Latin Works*, 3.337.)
[114] *Excuse*, CR 6.595. ("Maistre Fifi" is a sixteenth-century French slang term for a latrine or sewer cleaner.)
[115] *Commentary on the Last Four Books of Moses*, CR 24.386.

The argument against miracles

All of this would still remain rather academic and subject to dispute, though, if Calvin were not also to deny the metaphysical reality that the Catholics claimed for their worship. Catholic piety was defended through the example of the numerous miracles, ancient and contemporary, that had been performed through the agency of material objects of worship, especially through relics.[116]

Catholics argued that Protestant worship could be proven false through its lack of miracles. Calvin answers this charge by reinterpreting the role played by miracles in the Christian church, and by denying that there is any real substance to Catholic claims.[117] What they adduce as the strongest, physical evidence of the truth of their worship, says Calvin, is but its subtlest and most heinous deception. Calvin asserts that the only function of miracles is to strengthen the authority of God's messengers, not to alter the fabric of material reality. This is especially evident in the cases of Moses[118] and the apostles of Christ.[119] In regard to the message of the New Testament, miracles must be regarded as "seals of the Gospel," that is, as the signature of God upon the work being carried out by Christ and the apostles.[120] Calvin argues it is wrong for Catholics to demand miracles from the Protestants for this very reason, because they are not forging some new Gospel, but are instead "retaining that very Gospel whose truth all the miracles that Jesus Christ and his disciples ever

---

116 "Prefatory Address to King Francis I of France" (1536), included in the McNeill edition of *Institutes*, p. 16. In the *Commentary on Acts*, Calvin mentions that "the papists do object unto us miracles again and again."

117 For a detailed analysis of Calvin's view of miracles consult: H. Schützeichel, *Die Glaubenstheologie Calvins* (Munich, 1972), pp. 258–65; E. Saxer, *Aberglaube*, pp. 44–5; and Bernard Vogler, "La Réforme et le Miracle," *Revue d'Histoire de la Spiritualité*. 48: 145–9 (1972).

118 *Institutes*, I.8.5–6.

119 *Commentary on Acts*, 5.15, CR 48.104; *Commentary on Matthew*, 10.1; *Commentary on John's Gospel*, 2.11.

120 "Prefatory Address," McNeill (ed.), *Institutes*, p. 16; *Commentary on Matthew*, 10.1. In the *Commentary on John's Gospel*, Calvin says: "Tenendus est enim duplex miraculorum usus, nempe ut vel ad fidem nos praeferant, vel in fide confirment" (CR 47.270). In connection with this point, Calvin adds that miracles do not produce faith in and of themselves, and that in order to benefit from miracles, men must have their hearts purified. Otherwise, how would it have been possible for the Jews to be angered by the resurrection of Lazarus? Even "if heaven and earth were mingled" (the greatest miracle imaginable for Calvin), this would do nothing to change a heart that has no fear of God to begin with. Miracles, then, cause no objective change in those who behold them (CR 47.271).

wrought serve to confirm."[121] This is the principal point of Calvin's response to the Catholic argument, and it is a significant point. He asserts that miracles ceased at the end of the Apostolic Age. But, then, what becomes of the numerous miracles claimed by the Catholic church? Calvin has a ready answer, taken from scripture: They are not really miracles, but humanly devised deceptions that give the impression of being more than they really are.

> We may also fitly remember that Satan has his miracles, which, though they are deceitful tricks rather than true powers, are such a sort as to mislead the simple-minded and untutored [II Thes, 2:9–10] . . . Idolatry has been nourished by wonderful miracles, yet these are not sufficient to sanction the superstition either of magicians or of idolaters.[122]

Calvin, then, will grant miracles neither to God nor to the devil.

Like Bucer before him, Calvin realized that the miracles claimed by the Catholics were one of the mainstays of their piety.[123] "For whence," he asked, "come so many superstitious worshipings of saints, save only from the abuse of miracles?"[124] Since the numerous New Testament examples of miracles performed through the agency of physical objects provided the Catholics with a scriptural argument, Calvin had to develop a different interpretation of the nature and function of miracles. One example often cited by Catholic polemicists was the story of the miracles performed by Peter's shadow as it fell upon the sick (Acts 5:15). Calvin comments on this particular case:

> The papists abuse this text, not only to the end they may commend feigned miracles, which they say are done at the graves of martyrs, but also that they may try to sell us their relics. Why, say they, shall not the grave, or garment, or the touching of the bones of Peter have as much power to heal, as his shadow had?[125]

Calvin refutes the Catholic argument by saying it is wrong to think that Peter's healing power is a universal and everlasting characteristic of sainthood. The gift of miracles in the Church was restricted to a specific time, he says, and its only purpose was to spread the truth of the Gospel among the heathen of antiquity.[126]

---

[121] "Prefatory Address," McNeill (ed.), *Institutes*, p. 16.

[122] Ibid., p. 17. Calvin adds to this argument the testimony of Augustine, who attacked the "miracles" of the Donatists in the same manner (Augustine, *Commentary on John's Gospel*, 13.17).

[123] M. Bucer, *Summary* (1523), DS I, 112.

[124] *Commentary on Acts*, 3.9: CR 48.65; *Sermons on Deuteronomy*, 4.5: CR 28.208.

[125] *Commentary on Acts*, CR 48.104.

[126] Ibid., CR 48.104.

The same issue surfaces again in connection with the story of the healing power of pieces of clothing touched by St. Paul (Acts 12:2). These miracles, says Calvin, are temporary testimonies of the power of God, not a permanent condition of Christian religion. Calvin argues that Paul was given this power so that his doctrine would have greater authority, and that he was the minister of this power, not its source. All miracles are performed to increase knowledge of the glory of God, he continues, not to further the glory of the saint performing them or, even less, of the articles through which the miracles are performed.[127] The miracles claimed by Rome for its relics are utterly false, he concludes, because they accomplish the opposite effect: They lead men away from the true worship of God.[128]

Calvin thus applies his transcendentalist hermeneutic to the miracle stories of the New Testament, and therefore skirts having to consider the possibility of miracles being wrought through the agency of material objects. He does not deny that God chose such means to reveal His truth to the Jews and to propagate the Gospel, but he argues that the time has passed when such things would occur.[129] In reference to the miraculous effects obtained by the apostles through chrism and unction, for instance, Calvin advised that it was no longer possible to expect these material objects to be of any use. Now that the gift of miracles had ceased, he said, the figure ought no longer to be employed, and such things should be banished from the Church.[130] The historical argument for the usefulness of miracles, therefore, removes from Calvin the responsibility of having to admit that miracles can be performed through objects that may lead to idolatry. Calvin bypasses the potentially troublesome subject of a scriptural warrant for the existence of miraculous cures, and instead ridicules the Catholics in a superficially polemical manner:

---

[127] "Prefatory Address," McNeill (ed.), *Institutes*, p. 17.

[128] *Commentary on Acts*, CR 48.104: "Hic enim finis est, ut mundus a Christo abductus ad sanctos transfugiat."

[129] Martin Luther had also at times argued that although physical miracles could not occur in the post-Apostolic age, the Word of God continued to work spiritual miracles. "A Sermon on Keeping the Children in School" (1530), WA 30/2.534ff. Also: Vogler, "La Réforme et le Miracle," pp. 146–7; Berger, *Calvins Geschichtsauffassung*, pp. 108–10.

[130] *Institutes*, IV.29.4–13; IV.19.18–21. Although Calvin and the other Reformers abandoned the use of chrism as a method of healing, they never abandoned hope in the power of God to cure illness as He wished. Vogler maintains that through this interpretation of the miraculous, the Reformation separated medicine and religion. He feels this is distinctly "modern" and in keeping with the spirit of the Renaissance ("La Réforme et le Miracle," pp. 148–9).

For which cause the Papists are more absurd, who wrest this place unto their relics; as if Paul sent his handkerchiefs that men might worship and kiss them in their honor; as in Papistry they worship Francis' shoes and mantle, Rose's girdle, St. Margaret's comb and such like trifles.[131]

Calvin points to the will of God as the source of miracles. Nothing, after all, is impossible for the Almighty,[132] but He restricts their employment to dramatic revelational events. The momentous changes brought about in man's knowledge of God through the work of Moses, Jesus, and the apostles completely overshadow the relatively small service rendered by the miracles that accompanied the revelation. At the heart of Calvin's argument against the miracles of the Catholic church may be seen his deep distrust of the religious value that men come to place on material objects. He has to accept the possibility of having miracles occur through material mediation, but he does so reluctantly, removing this possibility to remote and specific instances, and keeping them as divinely chosen instruments that aid the revelation of the spiritual reality of God.

Calvin's denial of miracles in the material sphere is the capstone of his metaphysical assumptions. Uneasy with any intermingling of spiritual and material, he takes the miraculous out of the ordinary and moves it into the realm of revelation. Only when God decides to break into this world to communicate with humans does He appoint specific instances where the natural, material order is changed. Aside from such extraordinary events, which God intends as proof of His revelation, and not as ends in themselves, there is no intrusion of the divine, spiritual sphere into the material. This world operates on its own divinely appointed principles. Religion, then, does not seek to change the way the material world operates, but rather to understand it as it is: eternally subject to God's will and as always incapable of transmitting any spiritual power in and of itself. To believe otherwise, says Calvin, is to transfer God's glory to His creation, and this is the trap of idolatry.

131 *Commentary on Acts*, 19.11–12. CR 48.445.
132 For a discussion of Calvin's use of the nominalist concepts of the "potentia Dei absoluta" and "potentia Dei ordinata," see F. Wendel, *Calvin*, p. 127ff. The same issue is also analyzed by Karl Reuter, *Das Gründverstandnis der Theologie Calvins, unter Hinbeziehung Ihrer Geschichtlichen Abhängigkeiten* (Neukirchen/Vluyn, 1963), pp. 143–52; and K. McDonnell, *Calvin*, pp. 8–12. For a general discussion of the concept of God's authority in Calvin's theology consult Bohatec, *Budé und Calvin*, pp. 325–45.

POLLUTION AND PUNISHMENT:
THE DANGERS OF MISDIRECTED WORSHIP

Because Calvin sees human nature as inherently prone to idolatry, he constantly warns that it is dangerous to accept even the most insignificant form of material worship in the Church, for "men's folly" cannot restrain itself from falling headlong into superstitious rites.[133] The acceptance of materiality in worship presents a threat to the purity of religion, and Calvin cautions so much against idolatry because he considers it a contagious and fertile evil: "Idolatry is certainly so very fertile, that of one feigned god there should quickly be begotten a hundred; that a thousand superstitions should bubble up from one."[134] Calvin believes that idolatry progresses gradually, but warns that once the process of idolatry has begun there can be no turning back. He attributes this to the great speed with which the seed of false belief takes root in men's hearts: "Experience teaches us how fertile is the field of falsehood in the human mind, and that the smallest of grains, when sown there, will grow to yield an immense harvest."[135]

The amazing speed with which idolatry propagates is due to the fertility of the soil in which its seed is planted. It is also due, as has been seen, to the punishment inflicted by God on man. The more men persist in worshiping God in their own way, the more He abandons them to their own desires, and the greater the number of false ceremonies becomes. Relating this concept to the situation in his own day, Calvin remarks that those who attend Catholic ceremonies, even without intent to worship, are forced by God to attend more ceremonies.[136] Idolatry, then, is also its own punishment.

Taking these factors into consideration, Calvin warns that it is necessary to keep the seed from ever coming into contact with the soil; in other words, that every effort must be made to ensure that worship remains "spiritual." The image of idolatry as fertile is accompanied by that of idolatry as highly inflammable. Calvin cautions that when men begin to accept objects such as images into worship, they are playing with fire:

So innate in us is superstition, that the least occasion will infect us with contagion. Dry wood will not so easily burn when coals are put under it, as

133 *Institutes*, I.11.3.
134 *Commentary on Acts*, 7.42: CR 48.155.
135 *Letters*, CR 13.85.
136 *Petit Traicté*, CR 6.555.

idolatry will seize and occupy the minds of men, when the opportunity presents itself to them. And who does not see that images are sparks? What! sparks do I say? nay, rather torches, which are sufficient to set the whole world on fire.[137]

Keeping in mind the conflagration that can be produced by the smallest distortion of spiritual worship, Calvin maintains that images are inseparable from idolatry and that once an image has been erected within a religious context, men cannot be stopped from worshiping it.[138]

Calvin's argument is that there is no such thing as an "innocent" religious image. Their acceptance alone is an act of idolatry, so that as soon as images appear, religion is corrupted and adulterated.[139] Calvin also asserts that the prohibition against images voiced in the second commandment contains two distinct injunctions. The first prohibits the erection of any graven image, or any such likeness; the second forbids the payment of honor to any of these "phantoms or delusive shows."[140] By divine law, therefore, all believers are prohibited from taking the first step toward idolatry.

The same argument is used by Calvin in regard to relics. One cannot keep these material reminders of someone else's holiness without falling prey to one's baser instincts, that is, without eventually believing that God's power can be harnessed through the relic. Calvin argues that no distinction can be made between the preservation of relics and the worship of relics, because "experience teaches them one is never present without the other,"[141] and that, inasmuch as they "degenerate into idols," the pollution and defilement they bring about ought not to be tolerated by the Church.[142] Relics pervert the Christian faith because they make men cleave to things "vain and perishing."[143] Their presence in the Church is inexcusable, Calvin concludes, for it is most rare for anyone to be devoted

---

[137] *Commentary on I John*, CR 55.376.
[138] *De fugiendis*, CR 5.253–4. Zwingli had warned against this danger in *De vera et falsa religione:* "Since sure danger of a decrease in faith threatens wherever images stand in the churches, and imminent risk of their adoration and worship, they ought to be abolished in the churches and wherever risk of their worship threatens" (*Latin Works*, 3.336).
[139] *Institutes*, II.8.17.
[140] *Commentary on the Last Four Books of Moses*, CR 24.377: "spectra illa, vel fallaces pompas."
[141] *Inventory of Relics*, CR 6.410.
[142] Ibid., CR 6.450.
[143] Ibid., CR 6.411.

to relics without also being polluted by some degree of superstition.[144]

But the greatest danger involved in false worship is the punishment it can bring from God.[145] The ultimate result of all misdirected worship is to bring additional calamities upon the human race: unreasonableness, famine, pestilence, and war. This, Calvin insists, is another reason why idolatry needs to be removed from every town and nation. Even though Calvin regarded all idols as false and powerless in any real, divine sense, he still believed that they were an objective danger, a source of pollution for body and soul.[146] Calvin does not say that all idolatrous paraphernalia are dangerous in themselves, as if they objectively exude a contagious pollution to all who come in contact with them. There is no more pollution involved in looking at a statue, he says, then there is in looking at a stone. Yet, he adds, one must be cautious. Danger increases when the faithful are surrounded by idolatry on all sides and are continually incited to participate in false worship.[147] The best policy to follow concerning idols, says Calvin, is to keep away from them:

He alone keeps himself free, who does not even allow himself any faked imitation of idolaters, but is abstinent to such an extent that he contracts no guilt or stain either by look, access, or nearness; approving his constancy to the Lord all the more, because while surrounded by hostile forces, he does not allow himself to be conquered.[148]

A final consideration Calvin takes into account is that all impure worship not only displeases God, but goes to Satan as well. Those who become embroiled in idolatry, he points out, are handing themselves over to the devil, because the ultimate result of false worship is abandonment by God:

As long as we keep this rule (that one conform to the pure doctrine of God), we know that God will approve the worship that is rendered by us; but if we

---

144 Ibid., CR 6.410.
145 The threats made by God to sinners and idolaters are described by Calvin in the *Institutes*, II.18–21. Also: *De necessitate*, CR 6.502: "Scimus quam execrabilis Deo sit idolatria: et quam horrendis poenis eam ultus sit tum in populo israelitico, tum in aliis gentibus, passim narrant historiae."
146 *De fugiendis*, CR 5.250.
147 Even when one's life is threatened by idolaters, says Calvin, one must never give in or manifest the slightest indication of outward consent to any form of material worship. This would be Calvin's main argument against the Nicodemites (which shall be treated in the next chapter). *Response à un Holandois*, CR 9.604.
148 *De fugiendis*, CR 5.265.

add any of our fantasies or borrow anything from men, everything will be perverted and corrupted. And then the devil will be placed in charge of everything we do.[149]

The practical implications of Calvin's warnings about the dangers of idolatry are significant. Since idolatry is a fertile danger, the true Christian must maintain a strict separation from all kinds of misdirected worship. Catholic piety, therefore, must be avoided as a contagious plague. There is a vast gulf separating the Protestants, who worship spiritually, and the Catholics, who worship wrongly – a gulf that can never be bridged without endangering the purity of spiritual religion. As shall be seen in the next chapter, this attitude deeply affected the course of Protestantism in France from the 1540s onward, through the Wars of Religion.

CALVIN'S CHALLENGE

In many ways, it is fitting that Calvin's most popular published work against idolatry was not one of his many theological tracts, but rather the *Inventory of Relics* (1543), a sarcastic exposé of the "falsehood" of Roman Catholic piety written in an Erasmian vein.

The *Inventory* is primarily what the title implies: a catalogue of various relics held and venerated throughout Europe. In this work, Calvin lists numerous items, one after the other in quick succession, always pointing out how absurd they are; trying to show his readers that their falsehood can be easily proven through the use of reason. It is this last point that Calvin wants to stress: The worship of relics is "against reason,"[150] "some foolish desire that has no foundation in reason,"[151] "too absurd even to amuse children,"[152] or even "madness" (folie).[153] In fact, he says that the purpose of the *Inventory* is not really to show *why* the cult of relics is wrong, but rather to point out that it is foolish and fraudulent. Calvin says he hopes to reveal the "blindness" of idolaters through a display of the most obvious deceptions of the Catholic church.[154] If men cannot be convinced of the theological error involved in relic worship, then at least they might be able to see that its actual practice is insulting to human reason.

This remarkable exposé, one of the few places in all of his work

---

[149] *Sermons on Deuteronomy*, CR 28.715; *Petit Traicté*, CR 6.548.
[150] *Inventory*, CR 6.451.
[151] Ibid., CR 6.411.
[152] Ibid., CR 6.442.
[153] Ibid., CR 6.416.
[154] Ibid., CR 6.449.

where Calvin allows some humor to surface, is a good lens through which to peer into the inner texture of Calvin's theology of idolatry. In the first place, it is significant that the piece is so obviously a part of the Erasmian heritage to which Calvin and the Reformed tradition were indebted. The *Inventory* reveals the ideological roots of the war on idolatry very clearly. At times, in fact, Calvin even borrows freely from Erasmus, almost word for word, as in this joke about the relic of the true cross: "In brief, if all the pieces which could be found were collected into a heap, they would form a good ship-load, though the gospel testifies that a single man was able to carry it."[155]

The *Inventory*, which went through numerous editions and translations,[156] is not only a fitting homage to Erasmus by one of his intellectual grandchildren (even if the humanist would have objected to its "vehemence"), but also a convincing testimony to the enduring power of the Erasmian critique and its influence on the Reformed. No matter how much the conclusions reached by Erasmus and Calvin may have differed, their approach to piety remained similar, as did their style, and more importantly, their intention. Erasmus had wanted to turn piety from the outer to the inner, from the visible to the invisible. He also reveled in poking fun at what seemed irrational, nonsensical, or grossly stupid. Seven years after Erasmus's death, Calvin was trying to do the same thing, only with a more urgent sense of purpose.

This brings us to another point: Unlike Erasmus, who seems to have delighted in the mere act of ridiculing folly or absurdity, Calvin joked in a most serious manner. The comic face of the *Inventory* is not graced with an ironic smirk, but rather with the frozen smile of victory, of triumph over an opponent. Calvin's *Inventory* is a good complement to the first few chapters of the 1559 *Institutes*. If one keeps in mind what Calvin says about *cognitio* in his later work, then it is easy to see that the *Inventory* is a manifesto of the very same human powers that are fulfilled by this knowledge. True *cognitio* of God and self does not allow for nonsense.

The unreasonableness of relics, and of all misdirected worship as well, plays an important role in Calvin's polemic against Catholicism. By arguing that idolatry is not only wrong but wrongheaded, Calvin can compare idolaters to unreasoning beasts. Those who do not direct

---

[155] Ibid., CR 6.420. Also: Erasmus, "Pilgrimage," *Ten Colloquies*, p. 68.
[156] Between 1543 and 1622, the *Inventory of Relics* appeared in at least twenty different editions, including seven French, one Latin, six German, two English and four Dutch. CR 59.461–96. "Catalogis operum Calvini chronologicus."

every thought and action to the goal of worshiping God as He commands degenerate from the law of their creation, which is to come to know and worship God correctly. Calvin even argues that men become more miserable than beasts when they fail to worship properly.[157] He warns his readers to take stock of their position as rational beings and not let themselves be deprived of their humanity:

Let everyone, then, be on his guard, and not allow himself to be led along like an irrational animal, and as if he were incapable of discerning any way or path by which he might be guided safely.[158]

In other words, Calvin is here arguing about reality and the way it is to be perceived, just as he does in the *Institutes*. The purpose of human existence is to know God and worship Him correctly. In doing this, one also knows oneself and is fulfilled. There is but *one* reality to perceive: God's reality. Yet, this involves knowing that there is a fundamental division between material and spiritual and that one cannot approach the spiritual through the material.

Which means, of course, that once one knows that the divine – human relationship can only be transacted in spiritual terms, the material world assumes its proper place. It, too, is definitely real, but only in a contingent, finite way. But the important thing is this: It operates according to its own laws, as determined and directly controlled by God. It functions as it is supposed to function, as created, as material, as finite. (Two centuries later, the material world in its operations, stripped of God's direct guidance, would be referred to as a "machine.") Material reality cannot be usurped by spiritual reality: In fact, it is incapable of being altered by its superior. *Finitum non est capax infiniti.* Miracles can occur only because God, at rare moments, in His infinite power, decides to use them as proof of His revelation. But they are not the order of the day: They have not occurred since the time of the apostles, and would not occur again. Even then, when they did take place, they never went against human perception or reason, but depended primarily on faith.[159]

Calvin says over and over in the *Inventory* that what one sees, or observes as real, *is* real in this material sphere. If something is contrary to experience, or reason, then it must be considered false. This is why he lashed out with such comic fury against "pious frauds," using a keen empirical eye to unmask inconsistencies, and sharp measured descriptions to demolish absurd claims. What fish ever

---

[157] *Institutes*, I.3.3.
[158] *Inventory of Relics*, CR 6.452.
[159] *Commentary on John's Gospel*, CR 47.271.

lasted over 1,500 years?, he asks. How, then, is it possible that the fish distributed by Jesus can still be around? This is not the way the world works. What object ever multiplied itself endlessly? How then is it that there are so many duplicated relics? Has any ancient object ever taken on the appearance of something new? How, then, is it that St. Peter's robes look just like those of contemporary clerics? Or that the wine jars from Cana are all in different styles, shapes, and sizes? Or that so many of Jesus' household items are strikingly contemporary in appearance?[160] The point Calvin wants to make is that if anyone claims that these objects are *real* (as the Catholic church did in many cases), then it naturally follows, by reason and common sense, that the one making such claims should not be heeded.

This is the application of the new Renaissance metaphysics as adopted in the Reformed tradition. Although Calvin's argument in the *Inventory* is based on a theological and scriptural foundation, the hermeneutic is formed by metaphysical considerations about the fabric of reality. The intended audience of the treatise is a new phenomenon too. The *Inventory* aims to convince the educated, those who take pride in their thinking abilities, the cultured, urbane men and women of the Renaissance. Though theological from top to bottom, Calvin's attack on idolatry as something "unreasonable" is a product of the humanist tradition, and it indicates that the Reformation succeeded in part because of its affinity with certain aspects of the intellectual climate of the sixteenth century.

The metaphysical assumptions of this most Erasmian of Calvin's works force us to consider how Calvin finally shapes the Reformed notion of transcendence. As far as the fundamental principles are concerned, he adds nothing new. He is very faithful in maintaining a tradition, defending the principles of *finitum non est capax infiniti* and *soli Deo gloria*. His contribution lies principally in the clarification, expansion and application of these principles.

Calvin makes three crucial contributions to the Reformed theology of transcendence. First, he refines a point that Zwingli, Bullinger, and others had not fully developed. Calvin, like his predecessors, places the blame for idolatry in human beings, not in the material world.[161] This anthropological perspective is more than a matter of emphasis. Calvin makes it central to this theology, turning it into an essential component of his doctrine of the Fall. Whereas Zwingli had concen-

---

160 *Inventory of Relics*, CR 6.415–17. In another place, Calvin remarks on the incompatibility of faith and absurdity: "Ie m'en rapporte aux plus povres idiotz qu'on pourra trouver, si on dont adiouster foy à des choses tant absurdes" (CR 6.445).
161 *Institutes*, I.5.12.

trated more on the psychology of idolatry, Calvin now focused, theologically, on the human condition itself.[162] The problem on which Calvin focuses is the endemic corruption of human nature and the fact that the material world itself is not evil. Men are evil. Religion is a human phenomenon, a human response to the reality of God, but since men are corrupt, religion, too, shares in this corruption. Because they try to reverse the order of creation by attempting to bring God down to their level, men are inherently idolatrous. By stressing this point as a universal rule, Calvin makes idolatry an ever-present danger, a contagious disease of sorts, and he closes the door on compromise with any kind of religion that is not by his definition "spiritual." In juxtaposing the objective reality of God with the infinite number of subjective opinions that fallen humans create about Him, Calvin makes it a doctrine that men are metaphysically deranged, naturally inclined to reverse the order of things. Idolatry, then, is a permanent condition of the human race, something against which humans must always struggle.

In connection with this anthropological and metaphysical focus, Calvin makes a second and perhaps greater contribution toward the development of a theology of idolatry. Calvin defines the place of worship as none of his predecessors had done before. Though they had struggled against idolatry, their theology was somewhat fundamentalistic and more inclined towards action than systematic exposition. Calvin clears whatever doubt anyone could have had about the theological foundations of the Reformed struggle for "pure worship." Calvin states plainly that the war against idolatry is not merely blind obedience to scripture, but also something reasonable. Worship, he says, is *the* central concern of Christians. It is not some peripheral matter, but "the whole substance"[163] of the Christian faith. It is the reason for human existence, the fundamental principle that alone can bring true *cognitio* to human beings, and therefore true fulfillment, since the proper end of human existence is knowledge of God and of ourselves. By making worship a necessary existential component of knowledge, Calvin turns it into the nexus between thought and action, between theology and its practical application. It is a very practical sort of theology that Calvin develops as a result of this. Religion is not merely a set of doctrines, but rather a way of worshiping, and a way of living. "True piety begets true confession."[164] This is enor-

---

[162] Charles Garside, *Zwingli and the Arts* (New Haven, 1966), pp. 161–6.
[163] *De necessitate*, CR 6.459.
[164] *De fugiendis*, CR 5.244.

mously significant. One may even argue that it becomes the fundamental defining characteristic of Calvinism.

The Reformation for which Calvin struggled was not so much one of doctrine, but rather one of piety, which involved profound social and cultural changes. To be properly "Reformed," a community would not only have to change its theology, but also its outward expression of faith, not to mention its attitude toward the material world. Though this was already part of the Reformed tradition long before Calvin entered into the fight, it is Calvin, more than anyone else, who turned this into an explicit guiding principle and devoted his energies to making it understood. This, too, would have serious consequences when it came to considering any compromise on religion.

Calvin's third contribution is closely related to his second, and this is his analysis of reverential acts. In connection with his theology of worship, Calvin develops a univocal interpretation of reverential acts that, on the one hand, is an affirmation of his metaphysical assumptions, and on the other, is a practical application of these principles. By carefully defining what goes on in worship, how human actions relate to the spiritual reality of God, regardless of man's intentions, as some sort of spiritual commerce, Calvin finally drives the Reformed attitude toward worship to its logical conclusion in a clear, forceful manner. It is this point, because of its practical nature, that will allow Calvin to wage a new kind of war against idolatry. Unlike his predecessors, Calvin faced the task of teaching Protestants who did not have the power to overcome the "idolatrous" societies in which they lived. Instead of fighting against the idols by knocking them down, Calvin looked for a more effective way of undermining the system that supported their existence. It was to prove a long, hard battle, but without this understanding of reverential acts, or of the place of worship in human life, or of the dangers of idolatry, it is doubtful that the war against the idols could have become as serious a challenge to Catholicism as it eventually became wherever Calvin and his ideas were taken seriously.

CHAPTER 7

Calvin against the
Nicodemites

In the heart of winter 1545, as Protestants in France grew increasingly restless with Calvin's refusal to compromise on the issue of worship, the Genevan reformer wrote a letter to the ailing Martin Luther.[1] It was the first time that Calvin, not yet firmly established in his position as leader of the Reformed cause, attempted to cross the personal chasm that separated him from the great, and by now almost mythic Luther. After this one attempt, Calvin would never write him again.

What prompted Calvin to take this step was the issue of idolatry, more specifically, the occurrence of dissembling behavior among Protestants, or as Calvin himself called it, Nicodemism. Calvin asked Luther to voice his opinion on this problem, to lend support to his own position, and thus help convince wavering Protestants that there could be no compromise of any kind with Catholic worship. It was a risky move on Calvin's part, but unavoidable. He knew that Luther harbored little sympathy for the Reformed. Luther had only recently written his *Short Confession Concerning the Lord's Supper*, where, as Calvin himself said to Bullinger, Luther had "erupted into savage invective, not just against you, but also all of us."[2] Calvin knew that a few terse, negative words from Luther could do great damage to his reputation among the French, who seemed eager to find a more conciliatory leader.[3] But Calvin had no choice. Hoping, perhaps, to get to Luther before the Nicodemites, he agreed to act as a go-between.[4]

To lessen the risk of another "savage" blast from Luther, Calvin first approached Melanchton, whom he considered a friend. He addressed a cover letter to him, and asked that he pass the other epistle to Luther, along with two books on the subject of compromise that

[1] CR 12.7.
[2] CR 11.774.
[3] CR 12.10.
[4] CR 12.9.

Calvin had translated into Latin just so Luther could read them. Calvin also requested that Melanchton use his own good judgment and "dexterity," and not do anything that he might deem "rash" or likely to produce "unhappy" results.[5]

For all its warmth and goodwill, Calvin's letter went unread by Luther. Though Calvin addressed him as "my most respected father," and closed by saying that he wished he could fly to him, to spend a few hours talking about this and other matters, Melanchton thought it best not even to let Luther know about the letter or the treatises, much less read them. Apparently, Luther was in no mood to consider requests from the Reformed, especially regarding the subject of worship. As he had done on so many other occasions, with other correspondents, Melanchton covered politely for his superior: "I have not shown your letter to Pericles [Luther]. For, truly, he interprets many things suspiciously, and does not want his replies to the kinds of questions which you proposed to him to be circulated."[6]

Once again, an instance of human contact between two different traditions had ended in a disappointment; though this was not as disastrous as Luther's meeting with Karlstadt upon his return from the Wartburg, or Farel's meeting with Erasmus, or even Calvin's visit to Lefèvre. Melanchton wrote the statement that Calvin needed from the Lutherans, agreeing with his position, and the Nicodemites suffered a worse disappointment than Calvin. That Calvin would risk such trouble, though, or seek another opinion to solidify his own position among the French, points to the gravity of the issue. Nicodemism was a very serious matter for Calvin. It not only posed a real threat to his leadership, but also to the Protestant cause. It was an insidious variation of "idolatry," and as such, Calvin gave it his undivided attention. But what exactly was this phenomenon, and how did it come to cause such dissension?

CALVIN'S INVOLVEMENT WITH NICODEMISM

Calvin's concern over idolatry was not directed so much at his flock in Geneva as it was to his followers in France, where the spiritual dangers were particularly intense. French Protestants lived in an environment that was hostile to their beliefs and practices, making the threat of idolatry even greater. They were faced not only with a royally supported Catholicism, but also with the threat of persecution, es-

5 CR 12.10.
6 CR 12.61.

pecially after 1540, when the crown initiated a more aggressive campaign against heresy.[7] In the face of such pressure, some Protestants assumed the attitude of compromise and deceit that came to be known as Nicodemism. Theodore Beza described it as follows:

> At this time also there were some persons in France, who, having fallen away at first from fear of persecution, had afterwards begun to be satisfied with their conduct as to deny that there was any sin in giving bodily attendance on Popish rites, provided their minds were devoted to true religion. This most pernicious error, which had been condemned of old by the Fathers, Calvin refuted with the greatest clearness . . . The consequence was that from that time, the name of Nicodemite was applied to those who pretended to find a sanction for their misconduct in the example of that most holy man Nicodemus.[8]

Although this phenomenon was not exclusively French, Calvin's involvement with the problem was largely limited to France.[9]

Calvin was not the first Protestant theologian to face the question of participation in Catholic rites. Ulrich Zwingli had treated the problem briefly in his *Commentary on the Four Gospels* (1528). Zwingli was opposed to any participation in Catholic ceremonies, as was his successor Heinrich Bullinger. In his *Commentary on the Acts of the Apostles* (1533), Bullinger openly attacked the notion that one could participate in Catholic ceremonies out of charity for the "weaker brethren."[10] The same opinion was repeated again by Bullinger in his *Commentary on I Corinthians*, where he called for a strict separation from idolatry

---

[7] Auguste Bailly, *La Réforme en France jusqu'à l'Edit de Nantes* (Paris, 1960), p. 162ff. Also: G. Rothrock, *The Huguenots, Biography of a Minority* (Chicago, 1979), pp. 1–64; and N. M. Sutherland, *the Huguenot Struggle for Recognition* (New Haven, 1980), pp. 10–39.

[8] Theodore Beza, *Vita Calvini*, CR 21.138. English trans.: *John Calvin, Tracts and Treatises* (3 vols., Edinburgh, 1851; Grand Rapids, 1958), vol. I, p. lxxxvii.

[9] Nicodemism developed in Germany as well, especially after the Augsburg and Leipzig Interims of 1548 made it difficult for some Protestants to worship as they pleased. Wolfgang Musculus attacked the German Nicodemites in a satyrical dialogue entitled *Proscaerus*, published in Latin in 1549. This dialogue appeared in French the following year under the title *Le Temporiseur*. An English version entitled *The Temporisour* appeared in 1555, indicating that the phenomenon of religious deceit also troubled English Protestants under the reign of Queen Mary. That same year, a translation of a section from Vermigli's *Commentary on Judges* was published in Strassburg under the title *A Treatise of the Cohabitacyon of the Faithful with the Unfaithful*. This work also criticized simulation and compromise. Marvin W. Anderson, *Peter Martyr, A Reformer in Exile* (Nieukoop, 1975), p. 394 and bibliography. In addition to this evidence pointing to the existence of a Nicodemite problem throughout Europe – especially in times of persecution – stand the various German, English, and Italian translations of Calvin's treatises against dissembling behavior.

[10] Heinrich Bullinger, *In Acta Apostolorum Libri VI* (Zurich, 1533), p. 177.

and made an explicit comparison between the idolatry of the gentiles and the Catholic Mass.[11]

Martin Bucer and John Oecolampadius had also dealt with this problem in 1530, when emissaries from the Waldensian church of Piedmont came to them to ask for advice on several doctrinal questions. The two Waldensians, Georges Morel and Pierre Masson, traveled to Berne, Basel, Neuchâtel, and Strassburg, where they respectively consulted Berthold Haller, Oecolampadius, Guillaume Farel, and Martin Bucer, especially concerning the issues of free will, predestination, and clerical ordination. Bucer and Oecolampadius provided them with written opinions concerning the doctrinal questions, but they also added a strong condemnation of the Waldensians for their continued participation in Catholic ceremonies, especially in baptism and the eucharist.[12]

It is extremely difficult to pinpoint when, where, or how Calvin first came into contact with the problem of religious simulation because he says very little about this question. Undoubtedly, Calvin himself was faced with the dangers of idolatry and persecution while still in France, although he chose to flee in order to be able to worship "purely" and in peace.[13] One can only speculate about Calvin's contacts with Nicodemism. He refers to the problem as if he had firsthand knowledge of its occurrence, but he does not detail the extent or nature of his acquaintance with dissemblers. The best description provided by Calvin of his reaction to Nicodemism is found in his letter to Martin Luther. This information, however, is not too specific:

---

[11] *Commentarium H. Bullinger in omnes Apostolicas epistolas* (Zurich, 1540), I Corinthians 8–10. In the commentary on II Corinthians, Bullinger also prohibits contact with religious images: "Nihil ergo negotii est fideli cum simulachris," p. 296. Bullinger also wrote against compromise in his 1539 edition of *De origine erroris circa invocationem et cultum deorum ac simulachrorum.*

[12] On the story of the Waldensian emissaries: Jean Jalla, "Farel et les Vaudois du Piédmont," in *Guillaume Farel* (Neuchâtel, 1930), p. 285; G. Gonnet, "Les relations des Vaudois des Alpes avec les Réformateurs en 1532," *Bibliothèque d'Humanisme et Renaissance,* 23: 34–52 (1961); Eugenie Droz, *Chemins de l'Hérésie* (4 vols., Geneva, 1970), vol. I, pp. 89–91; also: *Ginevra e l'Italia* (Florence, 1959), p. 1–63, "I Rapporti tra i Valdesi Francoitaliani e i Reformatori d'Oltrealpe Prima di Calvino." On Oecolampadius's letter: E. Stahelin (ed.), *Briefe und Akten zum Leben Oekolampads* (Leipzig, 1934), vol. II, p. 787.

[13] In *Das Rätsel um die Bekehrung Calvins* (Neukirchen, 1960), Paul Sprenger asks the question "war Calvin Nikodemit?" Sprenger studies the possibility that Calvin might have dissembled shortly after his conversion, but concludes that it is not likely (p. 33). George H. Williams also considers this possibility, and cites Sprenger, but he leaves the question unanswered. *The Radical Reformation* (London, 1962), p. 602.

When I noticed that though many of our French people had been brought out from the darkness of the Papacy to the soundness of the faith, there were still some who had altered nothing as to their public profession, and that they continued to defile themselves with the sacrilegious worship of the Papists, as if they had never tasted the savour of true doctrine. I was altogether unable to restrain myself from reproving so great indolence in the way I thought it deserved.[14]

One obvious conjecture is that Calvin had known dissemblers during his early days as a Protestant in France, but that he refrained from attacking them at the time. It is not until 1537 that Calvin speaks out against simulation, when, as the author of the popular *Institutes* he could command respect from an audience. Calvin himself admits that he was at first reluctant to speak out, when he was "a mere novice," and that he entered his public career with great trepidation.[15] Another conjecture is that Calvin might have observed deceptive behavior at the court of the Duchess of Ferrara in April 1536.[16] Renée of France, Duchess of Ferrara and daughter of King Louis XII, was still a Catholic at the time of Calvin's visit to her court, but, like her cousin, Marguerite of Navarre, showed an interest in Protestantism, allowing Lutherans to live at her court. Calvin stayed at the palace for about three weeks, and it is quite possible that he observed some of the deceptive behavior of people at court.[17] The sycophant Nicodemite was later singled out by Calvin as one of the more despicable types of dissemblers.[18] A third conjecture is that Calvin received oral reports about Nicodemites from Frenchmen traveling through Geneva. A combination of these three factors, then, probably contributed to Calvin's awareness of Nicodemism.

---

[14] Letter to Martin Luther, 21 January 1545, CR *12.7*.

[15] For Calvin's own description of his timidity see the preface to the *Commentary on Psalms*, CR 31.21–6. An even more revealing statement is found in one of his sermons. Speaking about the horrors of persecution during his youth in France, Calvin confessed to his congregation at Geneva that there had been a time when he had been less than valiant: "Et je puis dire qu'il y a vingt ans et quasi trente, que j'ay esté en ces destresses la, que i'eusse voulu estre quasi mort, pour oster ces angoisses de devant mes yeux; pour moins, i'eusse desiré d'avoir la langue couppée, pour ne dire le mot." Sermon on II Samuel 5.13.17, *Supplementa Calviniana: Sermons Inédits*, E. Mulhaupt, ed. (Neukirchen, 1961 –), vol. I, p. 122.

[16] Eugenie Droz considers this possibility, and presents Calvin's stay at the court of Ferrara as his introduction to Nicodemism, without considering any other possibilities. *Chemins de l'Hérésie*, vol. I, 132–3.

[17] Emile Domergue, *Jean Calvin, les hommes et les choses de son temps* (7 vols., Lausanne, 1899–1927), vol. II, p. 20.

[18] CR 6.598–9, *Excuse à Messieurs les Nicodémites* (1544).

Calvin obviously had detailed information about Nicodemism that no longer exists, or has not yet been discovered. He attacked Nicodemite arguments point by point in some instances, but there are no extant "Nicodemite" treatises that correspond to his writings; nor are there any other documents indicating the sources of Calvin's information. The only anti-Nicodemite treatise of Calvin that refers to a known work is the *Response à un Holandois*, written in 1562 against Dirk Coornhert. Calvin, however, does not name his opponent, and does not even call him a "Nicodemite."[19] It is unfortunate that we do not possess the same information used by Calvin, and that we have no access to more documents that might shed light on the origins and character of Nicodemism, or of Calvin's contact with dissemblers.

On this account I differ radically with the interpretation of Carlo Ginzburg, who has proposed that Nicodemism was a unified and clearly defined European phenomenon in the sixteenth century.[20] Ginzburg argues that Nicodemism was not a fearful and disorganized reaction to persecution, or the result of half-hearted evangelism, but rather a conscious adherence to a definite tradition of spiritualizing principles. He traces this tradition to Otto Brunfels, whose work *Pandectae veteris et novis testamenti* (1527) he considers to be the first Nicodemite document. Ginzburg claims that Brunfels recruited several influential disciples, all of whom helped spread the "message" of Nicodemism: Wolfgang Capito in Strassburg; Bartolomeus Westheimer in Basel; Sebastian Franck, Johannes Brenz, and Clement Ziegler in Germany; Camilo Renato in Italy; and Jacques Lefèvre D'Etaples in France. Ginzburg's thesis, though somewhat seductive, is based largely on circumstancial evidence, and, in the end, fails to convince. Nicodemism appears not to have developed from preconceived theories, nor does it seem to have been unified or consciously organized as a philosophy in the way in which Ginzburg describes it. Calvin himself attacked all dissemblers, and admitted that he was addressing a varied crowd. But no matter what the nature of Nicodemism might have been, one thing is clear: Calvin assessed the problem as urgent, and he attacked it vigorously.

---

[19] Calvin may not have known the identity of the "Dutchman." Coornhert's work was translated into French and sent to Calvin by a church in the Low Countries, so that he could read it and give his opinion on the subject. Calvin mentions this in the *Response*, CR 9.585.

[20] Carlo Ginzburg, *Il Nicodemismo* (Turin, 1970). For my critique of Ginzburg see "Calvin and Nicodemism: a Reappraisal," *Sixteenth Century Journal*, 10.1: 45–69 (1979).

CALVIN'S ANTI-NICODEMITE WRITINGS

The war against simulation was begun by Calvin in two letters written to personal acquaintances during his sojourn in Italy in 1536. Although these were private letters, Calvin soon had them published in 1537 as his concern over simulation increased. The first, addressed to Nicholas Chemin (or DuChemin),[21] was entitled "De fugiendis impiorum illicitis sacris." This is one of Calvin's most forceful attacks on the idolatry of the Catholic Church, and was prompted by Chemin himself, as Calvin points out in the letter:

> You consult me, asking in what manner you may be able, while compelled by the times and circumstances of your situation, to live amidst this abominable sacrilege and Babylonish pollution, and keep yourself pure and unpolluted before the Lord.[22]

Calvin's advice to Chemin was harsh and uncompromising: He was to have no contact with the idolatry of Rome. Chemin, who had recently accepted an appointment to the bishopric of Le Mans, was apparently dissatisfied with Calvin's advice, because this letter marks the end of a long-standing correspondence between the two men.[23]

The letter to Chemin was published together with another letter under the title *Epistolae duae de rebus hoc saeculo cognitu necessariis*. The second letter, entitled "De sacerdotio papale," was addressed to Gerard Roussel and signals a break with the Fabrician reform. Roussel had originally been a member of the humanistic reform circle at Meaux, but had recently accepted the abbacy of Clairac and the bishopric of Oloron.[24] This letter dealt not so much with the problem of simulation as it did with the "evils" inherent in the priesthood, and with the guilt that could be incurred by those who participated in it. It can be considered anti-Nicodemite insofar as it counsels strict separation from Roman Catholic sacramental life, and warns that no true evangelical can serve as a Catholic priest. In the preface to the

---

[21] Calvin and Chemin had been fellow students at Orléans and enjoyed a cordial friendship. According to Beza, the two youths had roomed together while at Orléans. *Histoire Ecclésiastique des Eglises Réformées au Royaume de France*, P. Vesson, ed. (2 vols., Toulouse, 1882), vol. I., p. 6. Chemin wrote a book directed against the humanist lawyer Alciati (*Antapologia*) for which Calvin wrote a preface. Herminjard 2 no. 328.

[22] *De fugiendis*, CR 5.239.

[23] The correspondence between Calvin and Chemin is partially preserved in Herminjard 2 (nos. 328, 338, 365).

[24] For more on Roussel: C. Schmidt, *Gerard Roussel, Prédicateur de la Reine Marguerite de Navarre* (Paris, 1845; republished at Geneva, 1970); M. Mann, *Erasme et les Débuts de la Réforme Française* (Paris, 1934); R. J. Lovy, *Les Origines de la Réforme Française: Meaux 1518–1546* (Paris, 1959).

two letters Calvin identifies himself with the prophet Ezekiel, and cautions the faithful that they must choose between the worship of Baal and the worship of God.[25] This is a theme Calvin would never tire of repeating. Beza provides a short narrative of the circumstances surrounding the publication of the *Epistolae duae:*

In the year 1537, Calvin, seeing many persons in France, though they had a thorough knowledge of the truth, yet consulting their ease, and holding it enough to worship Christ in mind, while they gave outward attendance on Popish rites, published two most elegant letters, one on shunning idolatry, addressed to Nicholas Chemin, whose hospitality and friendship he had enjoyed at Orléans, and who afterwards was appointed to an official situation at Lorraine, and the other on the Popish priesthood, addressed to Gerard Roussel . . . who being presented first to an abbacy, and thereafter to a bishopic, when the Parisian disturbance was forgotten, not only failed to keep the straight course, but even gradually misled his mistress the Queen of Navarre.[26]

The second piece written by Calvin on the subject of compromise and simulation was a letter to the Duchess of Ferrara, written in 1540. In this letter (which was never published as a separate treatise), Calvin deals openly with the problem of simulation, especially in regard to the Mass. The letter was intended to warn the Duchess against the dissembling attitude of her new almoner, François Richardot.[27]

Calvin's third attack on simulation was written in September 1540, but was not published until 1543. This piece is a short letter, and is addressed to those of his "friends" who had sought his counsel concerning participation in Catholic ceremonies.[28] The identity of the friends remains unknown. The letter was published in 1543 as an "accompanying epistle" to his next anti-Nicodemite work, the *Petit Traicté.*[29]

The *Petit Traicté* is very similar to the first of the *Epistola duae* of 1537

---

[25] E. Droz prints the French translation of this preface in full: *Chemins de l'Hérésie,* vol. I, pp. 137–8.

[26] Beza, *Vita Calvini* (CR 21.127), English trans.: *Tracts and Treatises,* vol. I, p. lxix.

[27] Francois Richardot had advised the Duchess to attend the Mass and then to have a secret evangelical Lord's Supper afterward. Calvin cautioned the Duchess against this duplicity: "Car ie nay auiourdhuy si grand guerre a personnes que a ceux qui soubs umbre de levangile caphardent envers les princes, les entretenans tousiours par leurs finesses et cauteles enveloppez en quelque nuee, sans les mener au droict but" (CR 11.326).

[28] Herminjard 7.307–19.

[29] E. Droz claims that this letter was "More precise but less intolerant than the previous texts, possibly due to Bucer's influence" (*Chemins de l'Hérésie,* vol. I, p. 168). Droz exaggerates the irenic influence of Bucer on Calvin: this letter is no less opposed to compromise than any other of Calvin's works.

("De fugiendis") both in content and in style, and has many passages that are merely French translations of the earlier Latin work.[30] Despite the similarities, though, the two treatises are not entirely identical, and must be regarded as separate works.

The fifth and most significant treatise appeared in 1544: *Excuse à Messieurs les Nicodemites, sur la Complaincte qu'Ilz Font de Sa Trop Rigeur.* The exact origin of the epithet "Nicodemite" is difficult to ascertain. Although Calvin ascribes the creation of the name to the dissemblers themselves, there is no evidence available to prove this charge. According to Calvin, the Nicodemites took their name from Nicodemus, one of the leading Pharisees of Jerusalem, who, afraid of being seen with Jesus, visited him secretly at night. Apparently, some of the dissemblers adopted the name as an honorable defense.[31] The example of Nicodemus, being of scriptural origin, was readily available for anyone to use: It could describe those who seemed to lack the courage to display their inner convictions. The epithet "Nicodemisch" appears in the 1529 letter of Johannes Brenz, where it refers to people who are afraid of openly confessing their faith. This, however, is not entirely in character with Calvin's use of the term.[32] Antoine Fromment, the Genevan reformer and chronicler, used "Nycodemistes" to describe clerics who pretended to give up their benefices.[33] He also used the epithet in a more traditional sense when he described some of Geneva's dissembling council members.[34] By 1532, the use of the term was apparently widely accepted, as the Protestants of Payerne wrote to those of Geneva about "Nycodemysans" who had changed

[30] On this point: Droz, *Chemins de l'Hérésie*, vol. I, p. 169; and T. W. Street, *John Calvin on Adiaphora*, Th.D. Thesis (Union Theological Seminary, New York, 1954), p. 248.

[31] *Excuse*, CR 6.608: "Ces gens empruntent le nom de Nicodeme pour en faire un bouclier, comme s'ils estoyent ses imitateurs, je les nommeray ainsi pour ceste heure."

[32] *Anecdota Brentiana*, T. Pressel, ed. (Tübingen, 1868), pp. 31–3. Brenz writes to Chancellor Vogler, who is in service to Margrave George of Ansbach. Vogler had apparently referred to the delegates from Schwäbisch Hall to the Second Diet of Speyer as "Nicodemisch," because they had refused to sign the famous Protestation raised at the Diet. Brenz mentions his own disappointment over this development, and makes mention of Vogler's epithet in the process.

[33] Antoine Fromment, *Les Actes et Gestes Merveilleux de la Cité de Genève* (1544), reissued by J. G. Fick (Geneva, 1854), p. 99: "mais en y a d'aultres qui viennent et sont plus scaiges que nulz aultres; car avant que venir ilz vendent leurs benefices . . . Et aulcunz les resinent à leurs parens, freres, amys, ou nepueux, retenans toutefoys le moytié ou tout le revenu du benefice leurs vies durant: et avant qu'ilz abandonnent ces benefices, ilz usent encore d'une tres grande prudence, c'est qu'ilz font des Nycodemistes, ou des loups avec les loups."

[34] Ibid., p. 73: "Mais Michel Balthesard, et certaines aultres du conseil qui faysoint des Nycodemistes renversent la sentence du Conseil par plusieurs raysons."

their behavior and openly manifested their faith.[35] Erasmus was also occasionally called "amphibious," "two faced," and a "Nicodemus who came to see Jesus only by night."[36] These examples show that the figure of Nicodemus was widely recognized and variously employed in reference to dissembling behavior during the early years of the Reformation.

Calvin himself was never fully satisfied with the name "Nicodemite." He points out that Nicodemus was never really the prototype of the religious dissembler: Although he came to Jesus secretly at first, Nicodemus later professed his acceptance of the Messiah and even asked Pilate for the body of the crucified Jesus (John 19:39). Calvin argues that since the cowardly Nicodemus changed into an honorable and courageous Christian, it is not right to use his name as a defense for timid simulation.[37] (Johannes Brenz had defended the honor of Nicodemus in a similar manner.[38]) Calvin accepts the name "Nicodemite" with reservations in the 1544 edition of his *Excuse à messieurs les Nicodemites*, but subsequent editions display an ever greater hesitancy. The 1549 Latin translation bears the title *Excusatio ad pseudo nicodemos*. The 1569 French edition of Calvin's theological treatises (*Recueil des Opuscules*), published by Beza after Calvin's death, also reflects a certain reservation in accepting the epithet. The title page to the *Excuse* uses the name "Nicodemites," but every subsequent page carries the title "Faux Nicodemites." By 1562, when Calvin wrote against the Dutchman Dirk Coornhert, he had stopped using the name as an automatic label for religious dissemblers.[39] Re-

---

35 Herminjard 2.429: "Et vous prions de rechief, que faictes apparoir le tesmoignage de vostre foy laquelle est desja anuncé par tout le pays de deça, par laquelle plusieurs nycodémysans se declairent et manifestent."

36 Roland Bainton, *Erasmus of Christendom* (New York, 1969), p. 215. Also: Allen VIII, 1889, and V, 1276, n. 9.

37 *Excuse*, CR 6.609: Calvin's own description of Nicodemus is as follows: "Il ne craint point la honte et l'opprobre. Il ne craint point la haine. Il ne craint point le tumulte. Il ne crainte point les persecutions. Voila Nicodemiser: si nous prenons Nicodeme Chrestien, et non pas en son ignorance . . . Voila donc la vraye façon de Nicodemiser. C'est de confermer avec les temps pour s'avancer iournellement a donner gloire à Dieu."

38 Brenz had turned Chancellor Vogler's epithet around to point out that someone truly "Nicodemisch" should be a courageous follower of Christ. Brenz says that Nicodemus' faith and courage were so exemplary that he would gladly take the name of Nicodemus for himself: "Yedoch bin ich erfrewt worden, das Ir dannocht meine herrn lasst Nicodemisch bleiben. Ich nim das wort [Nicodemus] für mich an" (*Anecdota Brentiana*, p. 32).

39 *Response à un Holandois*, CR 9.585ff. The fact that Calvin does not call Coornhert a Nicodemite is probably due to his dissatisfaction with the term he had popularized. This does not mean, however, that he stopped using the name altogether. The

servations notwithstanding, the name "Nicodemite" became widely accepted as a proper epithet for dissemblers and was adopted by historians to describe the phenomenon of religious simulation in the sixteenth century.[40]

Beza describes Calvin's *Excuse* as a well-received condemnation of simulation and as the source of the negative connotations attached to the name "Nicodemite."[41] Calvin lists four different types of Nicodemites in this treatise, and he sharply rebukes each type for playing with the faith as if it were a matter of little importance. The first type comprises those whose primary interest is to obtain lucrative benefices, but still pretend to preach the Gospel. Calvin probably had Nicholas Chemin in mind when he made this accusation.[42] The second type includes those who try to convert ladies of high birth and are favorites at court, but do not really take the Gospel seriously.[43] Gerard Roussel and Francois Richardot are two possible targets, as is Mellin de Saint Gelays.[44] A third type mentioned by Calvin comprises those who try to reduce Christianity to a philosophy, and whose

epithet "Nicodemite" shows up in some of Calvin's later commentaries: *Acts* (1554), CR 48.486; *Psalms* (1556), CR 31.153; *Hosea* (1557), CR 42.290; *Jeremiah* (1563), CR 38.74–5.

[40] The epithet "Nicodemite" shared the limelight with other labels, such as "moyenneur" (Latin: "mediator") and "temporiseur." These were more popular outside France, especially in England, where the term "temporisour" was frequently employed. Droz, *Chemins de l'Hérésie*, vol. I, p. 173.

[41] Beza, *Vita Calvini*, CR 21.138.

[42] *Excuse*, CR 6. Calvin's own description is as follows: "Les premiers sont ceux qui pour entrer en credit, font profession de prescher l'evangile: et en donnent quelque goust au peuple, pour l'amieller . . . leur intention est d'abuser de l'Evangile, et s'en servir a faire un maquerellage, pour leur gaigner quelques benefices, ou remplir leur bourse, comment que ce soit . . . Voila donc la premiere espece de ceux qui se mescontent de moy: assavoir les prescheurs, qui au lieu de s'exposer à la mort pour relever le vray service de Dieu, en abolissant toutes idolatries, veulent faire Iesus Christ leur cuisinier, pour leur bien apprester à disner" (pp. 597–8).

[43] Calvin referred to this group as the "delicate protonotaries": Il y a puis une seconde secte. Ce sont les prothonotaires delicatz, qui sont bien contens d'avoir l'Evangile, et d'en deviser joyeusement et par esbat avec les Dames, moyennant que cela ne les empesche point de vivre à leur plaisir. Ie mettray en un mesme rang les mignons de court, et les Dames que n'ont iamais apprins que d'estre mignardées, et pourtant ne savent que c'est d'ouyr qu'on parle un peu rudement à leur bonne grace" (CR 6.598–9).

[44] Josef Bohatec singles out as a "protonothaire" Mellin de Saint Gelays, the "aumonier" of the future Henry II. *Budé und Calvin* (Graz, 1950), p. 146. For more on Mellin: H. J. Molinier, *Mellin de Saint Gelays: Etude sur Sa Vie et sur Ses Ouvres* [Thesis, Université de Toulouse (Rodez: Carrere, 1910)]. Bohatec does not analyze the problem of Nicodemism, but merely tries to provide some names to correspond with Calvin's attack on the various types of Nicodemites – especially in regard to the humanist community in France. (Bohatec stresses Calvin's break with the humanists.)

minds are awash in Neoplatonism.[45] It is very difficult to pinpoint which individuals Calvin had in mind in regard to this type.[46] The fourth and last type includes the merchants and common people, who are afraid of danger.[47]

Whether Calvin seriously considered these types to be fully descriptive is debatable. He did not differentiate among different types of simulation, since to him all simulation was evil. These descriptions are most likely intended as personal attacks on some of his former friends, such as Roussel and Chemin, since they had continued to observe Catholic rites in spite of Calvin's warnings. The first three types are all influential people: minions at court, protonotaries, and men of letters. They naturally form a relatively small social group. Although it is more likely that the fourth group – the merchants and the common people – formed the bulk of the Protestant community in France, Calvin seems to devote more attention to the first three types. This is due to Calvin's concern for support from the nobles. If the influential and powerful could be won over, then the success of the evangelical cause could be more easily ensured.

The *Petit Traicté* and the *Excuse* were put into further service by Calvin in a second edition in 1545. Included in this reissue were the opinions of several well-known Reformers concerning simulation and compromise. These addenda were intended to lend support to Calvin's position in the face of internal dissension among French Protestants. Some members of the Paris community agreed with Calvin's strong anti-Nicodemism, but others felt he was unduly harsh. To settle the controversy, the opinions of other Reformers, such as Bucer

---

45 "Il y a la troisieme espece, de ceux qui convertissent à demy la Chrestienté en philosophie . . . Davantage il y a une partie d'eux, qui imaginent des idées Platoniques en leurs testes, touchant la façon de servir Dieu, et ainsi excusent la pluspart des folles superstions qui sont en la Paupete, gens de lettres. Non pas que toutes gens de lettres en soyent" (CR 6.600).

46 Calvin himself says that this group includes "almost all the men of letters," therefore making it even more difficult to name individuals. Bohatec points to Etienne Dolet as one possible target; as well as Marguerite de Navarre, since she was the "Minerva of France" and still attached to Catholic ritual. Bohatec points out that the Neoplatonism of Ficino and Pico had won many adherents among the humanists of France, but Rabelais is not included as a member of this third group by Bohatec, nor are Catholic Platonists (*Budé und Calvin*, p. 144). Bohatec argues that Calvin attacked most humanists as irreligious in another treatise (*De scandalis*), and he devotes a large portion of his study to this work. Among the men attacked by Calvin in *De scandalis*, Bohatec includes the following: Pierre Bunel, Aggrippa von Nettesheim, Etienne Dolet, Simon Villanovanus, Rabelais, and Jacques Gruet. *Budé und Calvin*, pp. 149–240.

47 "Il mettray en la quatrieme espece les marchans et le comun peuple: lesquelz se trouvant bien en leur mesnage, se faschent qu'on les viene inquiter" (CR 6.601).

and Melanchton, were sought out. This affair is reported by Beza in his *Histoire Ecclesiastique*:

There also arose at that time [1545] a question among some men of rank in Paris who had a knowledge of the truth. This was occasioned by the fact that John Calvin, knowing how many people deluded themselves there about their infirmities, even to the point of polluting themselves with the manifest abominations of the Roman Church, had burdened them with a certain treatise [the *Excuse*] that was too bitter for their taste. Those there who would later be called Nicodemites maintained that one could attend Mass, providing that one's heart did not consent to it – and who knows what other conditions. The others, in contrast, said that one should serve God purely with body and soul, guarding oneself from all pollution. This disagreement resulted in the sending of an emissary not only to Geneva and Switzerland, but also to Strassburg, and even to Saxony; and all these responses were later published together.[48]

As has already been pointed out, Calvin himself solicited the opinion of Melanchton and Luther, and translated the *Petit Traicté* and the *Excuse* into Latin so they could read them and comment on the problem. The letter to Melanchton contains Calvin's fullest description of his involvement in the Nicodemite controversy, and provides a revealing glimpse of Calvin's own interpretation of the problem:

I had published a little book in French, in which I reproved the dissimulation of those people who had been given the light of the Gospel, but still failed to abstain from any of the popish rites which they knew to be accursed and full of sacrilege [*Petit Traicté*, 1543] . . . When I heard that many people complained about my strictness, especially those kinds of people who think that their wisdom increases proportionately to the care they take in protecting their lives, I wrote an apology which made their ears twitch even harder than the first book [the *Excuse*, 1545]. Many people who live by religion instead of philosophy look down on all of this, untroubled. Others who seriously fear God are, at least, beginning to feel displeased with themselves. But since they still consider the matter confusing, they continue to doubt, and want to see it confirmed by your authority and that of Doctor Luther. And I fear, in truth, that they only consult you because they hope you will be kinder to them.[49]

The letter to Luther is even more detailed in some respects. Here, Calvin lists the reasons for which so many French Protestants still

---

[48] Beza, *Histoire Ecclésiastique*, vol. I, p. 28. E. Droz discards Beza's account of the Nicodemite controversy, saying: "N'oublions pas que cette *Histoire*, écrite peu après la mort de Calvin, relève de l'hagiographie" (*Chemins de l'Hérésie*, vol. I, p. 141). Droz argues that the true spirit of the French reform in the 1540's was more conciliatory than Calvin, and that the Paris community was "scandalized" by the *Excuse* (p. 169). This issue will be discussed later.

[49] CR 12.9–10.

refused to accept his uncompromising position. Calvin briefly explains the *Petit Traicté* and the *Excuse*, asks Luther to glance over
them, and goes on to say:

In reading these books, indeed, quite a few of our people, who were previously fast asleep in a false security, have awakened and begun to think
about what they ought to do. But because it is difficult to cast aside all regard
for self and expose their life to danger, or to endure the violence of mankind
and the hatred of the world, or to relinquish all their possesions at home and
enter into voluntary exile, they are restrained by these hardships and kept
back from reaching a decision. They plead as an excuse other reasons as well,
and rather specious ones at that, whereby one can see that they only want to
find some pretext or another. Moreover, since they hesitate somehow in
suspense, they are eager to hear your opinion, which as they rightly revere,
so shall it serve as a great confirmation to them.[50]

As has been mentioned, Melanchton responded to Calvin's request,
but prevented Luther from receiving his letter or from reading the
treatises.

All the opinions obtained in this search for a consensus were collected, translated, and appended to the 1545 edition of the *Petit Traicté*
and the *Excuse* (along with other brief pieces by Calvin: two letters
and a final "Conseil et conclusion," which really said nothing new
about the problem). In 1549 and 1550 the whole collection was published again under one title, and in Latin, as *De vitandis superstitionibus*. Since the "Consensus Tigurinus" had been concluded between Geneva and Zurich (although it had not yet been published),
and there was a new feeling of unity among Swiss Protestants, an
additional opinion from the Zurichers, prefaced by Bullinger, was
included in this edition. The final appendix, thus, came to be an
impressive collection of opinions.[51] The Zurich statement completed
the consensus of all German-speaking evangelical theologians in supporting Calvin against simulation, and it was a major victory for
Calvin in his struggle against compromise.[52]

A few years later, in 1552, Calvin again felt compelled to speak
about simulation, because the problem continued to plague French

[50] CR 12.7–8.
[51] Calvin's position was defended by Martin Bucer, Philip Melanchton, Peter Martyr,
and Heinrich Bullinger.
[52] Beza assessed the episode as a total triumph for Calvin: "Or combien que par icelles
[responses] les Alemans accordassent quelque accord qu'on ne peut servir à deux
maistres, ce qui ferma la bouche pour lors a ceux qui s'estoient voulu couvrir d'un
fac mouillé: et fut cause ce differend d'un tres grand bien, plusieurs s'estans résolus
de se dedier du tout à Dieu, qui s'endormoient au paravant en l'ordure" (*Histoire
Ecclesiastique*, vol. I, p. 28).

Protestants, and because, as he says, he continued to receive requests for advice:

> Even though I have previously written two very adequate treatises showing that it is not lawful for a Christian who knows the pure doctrine of the Gospel, when he lives in Popery, to pretend in any manner that consents or adheres to the abuses, superstitions and idolatry that reign there: there are still people who daily ask for my advice again, as if I had never spoken to them. I also know that there are others who never cease to level their rejoinders and evasions against that which I have written.[53]

The resurgence of the Nicodemite controversy was largely due to an increase in religious repression after the ascension of Henry II to the throne of France (1547–59). Of all the Valois kings, he was the most rigidly anti-Protestant.[54] Since his reign coincided with a marked rise in Protestant activity,[55] the resulting tension made the issue of compromise and simulation even more pressing.

This new publication was a collection of four sermons in French that treated the issue of cohabitation with idolaters. It was entitled *Quatre Sermons de M. Iehan Calvin Traictans des Matières Fort Utiles pour Nostre Temps*. The first sermon was intended to warn the faithful against compromise with the evils of idolatry.[56] It covers much of the same ground covered by the *Petit Traicté* and the *Excuse*, but condenses the material into a shorter version. Calvin maintains that the purpose of this work is to provide instruction and to silence those who try to corrupt the true spiritual religion of God through their vain excuses.[57] The second sermon[58] deals with the problem of persecution, and consists largely of a series of exhortations intended to strengthen the faithful in time of trial. This sermon is full of encouraging words, promises of eternal life, and admonitions to remember the example of the martyrs. It is not a profound treatise, and is intended merely to make persecution seem one of the best opportunities provided for Christians, even though, as Calvin admits, the idea seems repugnant to human reason.[59] The third and fourth sermons are very

---

[53] *Quatre Sermons*, CR 8.374. Beza's opinion notwithstanding, it appears that Calvin did not achieve a thorough victory over Nicodemism in 1545.

[54] A. Bailly, *La Réforme en France*, p. 183 ff.

[55] Ibid., pp. 177–82.

[56] "Sermon auquel tous Chrestiens sont exhortez de fuir l'idolatrie exterieure" (CR 8.377–92).

[57] CR 8.374.

[58] "Le second Sermon, contenant exhortation a souffrir persecution pour suyvre Iesus Christ et son Evangile" (CR 8.393–408).

[59] "C'est une doctrine repugnante au iugement humain, ie le confesse" (CR 8.400).

similar in content. The third[60] explains the benefits of being able to serve God purely, and is an apologia for the necessity of a visible Church and the need to emigrate.[61] The fourth and final sermon[62] expands on the ideas of the third, providing a more detailed explanation of the benefits provided by a community that worships God purely and in peace.[63] In addition to the sermons, Calvin also includes an exegesis of Psalm 87, which is an exposition of the triumph of the Church. It is intended to give hope and courage to those who despair of the present condition of the Church. Although it does not deal directly with the problem of idolatry and compromise, it treats the questions of exile and martyrdom, which are the only alternatives open to those who are forced to commit idolatry.

Calvin's final work against simulation appeared in 1562. This was an attack on the work of Dirk Coornhert, and was entitled *Response à un Certain Holandois, Lequel sous Ombre de Faire les Chrestiens Tout Spirituels, Leur Perment de Polluer Leurs Corps en Toutes Idolatries.*[64] Although Calvin does not apply the epithet "Nicodemite" to his opponent, this treatise is a thorough summation of Calvin's anti-Nicodemite thought. Calvin attacks, point by point, the assertions of a man that had come to the following conclusion:

[60] "Le tiers Sermon, remonstrant combien les fideles doibvent priser d'estre en l'Eglise de Dieu, ou ils ayent liberté de l'adorer purement" (CR 8, 409–24).

[61] "Le troisieme sermon est pour declarer quel thesor c'est d'avoir liberté, non seulement de servir purement a Dieu et faire confession publique de sa foy, mais aussi d'estre en Eglise bien reiglee et policee ou la parolle de Dieu se presche, et ou les sacramens s'administrent comme il appartient . . . Or il m'a semble que cest argument estoit auiourd'huy bien necessaire, pource qu'il y a beaucoup de Chrestiens imaginatifs qui se mocquent de ceulx qui prennent peine de venir en pais estrange et loingtain pour iouir d'une telle liberté" (CR 8.375).

[62] "Le quatrieme Sermon, monstrant combien on doibt prendre de peine pour rechercher la liberté de servir Dieu purement en Eglise Chrestienne" (CR 8.425–40).

[63] "Ainsi la somme de quatriemme sermon est, quand nous avons le privilege d'ouir la parolle de Dieu purement preschee, d'invoquer son nom et user des sacramens, que cela est bien pour recompenser tous les ennuis, troubles et molestes, que Satan pourra susciter contre nous" (CR 8.375).

[64] CR 9.585ff. George H. Williams has identified the previously unknown "holandois" as Dirk Volkerts Coornhert (b. 1522), whose thought resembled that of Sebastian Franck, but who never openly left the Catholic church. Coornhert belatedly answered one of Calvin's anti-Nicodemite treatises (the *Petit Traicté* of 1543) in 1562 with a work entitled *Vershooninghe van de Roomische Afgoderye.* It is this work that prompted Calvin's *Response* the same year. Williams, *Radical Reformation*, p. 774. For more on Coornhert: Hendrik Bonger, *Leven en Werk van D. V. Coornhert* (Amsterdam, 1978); reviewed at length by Willem Nijenhuis in *Nederlands Archief voor Kerkgeschiedenis*, 60: 90–106 (1980). Also: H. Bonger's earlier work, *Dirck Volckertzoon Coornhert: Studie over een Nuchter en Vroom Nederlander* (Lochem, 1941); and B. Becker, "Coornhert, de 16 eeuwsche apostel der volkmaaktheid," *Nederlands Archief voor Kerkgeschiedenis*, 19: 59–84 (1926).

That if no service is agreeable to God, except that which comes from an honest conviction: the opposite holds true, that no simulation can displease him, when one only pretends to adore the idols without having devotion in order to please the unbelievers.[65]

The *Response* is one of the clearest expositions of Calvin's theological opposition to simulation: Here he argues most forcefully against the separation of body and soul in worship, calling, as he had done so often before, for total abstinence from idolatrous worship. Ironically, the very writing of the *Response* shows that Calvin's vigorous struggle against simulation and compromise had not ended, and that his victory over Nicodemism had not been complete.

Along with these major works against compromise and simulation, Calvin also wrote various letters and *consilia* to different individuals throughout his career advising them how to deal with Catholic worship.[66] Other treatises that criticize Catholic worship, such as the *Inventory of Relics* (1543) and *On the Necessity of Reforming the Church* (1543), counsel against compromise with Rome, but they do not specifically attack Nicodemism.[67]

This list of anti-Nicodemite works by Calvin shows that the issue of simulation caught his full attention, and embroiled him in a lifelong struggle against compromise with Catholicism. It was a protracted struggle that apparently remained unresolved up to the time of Calvin's death, yet Calvin's adamant refusal to accept compromise helped establish French Protestantism as a separatist religion, and laid the foundations for a vibrant Huguenot church.

THE EVIDENCE RECONSIDERED

The controversy over the nature of Nicodemism, which Carlo Ginzburg sought to put to rest with his revisionist thesis, cannot be

---

[65] *Response*, CR 9.613.

[66] For the *consilia:* CR 10a.196ff.

[67] Oddly enough, a complete accurate list of Calvin's works against simulation has never been prepared. Some have omitted central works, while others have included treatises that deal with different problems. Albert Autin, *La Crise du Nicodemisme 1535–1545* (Toulon, 1917), omits the *Sermons* of 1552 and the *Response* of 1562, as well as the letter to the Duchess of Ferrara (which is understandable, given the fact that it was never published separately). He includes Calvin's treatise *Contre les Libertines* (1548) as anti-Nicodemitic, failing to distinguish between Libertinism and Nicodemism. Ewald Rieser, *Calvin – Franzose, Genfer oder Fremdling?* (Zurich, 1968), omits the first and last treatises against Nicodemism (the *Epistolae duae* and the *Response*), and instead includes *De scandalis*, which is really a treatise against the irreligiousness of humanists. Eugenie Droz (*Chemins de l'Hérésie*) omits the last two of Calvin's anti-Nicodemite works: the *Sermons* and the *Response*.

fully appreciated without taking into consideration the original evidence provided by Calvin and Beza. First, one must consider that a substantial part of the "problem" of Nicodemism rests with Calvin's terminology. Calvin's use of the epithet "Nicodemite" has led most scholars to assume that there must have been a unified group of dissemblers. This, in turn, has spurred the search for Nicodemite origins. What must be kept in mind, however, is that Calvin was attaching a label to a common attitude, not to a unified group. Calvin's fondness for indiscriminate labeling has to be considered when dealing with any position he attacked under a common name, and Nicodemism is no exception. Seeing that Calvin did not usually shrink from attacking any of his opponents by name, one must wonder why he never revealed the identity of his Nicodemite adversaries. Had there been an organized group with a definite theology, Calvin would have met the challenge by attacking personalities as well as ideas. Calvin himself testifies to the amorphous nature of his classification in the *Excuse*, where he mentions various types of dissemblers, all of whom differ substantially from one another.[68] In fact, Calvin attacked simulation before he applied the name "Nicodemite" to this attitude. Anyone who compromised his faith by simulating adherence to Catholicism was a "Nicodemite" for Calvin. This nomenclature covered a very diverse group of people.

A second point to consider is how Ginzburg's theory compares to the historical facts provided by Calvin and Beza. This evidence, as incomplete and biased as it may be, cannot be lightly dismissed, since it is the only contemporary information available about the problem of religious simulation. Ginzburg argues that the philosophy of Nicodemism preceded its practice, but the original evidence points in a different direction. Beza, for instance, reports that Nicodemism arose at first from "fear of persecution," saying that it was only after dissemblers found their position to be comfortable that they began to defend their behavior with theories.[69] Calvin seems to have sensed that the major obstacle to convincing the Nicodemites of their sin was their fear of persecution, and he referred to Nicodemite behavior as "sloth and negligence."[70]

---

[68] CR 6.597ff., *Excuse*.

[69] Beza, *Vita Calvini*, CR 21.138.

[70] CR 12.9. As early as 1531, Guillaume Farel was saying to Ulrich Zwingli that the French evangelicals preferred the silence of bondage to the open confession of Christ's name. Herminjard 2.356: "Verum deliciae Gallicae ita detinent captivos, ut malint sine fructu perire, et mussitabundi latere sub tyrannis, quam palam Christum profiteri."

It appears, then, that Nicodemism was caused just as much by fear and confusion as it might have been by theoretical considerations. This is another shortcoming of Ginzburg's thesis. He argues for the existence of a unified and aristocratically inclined Nicodemite movement that emphasized exclusive religious knowledge and concentrated on the interior and subjective nature of worship, as well as on the freedom of the Christian. When the reports of Calvin and Beza are examined, however, it appears that among the Nicodemites addressed by Calvin there were many devout evangelicals who were groping for a solution to a serious dilemma. It is more likely that the "typical" Nicodemite was not a cryptospiritualist, but rather a concerned Protestant, and that his motivation was at first largely atheoretical. Calvin insists that some of those whom he addresses have already been brought "out of darkness" to the soundness of the Gospel, and he speaks of them as full members of the Protestant community – except for the fact that they continue to observe Catholic rites out of fear.[71] In the *Histoire Ecclesiastique* Beza speaks of the Nicodemites in the same manner, considering them full members of the Protestant church of Paris.[72] His report of the dispute over simulation in Paris and of the search for answers from the major Reformers indicates that Nicodemism was not some kind of spiritualist movement. Cryptospiritualists would not have felt obliged to obtain permission from anyone else to defend their behavior, much less from those whom they could only expect to condemn their position. What spiritualist ever felt the need to ask for Luther's opinion? The evidence provided by Calvin and Beza thus points to the existence of concerned, practicing evangelicals who wished to feign their Catholic orthodoxy but for whom theory was a secondary consideration.

Ginzburg's claim that Nicodemism was a fully developed *a priori* theory rather than an *a posteriori* reaction fails to prove convincing. This is not to say that dissembling behavior could not have been supported by ideology, or that in some cases theory might have preceded practice. Ginzburg's error lies in overlooking the opposite and most obvious probability. Ideology can support dissembling behavior, but it does not necessarily have to be the source of the deceit or its organizing principle. Simulation generated by fear of persecution needs no theory to support itself initially: It is an automatic defensive response. Theories might be sought for as conditions continue to demand outward conformity from the persecuted, but these arise as *a*

---

[71] CR 12.9.
[72] Theodore Beza, *Histoire Ecclésiastique*, vol. I, p. 28.

posteriori rationalizations. Should this perfectly normal possibility be ignored?

Nicodemism was a far more complex phenomenon than has been assumed by scholars in the recent past: It was international in character, lacked unity, and could not have been the creation of one specific group of individuals.[73] The Nicodemism attacked by Calvin in France was but one manifestation of a European phenomenon in the sixteenth century, and was composed of various types of dissemblers. The Nicodemites attacked by Calvin range from someone like Coornhert, who was indeed a cryptospiritualist and rejected the value of outward worship; to others like the concerned evangelicals at Paris, who sought the advice of Luther and Bucer; and even to those who were not yet fully converted to Protestantism, like Nicholas Chemin. Various influences played a part in the development of Nicodemism, but none, outside of fear of persecution, can be considered as central. The correlation between periods of persecution and Nicodemite activity clearly shows that dissembling behavior becomes a concern only when free worship is denied.[74] Nicodemism appears not to have been developed from preconceived theories, nor does it seem to have been unified or consciously organized as a philosophy. None of the evidence presented to date proves it to be otherwise. Calvin himself attacked all dissemblers, regardless of their motivation, and openly admitted that he was addressing a varied crowd. Nicodemism, then, was an amorphous phenomenon. An attitude rather than a movement, Nicodemism was composed of various types of dissemblers whose intellectual motivation was diverse and far from unified.

---

[73] Albano Biondi has made this point: "E impossibile . . . fare della simulazione religiosamente motivata l'ideologia di un gruppo specifico" ["La Giustificazione della Simulazione nel Cinquecento," *Eresia e Riforma nell'Italia del Cinquecento* (Florence/Chicago: The Newberry Library, 1974), p. 59]. His objection, however, is centered on a very broad interpretation of the problem of simulation in the sixteenth century – one that still looks for specific ideological sources, in the church fathers, Erasmus and Lefèvre.

[74] Religious simulation had been a problem in the early Church, especially in the third century, when persecution increased. The controversy over the "lapsed" greatly disturbed the Church and eventually led to the Donatist schism. The relationship between persecution and simulation is just as clear in the sixteenth century. German "Nicodemism" flourished during the period of the Augsburg and Leipzig Interims. English treatises dealing with dissembling behavior correspond with the era of Marian persecution. Calvin's own treatises against simulation appear as persecution increases in France. The revocation of the Edict of Nantes also caused a resurgence of anti-Nicodemite literature in the seventeenth century. (Jean Graverol published a work entitled *Instructions pour les Nicodemites* in 1687. This was again reissued at Amsterdam in 1700.)

Nevertheless, no matter what the nature of Nicodemism might have been, one fact remains undisputed: Calvin assessed the problem as urgent, and he attacked it with all his might.

THE POLITICAL DIMENSIONS OF CALVIN'S OPPOSITION TO COMPROMISE

Calvin's unrelenting struggle against Nicodemism was not appreciated by all French Protestants. In late 1543, his friend Antoine Fumée, a member of the Paris Parlement, wrote him to say:

> a number of people think your assertions are thoroughly wretched. They accuse you of being merciless and very severe to those who are afflicted; and say that it is easy for you to preach and threaten over there, but that if you were here you would perhaps feel differently.[75]

Theodore Beza also reports that even though Calvin knew his position was "too bitter" for the taste of many,[76] he continued to write treatises that made the Nicodemites' ears "twitch even harder."[77] Why such intransigence on the part of Calvin? And why such vehemence in the face of opposition from French Protestants?

Aside from predestination, few other aspects of Calvin's theology have given rise to as much misunderstanding as his refusal to compromise on worship. While French Protestants considered Calvin "merciless" and his theology misinformed ("if you were here you would perhaps feel differently"), Catholics considered him seditious. Catholic polemicists argued that Calvin's opposition to Nicodemism was not misinformed, but rather too well informed: It was a shrewd political crusade, an attempt to incite revolution.[78] Lutherans, too, leveled the same charge, showing a mixture of fear and embarrassment over this issue.[79] Some in Geneva and France also considered

---

[75] CR 11.646.
[76] Beza, *Histoire Ecclésiastique*, vol. I, p. 28.
[77] CR 12.9.
[78] The English Jesuit William Allen singled out Calvin as the "grand maister" of Protestant sedition in *A True, Sincere, and Modest Defence of English Catholics* (1584). [Facsimile edition in *English Recusant Literature, 1558–1640*, D. M. Rogers, ed. (Menston, England, 1971), vol. LXVIII, pp. 77–84]. M. Audin gives voice to the Catholic charge as follows: "Les deux ouvrages de Calvin, *De vitandis superstitionibus* et *Excusatio ad pseudonicodemitas*, sont moins des ouvres de controverse que de pamphlets politiques" [*Histoire de Calvin* (Paris, 1854), p. 319]. For further examples of Catholic polemics see M. J. Spalding, *The History of the Protestant Reformation* (2 vols., Baltimore, 1870), vol. I, pp. 370–92, esp. p. 467.
[79] As the Lutheran leader Christoph von Würtenberg put it: "Calvinism is seditious in spirit, and wherever it enters it is determined to usurp dominion, even over magistrates." A. Kluckhorn (ed.), *Briefe Friedrichs des Frommen* (Braunschweig, 1868), vol. I, p. 271. Also: Donald Kelley, *The Beginning of Ideology* (Cambridge, 1982), p. 258.

the affair as untheological, but for a different reason, arguing it was part of Calvin's scheme to undermine the political power of native Genevans by attracting French refugees to the city.[80]

The issue that needs to be addressed, then, is that of the relationship between religion and politics in Calvin's opposition to Nicodemism. On one level, we need to examine the charge made against Calvin by some of his contemporaries. Was there some hidden agenda in Calvin's refusal to compromise? Was this really a political ploy carefully disguised in theological language? On another level, going beyond a univocal interpretation of theology and politics that would not allow for theology itself to be political (or politics to be theological), we also need to look at this particular case as an example of the way in which ideology was shaped in the sixteenth century. More specifically, we need to consider the intricate relationship that existed between ideas and events in order to arrive at a fuller understanding of the way in which Calvin formulated his theology, and how that theology, in turn, affected his contemporaries.

In one of his earlier treatises, Calvin mentions that everything that the scriptures have to say about idolatry has been intended for the sake of those living among nations ignorant of God.[81] The same observation may be made about Calvin's writings against idolatry, which were directed to those living in what he viewed as a predominantly godless society.

Calvin considered the struggle against idolatry to be an unending task, and thought that the situation of sixteenth-century evangelicals paralleled that of the ancient Israelites: They were the chosen few, surrounded by peoples immersed in idolatry and superstition. Like their Old Testament forebears, sixteenth-century Reformed Christians had to be prepared to deal with the contagion of idolatry. Even in a Reformed community, Calvin insisted, it was necessary to speak to the faithful about the corruption around them, lest they become complacent. As had been the case with the Israelites, purity of worship was expected to be the primary response to the convenant between God and his people; and for Calvin the true Christian church always had to be reminded of the fact that it had been rescued from idolatry.[82] This means, of course, that Calvin regarded the Church as a sort of real, spiritual nationhood, and that he expected commitment

---

[80] "Troisieme Sermon," CR 8.412. Recently, this argument has again been revived. Droz, *Chemins de l'Hérésie*, vol. I, pp. 169–70.
[81] *De fugiendis*, CR 5.246.
[82] "Sermon auquel tous chrestiens sont exhortez de fuir l'idolatrie extérieure," CR 8.377–8.

to the purity of the covenant to eclipse any allegiances that opposed it, even if these allegiances were demanded by one's earthly nation. This is the conflict presented to sixteenth-century Reformed Protestants by Calvin: Regarding worship, they had to choose between the demands of earthly kingdoms and the responsibilities of the spiritual kingdom of God.

CALVIN'S ANTI-NICODEMITE THEOLOGY

Calvin's opposition to Nicodemism was solidly anchored in theology, particularly on his metaphysical interpretation of the nature of reverential acts and on a strong rejection of the separation of body and spirit in worship. Calvin's own definition of simulation is found in the *Petit Traicté* (1543), where he distinguishes between two types of dissembling behavior; one acceptable, the other deplorable. The acceptable form of deception is called "dissimulation" by Calvin. This merely involves keeping hidden in one's heart what one truly believes: As long as one does not deny these beliefs by word or action, even in trying circumstances, there is no sin involved. The unacceptable type of behavior is "simulation," that is, pretending to believe what one knows is false while keeping one's true faith a secret. Simulation is a hideous sin, says Calvin, because it entails a doubly idolatrous act:

In order to define this question it must be noted that, since we owe God a dual honor: which is comprised of the spiritual service of the heart, and of external adoration: likewise there is a contrary kind of dual idolatry (double espece d'idolatrie). The first is, that which occurs when man, through a false fantasy conceived in his own spirit, corrupts and perverts the spiritual service of the one God. The other occurs when, for any reason whatsoever, man transfers the honor belonging to the one God to any creature, such as an image.[83]

Calvin would never permit the act of worship to be considered subjectively, from the worshiper's point of view. Body and spirit had to participate in offering to God a worship that was spiritual in nature and did not seek grace from material objects.[84]

Nicodemism did not agree with Calvin's interpretation of the nature of worship because it assumed that without inner consent there could be no idolatry. Calvin was struggling against an attitude,

---

[83] CR 6.546.
[84] *Commentary on the Four Last Books of Moses*, CR 24.387.

then, that separated interior belief from outward worship.[85] Ironically, this position is founded on a concept of spiritual worship: God is only pleased by the spiritual worship that he has commanded; therefore, if one offers this to God, but has to go through the motions of any other kind of worship, there can be no harm done to the glory of God. The dissembling Nicodemite asks: If one merely goes through the motions of idolatrous worship with full knowledge of its falsehood, why should God mind?

Calvin's strict interpretation of the transaction of honor involved in worship does not allow him to accept the distinction made in Nicodemism. Feigned idolatry is still false worship as far as Calvin is concerned: "There is a real kind of idolatry when one performs an external act that is contrary to the true service of God, even if it is done only for deception."[86] Those who insist on paying external honor to idolatrous services are harming themselves and denying God his glory, says Calvin, because the physical act of participation in false worship is objectively misdirected and evil, regardless of the intentions of the worshiper.[87] One is not to use one's body incorrectly, he adds, because external acts of reverence are objective signs of spiritual honor, and as such carry with them the full intent of the reverential act. Bodily gestures cannot be separated fom the honor they automatically effect.[88] Calvin will not admit a separation of internal belief and external confession; to him, faith entails an honest outward profession:

---

[85] In a letter to the Duchess of Ferrara (1541), Calvin says, for instance, "Si quelquun objecte qu'il ne peult chaloir des choses exterieures, mes que le coeur soit droict par dedans, a cela nostre Seigneur respond qu'il veult estre glorifie en nostre corps lequel il a rachapté par son sang, qu'il requiert de nous confession de bouche, et que toutes les parties de nous soient consacreé a son honeur, nestant aulcunement contamines ne polules par les choses qui luy sont desplaisans (CR *11*.328). Later, in the *Petit Traicté*, Calvin again alludes to a Nicodemite argument: "C'est donc une excuse frivole, et qui ne faict qu'aggrever le peché, d'alleguer que Dieu se contente de couer. Car nous voyons le contraire; d'alleguer semblablement que l'idolatrie procede de superstition: et pourtant qu'elle ne se peut commetre que le couer n'y soit" (CR *6*.547–8).

[86] "Sermon Contre l'Idolatrie," CR *8*.380.

[87] *Petit Traicté*, CR *6*.570.

[88] *Excuse*, CR *6*.611: "C'est desia un grand crime de commetre idolatrie exterieure, abandonnant son corps, qui est le temple de Dieu, à pollution telle que l'escriture condemne . . . et n'est pas une faute legiere, de transferer l'honneur de Dieu à une idole; ie dy mesme la reverence exterieure, qui est signe et tesmoignage de l'honneur spirituel." In the *Petit Traicté* Calvin also says: "Car encore qu'un homme se mocque de l'idole en soy mesme, en faissant semblant de l'honneur il ne laisse pas d'estre coulpable d'avoir transferé l'honneur de Dieu à la creature" (CR *5*.548).

How, indeed, can this faith, which lies buried in the heart within, do otherwise than break forth in the confession of faith. What kind of religion can that be, which lies submerged under seeming idolatry?[89]

Consequently, Calvin argues against those who strive to divide belief and worship into separate, self-contained realities, saying that it is an affront to God to insist that the only important aspect of religion is one's interior life. Those who reject the significance of external acts of worship are misinterpreting the true nature of "spiritual" religion. Calvin protests that although he has written against the exaggerated importance of external worship, he has always maintained that "confession is an accessory of faith" and that "the two cannot be separated."[90] Calvin argues that although the service of God is primarily located in the heart, one still needs to make a public confession of faith through external actions. To conform to the "idolatry" of Rome (even as a form of deceit) is to deny the spiritual reality that needs to be manifested in the physical sphere through worship. It is a metaphysical inversion that denies that there is any real, concrete connection between the material and the spiritual.[91]

The full implication of Calvin's argument is that, while he draws a sharp dividing line between spiritual and material in worship, he does not admit the separation of the two principles within the person.[92] Human beings are spiritual–material entities: God has created both natures and demands that worship be returned by the whole person.

The Christian man ought to honor God, not only within his heart, and with spiritual affection, but also with external testimony. Now, after the Lord has rescued our body and soul from death: he has secured the one as well as the other, in order to be their master and ruler. Therefore, after both body and soul in man have been consecrated and dedicated to God, it is necessary that his glory shine forth just as much in one as it does in the other.[93]

To deny this, argues Calvin, is to deny God sovereignty over the physical world, and that is the heresy of the Manicheans. Taunting his opponents, Calvin remarks that it would be better if they con-

---

[89] Letter to Martin Luther, CR 12.7.
[90] *Response*, CR 9.610.
[91] CR 9.612: "Ie di que la foy n'est point ensevelie au coeur, mais qu'elle produit ses fruicts au dehors."
[92] As much as he insists on the integral unity of the two principles, Calvin still believes that the spiritual part is superior, as he points out in the *Petit Traicté*: "Ma doctrine est, que l'homme fidele se doit sanctifier et consacrer à Dieu, tant de corps que d'espirit: mais que l'espirit, comme le principal, aille en premier lieu" (CR 6.566).
[93] *Petit Traicté*, CR 6.580.

fessed to being "complete Manicheans" because, after all, they really deny that God is the creator of the total person.[94]

Maintaining a complicated balance between spiritual and material, Calvin argues that our spiritually dominated dual nature has been raised to a special level of prominence by Christ's death and resurrection. This makes it all the more important that one refrain from participating in idolatry: Since the ultimate goal of the human body is spiritual, one must always guard against pollution.[95] It necessarily follows, therefore, that the proper state of redeemed flesh is corrupted by the act of idolatry.[96] To worship spiritually does not mean to put away one's flesh, but rather to keep it unpolluted through the observance of true worship. Calvin, however, is careful to point out that he is not binding Christians to the mere observance of external ceremonies through this teaching. The dominant principle is always the superiority of the spiritual over the material:

Because we do not say that religion and sanctity consist in the external, in adoring God with the eyes, hands, or feet; but we say that external service is an appendage and accessory of spiritual service.[97]

Calvin maintains that although Christians are not bound to the "yoke of the flesh," they have not been completely excused from having to display their faith in some external manner. Christ's abolition of ceremonies only applies to specific practices, not to the whole of worship.[98] To try to skirt the issue by separating belief from action, as the Nicodemites did, was to expose oneself directly to all the dangers of "false worship."

CALVIN'S ALTERNATIVES TO COMPROMISE

Calvin's struggle against Nicodemism is the logical conclusion of his effort to avoid compromise with the worship of the Roman Catholic church. Calvin proposes a model form of conduct for all Christians, and he describes his opinion in detail as he deals with each of the

---

[94] "Sermon Contre l'Idolatrie," CR *8*.381. Ironically, Calvin himself has been accused of harboring Manichean tendencies. Roy Battenhouse speaks of a "dualism" of soul and body in Calvin: "The Doctrine of Man in Calvin and Renaissance Platonism," *Journal of the History of Ideas*, 9 (1948), p. 468. G. K. Chesterton goes much further, actually calling Calvin a Manichean: *St. Thomas Aquinas* (New York, 1933), p. 123.

[95] *Excuse*, CR *6*.593.

[96] Calvin bases this argument on I Corinthians 6:15–20, and he repeats it several times in his struggle against the Nicodemites. CR *8*.382, CR *6*.570, CR *9*.613.

[97] *Response*, CR *9*.597.

[98] CR *9*.590.

problems raised by the dissembling behavior of the Nicodemites. Calvin's principal dictum in regard to the Christian's relationship with "false religion" is that idolatry must be shunned at all costs, even at the risk of one's life; for as he says, the first lesson one should learn in the "school of Jesus Christ" is the renunciation of self.[99]

But what, specifically, is the individual living in a predominantly Catholic environment supposed to do if there is to be no compromise with Rome? How is all this theology to be brought to life in the harsh, practical world of politics? Calvin offers two alternatives to those who, as he says, are living in Babylon and cannot worship God correctly in public. The first is to emigrate: One can leave behind all corruption and seek a new location (such as Geneva) where true worship can take place. For those who find it impossible to flee (and Calvin grants that there are some for whom emigration is out of the question), the second alternative is to abstain from all idolatry: to remain "pure and immaculate before God, in soul as well as in body," even under duress.[100]

Calvin and the question of exile

In 1550, Calvin proudly wrote to Melanchton: "many, in order to avoid idolatry, are fleeing France and are coming to us in voluntary exile."[101] Calvin often refers to idolatry as if it were a plague: Once an area becomes infected with this virus, the only way the residents can escape contagion is by fleeing. Those who remain behind, surrounded by the disease, risk infection every day as long as they come into contact with its victims. Calvin was aware that not everyone was free to emigrate, but he continually stressed that for those who found it possible, it was the wisest course to follow:

Now, consider whether you can have peace with God and your own conscience while you persevere in your present state . . . We have no direct revelation commanding us to leave the country, but since we have the commandment to honor God in body and soul, wherever we may be, what else could we do? It is certainly to us, then, that these words are also addressed, 'Get thee out of thy country and from thy kindred' [Gen. 12:1]; as long as we are there constrained to act against our conscience, and cannot live for the glory of God.[102]

---

[99] *Petit Traicté*, CR 6.542.
[100] CR 6.576. Also: CR 55.280, CR 45.770.
[101] CR 13.596.
[102] CR 11.629–30.

Calvin adds that one should regard as "filth and dung" everything which hinders one from being a good Christian; if anything separates one from God, who is the true life, then it can only lead to death.[103]

Calvin called on the faithful to relinquish everything for the sake of pure worship, including one's native land. If one's country was opposed to the true worship of God, Calvin told his followers, then one should be ready to regard it as a foreign land. Recalling the words, "How shall we sing of the Lord in a strange land?" (Psalm 37), Calvin argues that the true Christian can never be at home in any land that forbids pure worship:

I admit that the kingdom of God is now everywhere, and that there is no longer any distinction between Judaea and other lands; but I say nevertheless, that any country where the worship of God is abolished and his religion is annihilated well deserves to be regarded as foreign and profane.[104]

This is a clear, forceful expression of Calvin's theological vision, a testimony to his conviction that "true religion" is the true nation of the Christian. Some Protestants, however, regarded these sentiments as improper, or even seditious, and they argued that emigration was an act of treason. Calvin denied this vigorously, saying that emigration could not be regarded an act of desertion or treason if the objective of the emigrant were to escape idolatry. After all, it was not a question of going over to an enemy country in order to join forces against one's king and country, said Calvin, but rather of merely seeking a place to worship God "purely" and in peace.[105] Calvin wanted to leave no doubt in anyone's mind that this was most correct, and he goes as far as to say that princes who deny their subjects the right to worship God as God has commanded, should expect to be deserted by them.[106]

---

[103] "Quatrieme Sermon," CR *8*.437.

[104] CR *8*.419. For a general treatment of the question of exile during the Reformation: Gottfried W. Locher, "The Theology of Exile: Faith and the Fate of the Refugee," in *Social Groups and Religious Ideas in the Sixteenth Century* (Kalamazoo, 1978), pp. 85–92. On Calvin's own exile: Ewald Rieser, *Calvin – Franzose, Genfer, oder Fremdling?* (Zurich, 1968).

[105] "Quatrieme Sermon," CR *8*.428.

[106] CR *8*.429: "Les princes terriens se rebecquent a l'encontre et veulent qu'on luy tourne le dos, ou bien, ils privent les povres ames de leur pasture ordinaire, et, au lieu de la face de Dieu, mettent devant les yeulx des masques de superstitions. Faut–il qu'ils soyent preferez au Dieu vivant? Si on escoute Dieu, il fault plustost aller mille lieues loing, pour veoir sa face ou il la monstre, que de croupir en son nid. Ainsi toutes fois et quantes que les princes attentent rien au preiudice de celuy qui ha toute autorité souveraine par dessus eulx, on ne leur faict nul tort en luy obeissant."

Calvin's opposition to compromise and his call to exile stem not only from his fear of the "contagion" of idolatry, but also from his ecclesiological doctrine. For Calvin, the visible church played a central role in Christian worship and in the controversy over compromise. In fact, the true "nationalism" of Christians was never something disembodied for Calvin – it was never merely an adherence to a certain kind of worship – but rather adherence to a certain social group: the "true" Christian church. The visible church was not the perfect church of God (it did not consist exclusively of God's elect), but it still offered a great assistance to the faithful.[107] Calvin maintained that there were great benefits to be derived from belonging to a community devoted to the pure worship of God, insisting that it is very beneficial to be able to worship freely, openly confess one's faith, pray, hear the Word preached, and participate in the sacraments established by God.[108] Calvin stresses the importance of the worshiping community against the dissemblers who scoff at his call to exile. Those who think they can do without the church, he says, know very little about the faith they claim to follow. Although God has done away with the earthly temple of the Jews and the organized priesthood of Aaron, there is still a divinely ordained need for organized worship. This need is met by the church.

I admit that there is no more material temple where it is necessary to go on pilgrimage to sacrifice to God, since we are now his spiritual temples and ought everywhere to raise our pure hands to heaven. However, the command to invoke His name in the company of the faithful endures forever: because this is not one of the figures of the Old Testament, but is a command which our Lord Jesus has given until the end of the world . . . It is certainly true that we are no longer like little children held under the tutelage of the Law of Moses; but we are still men and will continue to be men until God takes us from the world.[109]

The ecclesiological element of Calvin's call to exile is clearly established in this passage: Humanity is always in need of organized re-

---

[107] Numerous works treat the subject of Calvin's ecclesiology. Among the most useful are the following: Haro Höpfl, *The Christian Polity of John Calvin* (Cambridge, 1982); Leopold Schümmer, *L'Ecclesiologie de Calvin à la Lumière de l'Ecclesia Mater* (Bern, 1981); B. C. Milner, *Calvin's Doctrine of the Church* (Leiden, 1970); G. S. M. Walker, "Calvin and the Church," *Scottish Journal of Theology*, 16: 371–389 (1963); W. Niesel "Wesen und Gestalt der Kirche nach Calvin," *Evangelische Theologie*, 3: 308–30 (1936); A. C. McGiffert, "Calvin's Theology of the Church," *Essays in Modern Theology* (New York, 1911), p. 207–25; and P. Barth, "Calvins Verstandnis der Kirche," *Zwischen den Zeiten*, 8: 216–233 (1930).
[108] "Troisieme Sermon," CR 8.410.
[109] CR 8.418.

ligion. Although the shadows and figures of David's time have passed, Christians are still called to participate in public common worship, in the preaching of the Word, and in the partaking of the sacraments. This is not always possible in an idolatrous land, such as France, where the faithful are persecuted. Calvin adds that there is no choice in this matter, that Christians are required to use the aids that God has given them in the church, and that if these aids are not used one has fewer excuses before God.[110] This means, of course, that in cases where one has to choose between membership in the visible "New Israel" of the church, and citizenship in an idolatrous nation, preference is to be given to God's kingdom. To this extent, then, the visible church becomes a nation for Calvin, in that the ultimate allegiance required of all Christians (regardless of their place of birth) lies with God and his commandments, not with princes and their laws. And God is quite visible, making himself manifest in the church: "When God represents himself according to his good wishes, and gives us marks and signs so he can be known by us, then it is as if he took a face."[111]

Not surprisingly, Calvin's exhortations met with opposition and a bit of sarcasm. Some in France quipped that Calvin would not consider anyone a Christian or admit him into heaven unless he first passed through Geneva and had his ears blasted with sermons.[112] Calvin responded by saying that he was not trying to set up the Genevan church as the only valid church, but was instead seeking to make French Protestants realize the need for an organized religious community. He denied trying to bring anyone to Geneva, saying that his call to exile was not a requirement, but only sensible advice.[113] In fact, he added, if anyone were to remain in an idolatrous land and still manage to worship God purely, then his worship would be more meritorious than the worship offered at Geneva: "When a man lives purely and serves God as he should in the midst of Papist tyranny, I esteem him a hundred times more, point for point, than we, who enjoy freedom and peace."[114]

---

[110] CR *8*.421.
[111] "Quatrieme Sermon," CR *8*.426.
[112] "Troisieme Sermon," CR *8*.412: "Ie parle de nos philosophes de cabinets qui sont soubs la Paupeté. C'est bien a propos, disent-ils, qu'on ne soit point Chrestien, si on ne trotte à Genève pour avoir les oreilles conflictes de sermons, et user des ceremonies qu'on observe la!"
[113] E. Droz, *Chemins de l'Hérésie*, vol. I, pp. 169–70. Droz overlooks the theological dimensions of this phenomenon: "On cherche vainement les raisons théologiques à cette mise en demeure," p. 155.
[114] "Troisieme Sermon," CR *8*.412. Also: CR *6*.575; CR *51*.854.

Calvin's call to exile had dramatic results: Thousands of French Protestants fled their homeland in search of religious freedom. Nearly five thousand came to Geneva, significantly altering the social structure of the city.[115] Although it is true that the French refugees made it easier for Calvin to exert his control over Geneva, it would be wrong to ignore the theological dimension of Calvin's struggle against Nicodemism. Calvin may have benefited from the influx of refugees into Geneva, but this was not the sole motivation behind his inflexible position. Calvin was driven to oppose compromise principally through a set of theological principles that had a quite concrete, practical foundation. Besides, the effects of Calvin's call to exile extended far beyond the realm of his adopted city. Calvin's exhortations produced an exodus not only in France, but also in various countries where his treatises were translated and published. Other cities also served as havens for persecuted Protestants: English exiles, for instance, settled in Wesel, Emden, Frankfurt, Strassburg, Zurich, Basel, and Aarau.[116] The establishment of refugee churches throughout the continent in the sixteenth century, which proved to be so influential in the development of Protestant churches in their respective countries, owes much to Calvin's uncompromising stance against Roman Catholic worship.[117] Though he did not single-handedly cause the religious migrations of his day, Calvin had an enormous influence on their development.

Steadfastness: the other alternative

Those who cannot emigrate, and thus remain behind in "Egypt and Babylon," are not promised an easy life by Calvin, who persistently calls upon all the faithful to assume an uncompromising stance:

> see that you take courage to separate yourselves from idolatry and from all superstitions which are contrary to the service of God, and to the acknowledgement and confession which all Christians owe to him, for to that we are called.[118]

---

[115] Statistics for Genevan immigration are recorded in P. F. Giesendorf, *Livre des Habitants de Genève* (Geneva, 1957). A more reliable study of the refugee situation has been written by William Monter in *Calvin's Geneva* (New York, 1967).

[116] A. G. Dickens, *The English Reformation* (New York, 1974), p. 284; as well as Dan G. Danner, "The Marian Exiles and the English Protestant Tradition," *Social Groups and Religious Ideas in the Sixteenth Century* (Kalamazoo, 1978), pp. 93–101.

[117] D. Kelley, *Ideology*, p. 288.

[118] CR 14.638.

This doctrine of strict separation includes, as is to be expected, the possibility of having to suffer trials, encarcerations, and even martyrdom. In fact, Calvin published a sermon devoted entirely to the subject of martyrdom.[119]

Though Calvin accepts the possibility of martyrdom, he never advises this sacrifice as the norm for those who stay behind. Instead of calling for an aggressive struggle against "idolatry," Calvin calls for an assertive, but quiet withdrawal which is to be coupled with an exemplary adherence to the Gospel. Those living among idolaters, says Calvin, have to live out their faith as privately as possible in order to avoid controversy. Living as a nation within a nation, believers must be steadfast in their opposition to Rome, but not offensive. Only those in positions of authority had the right to take the offensive against "corrupt" religion. As early as 1537, Calvin was already prescribing this "rule of duty":

Consider it always forbidden to let anyone see you communicating in the sacrilege of the Mass, or uncovering your head before an image, or observing any kind of superstition . . . through which the glory of God is obscured, his religion profaned, and his truth corrupted.[120]

This rule included an admonition against confrontations. Calvin cautions that one should only raise suspicion about one's beliefs when one is forced to do so by circumstances. No one is to go out of his way to "make a display of contempt" against Catholic worship: "I do not ask you openly to profess your piety; all I ask is that you do not deny it for the profession of impiety."[121] In the *Petit Traicté*, Calvin is even more graphic, saying that it is not necessary for everyone to mount a pulpit or parade through the streets with trumpets. Rather, he says, each individual should give glory to God privately according to his state of life.[122] What Calvin asked of the individual was a constant

---

[119] "Le Second Sermon, Contenant Exhortation à Souffrir Persécution pour Suyvre Jesus Christ et Son Evangile," CR 8.393–408. Calvinist interest in the subject of martyrdom also found expression in martyrologies, a type of literature that became immensely popular in France, the Netherlands, and England in the latter half of the sixteenth century. Jean Crespin's *Histoire de Martyrs* (1564; reprinted Toulouse, 1885) was the prototype for all later martyrologies, including Foxe's *Actes and Monuments of these Latter and Perilous Dayes* (1563), commonly known as the *Book of Martyrs*. For more on this subject: J. F. Gilmont, *Les Martyrologes Protestants de XVIe Siècle* (Thesis, University of Louvain, 1966); L. E. Halkin, "Hagiographie Protestante," in *Mélanges Paul Pieters II* (*Analecta Bollandiana*, LXVII, 1950); and Hans Scholl, *Reformation und Politik* (Stuttgart, 1976), pp. 103–23.

[120] *De fugiendis*, CR 5.274.

[121] CR 5.276.

[122] *Petit Traicté*, CR 6.545.

private commitment to true worship, not to an iconoclastic crusade: Instead of trying to cleanse the temples and streets, the good Christian should rather guard his own body and soul from impurity.[123] It is the role of the government, not of the individual, to wage war on Roman Catholic worship:

> I do not require of the faithful, that upon seeing the Papists carry about their relics and other marmosets, they should wrench them from their grasp, or throw filth at them (because it is up to princes and superiors to correct such abominations), but rather that they should abstain from polluting themselves with them; and as long as it is illicit for them to adore God solemnly, that they should at least glorify Him in their hearts.[124]

At times, however, Calvin seems inclined to advise less caution. Although every Christian does not have the right to combat idolatry by force, he is bound by duty to despise it. Calvin points to the example of Christ's expulsion of the money changers from the Temple as a model for all Christians. He admits that it is not lawful for every person to "take up the whip," but asserts that it is right for all true believers to "burn with the zeal with which Christ was animated, when he vindicated the glory of the Father."[125]

Calvin's message could not help but be disruptive to society. While he admonishes the individual to keep his faith to himself and avoid confrontation, Calvin also tells him he should burn with zeal for the pure worship of God. By calling on his followers to withdraw from the customs of their society and to abhor these practices with zeal, Calvin helped create an explosive situation, especially when one considers that "confession" became a special Calvinist trait. For Calvinists, "confession" was a socially oriented concern that transcended whatever personal fulfillment any individual might find in the *fides* that was at the heart of the Protestant message. This impulse to offer witness publicly was rooted in Calvin's ecclesiology, particularly in his notion of the visible church as God's instrument of election, but it was further intensified by the need to combat Nicodemism. As we have seen, Calvin would admit no separation between private belief and public behavior, and this principle of confessional integrity went beyond mere passivity: It also called for an aggressive public rejection of the many social norms that supported "idolatry." To accept the Calvinist *credo*, body and soul, was to become an agent of change. More specifically, it meant becoming a

---

[123] "Sermon Contre l'Idolatrie," CR 8.385.
[124] *Petit Traicté*, CR 6.561.
[125] *De necessitate*, CR 6.507.

promoter of iconoclasm, even if indirectly. As one Huguenot pamphleteer put it in 1561, shortly before the outbreak of war, "Confession is demonstrating publicly that you consent in no way to idolatry, and communicating to others the same doctrine that you embrace."[126]

We can see here how, at the hands of some of his followers, Calvin's uncompromising advice could acquire a more aggressive character, and how the Calvinist hatred of idolatry could develop into a crusade. When interpreted by less cautious ideologues, the more volatile aspects of Calvin's teaching could be easily used to support violence,[127] and there were several occasions on which Calvin found it necessary publicly to distance himself from the excessive zeal of some of his followers. Whenever any illegal iconoclasm took place, Calvin was quick to disassociate himself from it. In 1561, for instance, he reprimanded some Parisians for having seized churches in the city, making it clear that he was not responsible for their actions.[128] In a similar manner, Calvin complained to Beza that his advice was not being heeded and that many were doing things of which he would never approve:

> What you write to me concerning the proposterous zeal of our brethren is certainly true, and yet no way of restraining it occurs to me, because they fail to heed sound advice. I proclaim far and wide that if I were a judge I would punish these furious attacks no less harshly than the King demands in his edicts.[129]

As religious violence erupted in 1561, Calvin tried to restrain the "preposterous zeal" for which he was partly responsible. In July the minister of the Protestant community at Sauve led his congregation in an iconoclastic riot; Calvin was infuriated by this incident and wrote a severe admoniton against the minister and his people. Launching into a lengthy condemnation of private initiative in the struggle against idolatry, Calvin laid bare the foundation of his opposition to such acts:

> God has never commanded the destruction of idols, except to each one in his own house and in public to those he arms with authority . . . By speaking in

---

[126] *Traitte du Devoir des Princes* (1561), cited by D. Kelley, *Ideology*, p. 96.

[127] Kelley, *Ideology*, p. 100: "Through such hatred of 'idolatry' and 'superstition' the cult of purified religion was easily transformed, by the temperaments of some enthusiasts, into a cult of violence."

[128] CR 18.378: "De seggaier beaucoup et occuper les temples, vous scavez que ce n'a iamais nostre advis, sinon par conge. Quant on la faict ça esté en nous mesprisant."

[129] CR 19.120–1.

this way we do not become defenders of the idols; no, we wish it were God's will that they were banished from the world even at the cost of our lives. But since obedience is better than sacrifice, we have to consider what is permitted, and restrain ourselves within bounds.[130]

In the spring of 1562 Protestant troops sacked the church of St. John in Lyons, and divided the spoils among themselves.[131] This incident prompted another angry letter from Calvin, who wrote to the Baron des Adrets asking him to condemn the actions of his soldiers.[132] Calvin also called on him to correct the one abuse that was "altogether insupportable," that is, the assumption that the troops had a right to "plunder the chalices, reliquaries, and other furniture of the temples."[133] Calvin could not condone unauthorized iconoclasm (though he considered it understandable), but even less could he approve of looting.

While Calvin argues that the sin of disobedience to established authority nullifies the good that one might do by removing idols, he also considers a very practical matter in connection with this issue. Calvin observes that individual acts of violence usually do more harm than good to the Protestant cause, because they give Catholics a further excuse for attacking the Protestants. Violence begets violence, and for an outlawed religious minority it is extremely risky to court retaliation.[134] Calvin rebuked the minister at Sauve for not taking this into account:

It is shocking that he should be so stupid as not to think of the opportunity he has given to the crafty to ruin everything . . . Now, since this is the case, dear brethren, we plead with you, that you have pity on the poor churches, and in order not to knowingly expose them to massacre, that you disavow this act, and openly declare to the people that it was wrong.[135]

---

[130] CR 18.581. As an example of good conduct, Calvin points to the ancient Jews who never hid their contempt for heathen idols while exiled in Babylon and yet refrained from destroying them. To those who consider exile, Calvin presents Abraham as a model: *Commentary on Acts*, CR 48.130–1; *Commentary on Hebrews*, CR 55.152. Ezekiel and Daniel are examples of restraint: They were faithful Jews who never took the destruction of idolatry into their own hands (CR 18.581). King Josiah, who lawfully destroyed the idols, is a model for all rulers (CR 13.73–4).
[131] Theodore Beza, *Histoire Ecclésiastique*, vol. II, p. 221.
[132] CR 19.412. The Baron des Adrets was at that time in charge of the government of Lyons. He later deserted the Protestant cause. J. H. M. Salmon, *Society in Crisis: France in the Sixteenth Century* (New York, 1975), p. 129.
[133] CR 19.412.
[134] Natalie Zemon Davis, "The Rites of Violence: Religious Riot in Sixteenth Century France," *Past and Present*, 59: 53–91 (May, 1973).
[135] CR 18.581.

Although he asked for restraint, Calvin did not abandon his struggle against idolatry. He always maintained that the only way to eradicate "false worship" was physically to remove the "materials" that caused it.[136] The agent of this action, however, should be the government; and while Calvin pleaded restraint with the faithful, he asked for war from those in power.

In the *Inventory of Relics* (1543), Calvin states that Christian princes should give "a little thought" to the abuses of the Catholic church, because it is their duty to prevent all offenses to God.[137] Calvin believed that those in power were the guardians of pure worship. In a letter to Protector Somerset of England, Calvin explains the religious duties of those in office, hoping that the Protector will institute a complete reform in the name of young King Edward. Calvin asserts that earthly princes ought to govern in the name of Jesus Christ, taking care that his authority should rule over all men alike. Calvin calls on Somerset to wipe out even the smallest traces of idolatry, warning that no one can afford to take chances with this problem:

> I admit that it is good to show moderation, and that too much rigor [*extremité*] is neither good nor useful, because it is necessary to accomodate ceremonies to the simplicity of the people. But one must not let that which comes from Satan and the Antichrist be accepted under this principle. This is why Holy Writ, when praising those kings who had attacked idolatry but failed to wipe it out altogether notes it as a shame, that nevertheless they had not cast down the small temples and places of deranged devotion.[138]

In 1544, Calvin gave similar advice to the King of Poland. In this letter, Calvin says that kings should not hesitate to wipe out idolatry in their land, because God has set them on high for the purpose of enlightening their people. Calvin further warns the Polish king that unless he calls his subjects away from the "filthy dissipation of Popery to the obedience of Christ" he shall incur serious blame before God.[139] In a letter written a year later, Calvin repeats the same admonition to the king, this time using the example of King David as the model monarch. King David, says Calvin, showed a great desire to build a temple for God; if such concern for an outward form of worship was undertaken by this ancient Jewish king, then how much

---

[136] *De necessitate*, CR 6.476: "Certum est, idolomania, qualiter nunc illa fascinatae sunt hominum mentes, non aliter quam subducta insaniendi materia, curari posse."

[137] CR 6.414.

[138] CR 13.73–4.

[139] CR 15.330: "Nam quum gregarios quoque discipulos lucernis similis esse velit Christus, quae in sublimi positae fulgorem suum longe emittunt: quid a rege exiget quem in summo dignitatis fastigio locavit ut aliis omnibus praeluceat?"

more should not the spiritual worship of God absorb a Christian monarch in the present day?[140]

As might be expected, Calvin met with some resistance, but he stood firm. When Fumée reported that many in France thought his assertions were "thoroughly wretched," Calvin replied by saying that his admonitions were not something he had dreamed up in some "shady nook," but rather something that had always been demanded of Christians, the very same principles for which the martyrs of old had died.[141] If Christians in the past were willing to suffer horrible tortures in order to avoid idolatry, asks Calvin, why should his fellow Frenchmen act any differently? Calvin refused to give in to criticism; he was convinced of the truth, and could not bring himself "to call that which is white black" to ease anyone's conscience.[142] He distanced himself from his advice by saying that it was not really "Calvin's" opinion, but the very truth of God.[143]

As early as 1536, however, Calvin knew that his opinion would not be warmly accepted. In his letter to Gerard Roussel, Calvin pleaded that his advice was not to be judged like the words of a poet or an orator (which need to be accepted with applause and signs of favor), but rather that it be considered as a doctrine of life (which can only be accepted through obedience), and as the word of God.[144] Calvin even began to accept his inflexibility as a necessary trait for anyone in a position of authority. In a letter to Philip Melanchton, Calvin reprimands him for being too "soft" and conciliatory with the Leipzig Interim, and comments on the merits of firmness:

I know how much the charge of unfeeling toughness horrifies you. But we must remember that popularity must not be regarded as greater than life by the servants of Christ . . . It is certainly hard and bitter to be regarded as an inflexible troublemaker . . . but your ears should have grown calloused against such talk long ago.[145]

Calvin himself turned a toughened ear on his opponents, and continued to wage an unrelenting war on idolatry and compromise.

---

[140] CR 15.894.
[141] *Petit Traicté*, CR 6.573.
[142] *Excuse*, CR 6.597: "De ma part, ie ne puis pas dire que le blanc soit noir, pour leur gratifier."
[143] CR 6.602. Also: *Response*, CR 9.594.
[144] *De sacerdotio papale abiiciendo*, CR 5.279ff.
[145] CR 13.595.

CALVIN'S AGENDA

Calvin's opposition to Nicodemism grew out of the struggle for the survival of the Reformed church in France. French Protestants were loosely organized and poorly directed through the 1540s. As Protestantism spread throughout the kingdom, so did Calvin's efforts to establish an organized church with regular congregations and well-trained ministers.[146] The 1550s may be seen as the great period of expansion and consolidation for French Protestantism, but all advances were threatened by the continual specter of persecution.[147] When these factors are taken into account, it becomes easier to understand Calvin's concern over the Nicodemites and their desire to compromise. Calvin's attack on Nicodemism was grounded on theological principles, but it was by no means an arid theological dispute. Overall, it may be seen as an attempt to salvage the Reformed cause from confusion and to mold it into a vibrant faith, distinct from Roman Catholicism. The compromise favored by the Nicodemites was repugnant to Calvin not just because it was a form of idolatry, but also because it denied the need for a church wholly dedicated to evangelical principles. Some have indicated that the Nicodemites were a serious threat to the Protestant cause in France.[148] Ideologically, at least, it is easy to see the threat they posed: Nicodemism could render the Protestant message useless through compromise, since it considered conciliation between the "corruption" of Rome and the "purity" of the Gospel to be possible. Nicodemism was a threat because it could easily paralyze the development of any outward reforms, or the establishment of any institutions. Because they refused to reject the authority of Rome openly, Nicodemites, were, in effect, advocating the existence of two churches, one "corrupt" and one "reformed." This attitude, even if intended only as a temporary measure, could greatly hinder the progress of religious change. One must always keep in mind that Calvin saw the "corruption" of Rome as an awesome evil that had to be shunned, and whenever possible, eradicated.[149] Anything that compromised this ideal was therefore also evil as far as he was concerned.

---

[146] On this point: Kelley, *Ideology*, pp. 89–128; and R. Kingdon, *Geneva and the Coming of the Wars of Religion in France, 1555–1563* (Geneva, 1956).

[147] A. Bailly, *La Réforme en France*, p. 177; Rothrock, *Huguenots*, pp. 1–64; Sutherland, *Huguenot Struggle*, pp. 10–39.

[148] Albert Autin has argued that Nicodemism threatened at one point to suffocate the Reformation in France: *La Crise du Nicodémisme, 1535–1545* (Toulouse, 1917).

[149] F. Higman comments on this point: "It is characteristic of the period, and of Calvin

By opposing Nicodemism and rejecting any kind of compromise, Calvin asserted the necessity of schism and laid a solid theological foundation for the establishment of Reformed churches throughout France and Europe. Moreover, by struggling against any compromise with "idolatry," Calvin drew a blueprint for social, political, and ecclesiastical strife. The implications of Calvin's position are quite disruptive. A choice must be made between Rome and the Gospel: Either one belongs to "the people of God," untainted by idolatry, or one belongs to the "false church" of the Pope.

To call for such a choice in the sixteenth century was to call for revolution. In an age when religion and nationality were closely intertwined, any religious schism could not help but also be political. The situation in France was particularly tense. As the monarch attempted to enforce the dictum, "one King, one law, and one faith" through the persecution of Protestants, Calvin continued to insist that there could be no compromise with the faith that the French king was trying to enforce by law. The civic unrest that troubled France through the 1540s and 50s, and that finally erupted into open war in 1562, can be blamed, to some considerable extent, on Calvin's rejection of compromise.[150] Similar conclusions can be drawn about Calvinist–inspired strife in England, Scotland, and the Netherlands during the second half of the sixteenth century. The old Catholic polemic that accused Calvin of political sedition for his attack on Nicodemism may have, after all, hinted at a truth, at least by sixteenth-century standards.[151] Though Calvin's primary objective was grounded on theological principles, chiefly on the necessity of maintaining "true" and "uncorrupted" worship in a visible church, the application of these principles in sixteenth-century society necessarily involved a very concrete kind of political challenge. By calling for separation and exile, and the creation of a "purified" church, Calvin was striking deep at the heart of the body politic; he was, in fact, calling into question the Christian's national identity and sense of allegiance.

While the ideological threat of Nicodemism is relatively clear, its actual extent and force are not. Some have claimed that Nicodemism

---

in particular, that such a rejection cannot be allowed to remain a polite divergence of opinion." *John Calvin: Three French Treatises* (London, 1970), p. 21.

[150] Autin, *Nicodémisme*, pp. 76–7; Higman, *Three Treatises*, p. 40.

[151] Hans Scholl argues even more forcefully for the political dimension of Calvin's struggle against compromise: "Die antinikodemitischen Schriften Calvins haben die berühmte Politisierung des französischen Protestantismus angeleitet und beschleugnigt" (*Reformation und Politik*, p. 78). See also Audin, *Histoire de Calvin*, p. 319.

was widespread and deep-seated among French Protestants before 1545. This assessment is not easy to verify. The dissembling nature of the movement itself has left little for us to trace: Since Nicodemites, by definition, hid their sentiments, they left few records behind; hence it is impossible for us to count heads. One conjecture that can be made by counting the number of published anti-Nicodemite treatises is that the phenomenon was pervasive, particularly in areas where a religious settlement was long in coming, such as in France. The traditional interpretation, supported by Beza's boast that Calvin put the Nicodemites to rest with his *Excuse*, is that Nicodemism began to wane after 1545; but the existing literary evidence suggests otherwise. Calvin himself admitted in 1552 that the problem still plagued the French Church,[152] and in 1562 he wrote against Coornhert's defense of dissembling behavior. The *Excuse* was reprinted in France in 1551 and 1582. Calvin's friend and close associate, Pierre Viret, also wrote many treatises against compromise[153]; and anti-Nicodemite books continued to be published in other languages throughout the sixteenth century, and even into the seventeenth.[154] It seems safe to assume, then, that although Nicodemism may have been weakened by the efforts of Calvin and others, it was never entirely eradicated. The real extent and force of Nicodemism in France can only be guess-

---

[152] *Quatre Sermons*, CR 8.374: "Combien que i'ay escript par ci devant deux traictez assez amples pour monstrer qu'il n'est pas licite a un Chrestien cognoissant la pure doctrine de l'Evangile, quand il vit en la Papaulté, faire semblant en facon que ce soit de consentir ou adherer aux abus, superstitions et idolatries qui y regnent; toutesfois il y a tous les iours gens que m'en demandent conseil de nouveau, comme si iamais ie n'en avoye parlé. J'enten aussi qu'il y en a d'autres qui ne cessent d'alleguer leurs replicques et subterfuges contre ce que i'en ay escript."

[153] The following are Viret's most important anti-Nicodemite treatises:
1541 *Epistre Consolatoire;*
1543 *Epistre Envoyée aux Fidèles Conversans entre les Chrestiens Papistiques;*
1547 *De la Communication des Fidèles qui Cognoissent la Verité de l'Evangile;*
1547 *Remonstrances aux Fidèles qui Conversent entre les Papistes;*
1551 *Du Devoir et Besoing qu'Ont les Hommes;*
1559 *Epistres aux Fidèles;*
1559 *Traitez Divers pour l'Instruction des Fidèles.*
For more on Viret, see J. Barnaud, *Pierre Viret* (Saint-Aman, 1911); and R. Linder, *The Political Ideas of Pierre Viret* (Geneva, 1964).

[154] The *Opera Calvini* lists the following translations of Calvin's anti-Nicodemite works:
De fugiendis: German, 1557; Italian, 1551, 1553;
Petit Traicté: English, 1548; German, 1589;
Excuse: Dutch, 1549, 1554;
Quatre Sermons: English, 1561.
One must also include the Latin translation of the *Petit Traicté* and the *Excuse*, which appeared together under one title, published along with the opinions of other Reformers, as *De vitandis superstitionibus*, 1549, 1550.

ed, but one thing remains clear: Regardless of their actual numbers or influence, religious dissemblers posed a serious ideological threat to French Protestantism in the sixteenth century – a threat that was checked and diminished, but never vanquished.

Can it be argued, then, that by opposing simulation, Calvin became the true founder of French Protestantism?[155] The complexities of the Nicodemite problem might not allow one to reach as specific a conclusion as one might wish, but it is possible to say that, by battling the Nicodemites, Calvin helped save the Protestant church from becoming invisible in France; in addition, by giving clear expression to the necessity of schism, Calvin also provided a formidable challenge to his age. As to the question of Calvin's motivation, the answer is clearer: While it is safe to say that he had no hidden agenda in opposing Nicodemism, and that his attack on compromise was motivated by a certain theological vision of the social and political order, it would be difficult to deny that his hatred of "idolatry" and his inflexibility had serious political repercussions. Among the many lessons to be learned from this case, perhaps one of the most important is that, when it came to questions concerning the social and political order, Calvin's theology was far from purely speculative or disembodied, and that it is very difficult indeed even to speak of "political motivations" or "theological reasons" as separate from one another. It would be even more foolish to regard them as mutually exclusive. Calvin's vision of the proper order of things and of the duties enjoined on true Christians, shaped as it was by the harsh realities of politics, could not help but encourage the development of more clearly defined political ambitions among his followers. Though Calvin himself publicly opposed the kind of aggressive campaign that some of his followers began against the "false religion" of the French monarchy, there was little he could do to stop them in the long run.

Theologians may write about society and politics, but they seldom have a chance to direct the application of their teachings; Calvin's struggle against compromise is a case in point. Once the Wars of Religion began, and theories of political resistance were developed that called for the removal of "idolatrous" rulers, the issue of Nicodemism faded into the background; however, the uncompromising spirit that had condemned it only intensified. It is appropriate to say that although Calvin did not intend to be seditious, his uncom-

---

[155] Autin, *Nicodémisme*, p. 10: "Dans cette evolution, Calvin n'est qu'un facteur, le plus important sans doute, puisque c'est lui qu a fixé la Reforme, comme un acide fixe une combination chimique."

promising stance against Roman Catholicism did become a prelude to sedition. By attacking the Nicodemites and ruling out compromise, Calvin developed the groundwork for a politics of "purity," that is, an understanding of the true Christian as exempt from certain civic obligations that demand pollution through idolatrous behavior. This righteous distancing, which under Calvin's direction was rather passive, helped many to take their first step away from total allegiance to their rulers, and also made it easier for others to develop a more active ideology of resistance against idolatry and the political order that supported it. He would have shuddered at the thought, but those Frenchmen who said that "the Gospel is the seed of rebellion" in 1577 probably had Calvin in mind when they said it, and with good reason.[156]

[156] Anonymous, cited by Kelley, *Ideology*, p. 89.

CHAPTER 8

From iconoclasm to revolution: the political dimensions of the war against idolatry

WHEN it came to matters of faith, John Calvin was more interested in doing what was "right" than about being liked or complimented; or at least he wanted to give that impression. As he told Melanchton, no servant of God should concern himself with being popular.[1] In December 1556, though, one Scottish refugee living in Geneva praised Calvin and his work as few others ever had, especially in the city itself. The man was John Knox, an aggressive Reformer who made Calvin and Farel seem timid in comparison. What he said about Calvin's Geneva has come to be regarded as perhaps the greatest testimony to the way in which Calvinism sought to turn its theological vision into a concrete social and political reality:

I neither fear nor ashame to say, [Geneva] is the most perfect school of Christ that ever was in earth since the days of the Apostles. In other places, I confess Christ to be truly preached; but manners and religion so sincerely reformed, I have not yet seen in any other place.[2]

Yet, only two years earlier, when Calvin and Knox first met, the two men had disagreed about the way in which such a state of affairs could be achieved in less receptive lands, such as England and Scotland. As in the other cases we have witnessed where pupil met master, Calvin could not bring himself to accept the new dimensions being given to his own teachings by this refugee. Consumed by the problem of "idolatry" in his native land, Knox had come to Switzerland to seek advice on questions dealing with religion and politics. He had apparently formulated a radical theory of religious

---

[1] CR 13.595.
[2] *The Works of John Knox*, D. Laing, ed. (6 vols., Edinburgh, 1846–64, reprinted, New York, 1966), vol. 4, p. 240.

revolution and was now looking for "official" approval, much as the Nicodemites had done with their very different proposals.

Having recently fled from Queen Mary's England, and also having previously spent nineteen months as a galley slave for the French as punishment for his participation in an abortive Protestant revolt at St. Andrews in 1547, Knox was anything but patient. He was extremely disturbed by the political situation in England and Scotland, where children and women could rule, forcing "idolatry" on their people. He asked Calvin four questions. The first queried whether it was necessary to obey a child-monarch; the second, whether a woman had any right to govern at all "by divine law"; the third and fourth rose in a revolutionary crescendo, asking

Whether it was necessary to obey a magistrate who enforces idolatry and condemns the true religion? . . . [and] to which party ought godly men to adhere if devout men of position resist an idolatrous king by war?[3]

Calvin sternly replied that under no circumstances was it ever lawful for subjects to rise up against an idolatrous ruler in an open act of rebellion, but he was not willing to dismiss Knox's questions altogether, and he wrote him a letter of introduction so he could also visit Pierre Viret in Lausanne and Heinrich Bullinger in Zurich. Knox left Geneva without a written response from Calvin, hoping to obtain a more favorable response from Bullinger.[4]

At Zurich, Knox found some encouragement. Though Bullinger agreed with Calvin, he left Knox a few openings. Yes, he said, children and women had every right to the throne under divine law, and no, there was no biblical sanction for any kind of revolt against lawful rulers. "But," he added, "the Lord will in his own time destroy unjust governments by his own people, to whom he will supply proper qualifications for this purpose, as he formerly did to Jerubaal, and the Maccabees." Hedging further, Bullinger added that although the apostle Paul had counseled obedience in the Epistle to the Romans, not rebellion, it was still "very difficult to pronounce" on this subject, that he would need to know the exact circumstances before he could offer an opinion, and that even then, "it would be very stupid" to try to "state any definite conclusions."[5] Bullinger sent a

---

[3] CR 15.90–1. On the identity of the "Scot" in question: Jasper Ridley, *John Knox* (New York, 1968), pp. 177–80.

[4] CR 15.125. Knox, *The Works*, "Certain Questions Concerning Obedience to Lawful Magistrates," vol. 3, pp. 217–26.

[5] CR 15.93: "difficile est mihi pronunciare quid agant hic fideles. Circumstantiae fere quid agi conveniat indicant. Quae quum nobis perspectae non sint, stultum esset

copy of his opinions to Calvin, and Calvin, in response, voiced his agreement.[6]

Knox went on to direct his own war against idolatry. A few years later, in 1562, after he had returned to Scotland and led an iconoclastic Reformation, he met face to face with his Catholic queen. Knox had been summoned to appear before Mary to discuss the vitriolic sermons he had been preaching against her "idolatry." Mary bluntly asked him how he could justify his doctrine that subjects had a right to rebel against their rulers: When Knox called on his congregation to rise up against her because she was Catholic and still attended Mass in her private royal chapel, was he not also calling on people to disobey God's commands? Knox answered Mary with a metaphor that was an inversion of the one used by Karlstadt in 1525. Knox compared the rebellion of subjects against an "idolatrous" ruler to children who resist their father when he tries to kill them in a frenzy. Just as the children are justified in snatching the sword from a crazed father's hand, he said, so are subjects justified in resisting an idolatrous ruler.[7]

Whereas for Karlstadt the danger came from a knife in a child's hand, and the knife represented the "idols" of the Church, now, for Knox, the danger came from the sword in the hands of a deranged parent, and the sword represented the government itself. The divine command to use force against idolatry had now shifted from the idols to the governments that supported the idols. This was the final step of the war against idolatry. It was now a full-fledged revolution.

The case of Knox proves that the uncompromising stance taken by Calvin and his followers against Roman Catholic worship was much more than a strictly intellectual theological squabble. From its inception in the early 1520s, the attack on idolatry had been the cause of much civic unrest. Under Calvinism, it became the sharp cutting edge of change, and wherever Geneva exported its theology, the social fabric was tested in two ways. In the first place, following the tradition established in Switzerland, the attack on idolatry inevitably pro-

---

definire velle certum aliquid. Paulus Romanorum armis contra coniuratos Iudaeos, sed idem nullis usus legitur armis, sed patientia pugnasse."

[6] CR 15.125.

[7] *John Knox's History of the Reformation in Scotland*, W. Croft Dickinson, ed. (2 vols., Edinburgh/London, 1949), vol. 2, pp. 13–20, esp. p. 17. Also: Richard L. Greaves, *Theology and Revolution in the Scottish Reformation* (Grand Rapids, 1980), pp. 111–68. For a full analysis of the thought of John Knox, and particularly of the way in which he developed his resistance theory, see Richard G. Kyle, *The Mind of John Knox* (Lawrence, Kansas, 1984). Kyle emphasizes the influence of the Old Testament on the formation of Knox's political theology.

duced iconoclasm and all its attending troubles. Secondly, and more significantly, it led to a reassessment of the political duties of citizens, and consequently to the development of revolutionary theories of resistance. Before turning to the second issue, which is the more complex of the two, let us first take a brief look at the way in which Calvinism continued the iconoclastic legacy of the Reformed tradition.

CALVINIST ICONOCLASM IN WESTERN EUROPE

Iconoclasm was an inevitable outcome of Reformed ideology. The iconoclastic tide that had earlier engulfed Switzerland and parts of Germany eventually reached other lands where Calvinism surfaced, most notably in France, England, Scotland and the Netherlands. It is Calvin who is largely responsible for this development, since it was under his direction that Geneva became the exporting center of the Reformed faith in Western Europe.[8]

In France, iconoclasm had been taking place since the 1520s, as has already been pointed out.[9] After all, the rejection of the Catholic cult was part of the religious atmosphere in which Calvin himself was nurtured. However, it was not until the 1560s when Calvinism had gained wide acceptance, that iconoclasm became an expression of massive religious discontent in France. The first cities to experience iconoclastic riots were Rouen and La Rochelle. A year later, in 1561, the iconoclastic fury spread to many other cities, especially Angers, Beauvais, LeMans, Paris, Pontoise, Touraine, and some towns of Languedoc. By the winter of 1561–2 iconoclastic riots had taken place in Abeville, Auxerre, Bayeux, Bourges, Caen, Lyons, Marseille, Meaux, Orléans, Sens, and Tours.[10] This unprecedented wave of image breaking, which many surprised contemporaries report as ex-

---

[8] Robert Kingdon firmly established Geneva as the exporting center of Calvinism in France. *Geneva and the Coming of the Wars of Religion in France, 1555–1563* (Geneva, 1956); and *Geneva and the Consolidation of the French Protestant Movement 1564–1572* (Madison, Wisc., 1967). Shorter studies of the influence of Geneva on other Western European countries incude: John T. McNeill, *The History and Character of Calvinism* (New York, 1967), pp. 237–352; and E. William Monter, *Calvin's Geneva* (New York, 1975), pp. 165–236.

[9] Jean Crespin, *Histoire de Martyrs* (1564; reprinted Toulouse, 1885), vol. I, p. 244; Herminjard 1.315; H. Heller, "Famine, Revolt and Heresy at Meaux, 1521–1525," *ARG* 68 (1977), p. 148.

[10] J. H. M. Salmon, *Society in Crisis: France in the Sixteenth Century* (New York, 1975), p. 136. In Louis Réan, *Histoire du Vandalisme: Les Monuments Detruits de l'Art Français* (2 vols., Paris, 1959), the inventory of damage done in the sixteenth century runs into forty pages.

cessively violent and destructive, was the prelude to the first War of Religion.

Although Calvin and his associates tried to moderate the violence, it only increased, stirring religious fervor and intolerance among both Catholics and Protestants. Once the wars commenced, iconoclastic destruction became the deliberate policy of Huguenot leaders. Though there were plenty of cases of vandalism and looting conducted by soldiers as a part of war, there is reason to believe that much of the destruction was carried out by the populace, and that it was done in defiance of the admonitions of the noblesse and the Calvinist pastors. Some of the revolutionary characteristics earlier displayed in Switzerland and Germany now surfaced in France.[11]

In the Netherlands, iconoclasm was even more dramatic. As in France, there had been isolated iconoclastic outbreaks since the early days of the Reformation, but never on a large scale. Suddenly, beginning on 10 August 1566, a terrifying outbreak of image smashing and church desecration swept the country. In less than two weeks, frenzied but well-organized mobs systematically vandalized churches in almost all of the seventeen provinces.[12] The extent of the destruction was such that in Flanders alone over four hundred churches were sacked. This outbreak prompted Philip II to send ten thousand troops under the Duke of Alva to crush heresy and rebellion, a move that only worsened the situation and eventually led to open rebellion against Spanish rule. Throughout the "Time of Troubles," iconoclasm continued to be the most characteristic form of religious violence among Protestants in the Netherlands, aside from warfare, of course.[13] Germany, too, saw its share of iconoclastic violence wherever Calvinism took root.[14]

In England, iconoclasm was "as complex as the making of the Reformation of which it was a product."[15] The iconoclastic legacy of

---

[11] Salmon, *Society in Crisis*, p. 137

[12] In addition to P. Mack Crew's *Calvinist Preaching and Iconoclasm in the Netherlands* (Cambridge University Press, 1978), see Solange Deyon and Alain Lottin, *Les "Casseurs" de l'Eté 1566: l'Iconoclasme dans le Nord* (Paris, 1981).

[13] Mack Crew, *Calvinist Preaching and Iconoclasm*, p. 354.

[14] Karl Czok, "Der Calvinistensturm 1592/93 in Leipzig – Seine Hintergründe und Bildliche Darstellung," *Jahrbuch zur Geschichte der Stadt Leipzig* (1977), pp. 123–44; and Hans Rott, "Kirchen- und Bildersturm bei der Einführung der Reformation in der Pfalz," *Neues Archiv für die Geschichte der Stadt Heidelberg*, 6: 229–54 (1905).

[15] John Phillips, *The Reformation of Images: Destruction of Art in England 1535–1660* (Los Angeles, 1973), p. 76. Phillips's book is the most complete study available on English iconoclasm. It is useful, but lacks depth in some areas, particularly in its assessment of the intellectual roots of Protestant iconoclasm and its treatment of religious factors.

Protestantism in England was erratic, since the changing policies of the English monarchs over a century and a half had a direct effect on the course of image breaking. Henrician policy was confused, engaging only in halfhearted iconoclasm and the despoliation of churches as a source of revenue. Henry VIII was responsible for establishing a policy that led to discriminatory iconoclasm: He decreed that only the "abused" images were to be removed, but provided no clear definition of the term. The same approach continued through succeeding reigns, with the exception of Mary's, until the time of Charles I and Archbishop Laud. With the triumph of Calvinism through the Puritan revolt in the seventeenth century, a more forceful iconoclastic policy emerged, and iconoclasm swept the country. In Scotland, meanwhile, the political situation had made it possible for Calvinism to triumph under the leadership of John Knox, and in 1559 the country was ravaged by iconoclasm.[16]

The revolutionary aspects of iconoclasm in German and Swiss communities have already been studied, but iconoclasm in Switzerland and Germany was only revolutionary in a localized sense. Since those countries were not centralized states, iconoclasm there was often the effort of certain individuals to establish the Reformation within one specific community. It was a challenge to the authority of local magistrates and Church authorities, but not to the nation as a whole: As a rule, Swiss and German iconoclasm took place within the framework of a fragmented and localized political system. Neighboring communities might have felt threatened, but the removal of the "idols" from one place did not offer any direct political challenge to anyone beyond that community's borders.

Iconoclasm assumes a different revolutionary dimension in centralized states. In France, for instance, Reformed communities were not able to challenge the religious life of any city or town without directly challenging the power of the monarch, who insisted on religious uniformity. As the adage "One king, one law, and one faith" indicated, the people of France were subject to the religious preference of their sovereign, and any act that challenged the Catholic Church also defied the king. The revolutionary implications of the attack on idolatry were thus magnified in France and other countries where Calvinist theology faced the opposition of a centralized government.

---

[16] On Scottish iconoclasm: Mary Paton Ramsay, *Calvin and Art, Considered in Relation to Scotland* (Edinburgh, 1938); and A. M. Renwick, *The Story of the Scottish Reformation* (London, 1960).

THE DEVELOPMENT OF THEORIES OF
RESISTANCE

The conflict between religious ideology and political reality in centralized states made the attack on idolatry revolutionary in another way, beyond iconoclasm. In order to uphold their uncompromising stance against idolatry and survive as an illegal religion, Reformed Protestants in France, England, Scotland, and the Low Countries needed to redefine the duties of subjects to their rulers.

Calvin's uncompromising stance assumed an even greater urgency in midcentury, as Protestants faced the threat of defeat, or even extinction, throughout Europe. As Protestantism expanded and consolidated its gains, the Catholics grew alarmed and soon began to respond vigorously. War, repression, and persecution followed in the wake of Protestant expansion.

The Lutherans in Germany were the first to feel the brunt of the attack. In 1543, Emperor Charles V moved his armies down the Rhine against the Schmalkaldic League, and in April 1547, he crushed the Protestant forces at Mühlberg. The Diet of Augsburg in 1548, then, promulgated the "Interim," outlawing the Lutheran church throughout the empire. For the first time in nearly thirty years, Protestants in Germany faced the threat of persecution on a grand scale. Even Bucer had to flee from Strassburg and seek refuge in England.[17]

A few years later, in 1553, the Reformation in England, too, suffered a crushing blow when the young Protestant Edward died and the Catholic Mary ascended the throne. In 1555, Stephen Gardiner, as Lord Chancellor, began the persecutions that would earn his queen the title "Bloody Mary." Many Protestants managed to escape to Switzerland, especially to Geneva, but over three hundred were arrested and burnt, including such leaders as Hooper, Latimer, Ridley, and Cranmer. More than the Lutherans in Germany, the English Protestants found themselves in a dangerous position.[18]

A similar reversal was also taking place in Scotland. During the 1540s, after the victory of the English at Solway Moss, a few advances had been made by Protestants under the aegis of the English. The aggressiveness of Protector Somerset against the Scots, though, drove them to form a political alliance with France; as a result, the Catholic church was strengthened. In 1547 a French naval force captured many leading Protestants at St. Andrews, sending off a good

---

[17] G. R. Elton, *Reformation Europe, 1517–1559* (New York, 1963), pp. 239–58.
[18] A. G. Dickens, *The English Reformation* (New York, 1964), pp. 259–82.

number to serve as galley slaves, including John Knox. In 1548, the young Queen Mary was betrothed to the French dauphin, and she left for France to be educated as a good Catholic. At home, her regent Arran was deposed and replaced by the very Catholic Queen Mother, Mary of Guise, in 1554. The following year, as in England, persecutions began against the Protestants.[19]

In France, where Calvinism had made immense inroads, the situation was even more treacherous. Whatever hopes the Calvinists may have had of converting some at the court, whether at the very top, with Francis I, or his sister Marguerite d'Angouleme, were dashed by 1540, when Francis promulgated the Edict of Fontainbleau, calling on his Parlements to persecute all kinds of heretics, and in the following years as this policy continued to be enforced.[20] Henry II only intensified the persecutions when he began his reign in 1547, establishing a special court for the trial of heretics, the Chambre Ardente, which convicted over five hundred French Protestants in its first three years.[21] In 1557 the Edict of Campiegne made leniency impossible for any judge, proclaiming that the only fitting punishment for heresy would be death. Two years later, when Henry II died and the crown passed to the young Francis II, the situation worsened. With the militantly Catholic Guises now in control of the government, the Calvinist Protestants (who now called themselves "Huguenots") found themselves threatened by a royal policy of extermination. By 1562, the country was sunk into civil war.[22]

The threat of persecution, which in most cases could only be resolved by exile, martyrdom, or apostasy, led some to ask the question: What is a subject to do when his sovereign tries to force him to commit idolatry? Should resistance to idolatry always be passive – that is, limited to exile or martyrdom – or do subjects have a right to defend themselves against such tyranny? More importantly, are Christians obligated in any way to wipe out idolatry by political revolution? Calvin's opposition to compromise with idolatry made this conflict between religious and secular demands one of the most

[19] Jasper Ridley, *John Knox*, pp. 59–65; Gordon Donaldson, *The Scottish Reformation* (Cambridge, 1960), pp. 30–1.

[20] Salmon, *Society in Crisis*, pp. 85–6.

[21] E. G. Leonard, *A History of Protestantism*, trans. J. M. H. Reid (2 vols., London, 1965–7), vol. 2, p. 110.

[22] Joseph Lecler, *Toleration and the Reformation*, trans. T. L. Westow (2 vols., London, 1960), vol. 2, p. 29; J. T. McNeill, *The History and Character of Calvinism* (New York, 1954), pp. 243–7. Also: Janet G. Gray, "The Origin of the Word Huguenot," *Sixteenth Century Journal*, 14.3: 349–59 (1983).

pressing questions for thousands of his followers, especially as their numbers increased and they became an ever-growing threat to the established religious and civil order.[23]

Because they faced persecution by their own governments, Calvinists throughout Europe naturally began to consider whether or not they had any right to resist, or even to overthrow, the powers that sought to wipe them out. This is not to say, of course, that each and every Calvinist pondered such questions, or that these theories were always a necessary precondition for revolution. For the most part, these theoretical formulations were the exclusive preoccupation of a relatively small group of leaders and ideologues, and their actual effect on the process of revolution is in many cases open to debate. What interests us here is not some larger question of causality concerning the relationship between revolutionary theory and revolutionary action, but rather a more particular question concerning the development of these Calvinist theories. Specifically, what we need to know in this case is how Calvinists used the issue of idolatry in their justifications for revolution.

Though the theories that developed were a response to a particular set of concrete political exigencies, they were informed, as is often the case with appeals to justice, by a complex series of precedents that involved a number of different political, legal, moral and theological issues.[24] Sixteenth-century theories of resistance, then, provided a justification for revolution that was at heart theological and exegetical, but that also depended on legal theory and appeals to natural law.[25] Though the language and the argumentation are at times markedly secular, and in some cases even ancient, it is possible to detect a common thread binding them together and giving them a distinctive shape. This is the issue of idolatry.

LUTHERANISM AND THE QUESTION OF RESISTANCE

Historians once used to credit French Huguenots with the development of theories of resistance. Recent research, however, has pro-

---

[23] Perez Zagorin, *Rebels and Rulers* (2 vols., Cambridge, 1982), vol. I, p. 156, argues that the increase in membership drawn from the nobility may have played a decisive role in the development of political resistance.

[24] W. D. J. Cargill Thompson: "Luther and the right of resistance to the Emperor," in *Church, Society and Politics*, Derek Baker, ed. (Oxford, 1975), esp. p. 161.

[25] Quentin Skinner, *The Foundations of Modern Political Thought* (2 vols., Cambridge, 1978), vol. 2, chap. 7. This point has been argued by Marvin W. Anderson in "Royal Idolatry: Peter Martyr and the Reformed Tradition," *ARG*, 69: 191 (1978).

posed that German Lutherans played an indispensable role in developing arguments later used by Calvinists.[26] It has also been shown that the idea of resistance was justified and generally accepted in secular and theological writings throughout the Middle Ages.[27] Some have even gone as far as to argue that the Calvinist theories actually posited nothing new or "distinctive," but rather rephrased medieval theories, or even parts of Justinian's *Digest*.[28]

No matter what the medieval background may have been, the roots of Calvinist resistance theories can be clearly delineated in Lutheranism.[29] Debate over the question of resistance began with the Lutherans in the Holy Roman Empire, who faced a determined Catholic opponent in Charles V. The primary aim of Lutheran theorists was not to wipe out idolatry, but rather to prevent the annihilation of their church; consequently, their resistance theories underwent a significant change between the 1520s and the 1530s, as the political situation in the empire became more threatening.[30]

At first, Luther and his associates opposed resistance to the emperor under all circumstances, arguing that the Gospel was a purely spiritual doctrine that should never be defended by force. Gradually, however, some of Luther's followers began to propose legal and constitutional arguments for resistance against an emperor who would persecute Protestants.[31] Curiously enough, these early arguments used the issues of worship and religion in a way opposite to that in which they would later be formulated in the "classic" theories of resistance. In 1529, for instance, Bugenhagen argued that the emperor's authority was legitimate only within a limited sphere. If he

[26] Thompson's article ("Luther") is the best study available on Lutheran resistance theories. Also useful is: Johannes Heckel, "Stellungnahme der Kirche der Reformation – Die Lutheraner," in *Widerstandsrecht und Grenzen der Staatsgewalt*, B. Pfister and G. Hildman, eds. (Berlin, 1956), pp. 32–44. A more recent contribution is that of Cynthia Grant Shoenberger, "The Development of the Lutheran Theory of Resistance: 1523–1530," *Sixteenth Century Journal*, 8: 61–76 (1977).

[27] Shoenberger, "Development," p. 62. Also: Johannes Spörl, "Gedanken um Widerstandsrecht und Tyrannenmord im Mittelalter," in Pfister and Hildman, *Grenzen der Staatsgewalt*, p. 11–31.

[28] This is argued rather forcefully by Quentin Skinner, "The Origins of the Calvinist Theory of Revolution," in *After the Reformation: Essays in Honor of J. H. Hexter*, B. Malament, ed. (Philadelphia, 1980). See also Skinner's magisterial *Foundations*, vol. I.

[29] Thompson, "Luther," p. 160.

[30] Thompson provides a very good survey of the political maneuvering that lay behind the development of Lutheran resistance theories ("Luther," p. 162ff.).

[31] Since Skinner, Shoenberger, and Thompson describe these arguments in detail, it is not necessary to recapitulate their summaries here. The primary sources dealing with German resistance theories have been ably collected by Heinz Scheible in *Das Widerstandsrecht als Problem der Deutschen Protestanten 1523–1546* (Gütersloh, 1969).

attempted to act in matters that rightly fell in God's sphere, that is, in matters of religion, the emperor was to be not only disobeyed, but also actively resisted by the princes.[32] In order to defend the Protestant cause against persecution, then, Bugenhagen argued that the emperor had no right to get involved in religious affairs. The primary consideration was resistance against persecution, not the maintenance of pure worship.[33]

This same theory was again presented in an anonymous theological opinion written at Wittenberg in 1530 to which Luther reluctantly agreed. This opinion stated that the sovereign could be resisted when he meddled in matters that were contrary to his charge or that did not belong to him and were really private matters. Religion was the "private matter" being referred to in this argument.[34]

A clear change occurred in the Lutheran position in 1536.[35] Whereas it had previously been argued that religion was outside the emperor's domain, it was now stated that all rulers had a duty to "protect and maintain Christians and the external worship of God against all unjust force." This opinion appeared in a landmark document signed by Luther, Melanchthon, Bugenhagen, Amsdorf, Jonas, and Cruciger.[36] The Lutheran position now clearly supported resistance on grounds of religion, stating that the Christian magistrate had a duty to uphold true religion, and that it was therefore incumbent upon the German princes to defend the Gospel:

In this case we conclude that every prince is responsible for maintaining and protecting Christians and their lawful, external worship against all unlawful powers; just as every prince is also responsible for protecting his pious subjects against all unlawful powers in regard to worldly affairs.

---

[32] Letter of Bugenhagen to Prince John of Saxony, in Scheible, *Widerstandsrecht*, p. 28.

[33] "Aber in den stucken, die Gott zugehoren, ist er noch keyser noch uberherr; er sol es auch nicht begehren; er ist auch noch nicht darzu von uns angenommen" (Scheible, *Widerstandsrecht*, p. 26.) In 1529 Luther was still opposed to resistance. Bugenhagen's opinion, then, supports Shoenberger's assertion that Luther is not the key figure in the development of Lutheran resistance theories (Shoenberger, "Development," p. 64).

[34] "Anonymes Theologisches Gutachten" (1530), in Scheible, *Widerstandsrecht*, p. 78. C. G. Shoenberger argues that the older Luther came to accept a notion of resistance based on constitutional and positive law, and finally even on natural law. "Luther on Resistance to Authority," *Journal of the History of Ideas*, 40: 3–20 (1979).

[35] Thompson provides a good analysis of the change ("Luther," pp. 190ff).

[36] This "Gutachten" is in Scheible, *Widerstandsrecht*, pp. 89–92. Thompson thinks this document was written primarily by Melanchton, but that Luther agreed with it ("Luther," p. 192).

These same theologians argued further, saying that the prince's duty to protect religion should be one of their highest priorities.[37] In the opinion of 1536 one finds three main lines of argument for a theory of resistance. The first has just been mentioned: Rulers have a duty to preserve true religion. The second is a constitutional argument that had previously been expressed in other Lutheran writings: The princes of the Empire are corulers with the emperor and have a say in running the empire. The third argument states that the emperor can be resisted when he attacks Christians as an agent of the pope.[38] The first two arguments were most influential for the subsequent development of Protestant political thought. It was out of a fusion of these two sets of ideas that there evolved the standard Protestant theory of resistance of the mid sixteenth century – the idea that the "inferior magistrates" had not only the right, but the duty to resist the supreme magistrate in defense of religion.[39]

Still, the Lutheran theories were limited in comparison to later Calvinist political thought. First, since Lutheran theories developed as a way of meeting the threat of religious persecution, they therefore remained more passive than aggressive. Secondly, Lutheranism made no attempt to make political resistance a way of waging war against false worship. In fact, the earlier theories had even tried to circumvent the worship issue when dealing with resistance to tyrants. The Calvinist theories, in contrast, would take an aggressive stance, making the issue of worship central to their argument and calling for a sustained political effort against "idolatry."[40]

CALVINIST THEORIES OF RESISTANCE

The Lutheran argument was adopted by Martin Bucer, who also stated that if the absolute power of a prince impaired the sovereignty of God, then the "inferior magistrates" had a right to call the prince to

---

[37] Scheible, *Widerstandsrecht*, pp. 89–90. "Das ist allein angezogen, damit des klarer sey, das fursten und alle oberkeiten schuldig sind, offentliche gewalt und unzucht, als ehezerreissung, zu weren. Und viel mehr sind sie schuldig, offentliche abgotterey zu weren, lauts den andern gebots."

[38] Thompson, "Luther," p. 199.

[39] Ibid., p. 200.

[40] Shoenberger makes the following observation about the difference between Lutheran and Calvinist resistance theories: "we may with justice, I think, call these later theories genuinely theories of revolution while the Lutherans had delineated no more than a notion of limited resistance" ("Development," p. 76).

account.[41] The same principle again surfaced in the Magdeburg *Bekentniss* (or *Confession*) of 1550, which was written against the efforts of Charles V to impose Catholicism on the city.[42] This tract, which was later used by Beza, is a direct link between the Lutheran and Reformed resistance theories. The *Bekentniss* states that a king who persecutes the true faith is no longer a legitimate ruler, because it is the duty of a king to defend the Law of God. It also affirms that such a king can be resisted by the territorial princes who have been established to uphold the will of God.[43] Although Bucer and the *Bekentniss* proved influential in the development of a theory of resistance on religious grounds, the clearest expression of these principles was left to some of Calvin's followers.

John Calvin himself made it clear that the individual had no right to resist a tyrant, since all rulers, good or bad, were appointed by God. "It is impossible," he said, "to resist the magistrate without, at the same time, resisting God himself."[44] It was the duty of the ruler to ensure true religion, but if he failed to fulfill this duty his subjects had only two options: to flee or face persecution. It has already been pointed out that while Calvin called on rulers to wipe out idolatry, he never advocated popular iconoclasm or armed resistance to idolatrous rulers.

It can be argued, however, that by consistently urging the people to hate idolatrous worship and abstain from it, Calvin was implicitly advising civil disobedience. There can be little doubt that Calvin's writings and the sermons and writings of Calvinist pastors helped bring the religious crisis to a head with their uncompromising attitude. Still, this type of disobedience is passive. There is little revolutionary thought in Calvin.[45] In every edition of the *Institutes*, from

---

[41] Hans Baron, "Calvinist Republicanism and Its Historical Roots," *Church History* 8: 36 (1939). Also: Shoenberger, "Development," pp. 68–70, 75.

[42] *Bekentniss, Unterricht und Vermanung der Pfarrhern und Prediger der Christlichen Kirchen zu Magdeburg* (1550). The circumstances surrounding the publication of this treatise were described by the contemporary John Sleidan in his *General History of the Reformation of the Church* (English trans. of the Latin original, London, 1689), pp. 436, 496. Also: Friedrich Hulse, *Die Stadt Magdeburg im Kampfe für den Protestantismus während der Jahre 1547–1551* (Halle, 1892). Robert Kingdon has ascribed a significant importance to the *Bekentniss*. "The Political Resistance of the Calvinists in France and the Low Countries," *Church History* 27: 227, 230 (1958). Also: Esther Hildebrandt, "The Magdeburg *Bekentniss* as a Possible Link Between German and English Resistance Theory in the Sixteenth Century," *ARG* 71: 227–53 (1980).

[43] *Bekentniss*, fol. K ii.

[44] *Institutes*, IV.20.23. Ernst Wolf, "Das Problem des Widerstandsrecht bei Calvin," in Pfister and Hildman, *Grenzen der Staatsgewalt*, pp. 45–58.

[45] It is not my intention here to debate whether or not Calvin was a pioneer of democratic thought. Different opinions about this question have been collected in

1536 to 1559, Calvin argues that popular magistrates "who have been appointed to curb the tyranny of kings" have a duty to overthrow idolatrous tyrants.[46] As an example of such magistrates Calvin pointed to the Spartan ephors, the Roman tribunes, and the Athenian demarchs. Although this statement has been interpreted to mean that Calvin espoused a theory of religious resistance,[47] there are limitations to this "theory." It is a troublesome issue that has led some to call Calvin a "master of equivocation."[48]

In the first place, Calvin always preached unlimited and unqualified obedience to established powers, arguing that the private individual had no right to resist. Secondly, Calvin never defined the role of the "inferior magistrates," nor did he say in what manner they were to correct tyrants. He also limited his examples to ancient history, making no direct reference to contemporary officials, such as the members of the Estates General in France. Finally, he made only a general reference to "tyranny" without specifying the issue of religious coercion. All in all, then, Calvin's thought on political resistance was rather sketchy.[49] It remained for his followers to create a forceful theory of resistance based on religious grounds.

Pierre Viret

Calvinist opposition to compromise with idolatry assumed a more aggressive political dimension at the hands of Pierre Viret, Calvin's

abridged form by Robert Linder and Robert Kingdon, in *Calvin and Calvinism, Sources of Democracy?* (Lexington, Mass., 1970). I do think, however, that Hans Baron and Winthrop Hudson place too much emphasis on the importance of Calvin's statement in the *Institutes*. Hans Baron, "Calvinist Republicanism and Its Historical Roots," *Church History*, 8: 30–42 (1939); and Winthrop S. Hudson, "Democratic Freedom and Religious Faith in the Reformed Tradition," *Church History*, 15: 177–94 (1946).

[46] *Institutes*, IV.20.31.

[47] In addition to the Baron, "Calvinist Republicanism," and Hudson, "Democratic Freedom," see John T. McNeill, "The Democratic Element in Calvin's Thought," *Church History*, 18: 153–71 (1949).

[48] "Calvin . . . who wrote a brilliantly logical prose, was a master of equivocation. His work possessed the great political virtue of ambiguity. It was subject not so much to a private process of internalization and emotional recapitulation, as to a public process of development, accretion, distortion and use." Michael Walzer, *The Revolution of the Saints: A Study in the Origins of Radical Politics* (Cambridge, Mass., 1965), p. 23.

[49] Calvin made minor modifications on his position, but no substantial changes, in his *Homilies on I Samuel* (1562–63; published 1604). CR 29.238–9. For the most recent discussion of Calvin's position see *Journal of Ecclesiastical History*, 32 (1981): H. A. Lloyd, "Calvin and the Duty of the Guardians to Resist," with a comment by Peter Stein (pp. 65–70); and Walter Ullman, "Calvin and the duty of the Guardians to Resist: A Further Comment," p. 499.

close friend and associate. At first sight, Viret's political theory seems to differ little from Calvin's. Viret accepted all authority, both spiritual and secular, as coming directly from God and based on the principle of God's will for the world.[50] Like Calvin, Viret always advised obedience to civil authorities, observance of law and order, and caution in political activities. He was opposed to illegal iconoclasm on the same grounds as Calvin, thinking that only those who had legitimate authority were empowered to remove idolatry from a community. Viret thought that the role of the true Christian prince and magistrate was to act as a "guardian" and "foster father" of the Church.[51] According to him, the implication of this teaching was that the ruler should protect the true Church from all injury, make sure it had the support of the law, and try to see that all the citizens had a chance to hear the Gospel message. It also meant that the magistrate was personally responsible for the abolition of idolatry:

> One ought to leave to the magistrate those things which pertain to his office. His duty is to cast down all the idols and instruments of idolatry, and to put an end to all public scandals in the Church, just as Ezekiel and Josiah did, according to the word of God.[52]

Viret always cautioned that it was not lawful for private citizens to remove images, statues, and altars from the churches without the consent of the government. He pointed out that too many Protestants were misreading the Deuteronomical injunction against idols as a license for wanton iconoclasm, because the "true" interpretation of these passages revealed that the faithful were not to remove the idols until they had political control of their nation.[53] The correct way to eradicate idolatry was to "first destroy the idols in the hearts of the people" through preaching and teaching and then allow the civil officials to destroy all traces of idolatry in the churches.[54]

---

[50] Robert Dean Linder, *The Political Ideas of Pierre Viret* (Geneva, 1964), p. 57.

[51] Pierre Viret, *Instruction Chrestienne en la Doctrine de la Loy et de l'Evangile* (2 vols., Geneva, 1564), vol. I, pp. 378, 604; *L'Interim, Fait par Dialogues* (Lyon, 1565), p. 335; and *Remonstrances aux Fideles qui Conversent entre les Papistes* (Geneva, 1547). I have used the 1559 edition of *Remonstrances*, which was published as *Traittez Divers pour l'Instruction des Fidèles qui Resident et Conversent en Lieus et Pais Esquels Il ne Leur est Permi de Vivre en la Pureté et Liberté de l'Evangile* (Geneva, 1559), pt. 5, pp. 27–30, and to which all subsequent references refer.

[52] *Remonstrances*, p. 27. The Lutheran influence seems evident here, but Viret himself never acknowledges it. This leads Robert Linder to ignore the Lutheran background, making Viret seem more of a pioneer than he really was.

[53] *L'Interim*, pp. 394–7.

[54] *Instruction Chrestienne*, vol. I, p. 168; *L'Interim*, pp. 204–7; *Remonstrances*, pp. 27–30; *Le Monde a l'Empire et le Monde Demoniacle* (Geneva, 1561), pp. 287–8; *Instruction Chrestienne*, vol. I, pp. 302–3; 452–3; *L'Interim*, pp. 459–61.

Yet, as can be deduced from what has already been said, Viret's call to obedience was equivocal. Mixed in with his pleas for obedience were, as Robert Linder has observed, "inflammatory language, revolutionary innuendos and stated qualifications to the Christian's obligation to obey political superiors."[55] And the basis for these reservations was the issue of "true religion" versus "idolatry."

Viret's view of the relationship between civil law and religion rested on the assumption that civil authorities should never legislate contrary to the Holy Scriptures. He made a clear distinction between "good laws" and "wicked laws," proposing that wicked laws were those "which are made contrary to all right and equity in order to hinder the course of the Gospel."[56] In this way, then, Viret separated laws into those which could be obeyed freely and those that should not be obeyed, weakening the concept of the absolute power of secular rulers.

In discussing the relationship between Christians and their civil rulers, Viret made it clear that the religious issue was of supreme importance. He dealt with the conflict between secular and religious duties by placing a hierarchy of values upon the Ten Commandments, saying that the First Table always took precedence over the Second. (It should be remembered that the First Table deals largely with questions of worship, and that it is the source of much of the Protestant argumentation against the "idolatry" of the Catholic Church.) According to Viret, man's relationship with God – as expressed in the first four commandments – came before man's ethical obligations to his fellow man. Thus, even though the Law commands one to obey one's parents, it would be wrong to obey them if they commanded idolatrous worship. Viret resolved conflicting commands by appealing to the supremacy of man's life of worship. Consequently, he was also able to say that the commands of irreligious magistrates did not have to be obeyed when they were opposed to the first four commandments of the Law.[57]

Viret's teaching on obedience to secular rulers was limited in still another way, and again the basis for the reservations was the issue of "pure worship" versus "idolatry." Viret made a distinction between

---

[55] Linder, *Political Ideas*, p. 129.
[56] *Instruction Chrestienne*, vol. I, p. 122.
[57] *Instruction Chrestienne*, vol. I, p. 280; *L'Interim*, pp. 158–9; *Romonstrances*, p. 240. Although Viret's treatment of the two tables in regard to civil matters is influential, it was not novel. In 1539 Martin Luther had argued that Christian magistrates had a duty to prevent blasphemy and could thus resist an emperor in defense of the first table of the law (WA 39/2.78). Also: Thompson, "Luther," p. 198.

"good magistrates" and "good princes" on the one hand and "tyrants" on the other, arguing that Christians should give their wholehearted allegiance only to "true kings and princes."[58] He noted that it was exceedingly difficult for even the most devout Christian to be obedient when he was being constantly abused by secular authorities for the sake of religion.[59] More specifically, he advised his readers to honor and obey magistrates in all matters of the physical body and earthly goods insofar as was possible without ever "consenting to idolatry,"[60] "going against our conscience,"[61] or "hurting our soul."[62] Even in his most sweeping and generalized statement of the obligation of Christians to their rulers, Viret slipped in a qualifying phrase. Again, the crucial issue is the proper honor and glory due to God:

> Moreover, I confess to you that it is always necessary to give honor and reverence to princes and that it is necessary to obey them in all things which relate solely to the body and to goods, and which do not affect adversely or infringe in any way upon one's salvation or the glory of God, even when they are tyrants who abuse their subjects with great extortions and violence.[63]

Viret thus hinted that resistance to political authority was justified when rulers sought to encroach upon religion against the glory of God. At times, Viret seemed to counsel a passive form of resistance, much like Calvin. For instance, he advised Christians to resort to prayer and patience as the "best arms" that they could use against tyranny, not only to defend themselves, but also to "fight and conquer."[64]

Nonetheless, Viret prescribed more than just passive resistance, urging his readers to confess Christ openly, even against the law. He conceived of instances when "righteous disobedience" to cruel political edicts that opposed true religion could be defended by God's Law. In fact, Viret would say that obedience to God always came before obedience to men when the civil and religious spheres came into

---

[58] *Instruction Chrestienne*, vol. I, p. 461.

[59] *De l'Authorite et Perfection de la Doctrine des Sainctes Escritures, et du Ministere d'Iclelle* (Lyon, 1564), prefatory letter, Sig. viii; *L'Interim*, prefatory letter, sigs. 1.vii verso and 2.i.

[60] *Epistre Envoyée aux Fideles Conversans Entre les Chrestiens Papistiques* (1543): *Traittez Divers*, pt. 1, p. 93.

[61] *Epistres aux Fideles pour les Instruire et Admonester et Exhorter Touchant leur Office* (Geneva, 1559).

[62] *Disputations Chrestiennes en Maniere de Deviz, Devisées par Dialogues* (Geneva, 1544), p. 91.

[63] *Le Monde a l'Empire*, p. 288.

[64] *L'Interim*, prefatory letter, sigs. 2.v–2.vi.

conflict.[65] Also, Viret made it clear that it was necessary sometimes to ignore certain laws, especially "wicked laws" that made it illegal for men to "truly serve God," or that set up the prince above God and the scriptures.[66]

Viret warned rulers on occasion that they could only push Christians so far without inciting rebellion. In the first place, he calls the judgment of God down on godless tyrants, saying that those who try to destroy true religion are often destroyed by God.[67] And not only are tyrants alone punished, but those who assist them as well:

Because the people who have taken pleasure in the tyranny of tyrants, or who have aided them will receive the same payment as those with whom they have been in league. Because the same God who judges and punishes them [the tyrants] still lives, and is as just and powerful with one as he is with the other.[68]

In this respect, then, Viret says that obedience to tyrants can be a punishable sin. He also tries to intimidate tyrants by saying that even a good horse with a noble spirit can become rebellious when pushed too far or mistreated too often. Even the most humble and obedient subjects, he warns, could rebel when pushed to the brink. Viret noted that the "popular furor" of the people is hard to control once they are angered and moved to action, and that unrestrained tyranny often causes bloody rebellions.[69]

Viret's unwillingness to compromise, so typically Calvinist, did much to increase the religious tension that finally erupted into war in the 1560s. Certain elements in Viret's arguments could easily justify the political resistance offered by the Huguenots, especially his belief that obedience to God in matters of faith and worship took precedence over obedience to secular rulers. For Viret, religion was always the supreme consideration and obedience to God the most important rule:

Though it is necessary to support the shortcomings of princes and of other people, there are faults and then there are faults. We cannot in good con-

---

[65] *Remonstrances,* p. 300: "Car ils ne peuvent estre vrais serviteurs de Dieu, s'ils ne craignent plus Dieu que les hommes, aussi ils craindront plus de luy desobeir et de l'offenser, que de desobeir aux hommes et de les offenser, si grans Rois et Princes puissent–ils estre."

[66] Ibid., pp. 241–2: "Car si les loix estoient mauvaises et contre Dieu, il n'y estoit point obliée. Si elles estoient bonnes, luy n'eust pas peché contre les loix, mais les tyrans pechoient contre icelles, condamnans celuy lequel les loix iugeoient innocent."

[67] Ibid., p. 110.

[68] Ibid., p. 119; cf. p. 309.

[69] *Le Monde a l'Empire,* pp. 295–302.

science stand for those things which God does not want us to support . . . for how can we best honor God if not by obeying him? And how can we dishonor him the most, if not by disobeying him?[70]

If it can be argued that the seeds of the idea of righteous Christian resistance are found in Calvin,[71] a much stronger case can be made for Pierre Viret. Pierre Viret criticized all secular rulers who persecuted the true church, calling them "tyrants," and also advised the faithful that it was not necessary to obey civil commands that went against the Gospel. Although Viret did not use specific historical examples of the rights of lesser magistrates to depose a sovereign, as did Calvin, he stated clearly that lesser magistrates could try to "correct" the government of a tyrant if they had a constitutional right to do so within their country.[72]

Viret's theory of the right of magistrates to resist a tyrant on religious grounds is one of the earliest Calvinist expressions of a theory of resistance. When the later Lutheran theories are taken into account it may seem as if Viret's significance is diminished, but Viret presented the Lutheran arguments in a more coherent and forceful manner. Consequently, his influence on the development of French constitutionalist thought and Huguenot resistance is significant, especially when his popularity is taken into account. In addition, the influence of Viret on other Calvinists offers "a tantalizing possibility for further investigation."[73] Among the heirs of Viret's theory are Theodore Beza, who was his close friend and colleague, Phillipe du Plessis-Mornay, John Knox, Christopher Goodman, and John Ponet. We shall deal with these men shortly.

With Viret, then, the issue of idolatry becomes a political question. Because he refused compromise, as a good Calvinist was required to do, Viret would not accept any corruption of the "true religion" or any attempt by secular rulers to impose idolatrous worship on the populace. One outcome of this attitude was the development of a theory of resistance long before the actual eruption of religious warfare in France.[74] Viret's work proves that a coherent ideology for

---

[70] *Remonstrances*, p. 359.
[71] McNeill, "Democratic Element," p. 162.
[72] *Remonstrances*, pp. 282, 287ff.; *L'Interim*, pp. 96–8.
[73] It has been argued that since Viret wrote about resistance in 1547, it is probable that he influenced the writers of the Magdeburg *Bekentniss* (1550). The *Bekentniss*, though, could just as well have relied on the Lutheran theories upon which Viret builds. Linder, *Political Ideas*, p. 140.
[74] Linder comments on the influence of Viret's political thought: "Viret's ideas on the subject of political resistance add weight to a growing body of evidence that Calvinism was in many ways a revolutionary religious organization . . . Viret provided

resistance was in fact developed prior to the outbreak of armed conflicts, and that the Hugenots did not have to look very far to find
theological and moral justifications for their actions. Furthermore, it
is significant that these justifications centered on the issue of "true
worship" versus "idolatry." Whether or not Viret's theories are an
honest reflection of the motivations of all Huguenot revolutionaries is
another question altogether – one that is beyond the scope of this
study. Again, what interests us here is the development of the justifications for revolution, not the causal relationship between theory and
action.

Nonetheless, the case of Calvinist resistance theories does provide
a good opportunity to observe, in a general way, how ideology influences revolution. As is the case in our own day with the Marxist *credo*,
the Calvinist call for change was formulated as a response to a complex set of circumstances. Revolutionary theory, whether Calvinist or
Marxist, has certain aims. These aims consist of grievances and demands that are generalized into programs for change, which are directed against the existing order. The rebel mentality, expressed in its
justifying beliefs and ideology, becomes the framework for the aims
and grievances, and therefore also functions as the conscious raison
d'être for the programs of the movement.[75] The ideology becomes
one grand symbolic package around which revolutionaries can rally
in their struggle against oppression (however that may be defined).
"Liberation" from a certain system is the objective of revolutionaries,
and their ideology is developed in a way that reflects the contrast in
values between the oppressors and the rebels in a simplified manner.
For Marxists it may be the catchword "capitalism" that automatically
conjures up the full meaning of oppression; for Calvinists it was
"idolatry." In either case, the reasons given for "liberation" as not
only proper, but absolutely necessary, are imbedded in the ideology
and its symbols. Revolutionaries need not understand how their ideology was generated, or even what it means, in order to march into
battle: The promise of change, formed as it is by specific grievances
against concrete circumstances, is the primary motivation. But this
does not make the ideology unnecessary: Even in its most simplified
form, even as a battle cry that is insincerely voiced, it becomes an
inescapable medium through which grievances and programs for
change are expressed.

the kind of justification for political resistance that could be extended rather easily to
include all kinds of popular uprising against oppressive governments" (*Political
Ideas*, p. 141).
[75] Zagorin, *Rebels and Rulers*, vol. I, pp. 39–40.

It is with such considerations in mind, then, that these theories of resistance may be viewed as inherently "religious," and that it becomes possible to say that religion was at the heart of Calvinist revolutionary ideology. It must also be kept in mind that when one speaks of "religious issues" behind the Wars of Religion, one is speaking about reactions to very concrete situations, and more specifically, about practical questions regarding worship and its social dimensions, rather than about speculative theological issues. Protestant hatred focused most often on the "idols" of the Catholic church and the oppression they came to represent.

THE FURTHER DEVELOPMENT OF CALVINIST RESISTANCE THEORIES

There were many causes of political disaffection in sixteenth-century France: judicial corruption, administrative inefficiency and ecclesiastical venality, to name a few. These problems, however, were not enough by themselves to generate the opposition that eventually surfaced against the monarchy in the mid sixteenth century. The catalytic element was the "religious issue."[76] It was Calvinist dissent that crystallized the long-standing opposition to the monarchy, especially since it was the influential social strata that were most attracted to Calvinism: the humanist elite, the bourgeoisie, and the nobility. Most important was the accession of converts from the nobility in large numbers, as well as the long delay in reaching a religious settlement.[77] But the nature of the Huguenot movement is not the issue here. Instead, we shall focus on how some of the intellectual leaders of this political coalition formulated a theory of resistance based on religious grounds, primarily on the issue of idolatry.

Theodore Beza's *On the Right of Magistrates* published in 1574, ten years after Calvin's death, revived the issue of political resistance in France during a time of great turmoil. It is based on the Magdeburg

---

[76] H. G. Koenigsberger has observed that it was the religious issue that made the existence of religious parties possible in France. "The Organization of Revolutionary Parties in France and the Netherlands during the Sixteenth Century," *Journal of Modern History*, 27: 336 (1955). The same point has been made somewhat indirectly by Julian H. Franklin, who observed that one of the most remarkable facts about the political agitation of sixteenth-century France was "the rapidity with which it subsided" once a religious settlement had been reached under Henry IV. *Constitutionalism and Resistance in the Sixteenth Century: Three Treatises by Hotman, Beza and Mornay* (New York, 1969), Introduction, p. 44.

[77] Franklin, *Constitutionalism and Resistance*, p. 18. For an analysis of the social complexion of French Calvinism: Salmon, *Society in Crisis*, pp. 117–45.

Bekentniss, and Beza makes his debt known in the subtitle.[78] A year before its publication, another work had also explored the issue of the right of magistrates to rebel: This was François Hotman's *Francogallia.*[79] Hotman's treatise was a significant contribution to the development of French constitutionalist thought. It was not so much a statement of the principle of resistance as an investigation of historical precedents for magisterial resistance in France. Beza's treatise transformed Hotman's reflections on French history into a general constitutionalist doctrine of the state, making the theoretical principles applicable to the contemporary situation, and placing a special emphasis on the religious issue.[80]

Beza says in the *Rights* that all earthly authority flows from God and that all obedience is due solely to God. The first question in the treatise asks: "Should magistrates as well as God be unconditionally obeyed?" The answer is straightforward:

The only will that is a perpetual and immutable criterion of justice is the will of the one God and none other. Hence Him alone we are obliged to obey without exception. Princes too would have to be obeyed implicitly if they were always the voice of God's commandments. But since the opposite too often happens, an exception is imposed upon obedience, when their commands are irreligious or iniquitous. Irreligious commands are those which order us to do what the First Table of God's Law forbids, or forbid us to do what it commands.[81]

Here we find Viret's principle of the Two Tables of the Law, the First demanding obedience over the Second. Thus, from the very start, Beza centers his theory of resistance on the question of religion and worship. This reveals a shift from Lutheran argumentation, and is typically "Calvinist." Whereas the Magdeburg *Bekentniss* had argued that it was lawful for the inferior magistrate to defend himself against the superior who compelled him to "forsake the truth," stressing the issue of conscience, Beza stressed the question of worship.[82]

---

78 *Du Droit des Magistrats sur les Subjects. Traitté Tres-necessaire en ce Temps, pour Advertir de Leur Devoir, Tant les Magistrats que les Subjects: Publiée par Ceux de Magdebourg, l'an MDL; et Maintenant Reveu et Augumenté de Plusieurs Raisons et Examples.*

79 François Hotman, *Francogallia* (1573). A partial translation of this treatise can be found in Franklin's *Constitutionalism and Resistance,* pp. 53–96. For more on Hotman: Donald R. Kelley, *François Hotman: A Revolutionary's Ordeal* (Princeton, 1973).

80 I disagree with Franklin on this point. He pays little attention to the religious issue in Beza, and even says that "his theoretical grounds are not, at bottom, theological" (*Constitutionalism and Resistance,* p. 32).

81 *Du Droit des Magistrats,* trans. J. H. Franklin, in *Constitutionalism and Resistance,* p. 101.

82 Q. Skinner, *Foundations,* vol. 2, p. 209.

In dealing with the issue of persecution, Beza asks, "Do subjects have any remedy against a legitimate sovereign who has become a notorious tyrant?" His answer is very similar to that of Viret and the later Lutheran theorists as well: He assumes that the protection and enforcement of true religion is an inherent obligation of the state. When a king becomes idolatrous and tries to force his subjects into idolatry, the people have a right to rebel through their magistrates if "correct" worship has been guaranteed by public law. Viret had cautiously founded the right of magisterial resistance on constitutional principles, but now Beza was establishing it on existing public law.[83] Like Viret, Beza also thought it was a *duty* of the lesser magistrates to offer resistance to "flagrant tyranny" by force of arms, if necessary, until such time as the proper legislative power could reestablish an appropriate government by "common deliberation."[84] All in all, then, Beza's *On the Right of Magistrates* was a forceful and clearly argued restatement of Viret's principles of resistance, and its major contribution was its presentation of Huguenot resistance as the defense of an established right that was sanctioned by law.

One of the most radical French expressions of the right of resistance was that voiced by Phillipe du Plessis-Mornay in his *Vindiciae contra tyrannos* (1579). Julian H. Franklin has said that Mornay was not a theologian trying to soothe conscientious doubts, "but a soldier and a statesman exhorting to revolt."[85] Still, Franklin himself is willing to admit that Mornay is more militant than Beza when it comes to considering the issue of resistance on religious as opposed to strictly political grounds.

Mornay does not let resistance depend on constitutional history or public law, as Viret and Beza did, but rather upon a general assumption that every government has an overriding religious obligation to maintain in all cases, and that if this obligation is breached anywhere, then the ruler can be deposed by his people. Mornay addresses this issue in the first question of the *Vindiciae,* where he asks, "Are subjects bound to obey princes if their orders contradict the law of God?" His answer explains the contractual agreement among God, rulers, and the people in feudal terms:

---

[83] Franklin points out that partial toleration had already been conceded to the Protestants by the edict of January 1562, which Beza himself had helped to draft, and that the resistance theory presented by Beza is therefore "the defense of an established right which has been sanctioned by the country as a whole" (*Constitutionalism and Resistance*, p. 39).

[84] *Du Droit des Magistrats*, in Franklin, *Constitutionalism and Resistance*, p. 112.

[85] *Constitutionalism and Resistance*, p. 39. For more on Mornay: Raoul Patry, *Phillipe du Plessis-Mornay, un Huguenot Homme d'Etat, 1549–1623* (Paris, 1933).

If the vassal does not keep the fealty he swore, his fief is forfeited and he is legally deprived of all prerogatives. So also with the king. If he neglects God, if he goes over to His enemies and is guilty of felony towards God, his kingdom is forfeited of right and is often lost in fact.[86]

Mornay extends this obligation to all nations, regardless of their constitutional history, basing his argument on what is commonly referred to as "covenant theology": The people and the king enter a covenant with God to maintain proper order, including, of course, proper order in worship. Each individual, as well as the king, is responsible for seeing that this covenant is fulfilled.

The importance of the worship issue for Mornay's covenant theory becomes apparent when he tries to provide a historical example. Mornay uses the case of King Josiah, indicating that the covenant between God and the Jews stipulated that "the king and his entire people would worship God according to the prescription of His Law as individuals and would act collectively to protect their worship."[87] Moreover, Mornay is not content with merely using this ancient covenant as an example. He insists that the same principles apply to his own day, arguing that Christian rulers stand in the place of the Jewish kings, and that it is their duty to ensure the fulfillment of God's Law.[88]

Mornay proposes that if the ancient Jews were enjoined to resist godless rulers, the same must surely hold for Christians. Mornay stipulates that it is the duty of the people to safeguard pure worship. When dealing with this issue, then, Mornay insists that the question of idolatry is of prime importance, particularly because the violation of "pure worship" and the persecution of the true Church are the principal grounds for resistance:

A religious people not only will restrain a prince in the act of doing violence to God's law, but will from the beginning prevent gradual changes arising from his guilt or negligence, for the true worship of God may be slowly corrupted over extended periods of time. Moreover, they will not only refuse to tolerate crimes committed against God's majesty in public, but will constantly strive to remove all occasions for such crime . . . It is, then, not only lawful for Israel to resist a king who overturns the Law and the Church of

---

[86] *Vindiciae*, trans. J. H. Franklin, in *Constitutionalism and Resistance*, p. 143. (All subsequent citations refer to the Franklin translation.)

[87] *Vindiciae*, p. 144.

[88] Ibid.: "The covenant remains the same; the stipulations are unaltered; and there are the same penalties if these are not fulfilled, as well as the same God, omnipotent, avenging perfidy. And as the Jews were bound to keep the Law, so are Christians to observe the Gospels."

God, but if they do not do so, they are guilty of the same crime and subject to the same penalty.[89]

The burden for maintaining pure religion, however, rests not on every individual, but on the magistrates who represent the people.[90] Mornay says that each individual is bound to serve God in the vocation to which he is called, but private persons have no political power. Since God did not "give them the sword," he says, He does not expect them to use it.[91] Mornay divides the religious duties of the magistracy and the private individual in a way that again places great emphasis on the purity of worship. He says that it is the duty of the magistrate to see that "the Temple of God is not ruined or polluted" and is safe from corruption and damage, both externally and internally. The private individual is solely responsible for his own person and has to see that his own body, "which is God's Temple," is pure and fit for the dwelling of God's Spirit.[92]

But what may private subjects do when a king drives them to idolatry? Mornay differentiates between two possible sets of circumstances. First, if the magistrates or officials empowered by the people should intervene against the king, then private persons are obliged to "obey and follow and use all their energy and zeal as soldiers on the side of God to support these holy enterprises." This is an open call to political revolution as a way of correcting idolatry. The second situation is one where the magistrates do nothing to resist the idolatrous commands of a king. In such cases, Mornay advises the people to flee to another country. Under no conditions would he sanction an uprising that was not led by the magistracy. Still, Mornay would sanction localized resistance. He believed that residents of towns and provinces, as the individual parts of a covenanted kingdom, were each responsible for the observance of the covenant among their people. Consequently, they were subject to divine punishment if they did not "at least drive idolatry beyond their borders." This meant, of course, that in some cases secession from the larger body politic was advisable.[93]

---

[89] Ibid., p. 149. Peter Martyr echoed this sentiment in 1554, writing "wherefore for as much as idolatry is the cause of captivity, pestilence and famine, and overthrowing of publique wealthes, shall it not pertaine unto the Magistrate to repress it, and to keep the true sound religion?" (*Commentary on Judges*, 1564 ed., fols. 266v–267r).

[90] Ibid.: "When we speak of the people collectively, we mean those who receive authority from the people, that is, the magistrates below the king who have been elected by the people or established in some other way."

[91] Ibid., p. 154.

[92] Ibid., p. 155.

[93] Ibid., p. 157.

Mornay was among the most forceful Calvinist advocates of armed resistance against idolatry. He argued that although the Church was not enlarged by arms, by arms it could be justly defended.[94] The theory of resistance grounded on opposition to idolatry had not yet been brought to the point of advocating open rebellion by the populace, but it had come far enough to sanction magisterially led revolutions and geographical secessions. It would be very difficult to find another orthodox French Calvinist who wrote more aggressively against governments that supported idolatry.[95]

The development of resistance theories among Calvinists was not restricted to France. A decade and a half before the political situation in France caused the issue of resistance to surface, three Marian exiles nurtured in Calvin's Geneva had already argued that the Christian people, like the Jews of the Old Testament, were obliged by a covenant with God to defend true religion at all costs. These spokesmen for resistance against "idolatrous" tyranny were John Knox, Christopher Goodman, and John Ponet.[96] Among them, the Calvinist theory of resistance reached even more radical conclusions. John Knox, for instance, became convinced that the nobility and the estates were responsible for putting all idolaters to death – including monarchs – at the command of God.[97]

---

[94] Ibid., p. 156.

[95] There were some French Calvinists who advocated popular rebellion, but their views were disowned by the leaders of the movement. One such example is the anonymous treatise entitled *La Defense Civile et Militaire des Innocents et de l'Eglise de Christ* (1565). Robert Kingdon describes its views in detail and comments on its impact among both Catholics and Protestants: *Geneva and the Consolidation*, p. 153ff.

[96] John Knox, *The First Blast of the Trumpet against the Monstrous Regiment of Women* (Geneva, 1558); *Appellation to the Nobility and Estates of Scotland* (Geneva, 1558); Christopher Goodman, *How Superior Powers Ought to Be Obeyed of Their Subjects, and Wherein They May Lawfully by God's Word Be Disobeyed and Resisted* (Geneva, 1558); John Ponet, *A Short Treatise of Politicke Power* (Strassburg, 1556).

[97] Greaves, *Theology and Revolution*. Also the two articles by Richard L. Greaves: "John Knox, the Reformed Tradition, and the Development of Resisitance Theory," *Journal of Modern History*, 48: supplement (September 1976); and "Calvinism, Democracy and the Political Thought of John Knox," *Occasional Papers of the American Society for Reformation Research*, 1: 81–91 (December, 1977). Dan G. Danner has written a brief, but helpful article on the work of Knox, Goodman, and Ponet: "Christopher Goodman and the English Protestant Tradition of Civil Disobedience," *Sixteenth Century Journal*, 8: 61–73 (1977). Robert Linder has studied the connections between Viret and these men in "Pierre Viret and the Sixteenth-Century English Protestants," *ARG*, 58: 149–70 (1967). Michael Walzer has compared the character of Goodman and Knox's attitude toward resistance with that of the Huguenots in *The Revolution of the Saints*, chap. 3, passim, esp. pp. 108–9. Also the article by Leo F. Solt: "Revolutionary Calvinist Parties in England under Elizabeth I and Charles I," *Church History* 28: 234–9 (1958). Another fine contribution to the study of English resistance theories is Marvin Anderson's "Royal Idolatry: Peter Martyr and the Reformed Tradition," *ARG*, 69: 157–200 (1978).

Knox was able to formulate such a policy by proposing a separation between the person of the ruler and the office he was supposed to fulfill. This is a distinctively Calvinist development, beyond Lutheranism. It had been the common assumption that all rulers and magistrates, whether or not they fulfilled their office properly, had to be regarded as powers ordained by God. Once it began to be emphasized that all such powers were established to fulfill a particular set of duties, the new question arose which asked whether a ruler who failed in his duties could still be considered as a genuinely ordained power. The Lutherans never broke completely with the older notion of all power being divinely ordained. It is only in the 1550s with Goodman, Knox, and Ponet, that the separation of person and office is finally effected.[98] Goodman, for one, makes the distinction very clear. First, he lays down a general principle:

> First we maye herof justlie conclude, that to obeye man in anie thinge contrary to God, or his precepts thoge he be in hiest actoritie, or never so orderly called there unto . . . is no obedience at all, but disobedience . . . there is no obedience against God which is not plaine disobedience.[99]

Then, almost in a literal sense, he moves in for the kill:

> For what is kinge, Quene, or Emperour compared to God? . . . Of the whiche we may justlie conclude, that by the ordinance of God, no other kinges or Rulers ought to be chosen to rule over us, but suche as will seeke his honor and glorie, and will commaunde and do nothing contrarie to his Lawe . . . But if they will abuse his power, liftinge themselves above God and above their brethren, to draw them to idolatrie, and to oppresse them, and their contrie: then are they no more to be obeyed in any commandments tending to that ende . . . For the same cause God commanded Moyses to hange up all the capitaynes and heads of the people, for that by their example they made the people idolatrers also: he had no respect to their auctoritie, because they were Rulers, but so muche the rather woulde he have them so sharplie punished, that is, hanged agaynst the sunne without mercy.[100]

By stating their case in this way, these theorists also promoted the development of the covenant theory. This development, in turn, had even more serious implications for revolution, and the focus, once again, was the issue of idolatry: for the "duties" that Goodman, Ponet,

---

[98] Skinner (*Foundations*, vol. 2, p. 398) argues that this "private law" agreement has its roots in Calvin himself.

[99] Christopher Goodman, *Superior Powers* (1558), in Edmund S. Morgan (ed.), *Puritan Political Ideas, 1558–1794* (Indianapolis, 1965), p. 2.

[100] Ibid., pp. 4, 5, 11.

and Knox thought determined the validity of the rulers office under this scheme were religious duties. Goodman says that the chief command God issues is to uphold His Law, "to root out evil, to repudiate all forms of idolatry and tyranny." Under the covenant principle, where God seals His promises to a certain nation only as part of a reciprocal agreement in which the people are expected to fulfill certain duties, each individual citizen is said to have promised God to uphold His Law. Each citizen, then, also has a sacred duty to help resist and remove all idolatrous or tyrannical magistrates.[101] Knox speaks of the covenant in a similar manner.[102]

Not to resist under this scheme, then, means not to obey the covenant. This is a sin, and all sin deserves punishment. Ponet promises that if the people submit to "idolaters and wicked livers, as the papists are," God will send them "famine, pestilence, seditions, wars," as punishment for breaking the covenant.[103] Goodman reminds his readers to turn away from "the great wrath of God's indignation" by removing all idolatrous and tyrannical rulers.[104] Knox said that "God will neither excuse nobility nor people" if they continued to submit to idolatrous rulers. "With the same sense of vengeance," God would punish the princes, people, and nobility for "conspiring together against Him and His holy ordinances."[105] Not to rebel, then, was to conspire; to conspire was to sin.

The Scots listened to Knox. In December of 1577 the leaders of the nobility signed a solemn covenant by which they constituted themselves as "the congregation of Christ" and bound themselves to oppose their Catholic enemies, "the congregation of Satan." This is the outcome of Knox's idea of "the people assembled together in one body of a Commonwealth, unto whom God has given sufficient force, not only to resist, but also to suppress all kind of open idolatry."[106]

On the continent, the Calvinist theory of resistance was also adopted and applied in the Low Countries during the revolt against Spanish rule. Although some Dutch leaders such as Louis of Nassau and John of Nassau (both brothers of William of Orange) voiced argu-

---

[101] Christopher Goodman, *Superior Powers* (Geneva, 1558), p. 180.
[102] John Knox, "The Appellation from the Sentence Pronounced by the Bishops and Clergy," in Laing (ed.), *Works*, vol. 4, p. 505.
[103] John Ponet, *A Short Treatise of Politicke Power*, reprinted in W. S. Hudson, *John Ponet, Advocate of Limited Monarchy* (Chicago, 1942), pp. 176, 178.
[104] Goodman, *Superior Powers* (1558), pp. 11, 93.
[105] Knox, "Appellation," *Works*, vol. 4, p. 498. Also: Greaves, *Theology and Revolution*, pp. 111–14.
[106] *Knox's History*, vol. 2, p. 122.

ments in favor of armed resistance against the "idolatrous" rule of Phillip II, no major theorist appeared among them. The significance of the Dutch revolt, therefore, lies in its application of the Calvinist theory of resistance rather than in its formulation.[107]

IDOLATRY AS THE CALVINIST SHIBBOLETH

On certain occasions, it is easier to argue for the validity of something when its existence is called into question. This is one such case. Recent scholarship has attempted to explode the myth that Calvinism is the source of theories of resistance. This trend began first by looking to Lutheranism, and then to the Middle Ages. Now, however, the demythologizing has turned on itself, and the claim has been made that there are really no "Calvinist" theories at all. Although it is difficult to take issue with the threads of influence traced by much of this recent work, it is possible to argue against the newer argument made by Quentin Skinner, that states that theology has little if anything to do with the issue of resistance, at least in any way that could reveal the uniqueness of some theories as "Calvinist."[108]

The tendency toward revisionism so evident in Skinner can be traced to Michael Walzer. Walzer's central thesis in *The Revolution of the Saints* is that Calvinism, especially as represented in English Puritanism, was "a response to disorder and fear, a way of organizing men to overcome the acute sense of chaos."[109] Walzer, then, sees psychology as the primary motivation for theories of resistance. "The Primary source of the saints' radical character lies in their response to the disorder of the transition period."[110] The Calvinist experience becomes an instance of "social-psychological reaction-formation," an obsession with identity in an age of confusion, not some fundamentally new theological vision. The net result of all of this, according to Walzer, is that Calvinism developed as a response to the chaos of its age with a heightened sense of the importance of repression and regimentation. Discipline became their hallmark, and the keynote of this discipline was repression.[111]

Under this interpretation, then, Calvinism must be viewed as a political rather than religious phenomenon. The blame is laid at the feet of Calvin himself, who is portrayed by Walzer as follows:

Detached from the traditional forms of theological and philosophical speculation, Calvin might be described most simply as a practical man of ideas: a

---

107 On Dutch developments consult: R. Kingdon, "Political Resistance," esp. pp. 228–30.
108 Skinner, "Origins," pp. 312–15, 325.
109 Walzer, *Revolution of the Saints*, p. 77.
110 Ibid., p. 312.
111 Ibid., p. 302.

French refugee intellectual caught up in Genevan politics. He was . . . not primarily a theologian or a philosopher, but an ideologist.[112]

According to Walzer, Calvin was seeking a resolution to the problem of alienation, disruption, and anxiety caused by the politics of his day. Calvin's solution was the development of an ideology of political absolutism.

Skinner, though arguing against Walzer, does not deny this premise, and also looks for a totally "secular" notion of resistance. Skinner finds the first "fully secularized and populist theory of resistance" in the work of George Buchanan, *The Right of the Kingdom among the Scots*. Buchanan, according to Skinner, is the first Calvinist to formulate a fully naturalistic concept of the state, one that proposed that government is not given by God, but invented by men themselves. This secularism is matched by a "radically populist view" of the right of the people to rebel.

Skinner, though, is not concerned with proving that populist revolutionary theories had their roots in Calvinism. He wants to deny that there was anything "Calvinistic" about them. He says that though the *men* who led and theorized about revolutions in the mid sixteenth century "were in general self-proclaimed Calvinists," there is reason to question the belief that their *arguments* were necessarily "Calvinist in provenance and character."[113]

In order to prove the error of "the Calvinist myth," Skinner focuses on the work of Walzer, as if his theories about the nature of Calvinism were the only ones worth disproving. Walzer, after all, traces political radicalism to Calvinism, even if for psychological and political reasons alone. Skinner, in addition to saying that Calvinist theories were rooted in medieval scholasticism, also wants to argue that "it still does not follow that Calvinist radicalism must have been a product and conceptualization of a distinctively Calvinist psychology and experience."[114]

Skinner begins to chip away at the "myth" by tracing Calvinist theories to Lutheranism. He concludes that Lutheran theories, in fact, existed long before the radical Calvinists began to write in the 1550s, and that these early Calvinist theorists did not break away from the Lutheran beliefs, but rather adopted them without making any signif-

---

[112] Ibid., p. 27. Walzer's thesis has been perceptively critiqued by David Little, "Max Weber Revisited, the 'Protestant Ethic' and the Puritan Experience of Order," *Harvard Theological Review*, 59: 415–28 (1966), esp. p. 417, n. 11.
[113] Skinner, "Origins," p. 314.
[114] Ibid., p. 315.

icant changes. Even the more radical ideas of Goodman and Ponet, he says, are already emphasized by Luther and Melanchton.[115]

Skinner digs further into the past to prove there is nothing new about the Lutherans either. They are direct heirs of medieval, scholastic political theories, going back even to Justinian's *Digest*, where the concept of repelling force by force (*vim vi repellere licet*) was already considered a right of Nature. The more immediate sources are Ockham, Gerson, the conciliar movement, Jacques Almain (1480– 1515) and John Mair, or Major (1467–1550). Major, a disciple of Gerson and Ockham, not only taught Almain, but also Calvin (at the College de Montaigu), and both John Knox and George Buchanan.[116]

Skinner's grand secularization of Calvinism is simply stated. He says that the domination of the concept of the "Calvinist theory of revolution" is now over. "Strictly speaking," he says, "no such entity exists." Skinner even casts doubt on the sincerity of the men who led these revolutions, at least, "strictly speaking," in the religious sense.

> The revolutions of sixteenth-century Europe were, of course, largely conducted by professed Calvinists, but the theories in terms of which they sought to explain and justify their actions were not, at least in their main outlines, specifically Calvinist at all.[117]

One is forced to ask, what are these "main outlines?" For Skinner, it seems simple: Buchanan, and all other Calvinists were only parroting what Mair had taught at the Sorbonne fifty years before, grafting medieval theory onto the Calvinist cause. At this juncture, though, one must also ask: If there is nothing "Calvinist" about these theories, is it possible to say there is also anything "Calvinist" about the cause? Skinner, in failing to address this question, is driven to say that Calvinist ideology and Calvinist practice were two very different things. He does not, however, define very clearly what "Calvinist ideology" is.

With the scholastic background uncovered, Skinner thinks it is possible to see that scholars have been asking "the wrong question" for a long time. Instead of asking, as they have, what could have prompted the Calvinists to develop their resistance theories, they ought instead to ask "what prompted the Calvinists to appeal so extensively to the existing theories of revolution developed by their Catholic adversaries."[118]

In saying this, Skinner sets the stage for a sweeping revision of

---

[115] Ibid., p. 318.
[116] Ibid., p. 324.
[117] Ibid., p. 325.
[118] Ibid.

Calvinism, turning it into a political Nicodemism of sorts. Calvinists are portrayed as rather cunning, but somewhat insincere revolutionaries who used religious language to cover more "secular" aspirations. Their "ideology" was a cover for a revolutionary practice. The significance of Skinner's question, he believes, "lies in the fact that it hints at the possibility of a new view of the relationship between the ideology of the radical Calvinists and their political practice."[119]

Because Skinner bases so much of his understanding of Calvinism on Walzer's definition, he thinks that this "new view" explodes the myth of the "Calvinist theory." Skinner criticizes Walzer for trying to define Calvinist ideology as "Calvinist," that is, as a means of self-definition and as a direct motive for revolution of the part of people who called themselves "Calvinists." The real nature of Calvinism, according to Skinner, was not self-definition, not this psychological need for order and discipline that Walzer proposes, but rather revolution itself. The "cause" was its own end, it seems:

Once we see, however, *how little of their ideology is distinctly Calvinist*, we are bound to ask whether they may have been concerned not only with efforts at self-definition, but also with appealing to the uncommited, seeking to reassure those who might be thinking of joining the cause, and above all attempting to neutralize as far as possible the hostile Catholic majority by showing them the extent to which revolutionary political actions could be legitimated in terms of impeccably Catholic beliefs.[120]

This view of Calvinism makes it no more than a political party. Though there is constant reference to ideology, the "ideology" to which Skinner refers is never religious. There is no room for theology in this interpretation. Skinner sees Calvinists primarily (or almost exclusively, it seems) as a small, radical political minority that promoted illegal and subversive behavior, and that, in order to broaden its base of support, resorted to Catholic arguments as a way of defusing the objections and denunciations of the Catholic majority.

If it were truly possible to reduce the Reformation to a political movement, in strictly social terms – that is, to present it solely as the case of a minority seeking to expand at the expense of the majority – or if it were possible to reduce its ideology exclusively into a quest for power and control, then it would be difficult to take issue with Skinner. Such reductionism, even if alluring to many, is sorely lacking in subtlety. Many questions can be raised about Skinner's thesis as soon as the religious dimensions of the Reformation, and of Calvinism in particular, are brought into the discussion.

---

[119] Ibid.
[120] Ibid. (italics mine).

To begin with, why is it that the Calvinist writers *do not* cite their Catholic sources openly if their main intention is to try to defuse the Catholic objections? Since no Calvinist ever appealed directly to this medieval heritage, one need also ask how many readers would have recognized Mair in Goodman, Viret or Knox, or even if they would have seen this argument as "Catholic."

If one defines "Catholic" as Skinner does, merely as "medieval," a further problem arises. Just what is it that the "Calvinists" are trying to get the "Catholics" to see in their revolution, in their "cause?" What is the "cause?" Are we caught in a vicious tautology?

If one defines "Catholic" and "Calvinist" in terms of religious values, as "theologies" rather than strictly political ideologies, then one can escape the tautology. Throughout his argument, Skinner makes no mention of a religious basis for anything that may be "distinctly Calvinist." If one views the Calvinist cause as the defense of a complex set of religious values, which of themselves include a certain social vision, then one can also dispute Skinner's point, and through him, also Walzer's.

What makes the Calvinist theories "distinctly Calvinist" is not the arguments themselves, but the reasons for the arguments, and beyond that, the reason for the theories and for the cause itself. This is the struggle against idolatry – and not just idolatry in the church, but as a social phenomenon, as something that needs to be wiped out from the body politic. If there is one concept or word that stands out as some sort of red blinking light in all the Calvinist theories from Calvin to Buchanan, it is precisely this issue of idolatry. If one accepts the religious issue as a real motivating force, as the ideological foundation of dissent, and not just some sort of tool insincerely used in a grand social and political plot, it is possible to say that the word "idolatry" and the concepts it signified became the Calvinist shibboleth in the sixteenth century.[121] It became an inescapable password. Even if one grants to Skinner that Calvinists used the concept of idolatry insincerely in their pursuit of power, the very use of the word betrayed the essentially religious origins of the conflict.

What I propose, against Skinner and Walzer, is that any definition of Calvinism needs to take theology into account as a real motivating force, especially as a vision of reality that becomes an ideology, a blueprint for behavior on the individual and social level. In regards to theories of resistance, the issue of idolatry assumes central importance. Calvinists resorted to revolution not just as a way of ensuring

---

[121] The Oxford English Dictionary defines "shibboleth" as "a catchword or formula adopted by a party or sect, by which their adherents or followers may be discerned, or those not their followers may be excluded."

their survival solely for its own sake, but rather to promote a new kind of social and political vision based on certain theological principles. "Right worship" and "true belief" are the heart of their ideology. Calvinists struggled not just against "tyrants" in a strictly political sense, but also, very clearly, against "idolaters." What made their "tyrants" deserving of resistance is not just political or social oppression, but rather the perversion of religion. When a ruler disobeys the First Table of the Law, when he breaks the covenant with God for pure worship, then and only then is revolution fully justified: This is what Calvinist theorists never tired of repeating.

One cannot, of course, dismiss the many interrelated sets of political, economic, and social exigencies which gave shape to Calvinist discontent. Theology alone was not the seed of resistance, nor could it have been uniformly and unequivocally perceived as such by every sixteenth-century Calvinist. Yet, it was through theology that the cause of revolution was defended, in conjunction with other causal factors; and it was largely through the reassessment of the religious responsibilities of the body politic that Calvinists made their grievances explicit.

In Jewish Cabalistic legend, it was believed that those who knew how to harness the creative power latent in the Hebrew alphabet could bring anything into existence, even another man. Such a man, however, was devoid of a soul. He could perform human functions, much as some kind of organic robot, but had no transcendent self, no eternal life force that needed to be redeemed from the contingency and corruption of material existence. This legend of the "golem" is told in one nineteenth-century version as follows:

> After saying certain prayers and observing certain fast days, the Polish Jews make the figure of a man from clay or mud, and when they pronounce the miraculous Shemhaphoras [the name of God] over him, he must come to life. He cannot speak, but he understands fairly well what is said or commanded. They call him golem and use him as a servant to do all sorts of housework. But he must never leave the house.[122]

What Skinner proposes is that Calvinists in the sixteenth century made a golem from medieval resistance theories. They used the scholastic material much as the Cabalists used clay and mud, to give form to their arguments; then, after somehow bringing them to life, to make them work for their cause without ever leaving their house, that is, without ever becoming explicitly "Catholic." By refusing to consider the full theological dimensions of Calvinist resistance theories,

---

[122] Cited in Gershom Scholem, *On the Kabbalah and Its Symbolism*, trans. R. Manheim (New York, 1969), p. 159.

Skinner has failed to take into account the one factor that gives Calvinism its soul.

In conclusion, it must be observed that the question of idolatry had evolved into a dramatic political issue by the second half of the sixteenth century. Not only had it contributed to iconoclasm throughout Western Europe, but also to theories that supported armed resistance against established rulers. In the 1520s, when the issue of "true" versus "false" worship first surfaced, the attack on idolatry was limited to the cultic objects of Roman Catholicism. By the middle of the century, however, the attack had been extended against the governments that supported "false" religion and tried to enforce it on all Christians. Luther's fears about iconoclasm might have been justified after all. The revolutionary aspect of the attack on idolatry began with Karlstadt's request that all Christians take the law into their own hands and remove idols from their midst; it culminated with Viret, Beza, Mornay, Knox, Goodman and Ponet asking that idolatrous rulers be resisted. Instead of being called upon to overturn statues and altars, Christians were now being called upon to overturn governments. The fact that resistance was limited, for the most part, to the magistracy does not make Calvinist theories any less significant. These theories supported serious challenges to established authority, and the various upheavals of sixteenth- and seventeenth-century Europe bear witness to this fact: the Wars of Religion in France, the Dutch Revolt in the Low Countries, and the Revolution of the Saints in England.

It is not my intention to argue that Calvinism was inherently "democratic." Calvinist resistance theories did not have in mind the establishment of democratic governments, but rather the abolition of idolatry and Catholic coercion. Because Calvinists were a minority in centralized states, there was something inherently "revolutionary" about their uncompromising attitude, and it is this point that I wish to stress.

Many factors played a role in the development of theories of resistance in the sixteenth century, but it was the issue of religion, and more specifically, the issue of idolatry, that assumed a central place in these arguments and distinguished them as "Calvinist." These theories, at first formulated to meet a religious crisis, eventually became the foundation of more radical politics. Though far from democratic, these theories influenced revolutions that would later usher in democracy in other places. Ironically enough, those later revolutions would also usher in religious toleration, and thus render useless the concept of "idolatry."

Conclusion

If, as literary wisdom proposes, it is best to "begin at the beginning,"[1] then perhaps it might also be good, in true humanist form, to return *ad fontes*, to the beginning, in search of an appropriate end. Going back once again to 1509, the year of Calvin's birth, we find Lefèvre D'Etaples expressing certain principles that reveal much about the origin of the war on the idols, as well as about its eventual legacy. Presenting his case for a return to the "pure" sources of scripture, the French humanist also argued in his *Commentary on Psalms* for a certain metaphysical understanding of reality. Without scripture, he said, everything became corrupt:

> from the moment these pious studies are no longer pursued . . . devotion dies out, the flame of religion is extinguished, spiritual things are traded for earthly goods, heaven is given up and earth is accepted – the most disastrous transaction conceivable.[2]

It is no accident, in an age when such statements were made about the metaphysical relationship between heaven and earth, that some men, such as Copernicus, should have also perceived, for the first time in human history, a new physical relationship between a revolving earth and the heavens through which it moves. Though the connections among Renaissance, Reformation, and "modernity" form a Gordian knot that no pen or sword can easily unravel, it makes sense to say that the scientific and religious revolutions of the sixteenth century share common traits. In spite of the fact that Calvin ignored Copernicus and continued to explain the cosmos in a geocentric fashion, there is a striking similarity between his approach to reality and that of the Polish astronomer. In fact, Galileo's praise of Copernicus

---

[1] Lord Byron, *Don Juan*, T. G. Steffan, E. Steffan, W. W. Pratt, eds. (4 vols., New Haven, 1982), vol. 2, p. 25: "My way is to begin with the beginning;/ The regularity of my design/ Forbids all wandering as the worst of sinning" (Canto i, st. 7).

[2] Introduction to the *Commentary on the Psalms* (1509), trans. P.L. Nyhus, in *Forerunners of the Reformation*, H. Oberman, ed. (New York, 1966), p. 297.

and his supporters (those who championed the mathematical intelligibility of nature), could also, with little alteration, be applied to Calvin and his followers. "They were able," he said, "to make reason so conquer sense that, in defiance of the latter, the former became the mistress of their belief."[3]

The revolution in physics that begins in the sixteenth century with Copernicus has its parallel in the revolution in metaphysics that Calvin championed. No longer was it requisite for "belief" to go against reason.[4] Calvin did not want a religion in which reason had at times to be denied or suspended. Faith was reasonable, it had to make sense. The separation of the heavenly and earthly spheres in metaphysics lay the groundwork for a more rationalistic interpretation of religion and the empirical world. As the divine began to be removed from creation into its own heavenly sphere, and as it began to be understood according to clearly defined and "unchanging" scriptural principles, religion became less mysterious and unpredictable. The wonder-working, fragmented, and sometimes capricious "parapolytheism" of late medieval religion was replaced, especially in Reformed Protestantism, by a transcendent God who is totally "other," and who rules the created world omnipotently according to unchanging principles. This is not to say that the Reformed vision of reality gave birth to rationalism, or Deism, or even modern science (Copernicus and Galileo were both faithful Catholics); but rather that by emphasizing the separation of spiritual and material and attacking idolatry and superstition, it lessened the importance of the miraculous and allowed for the material world to be understood on its own terms. In many ways, for Calvinists, almost as much as for Copernicans, reason became the mistress of belief. There were limits to the power of reason, of course. Since God was totally "other," human reason was still considered incapable of piercing through the mystery of His being, or the mystery of His will. Problems such as sin and salvation remained, at bottom, outside the realm of reason. Yet, faith was reasonable and had to correspond to sense experience. Though some mysteries remained inaccessible to the powers of the human mind, there were no historical events or any earthly phenomena since

---

[3] Galileo Galilei, *Dialogue Concerning the Two Chief World Systems – Ptolomaic and Copernican*, trans. Stillman Drake (Berkeley, 1953), p. 328. A good, brief summary of the problems involved in trying to relate the Reformation to modern science can be found in Brian A. Gerrish, "The Reformation and the Rise of Modern Science: Luther, Calvin, and Copernicus," in *The Old Protestantism and the New: Essays on the Reformation Heritage* (Chicago, 1982), pp. 163–78.

[4] *Inventory of Relics*, CR 6.445.

the time of the apostles that were regarded as contradictory to the natural laws of the physical realm.[5] This outlook helped intensify the rationalistic tendencies of the Renaissance that were mirrored so clearly by the Reformation itself and that would gradually contribute to the development of a new scientific mind-set in the seventeenth and eighteenth centuries.

The attack on Catholic piety also occasioned important cultural, social, and political changes. Perhaps the most tangible change was brought about by iconoclasm, as the cultic objects of previous generations were defaced, burned, or reduced to rubble. Iconoclasm, in turn, tested and strained the political systems of many localities, since it challenged civic as well as ecclesiastical authorities. In addition to destruction and unrest, the war on the idols also laid the foundation for a profound disruption of society. By pointing to a distinction between "true" and "false" worship and charging their followers to abstain from religious pollution, the Reformers – most notably Calvin – intensified the social divisions caused by theological disagreements. Moreover, this strident separatism further aggravated tensions by contributing to theories of resistance: Not only the idols, but the governments that supported them became subject to aggression. The social conflicts created by the rejection of Catholic worship were at heart religious, motivated by the belief that society ought to conform to certain theological principles; but by challenging the status quo, the war on idolatry indirectly laid a foundation for the more radical secularizing tendencies that surfaced in the following age.

But revolutions have a way of turning against the very principle of revolution. Once the old system is replaced with the new, the objectives shift from change to control. In some cases, as witnessed with chilling regularity in our own century, the revolutionaries who oust the tyrants impose a tyranny of their own in the name of revolution. It has been argued that in the Reformation the Protestants became "new Papists."[6] This is especially clear in the case of Calvin and Calvinism. Geneva became the Protestant Rome not just because it

---

[5] Max Weber argued at the beginning of this century that Calvinism was the "logical conclusion" of a broad process of rationalization that aimed at the elimination of magic from the world. *The Protestant Ethic and the Spirit of Capitalism* (1905–6), trans. Talcott Parsons (New York, 1958), p. 105. Though I am not in agreement with Weber's conception of this principle as the "complete elimination of salvation through the church and the sacraments" and the exaltation of the isolated personal spiritual experience, I am arguing for the "rationalism" of Calvinism in a Weberian sense; that is, as a move away from "magic" to a bureaucratically organized religion of transcendence.

[6] Steven Ozment, *The Reformation in the Cities* (New Haven, 1975), p. 164.

served as the exporting center of a vibrant faith marked by conviction and social and political activism, but also because it sought to crush dissent from within and to enforce conformity no less ruthlessly than Rome ever had. Amy Perrin and Pierre Vandel, two of the young iconoclasts who delighted in defying the Catholic powers in Geneva before Calvin's arrival, later became "Libertines" and foes of Calvin. As Perrin and Vandel had once humiliated the priests and demolished the images, so did Calvin later crush these men and drive them out of their own city.[7] Appropriately enough, when Perrin's property was confiscated by the city, the revenue was used to help build Calvin's new Academy. Thus did the revolutionaries pay against their will for the training of the ministers who would defend the new order.[8]

Iconoclasts are often also moralists. The iconoclastic spirit of Calvinism was inherently revolutionary, but its aim was not to destroy as much as to build. Though art lovers may often speak of Calvinists as vandals who engaged in wanton destruction, the situation was, in fact, quite the opposite. The new view of worship proposed by the Reformed, especially by Calvinists, was a social vision. Calvinists sought to destroy "false" ideas and concepts as well as their concrete expressions, and asked for the corporate political reality to change in ways that would reflect their new metaphysical concepts. The end result was the abolition of the old system, and this was something that could not be obtained without strife. The resulting turmoil was never considered as an end in itself, but rather a step on the way to a new social and political expression demanded by the new kind of worship. This was the enormous transforming power of the war against the idols.

Theologically, the rejection of the medieval *cultus* allowed for the development of a new interpretation of worship and the creation of new liturgical styles. This altered the day-to-day ritualistic life of a good part of the European population, dividing the continent into several types of religious societies, each visibly different from the other: not only Catholic versus Protestant, but Reformed versus Lutheran.

For those communities where Reformed Protestantism triumphed permanently, such as Zurich, Geneva, Scotland, or the Dutch Republic, the cultural changes were enormous. First, one must consider the aesthetic side of this upheaval, that is, the nearly total divorce

---

[7] R. W. Collins, *Calvin and the Libertines of Geneva* (Toronto/Vancouver, 1968).
[8] E. William Monter, *Calvin's Geneva* (New York, 1967), p. 113.

effected between art and religion. The impact of this separation on both religion and art was so profound and has so many ramifications that it falls entirely out of the scope of this study.[9] The stripped, whitewashed church in which the pulpit replaced the altar became the focal point of a cultural shift from visual images to language, the consequences of which shall be analyzed presently. Suffice it to say at this point that this shift from the visual to the verbal as a means of communication went beyond merely aesthetic considerations.

Another cultural change effected by iconoclasm, which deserves more attention than can be paid to it here, was an increased masculinization of piety. If, as recent studies have shown, nearly fifty percent of late medieval church art was devoted to Mary and the saints,[10] the removal of these feminine representations marks a definite shift away from a gender-balanced, feminized piety to a more strictly masculine one. God the Father, God the Son (the Word incarnate in the *man* Jesus), and God the Holy Spirit became the sole focus of devotion. The richly symbolic feminine aspects represented by the Virgin Mary as "Mother of God," and by other female saints, were suddenly replaced by those of a transcendent, but overtly masculine God.

In ecclesiastical terms, the war against idolatry gave rise to a new kind of lay piety, one that was more tightly controlled than had been the case under Catholicism. Exhuberance is replaced by restraint, not just in an aesthetic sense, but in all practical aspects. As also often happens in revolutions, those who actually fight the battles and bring the old system to its knees enjoy but a brief moment of glory. After all the victory celebrations are over, power is assumed once more by a relatively small elite.

In this case, the Protestant iconoclasts and revolutionaries, laymen for the most part, turned a certain theological vision into a concrete reality. It is fair to say that lay participation in the process of the Reformation, particularly through iconoclasm, is one of those rare instances of true partnership between the intellectual elite and the people at large. Though probably inspired to a large extent by sermons and literature that were generated by the intellectual elite, Reformation iconoclasts and revolutionaries took it upon themselves to bring about religious change. Once they had smashed the images and altars and chased away the priests, however, the laity once again

---

[9] The best study of this phenomenon, at least as it pertains to Lutheranism, is Carl Christensen, *Art and the Reformation in Germany* (Athens, Ohio, 1980).

[10] Ibid., p. 207.

found themselves restricted from above. They may have had a new kind of piety, but it was a carefully formulated and clearly dictated piety. More than had been the case before, religious expression began to be controlled from above, by the pastors and consistories. In Geneva, under Calvin, even the names one could give to one's children were carefully regulated: Those which had been previously linked with the cult of the saints were strictly forbidden. All this was sternly enforced in the name of "true piety."[11]

Having already mentioned the aesthetic dimensions of the cultural shift from the visual to the verbal, we must now consider a more subtle, but perhaps more significant aspect of this change in the means of communication and the exercise of authority.

While still a very visible and powerful social phenomenon, religion suddenly became, in many ways, an invisible, interior realm that depended on the guidance of a clerical elite. For Reformed Protestants, even more than for Lutherans, it was the power of the Word, as broadcast by the words of its ministers, that brought salvation. It was a cerebral, learned sort of religion, one that only allowed for the Word to stand as an image of the invisible reality of the spiritual dimension. In practical terms, this meant a very concrete shift from a world brimming over with physical, visible symbols that were open to a rather wide range of interpretations – some intentionally ambiguous – to one charged principally with verbal symbols that were subject to the interpretation of a carefully trained and ostensibly learned ministry. If nothing else, the old Catholic argument against absolute dependance on the Bible was turned on its head by Calvinists. Instead of producing an endless series of increasingly radical schisms (as had earlier been the case with some of the so-called *Schwärmer*), Calvinism seized on the Word as an instrument of control and uniformity.

Those who jokingly complained against Calvin, saying he would not consider anyone saved unless they first passed through Geneva and had their ears blasted with sermons, were pointing, in fact, to the way in which the shift from pictures and concrete symbols to words

---

[11] *Registres de la Compagnie des Pasteurs de Genève au Temps de Calvin*, R.M. Kingdon and J.-F. Bergier, eds. (Geneva, 1964–), vol. I, p. 29. Among the forbidden names are Suaire, Claude, Toussaint, Dimanche, and Sepulchre. Nicknames, too, were outlawed ("Monet" for Simon, "Tyvan" for Estienne); as were "bad-sounding" names such as Mermet, Sermet, and Allemand. The name Chrestien was forbidden "pour ce qu'il est commun à tous." For a detailed study of religious control in Geneva see William Monter, "The Consistory of Geneva, 1559–1569," *Bibliothèque d'Humanisme et Renaissance*, 38: 467–84 (1976).

made an interpretive elite necessary in Reformed Protestantism. When the vernacular Bible and the sermon replaced the stained glass window and the Mass as the primary didactic and liturgical nexus of faith and worship, especially in connection with the humanist insistance on the ultimate superiority of the original biblical languages, then was the mediation of a literate, almost professorial ministry made even more necessary for the survival of the church as guardian of the social myth.

Moreover, the spiritual return *ad fontes,* to the pure sources of scripture, not only required a more sophisticated clerical class to serve as interpreters, but also called for a more literate laity. With the Bible as the cornerstone of faith, and the Word as the only true symbol, the education of the Christian community became imperative. And as the importance of education increased, so did the opportunity for increased control and regulation: After all, it is generally easier and more efficient to indoctrinate unambiguously through texts than it is through images. By virtue of the fact that the limits of belief and practice were now more clearly defined for the laity in terms of a set of verbal symbols, the detection and correction of deviations became, in many ways, a simpler and more efficient process (at least from the perspective of those who exercised control). Thus it is that those who broke the law by overturning altars, smashing images, and feeding the host to animals eventually came, wherever they were truly successful in their revolt, under control of a consistory.

As a crusade against superstition and ignorance, or error and deception, this revolution in piety, especially as formulated by Calvin, called precisely for this kind of control. For Calvin lay piety, as something spontaneous and uncontrolled, was a danger. Left to their own devices, the Christian populace could not help but revert to idolatry. After all, had not this been the downfall of the early Church? Was this not the fatal oversight that had made the Reformation necessary? Calvin points this out in the *Inventory of Relics,* where he tells one of his very few childhood stories. What he says here about his fellow parishioners and their expression of piety shows his fear of the human propensity for error all too clearly:

I remember what I saw them do to images [*marmousetz*] in our parish when I was a small boy. As the feast of St. Stephen drew near, they would adorn them all alike with garlands and necklaces, the murderers who stoned him (or 'tyrants,' as they were called in common speech), in the same fashion as the martyr. When the poor women saw the murderers decked out in this way, they mistook them for Stephen's companions, and presented each with his own candle. Even worse, they did the same with the devil who struggled against St. Michael.[12]

It is precisely this kind of spontaneous, indiscriminate worship that Calvin and his followers sought to eradicate. Guided by a new metaphysical understanding of worship and its place in society, the Reformed attacked such practices with unrestrained fervor well into the seventeenth century. Thus does this first revolution of the modern age reveal the way in which conservatism and repression so often follow in the wake of liberation. By establishing new, efficient systems of social control, Calvinists tried to ensure that the "disastrous transaction" which Lefèvre criticized would become impossible, and that simple folk would never again deck statues with flowers, or even hope to find heaven close to earth.

---

[12] *Inventory of Relics,* CR 6.452.

Index